Solfege

Written & Illustrated by:
Fumi Yoshinaga

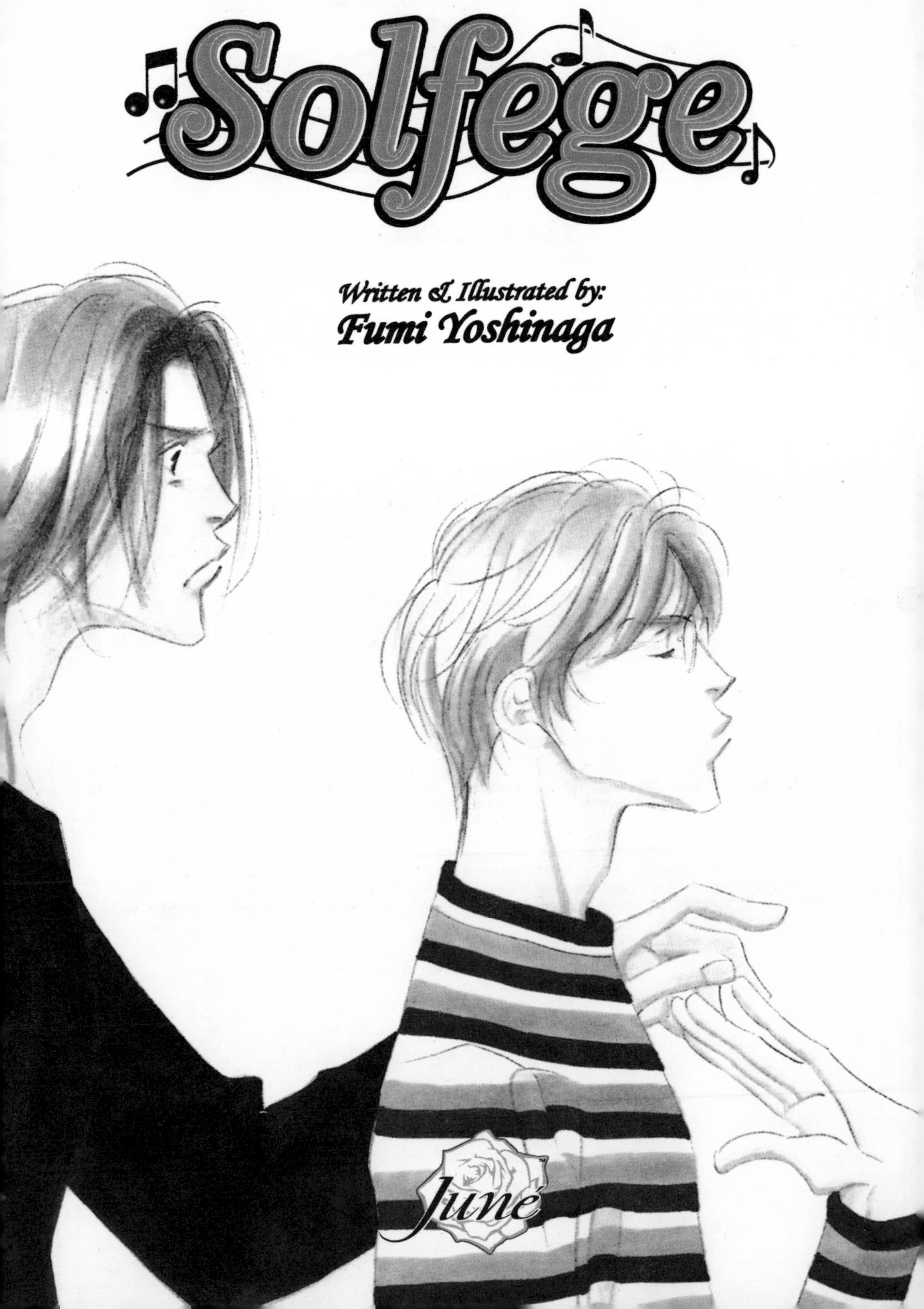
Juné

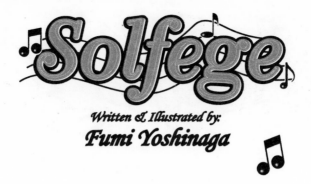

Solfége

Written & Illustrated by:
Fumi Yoshinaga

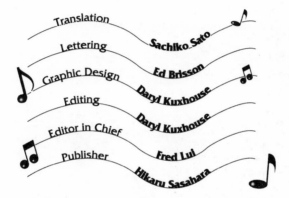

Translation	Sachiko Sato
Lettering	Ed Brisson
Graphic Design	Daryl Kuxhouse
Editing	Daryl Kuxhouse
Editor in Chief	Fred Lui
Publisher	Hikaru Sasahara

English Edition Published by
DIGITAL MANGA PUBLISHING
A division of DIGITAL MANGA, Inc.
1487 W 178th Street, Suite 300
Gardena, CA 90248

www.dmpbooks.com

First Edition: March 2007
ISBN-10: 1-56970-841-X
ISBN-13: 978-1-56970-841-5

1 3 5 7 9 10 8 6 4 2

Printed in China

ソルフェージュ
SOLFÈGE

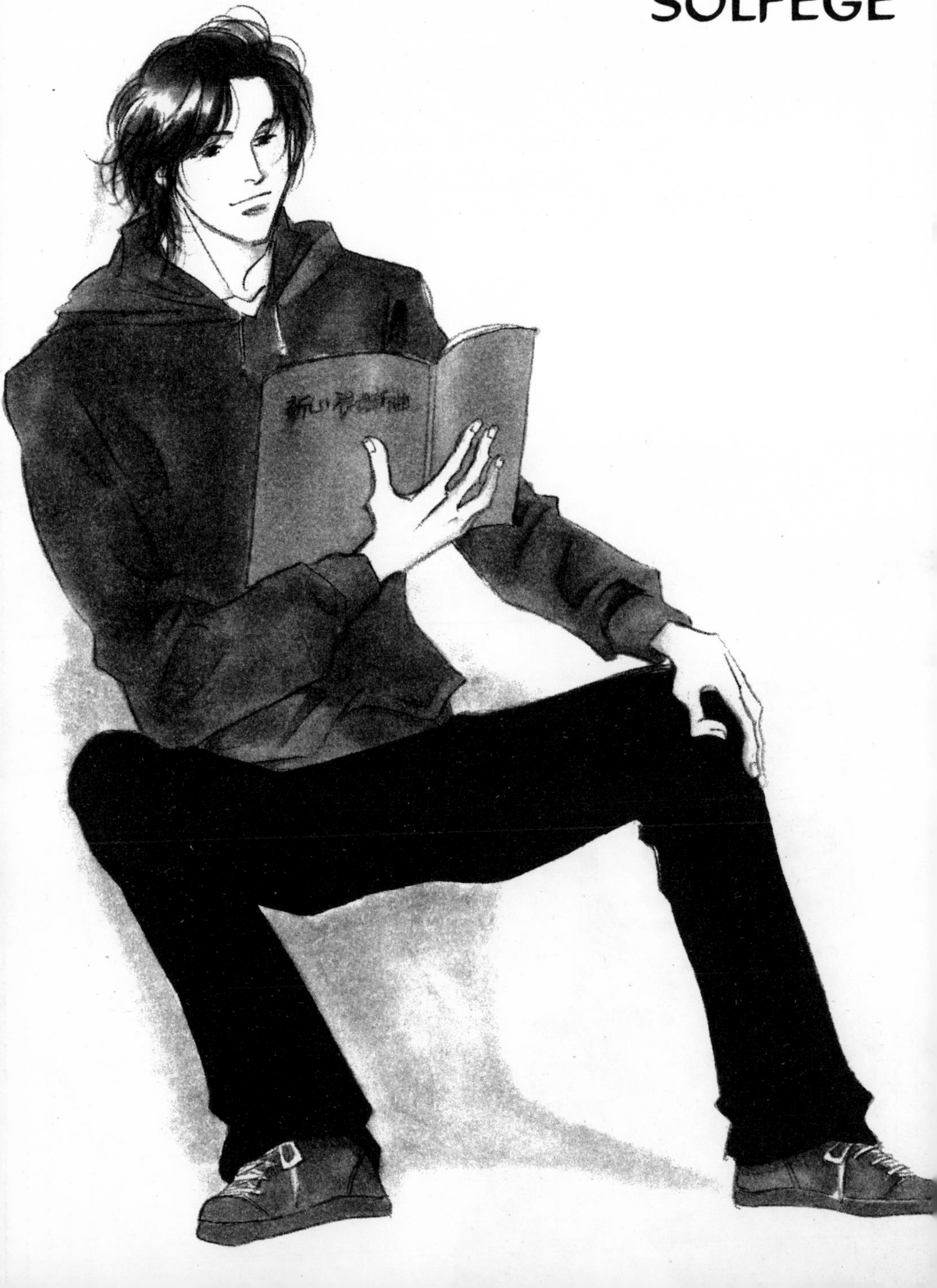

SOLFÈGE – THE BASICS OF MUSICAL STUDIES, SUCH AS LEARNING HOW TO READ MUSIC AS WELL AS TAKE MUSICAL DICTATION.

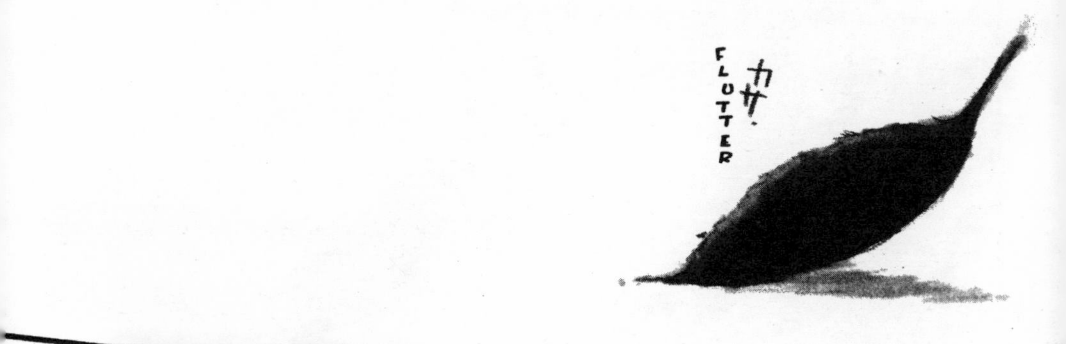
FLUTTER

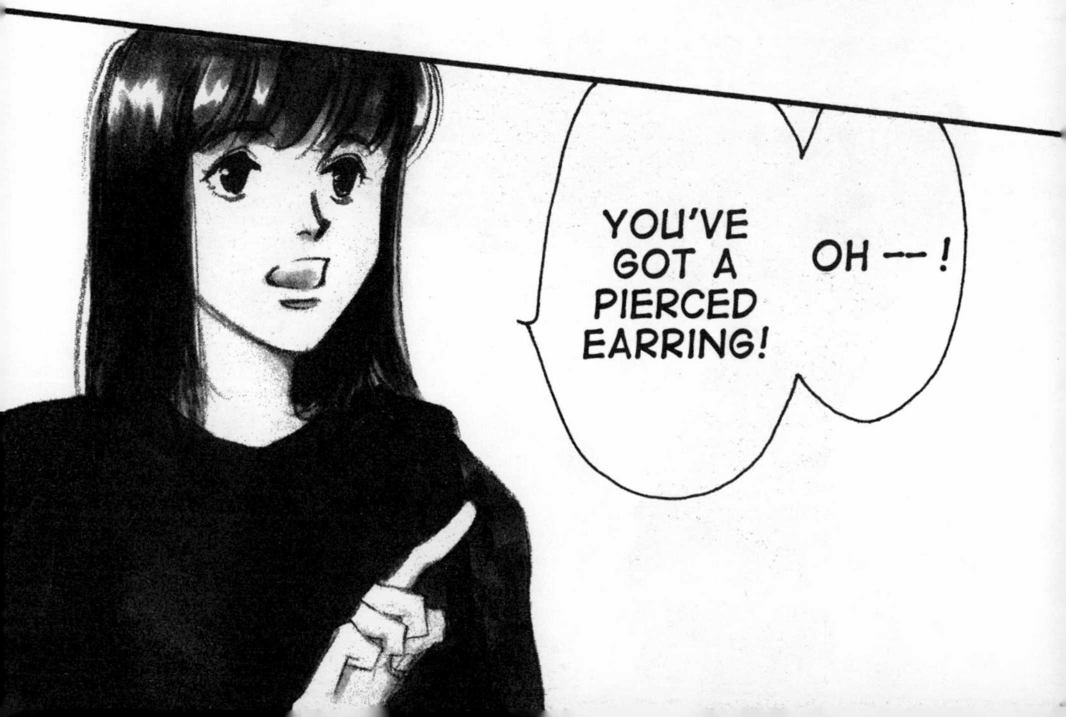
OH --!
YOU'VE GOT A PIERCED EARRING!

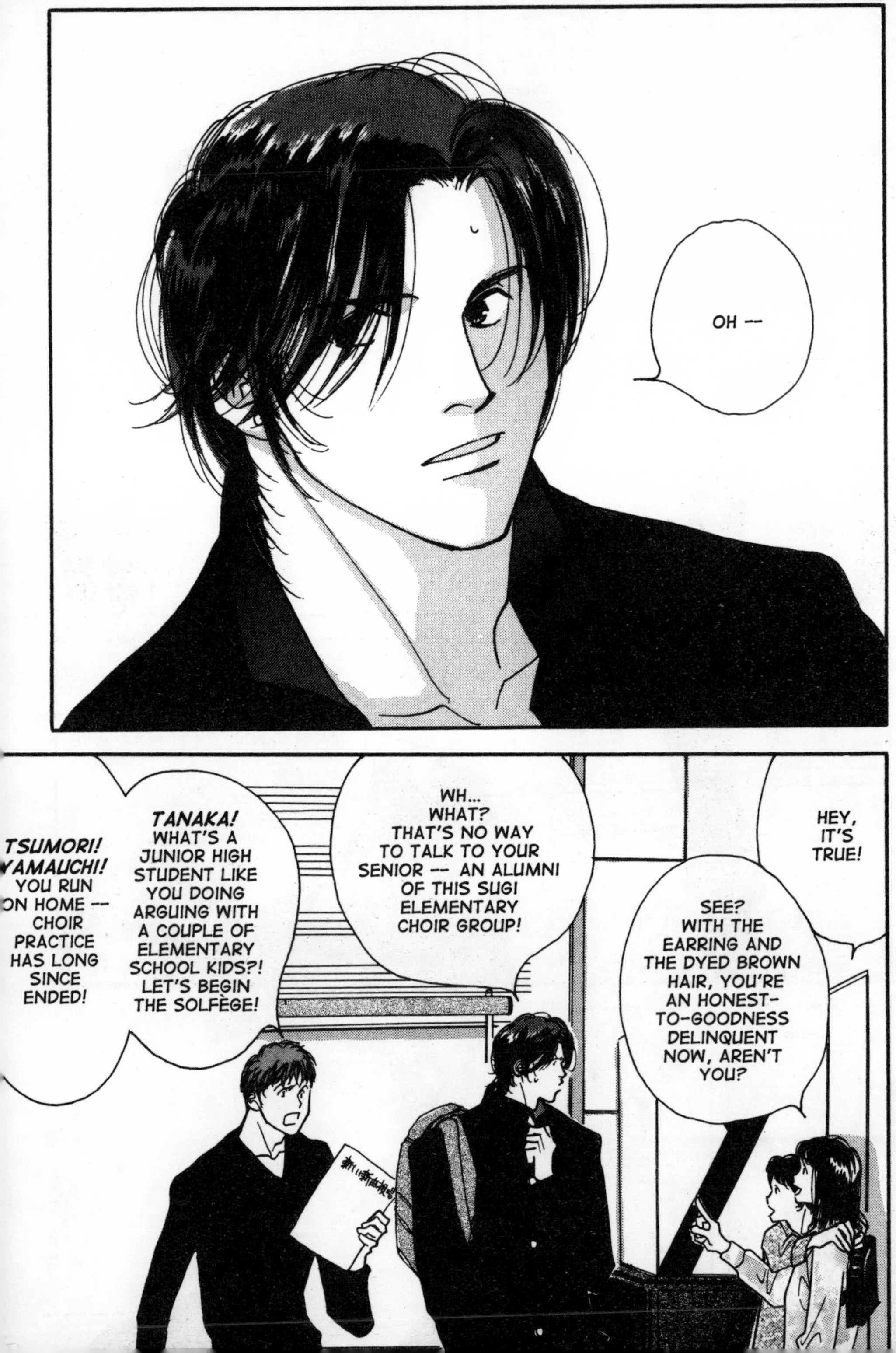
OH --
HEY, IT'S TRUE!
SEE? WITH THE EARRING AND THE DYED BROWN HAIR, YOU'RE AN HONEST-TO-GOODNESS DELINQUENT NOW, AREN'T YOU?
WH... WHAT? THAT'S NO WAY TO TALK TO YOUR SENIOR -- AN ALUMNI OF THIS SUGI ELEMENTARY CHOIR GROUP!
TANAKA! WHAT'S A JUNIOR HIGH STUDENT LIKE YOU DOING ARGUING WITH A COUPLE OF ELEMENTARY SCHOOL KIDS?! LET'S BEGIN THE SOLFÈGE!
TSUMORI! YAMAUCHI! YOU RUN ON HOME -- CHOIR PRACTICE HAS LONG SINCE ENDED!

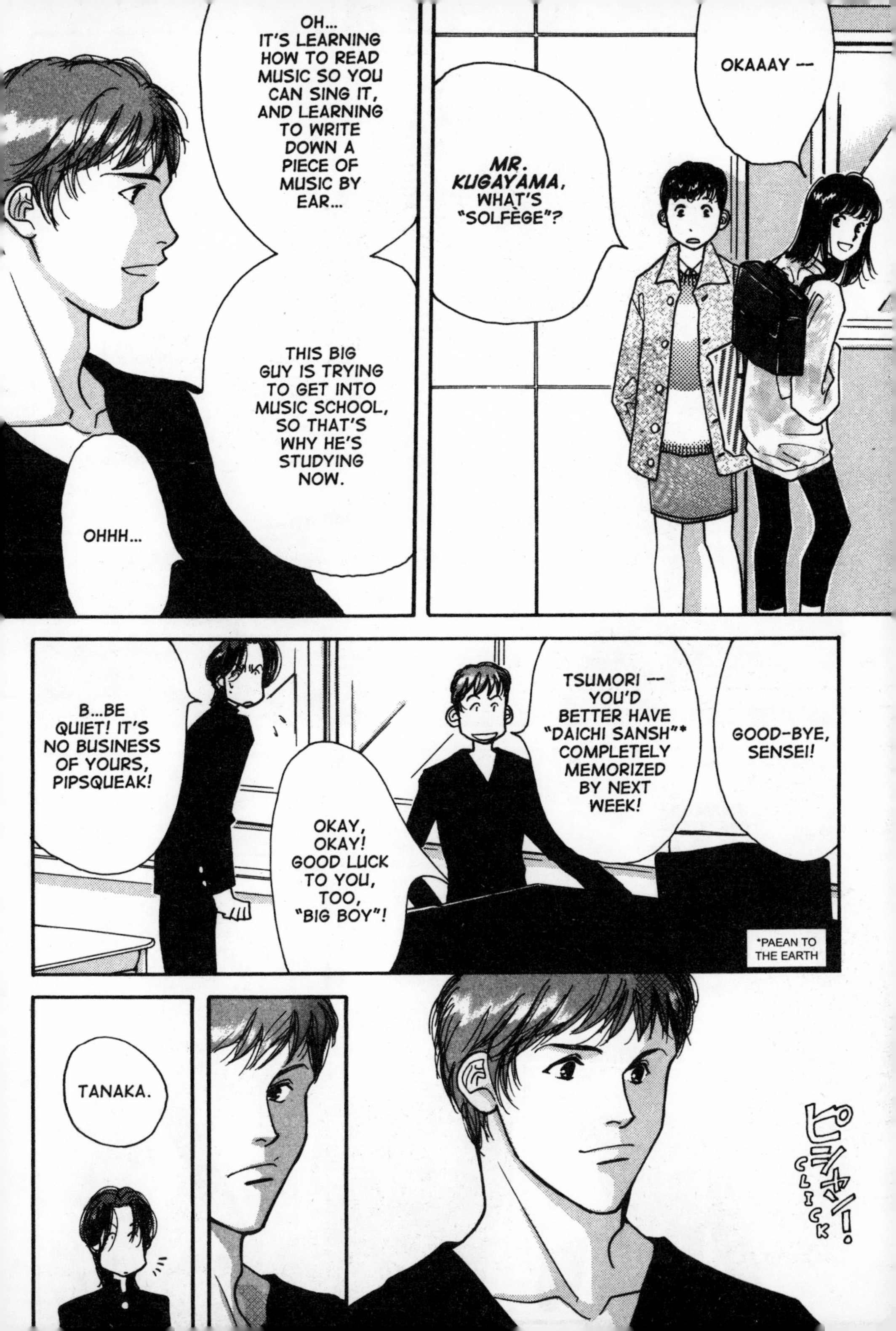
OKAAAY --
MR. KUGAYAMA, WHAT'S "SOLFÈGE"?
OH... IT'S LEARNING HOW TO READ MUSIC SO YOU CAN SING IT, AND LEARNING TO WRITE DOWN A PIECE OF MUSIC BY EAR...
THIS BIG GUY IS TRYING TO GET INTO MUSIC SCHOOL, SO THAT'S WHY HE'S STUDYING NOW.
OHHH...
GOOD-BYE, SENSEI!
TSUMORI -- YOU'D BETTER HAVE "DAICHI SANSH"* COMPLETELY MEMORIZED BY NEXT WEEK!
OKAY, OKAY! GOOD LUCK TO YOU, TOO, "BIG BOY"!
B...BE QUIET! IT'S NO BUSINESS OF YOURS, PIPSQUEAK!
*PAEAN TO THE EARTH
ピシャリ! CLICK
TANAKA.

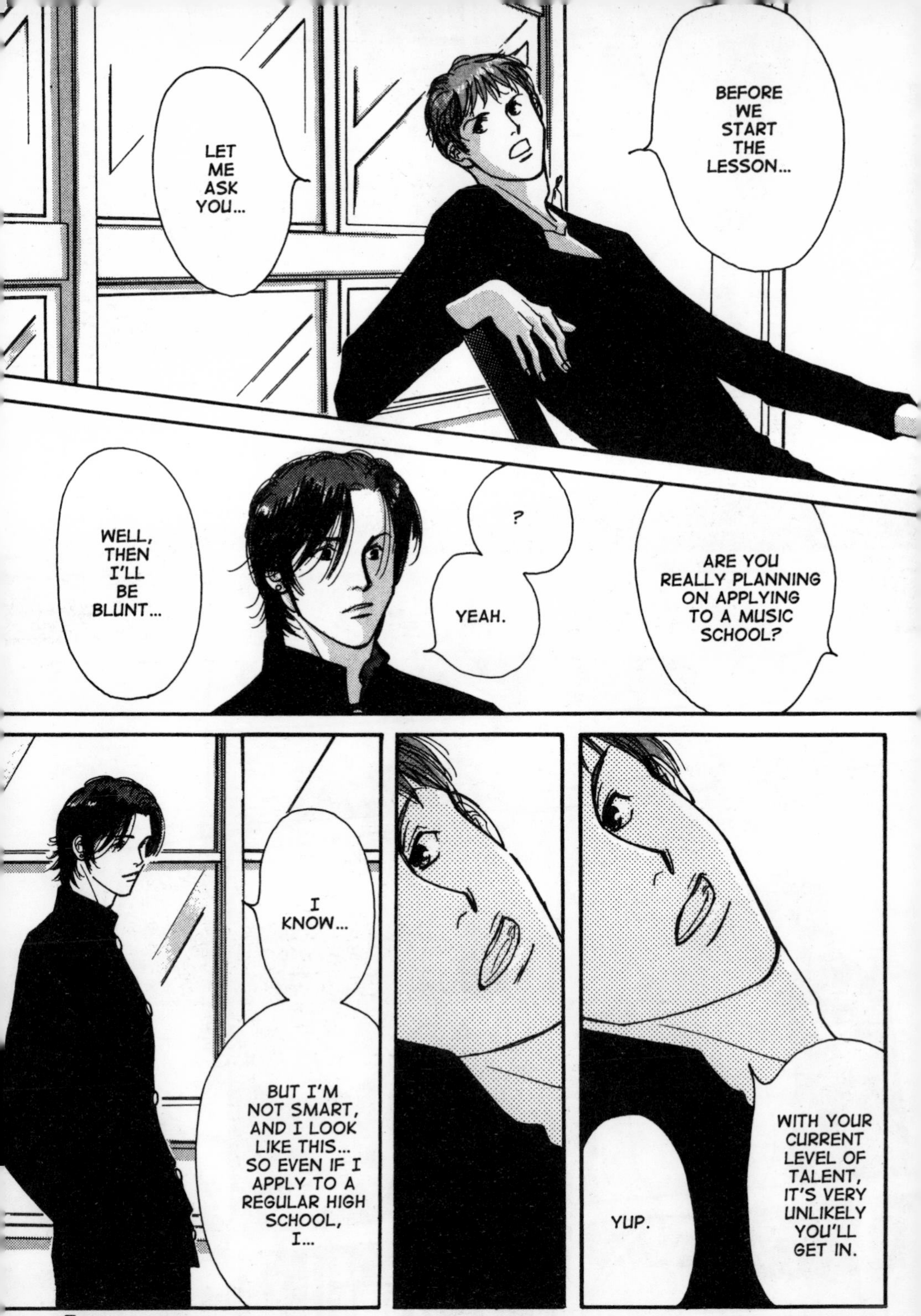
BEFORE WE START THE LESSON...
LET ME ASK YOU...
ARE YOU REALLY PLANNING ON APPLYING TO A MUSIC SCHOOL?
?
YEAH.
WELL, THEN I'LL BE BLUNT...
WITH YOUR CURRENT LEVEL OF TALENT, IT'S VERY UNLIKELY YOU'LL GET IN.
YUP.
I KNOW...
BUT I'M NOT SMART, AND I LOOK LIKE THIS... SO EVEN IF I APPLY TO A REGULAR HIGH SCHOOL, I...

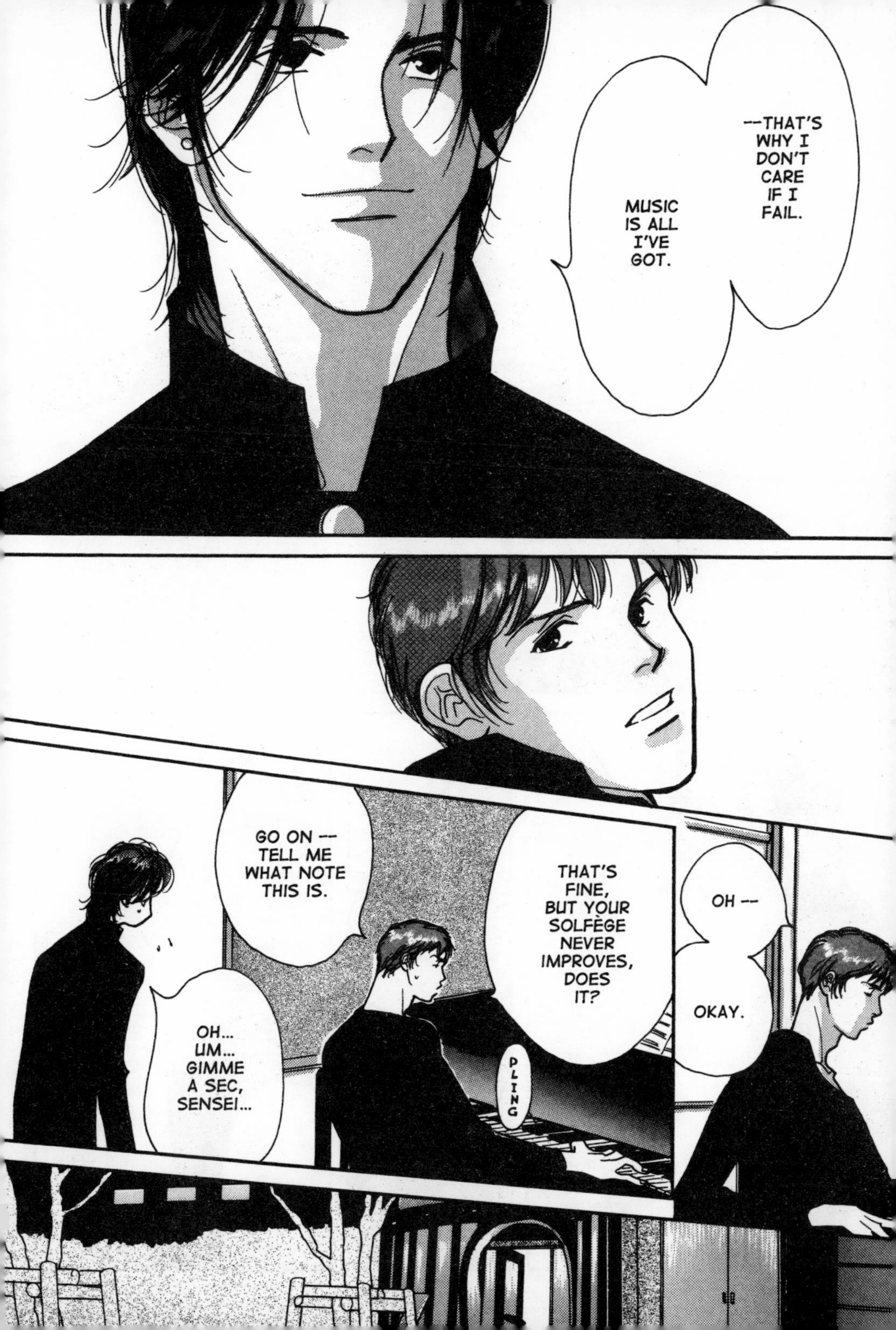
--THAT'S WHY I DON'T CARE IF I FAIL.
MUSIC IS ALL I'VE GOT.
OH --
OKAY.
THAT'S FINE, BUT YOUR SOLFÈGE NEVER IMPROVES, DOES IT?
GO ON -- TELL ME WHAT NOTE THIS IS.
PLING
OH... UM... GIMME A SEC, SENSEI...

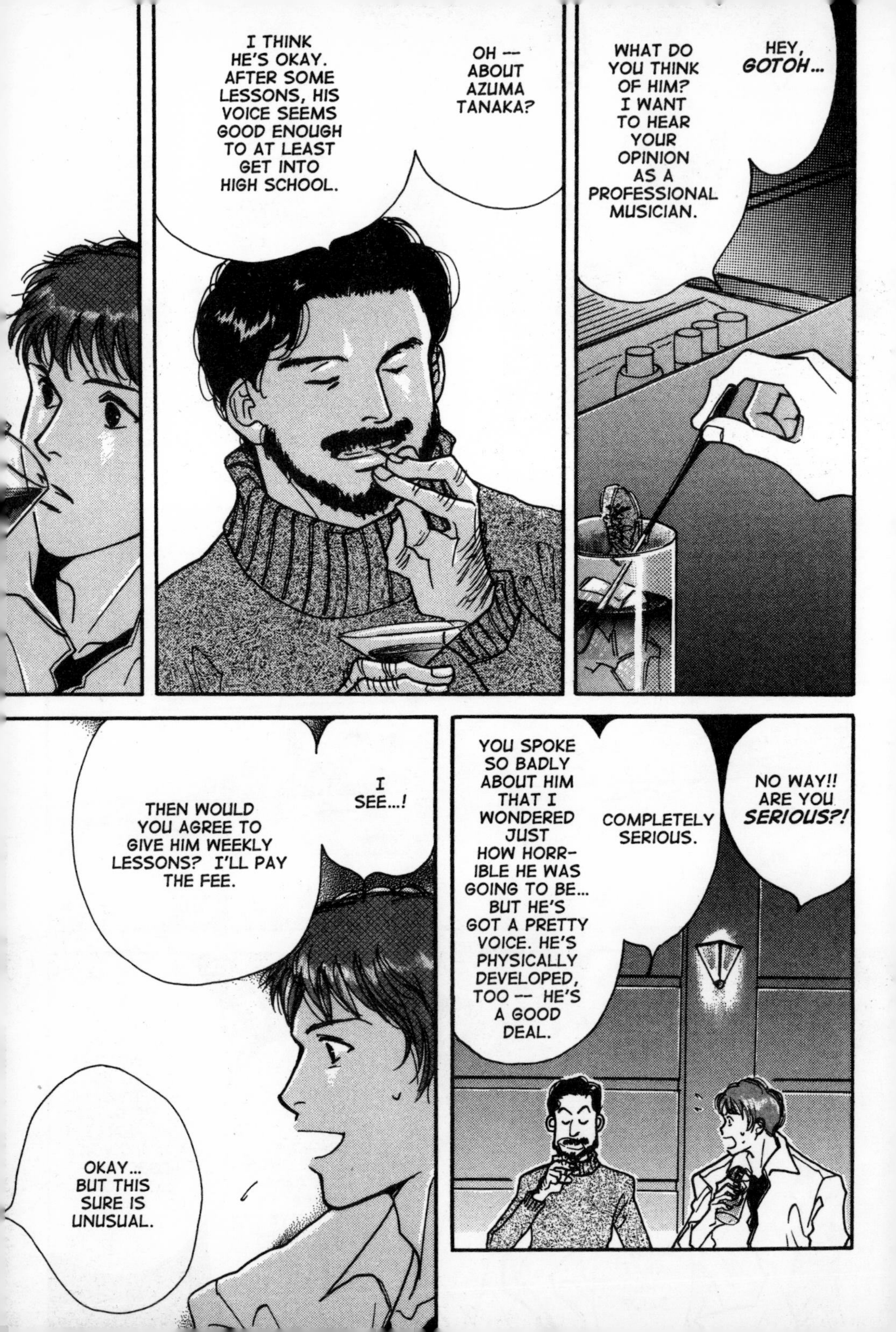
HEY, *GOTOH*...
WHAT DO YOU THINK OF HIM? I WANT TO HEAR YOUR OPINION AS A PROFESSIONAL MUSICIAN.
OH -- ABOUT AZUMA TANAKA?
I THINK HE'S OKAY. AFTER SOME LESSONS, HIS VOICE SEEMS GOOD ENOUGH TO AT LEAST GET INTO HIGH SCHOOL.
NO WAY!! ARE YOU *SERIOUS?!*
COMPLETELY SERIOUS.
YOU SPOKE SO BADLY ABOUT HIM THAT I WONDERED JUST HOW HORR-IBLE HE WAS GOING TO BE... BUT HE'S GOT A PRETTY VOICE. HE'S PHYSICALLY DEVELOPED, TOO -- HE'S A GOOD DEAL.
I SEE...!
THEN WOULD YOU AGREE TO GIVE HIM WEEKLY LESSONS? I'LL PAY THE FEE.
OKAY... BUT THIS SURE IS UNUSUAL.

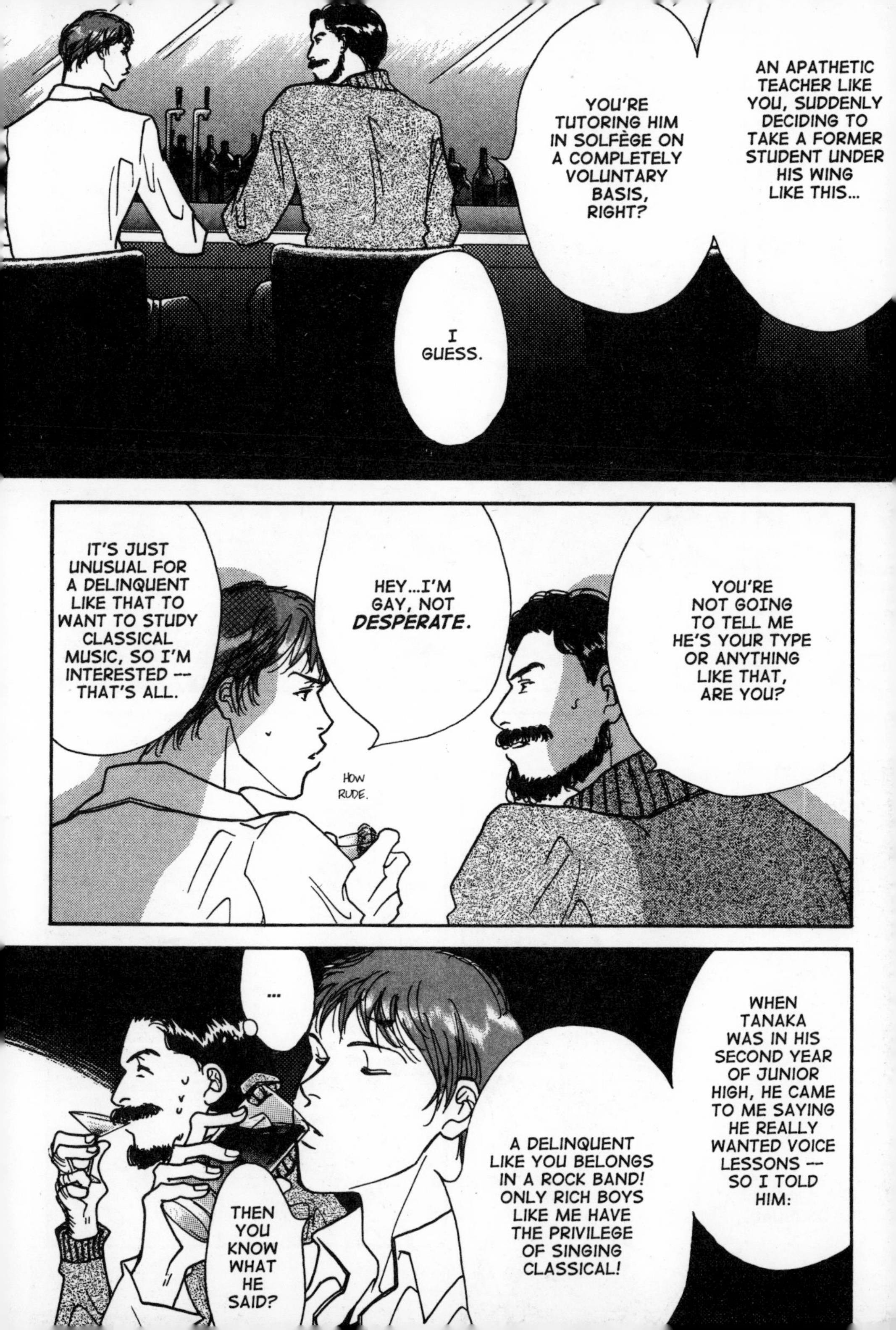
AN APATHETIC TEACHER LIKE YOU, SUDDENLY DECIDING TO TAKE A FORMER STUDENT UNDER HIS WING LIKE THIS...
YOU'RE TUTORING HIM IN SOLFÈGE ON A COMPLETELY VOLUNTARY BASIS, RIGHT?
I GUESS.
YOU'RE NOT GOING TO TELL ME HE'S YOUR TYPE OR ANYTHING LIKE THAT, ARE YOU?
HEY...I'M GAY, NOT *DESPERATE*.
HOW RUDE.
IT'S JUST UNUSUAL FOR A DELINQUENT LIKE THAT TO WANT TO STUDY CLASSICAL MUSIC, SO I'M INTERESTED -- THAT'S ALL.
WHEN TANAKA WAS IN HIS SECOND YEAR OF JUNIOR HIGH, HE CAME TO ME SAYING HE REALLY WANTED VOICE LESSONS -- SO I TOLD HIM:
A DELINQUENT LIKE YOU BELONGS IN A ROCK BAND! ONLY RICH BOYS LIKE ME HAVE THE PRIVILEGE OF SINGING CLASSICAL!
...
THEN YOU KNOW WHAT HE SAID?

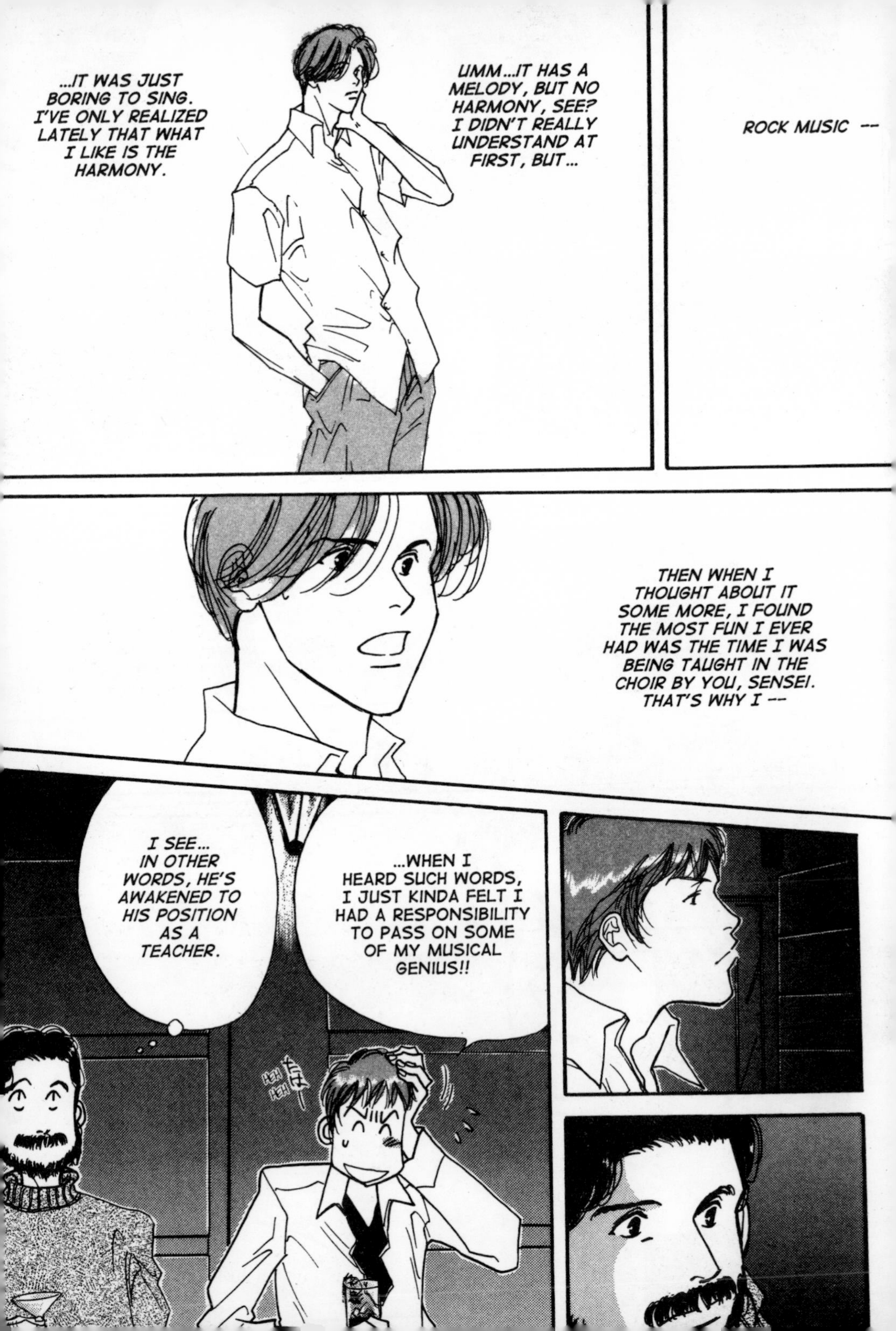
ROCK MUSIC --
UMM...IT HAS A MELODY, BUT NO HARMONY, SEE? I DIDN'T REALLY UNDERSTAND AT FIRST, BUT...
...IT WAS JUST BORING TO SING. I'VE ONLY REALIZED LATELY THAT WHAT I LIKE IS THE HARMONY.
THEN WHEN I THOUGHT ABOUT IT SOME MORE, I FOUND THE MOST FUN I EVER HAD WAS THE TIME I WAS BEING TAUGHT IN THE CHOIR BY YOU, SENSEI. THAT'S WHY I --
...WHEN I HEARD SUCH WORDS, I JUST KINDA FELT I HAD A RESPONSIBILITY TO PASS ON SOME OF MY MUSICAL GENIUS!!
HEH HEH
I SEE... IN OTHER WORDS, HE'S AWAKENED TO HIS POSITION AS A TEACHER.

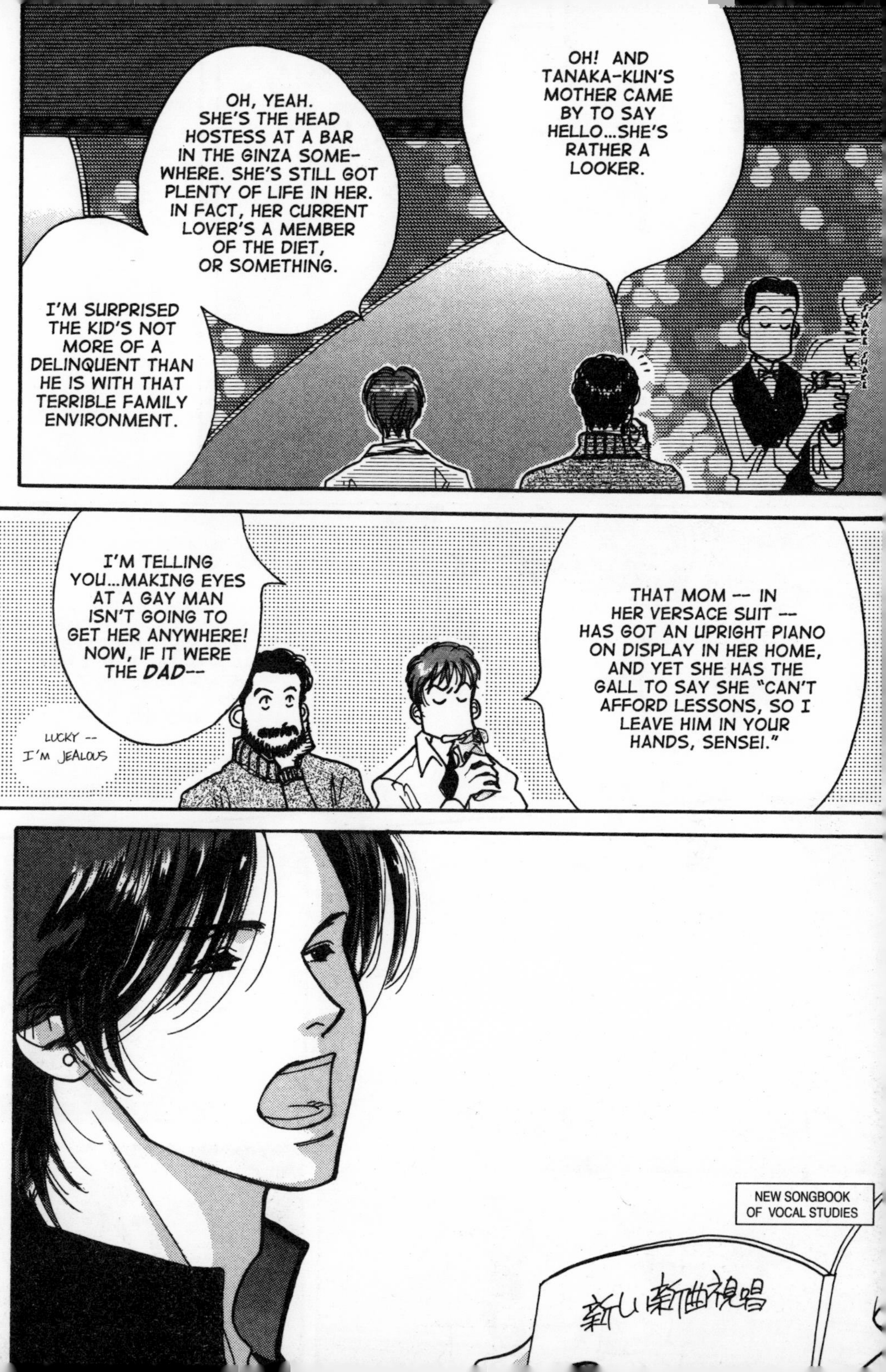
OH! AND TANAKA-KUN'S MOTHER CAME BY TO SAY HELLO...SHE'S RATHER A LOOKER.
SHAKE SHAKE
OH, YEAH. SHE'S THE HEAD HOSTESS AT A BAR IN THE GINZA SOME-WHERE. SHE'S STILL GOT PLENTY OF LIFE IN HER. IN FACT, HER CURRENT LOVER'S A MEMBER OF THE DIET, OR SOMETHING.
I'M SURPRISED THE KID'S NOT MORE OF A DELINQUENT THAN HE IS WITH THAT TERRIBLE FAMILY ENVIRONMENT.
THAT MOM -- IN HER VERSACE SUIT -- HAS GOT AN UPRIGHT PIANO ON DISPLAY IN HER HOME, AND YET SHE HAS THE GALL TO SAY SHE "CAN'T AFFORD LESSONS, SO I LEAVE HIM IN YOUR HANDS, SENSEI."
I'M TELLING YOU...MAKING EYES AT A GAY MAN ISN'T GOING TO GET HER ANYWHERE! NOW, IF IT WERE THE *DAD*--
LUCKY -- I'M JEALOUS
NEW SONGBOOK OF VOCAL STUDIES
新しい新曲視唱

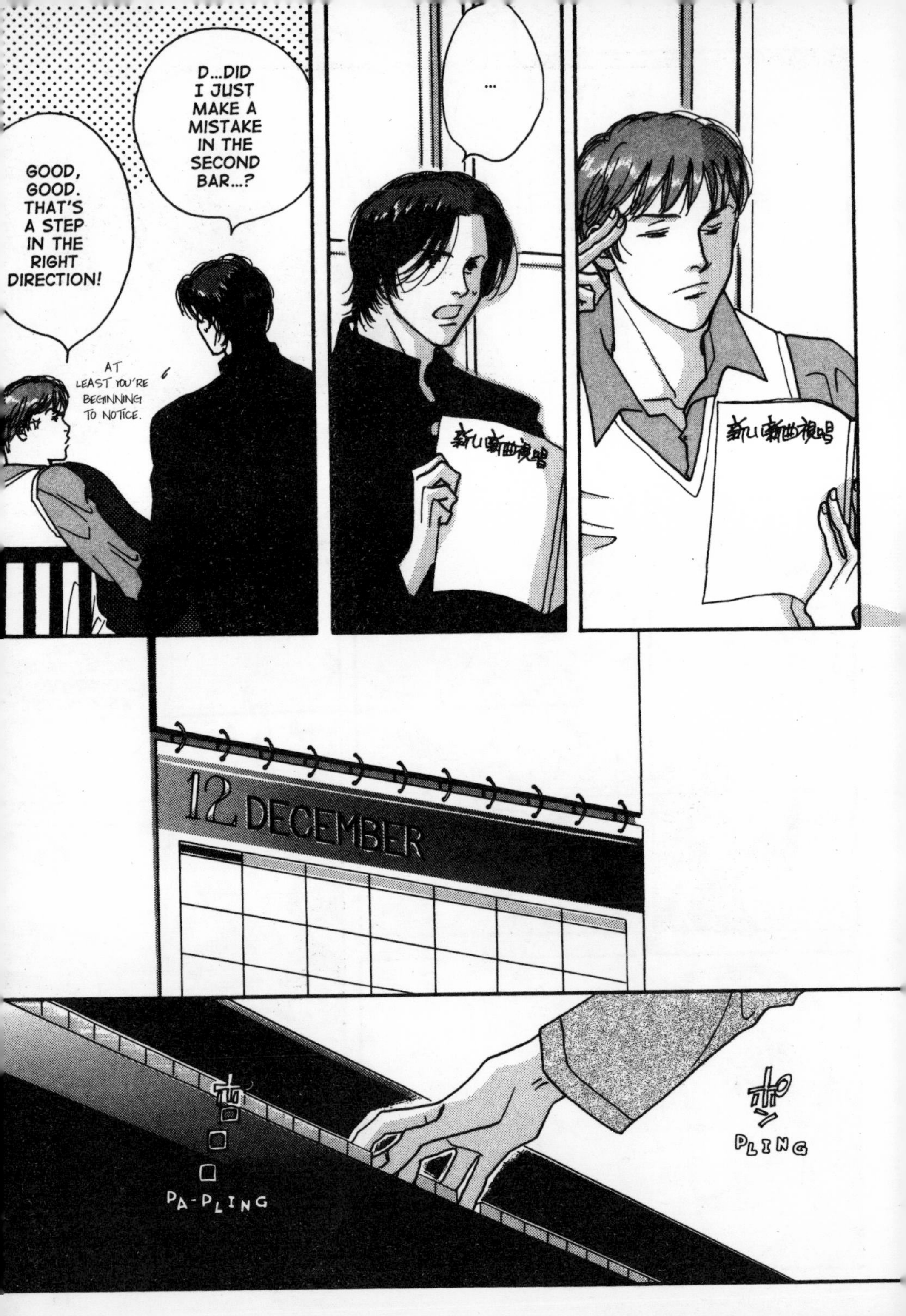
...
D...DID I JUST MAKE A MISTAKE IN THE SECOND BAR...?
GOOD, GOOD. THAT'S A STEP IN THE RIGHT DIRECTION!
AT LEAST YOU'RE BEGINNING TO NOTICE.
12 DECEMBER
PLING
PA-PLING

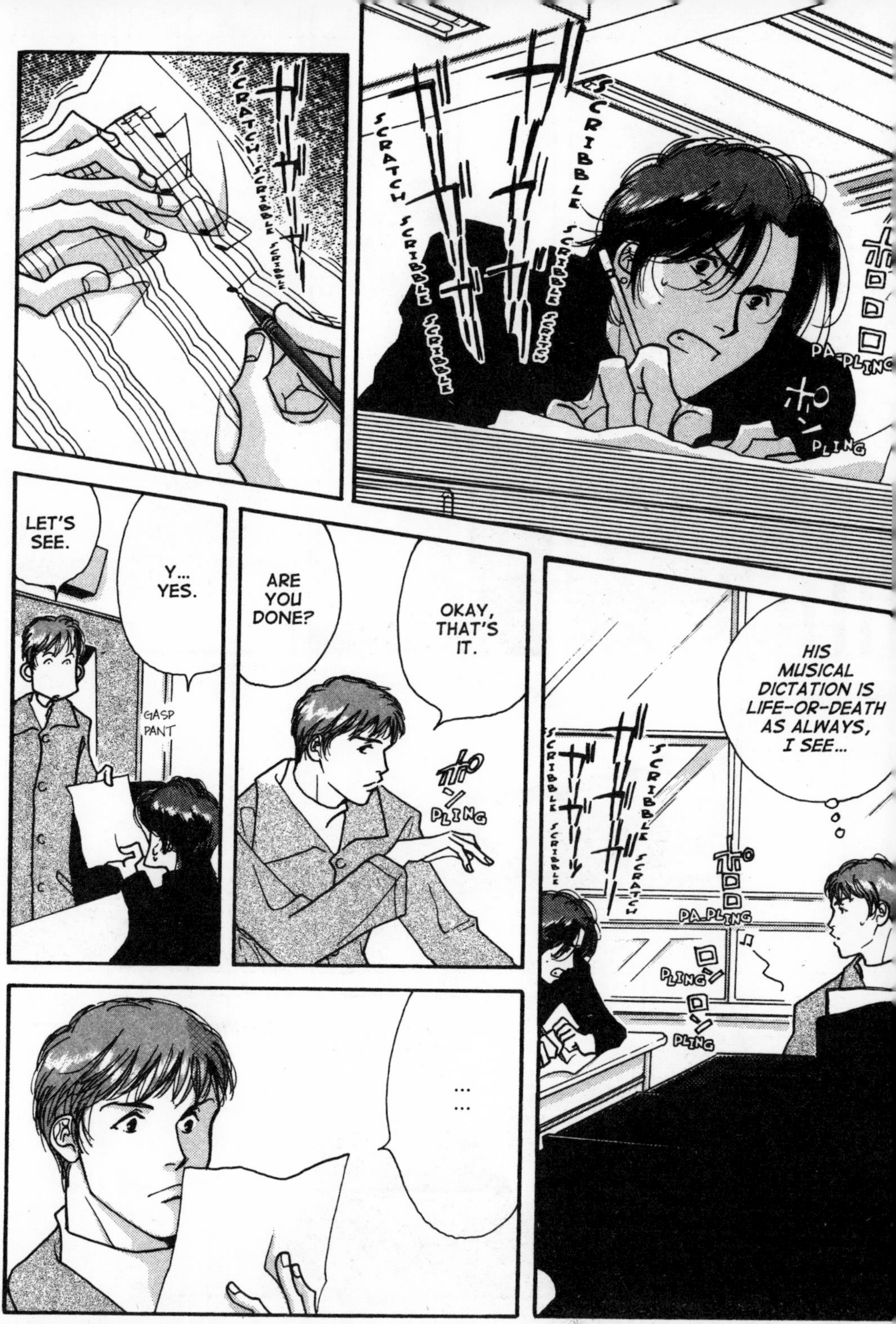

SCRIBBLE
SCRIBBLE SCRIBBLE
SCRATCH SCRIBBLE SCRIBBLE
PA-PLING
PLING
SCRATCH SCRIBBLE SCRIBBLE
HIS MUSICAL DICTATION IS LIFE-OR-DEATH AS ALWAYS, I SEE...
SCRIBBLE SCRATCH
SCRIBBLE SCRIBBLE
PA-PLING
PLING
PLING
OKAY, THAT'S IT.
ARE YOU DONE?
PLING
Y... YES.
LET'S SEE.
GASP PANT
... ...

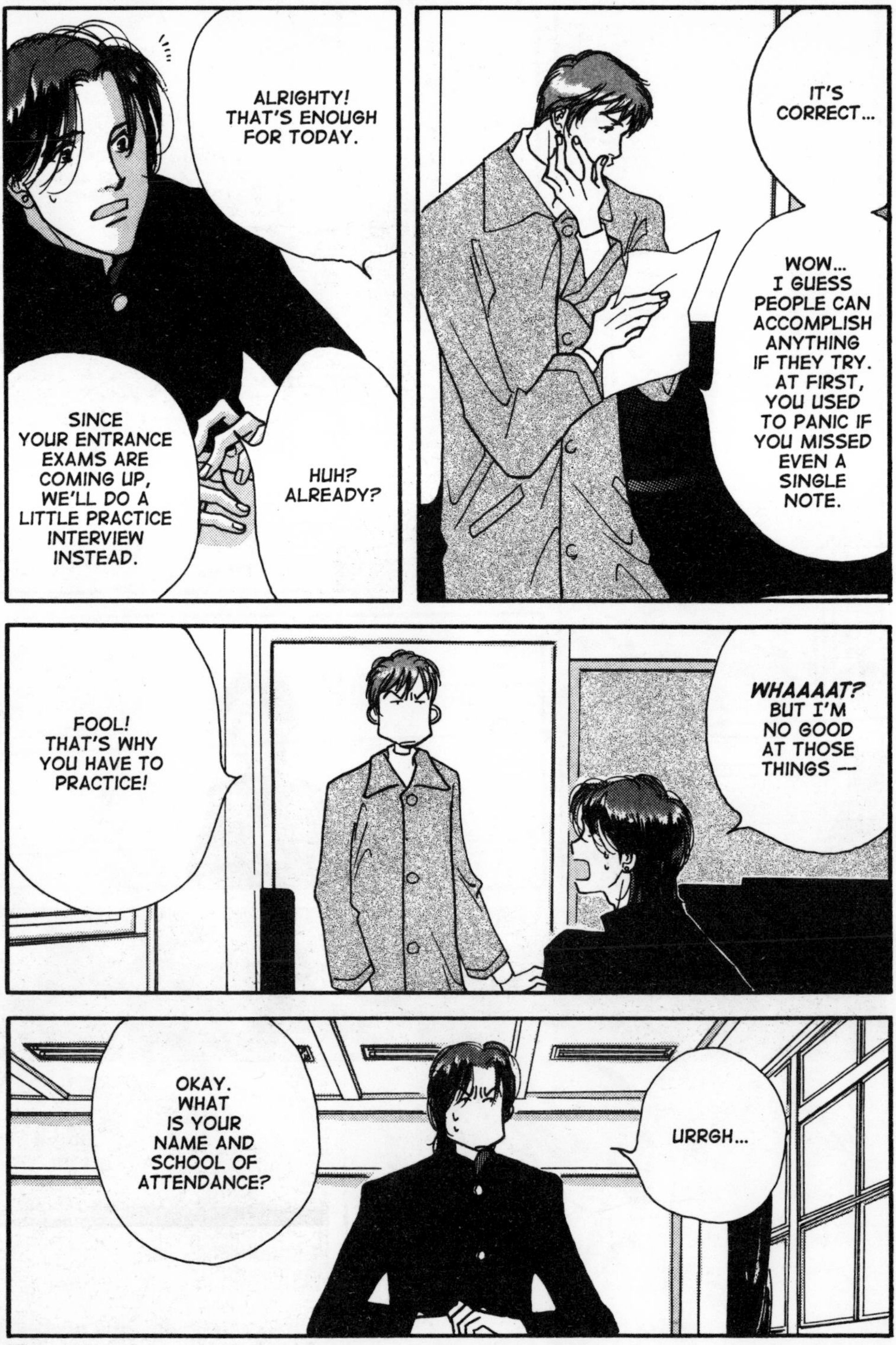
IT'S CORRECT...
WOW... I GUESS PEOPLE CAN ACCOMPLISH ANYTHING IF THEY TRY. AT FIRST, YOU USED TO PANIC IF YOU MISSED EVEN A SINGLE NOTE.
ALRIGHTY! THAT'S ENOUGH FOR TODAY.
HUH? ALREADY?
SINCE YOUR ENTRANCE EXAMS ARE COMING UP, WE'LL DO A LITTLE PRACTICE INTERVIEW INSTEAD.
WHAAAAT? BUT I'M NO GOOD AT THOSE THINGS --
FOOL! THAT'S WHY YOU HAVE TO PRACTICE!
URRGH...
OKAY. WHAT IS YOUR NAME AND SCHOOL OF ATTENDANCE?

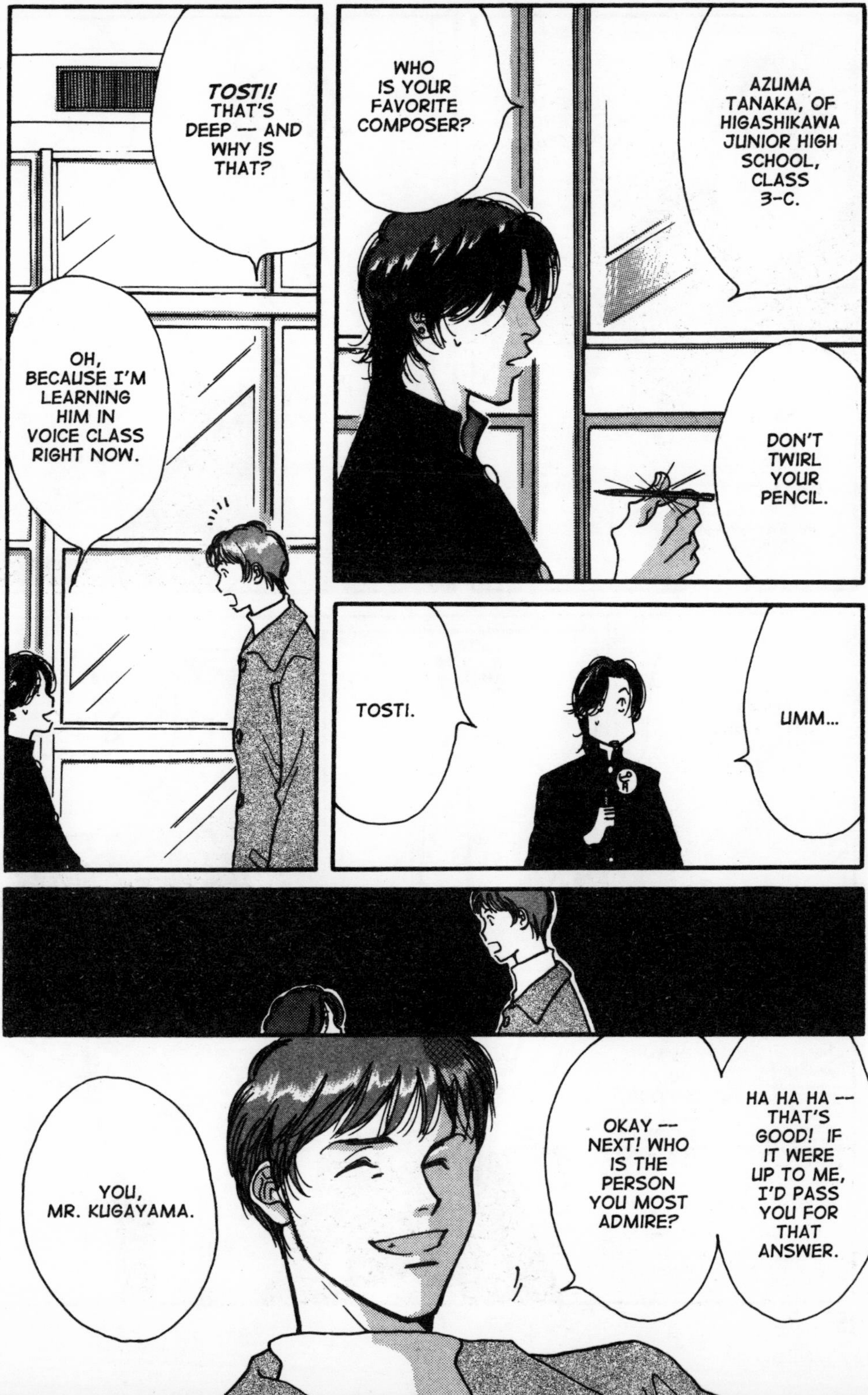
AZUMA TANAKA, OF HIGASHIKAWA JUNIOR HIGH SCHOOL, CLASS 3-C.
WHO IS YOUR FAVORITE COMPOSER?
DON'T TWIRL YOUR PENCIL.
UMM...
TOSTI.
TOSTI! THAT'S DEEP -- AND WHY IS THAT?
OH, BECAUSE I'M LEARNING HIM IN VOICE CLASS RIGHT NOW.
HA HA HA -- THAT'S GOOD! IF IT WERE UP TO ME, I'D PASS YOU FOR THAT ANSWER.
OKAY -- NEXT! WHO IS THE PERSON YOU MOST ADMIRE?
YOU, MR. KUGAYAMA.

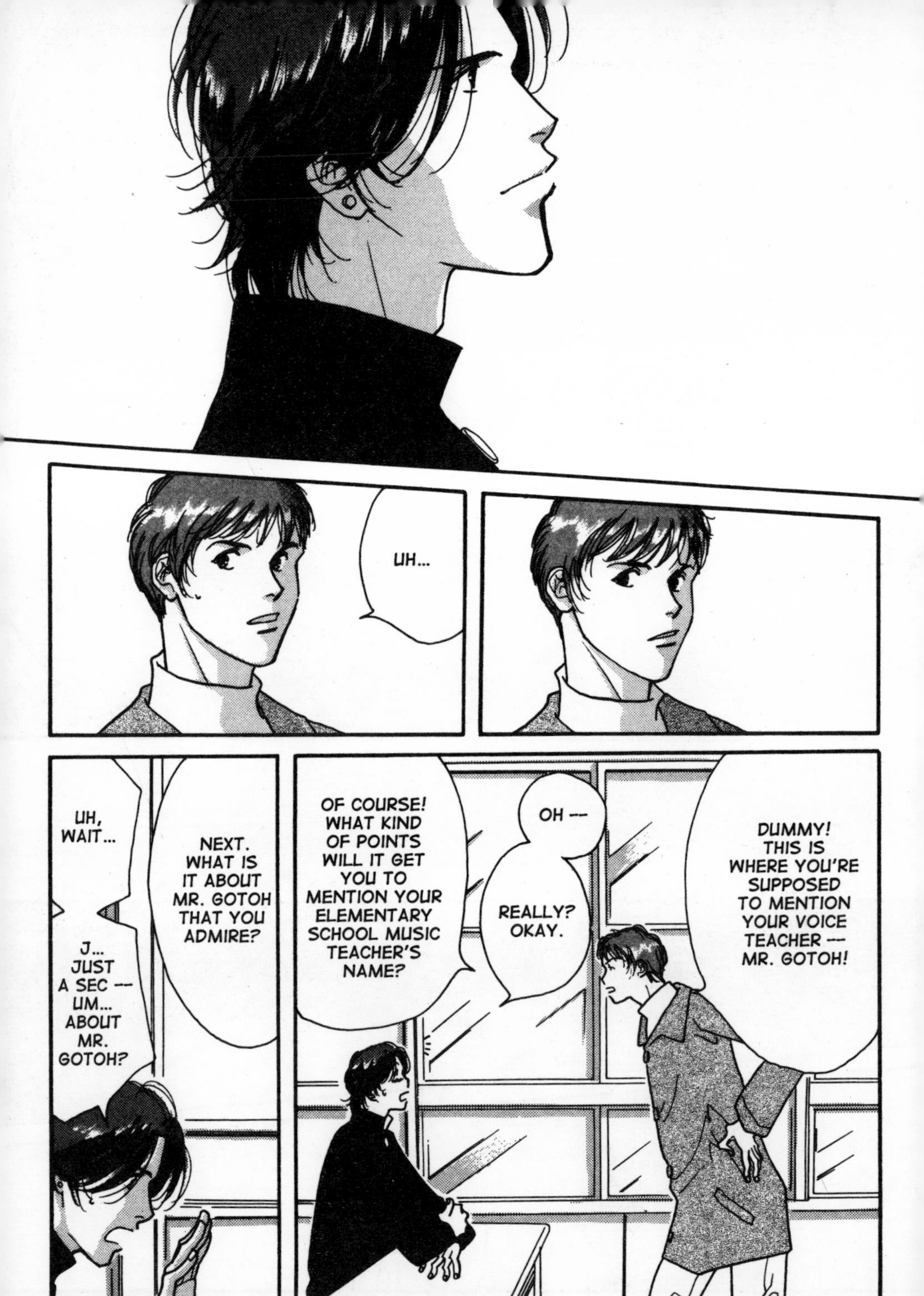
UH...
DUMMY! THIS IS WHERE YOU'RE SUPPOSED TO MENTION YOUR VOICE TEACHER -- MR. GOTOH!
OH --
REALLY? OKAY.
OF COURSE! WHAT KIND OF POINTS WILL IT GET YOU TO MENTION YOUR ELEMENTARY SCHOOL MUSIC TEACHER'S NAME?
NEXT. WHAT IS IT ABOUT MR. GOTOH THAT YOU ADMIRE?
UH, WAIT...
J... JUST A SEC -- UM... ABOUT MR. GOTOH?

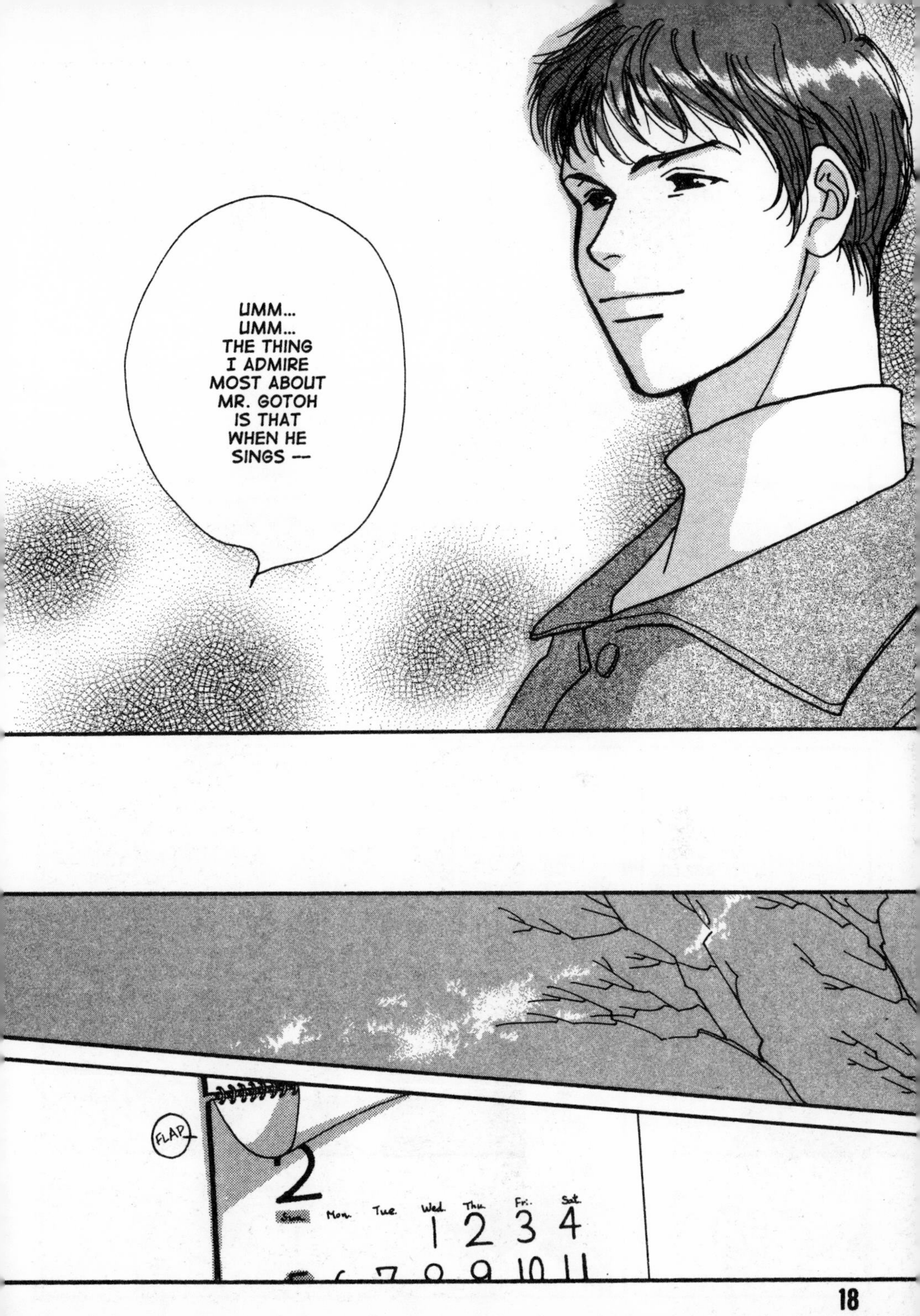
UMM... UMM... THE THING I ADMIRE MOST ABOUT MR. GOTOH IS THAT WHEN HE SINGS --
FLAP
2
Mon. Tue. Wed. Thu. Fri. Sat.
1 2 3 4

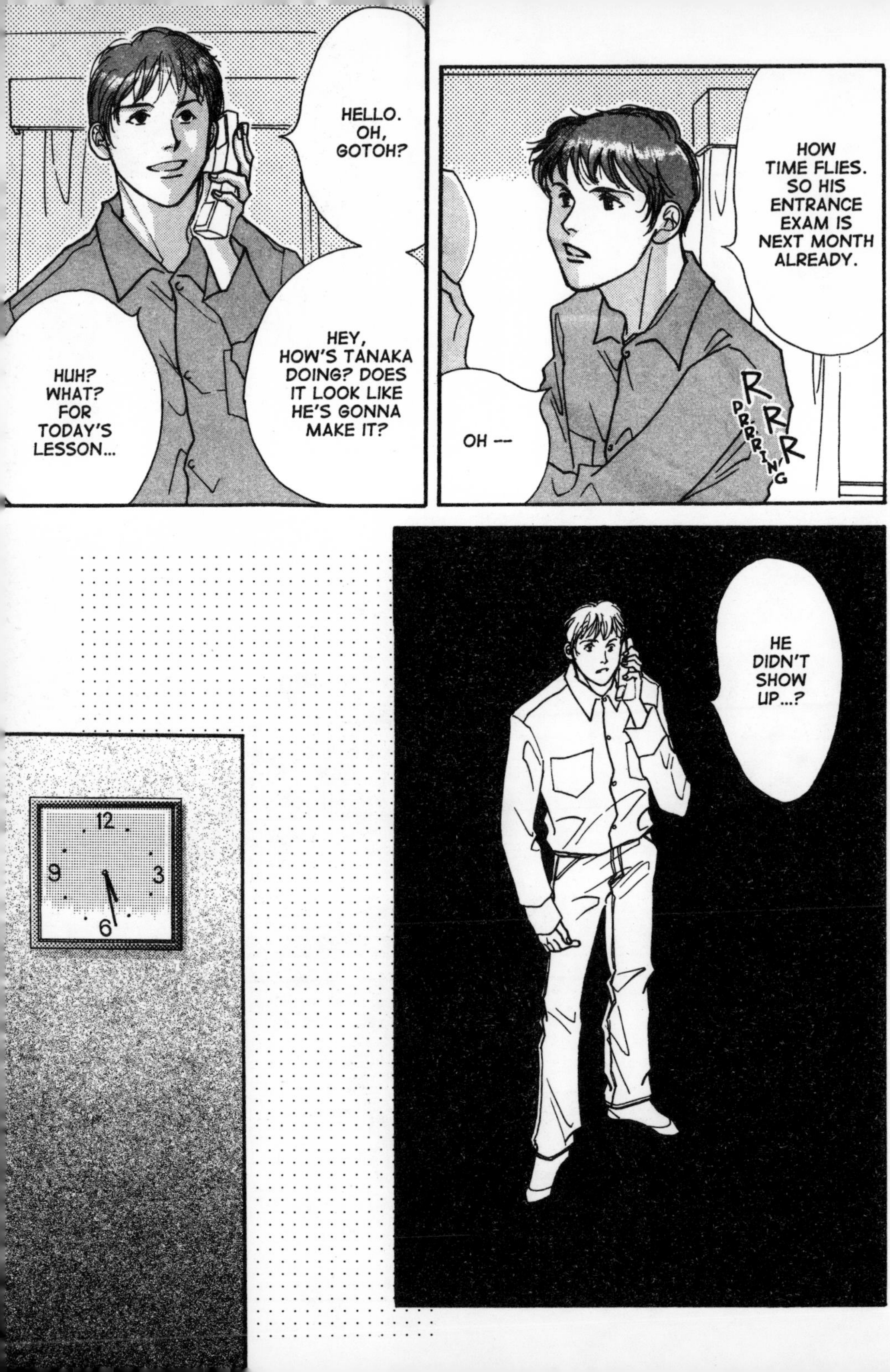
HOW TIME FLIES. SO HIS ENTRANCE EXAM IS NEXT MONTH ALREADY.
RRR
PRRRING
OH --
HELLO. OH, GOTOH?
HEY, HOW'S TANAKA DOING? DOES IT LOOK LIKE HE'S GONNA MAKE IT?
HUH? WHAT? FOR TODAY'S LESSON...
HE DIDN'T SHOW UP...?

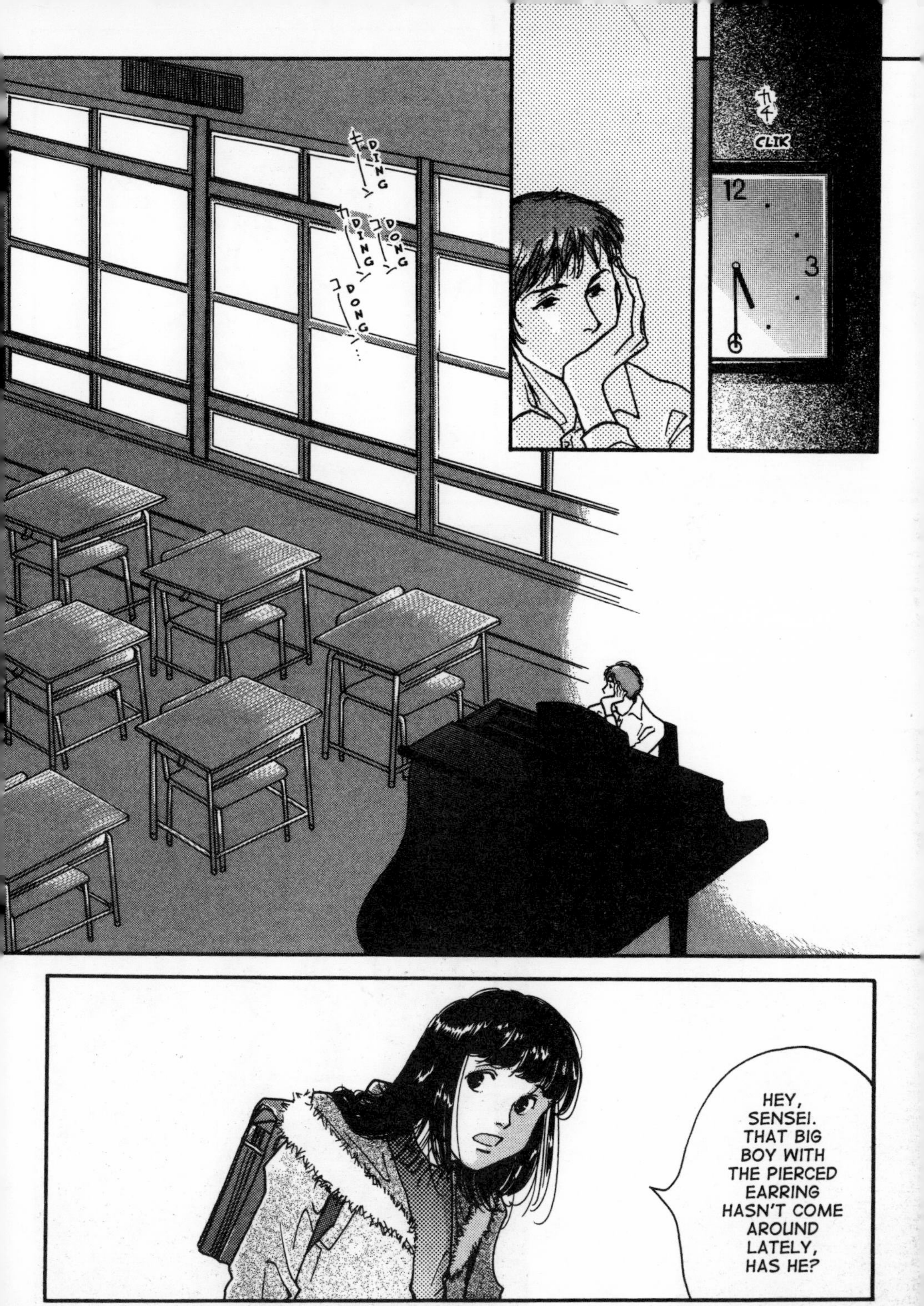
CLIK
DING DONG DING DONG...
HEY, SENSEI. THAT BIG BOY WITH THE PIERCED EARRING HASN'T COME AROUND LATELY, HAS HE?

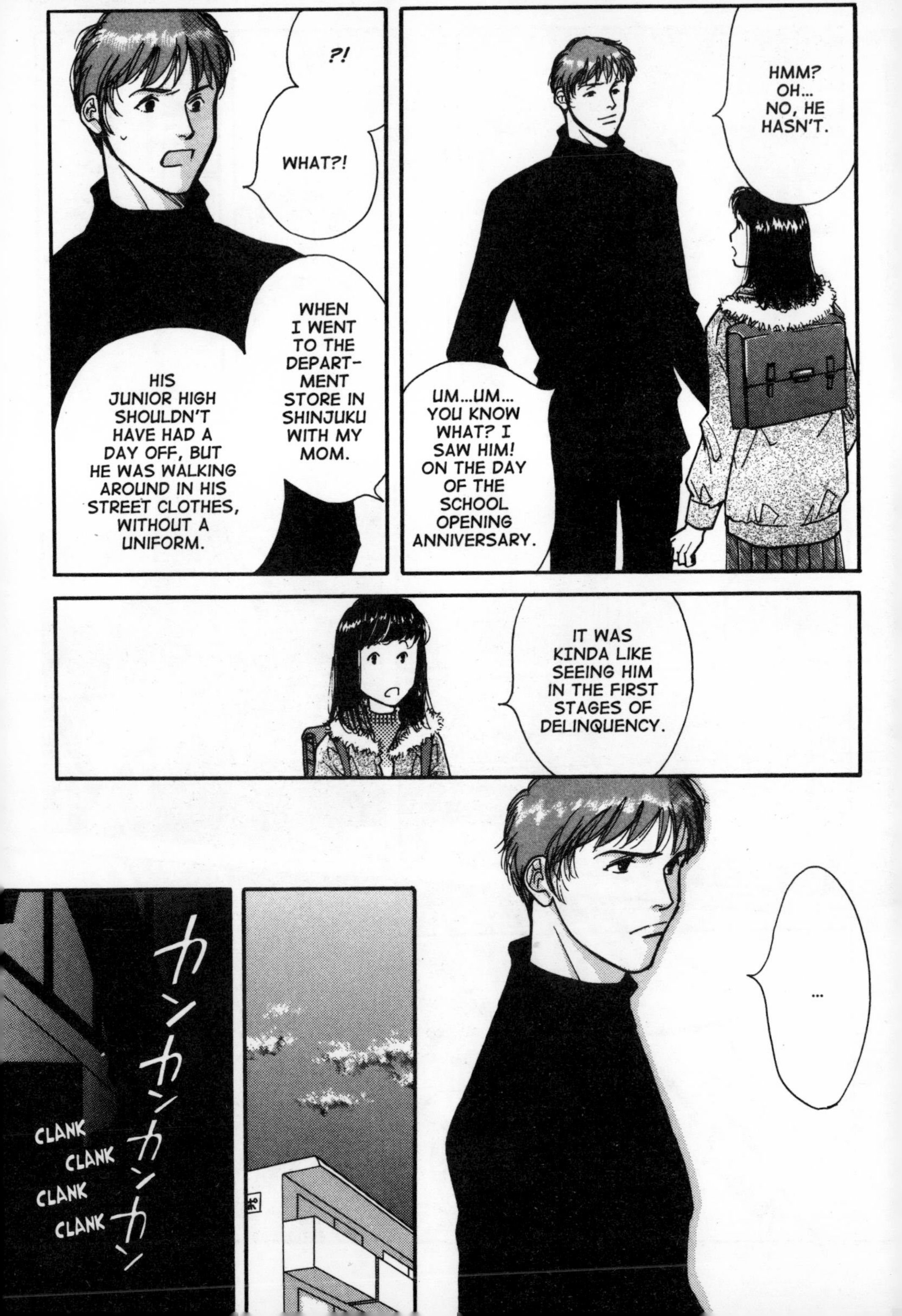
HMM? OH... NO, HE HASN'T.
UM...UM... YOU KNOW WHAT? I SAW HIM! ON THE DAY OF THE SCHOOL OPENING ANNIVERSARY.
?!
WHAT?!
WHEN I WENT TO THE DEPART-MENT STORE IN SHINJUKU WITH MY MOM.
HIS JUNIOR HIGH SHOULDN'T HAVE HAD A DAY OFF, BUT HE WAS WALKING AROUND IN HIS STREET CLOTHES, WITHOUT A UNIFORM.
IT WAS KINDA LIKE SEEING HIM IN THE FIRST STAGES OF DELINQUENCY.
...
カンカンカンカン
CLANK
CLANK
CLANK
CLANK

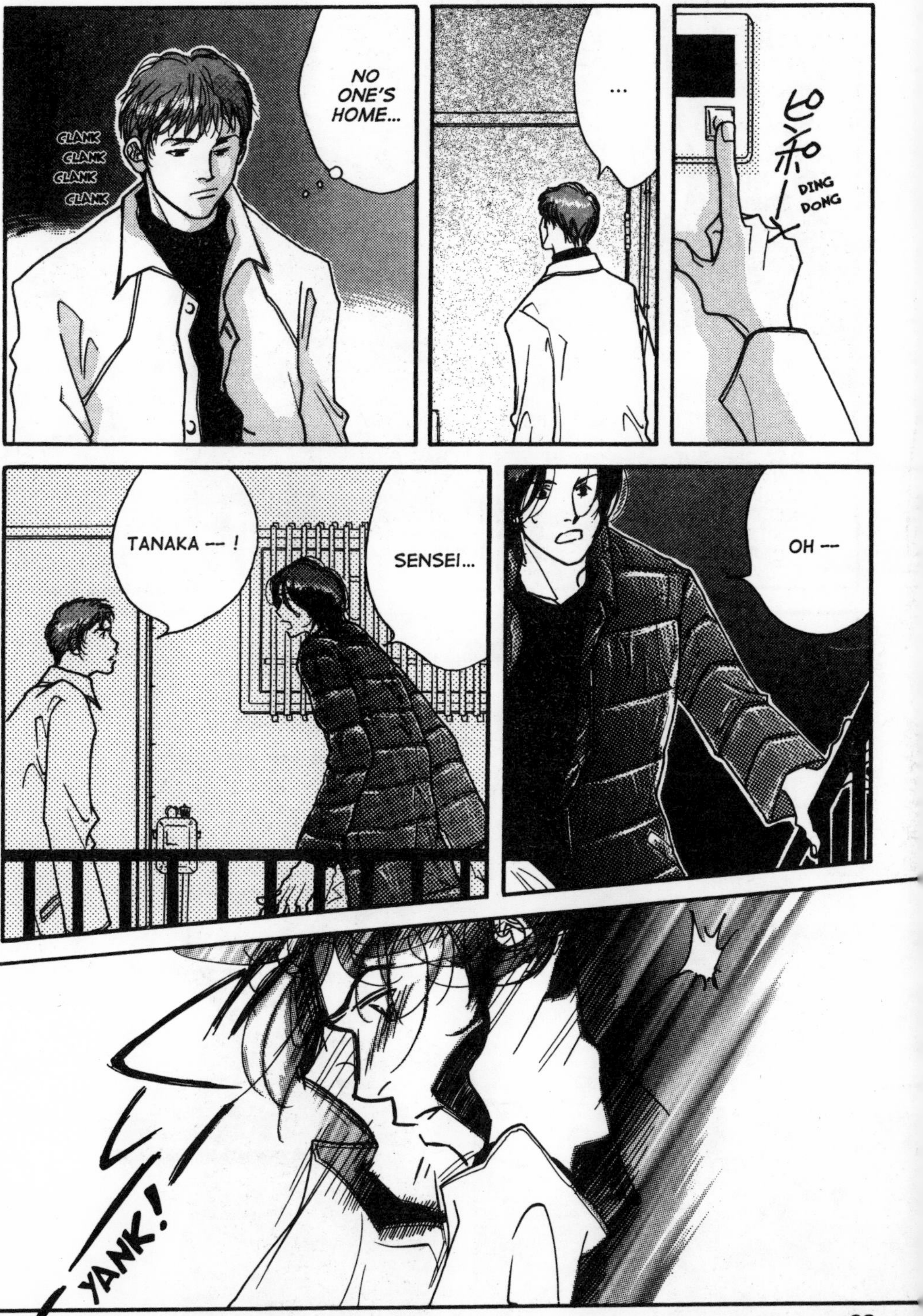
DING DONG
...
NO ONE'S HOME...
CLANK
CLANK
CLANK
CLANK
OH --
SENSEI...
TANAKA -- !
YANK!

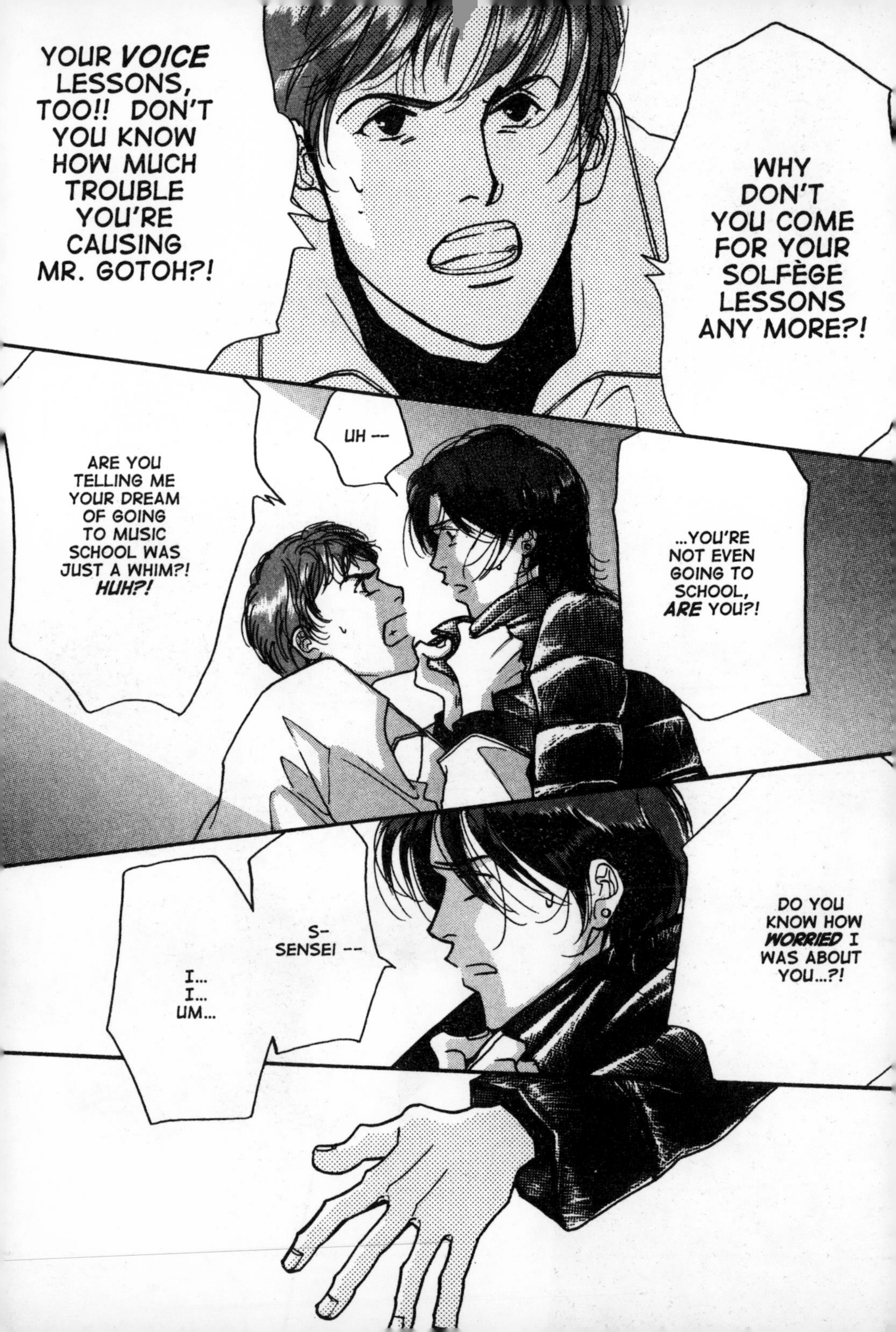
WHY DON'T YOU COME FOR YOUR SOLFÈGE LESSONS ANY MORE?!
YOUR VOICE LESSONS, TOO!! DON'T YOU KNOW HOW MUCH TROUBLE YOU'RE CAUSING MR. GOTOH?!
...YOU'RE NOT EVEN GOING TO SCHOOL, ARE YOU?!
UH --
ARE YOU TELLING ME YOUR DREAM OF GOING TO MUSIC SCHOOL WAS JUST A WHIM?! HUH?!
DO YOU KNOW HOW WORRIED I WAS ABOUT YOU...?!
S- SENSEI --
I... I... UM...

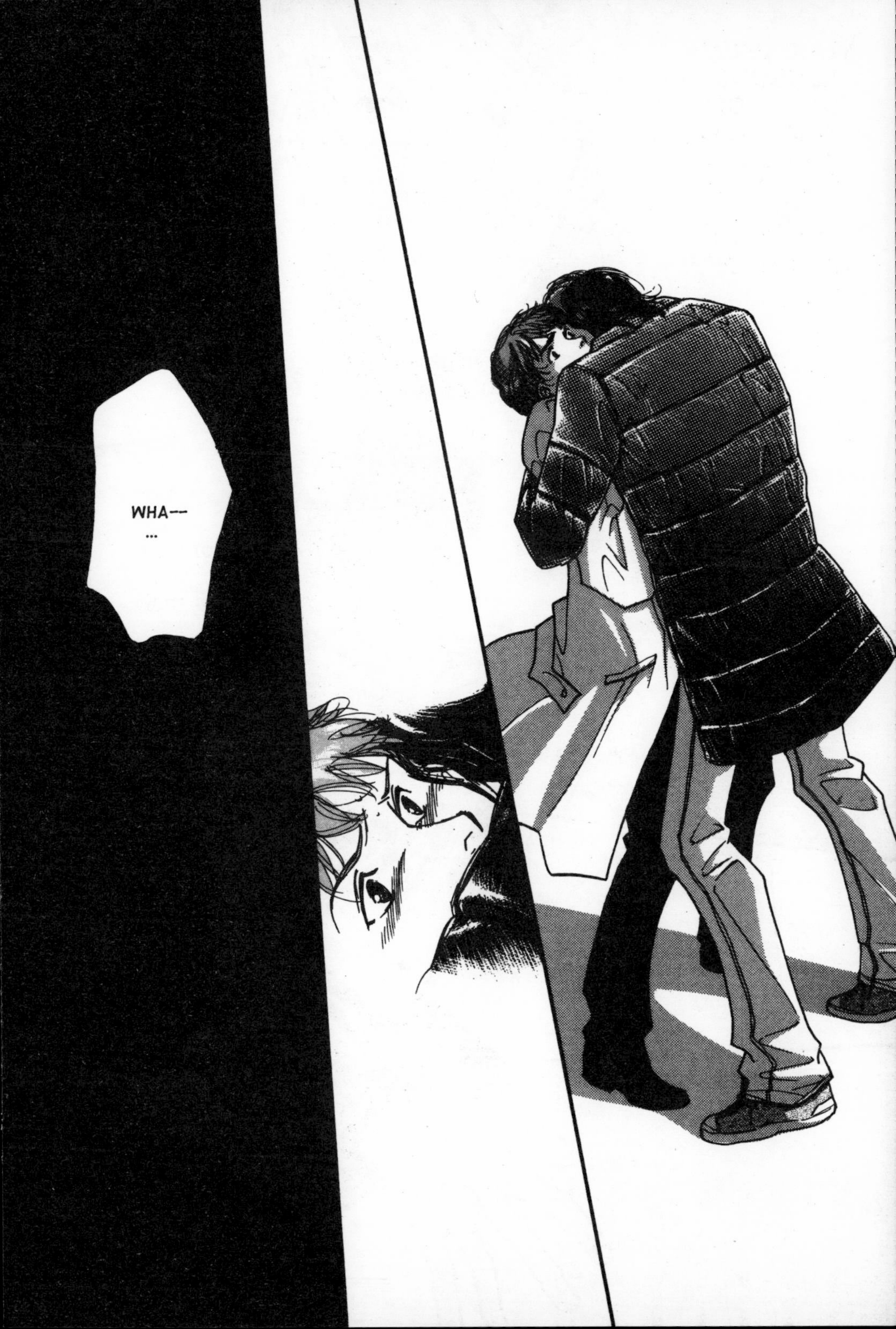
WHA--
...

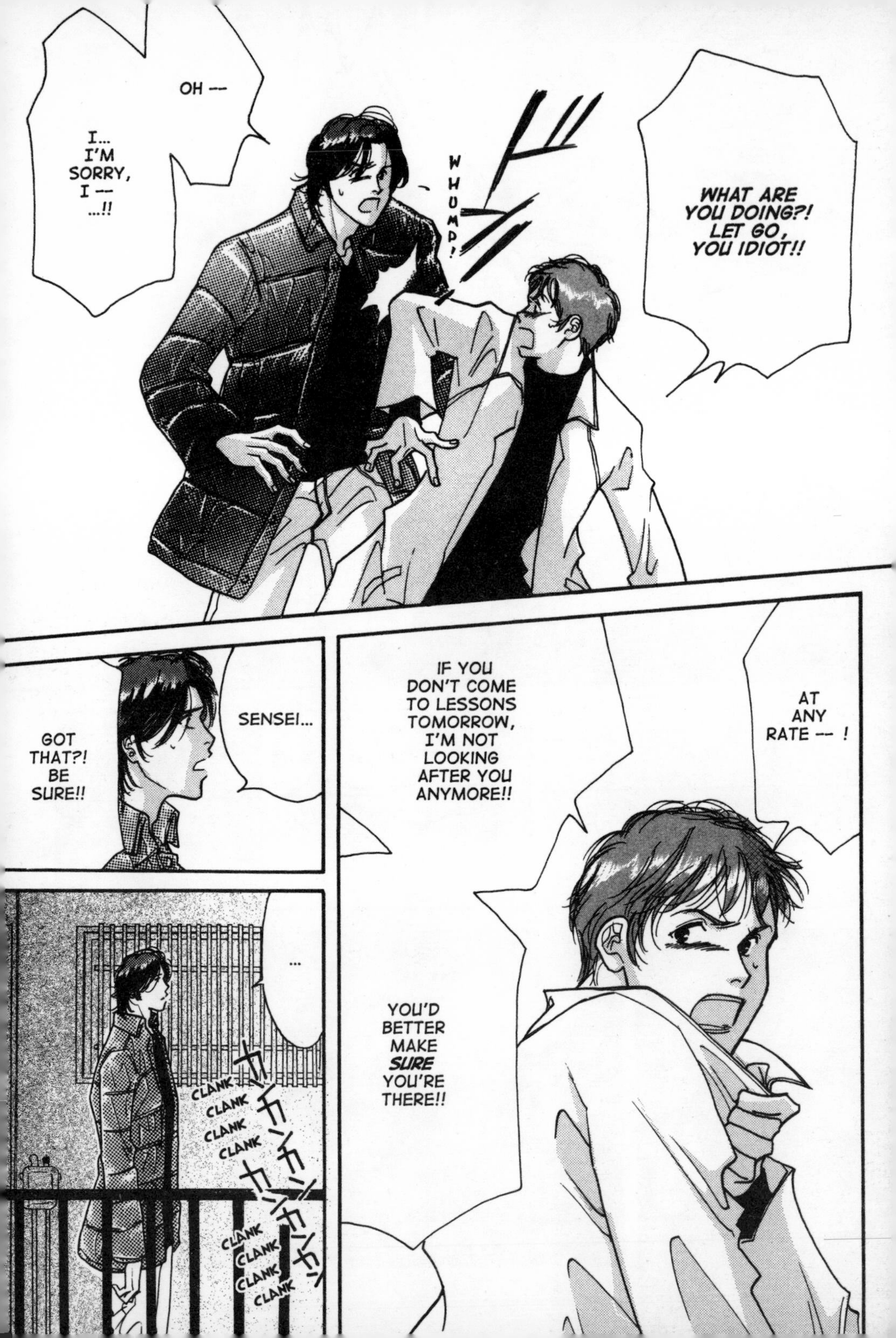
WHAT ARE YOU DOING?! LET GO, YOU IDIOT!!
WHUMP!
OH --
I... I'M SORRY, I --- ...!!
AT ANY RATE -- !
IF YOU DON'T COME TO LESSONS TOMORROW, I'M NOT LOOKING AFTER YOU ANYMORE!!
YOU'D BETTER MAKE SURE YOU'RE THERE!!
SENSEI...
GOT THAT?! BE SURE!!
...
CLANK CLANK CLANK CLANK
CLANK CLANK CLANK CLANK

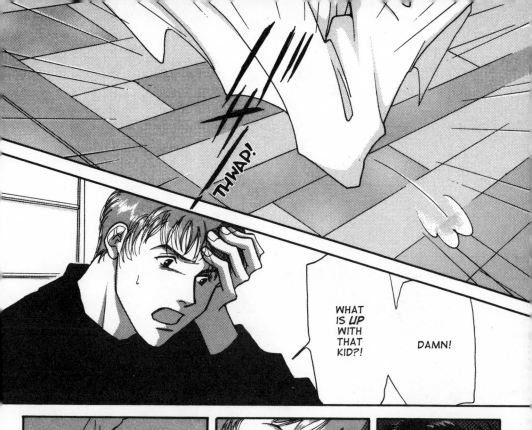

THWAP!

WHAT IS *UP* WITH THAT KID?!

DAMN!

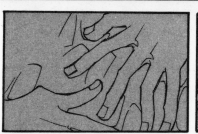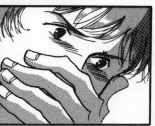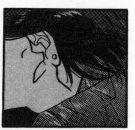

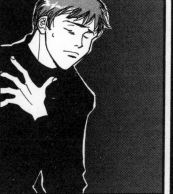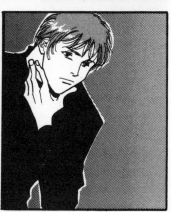

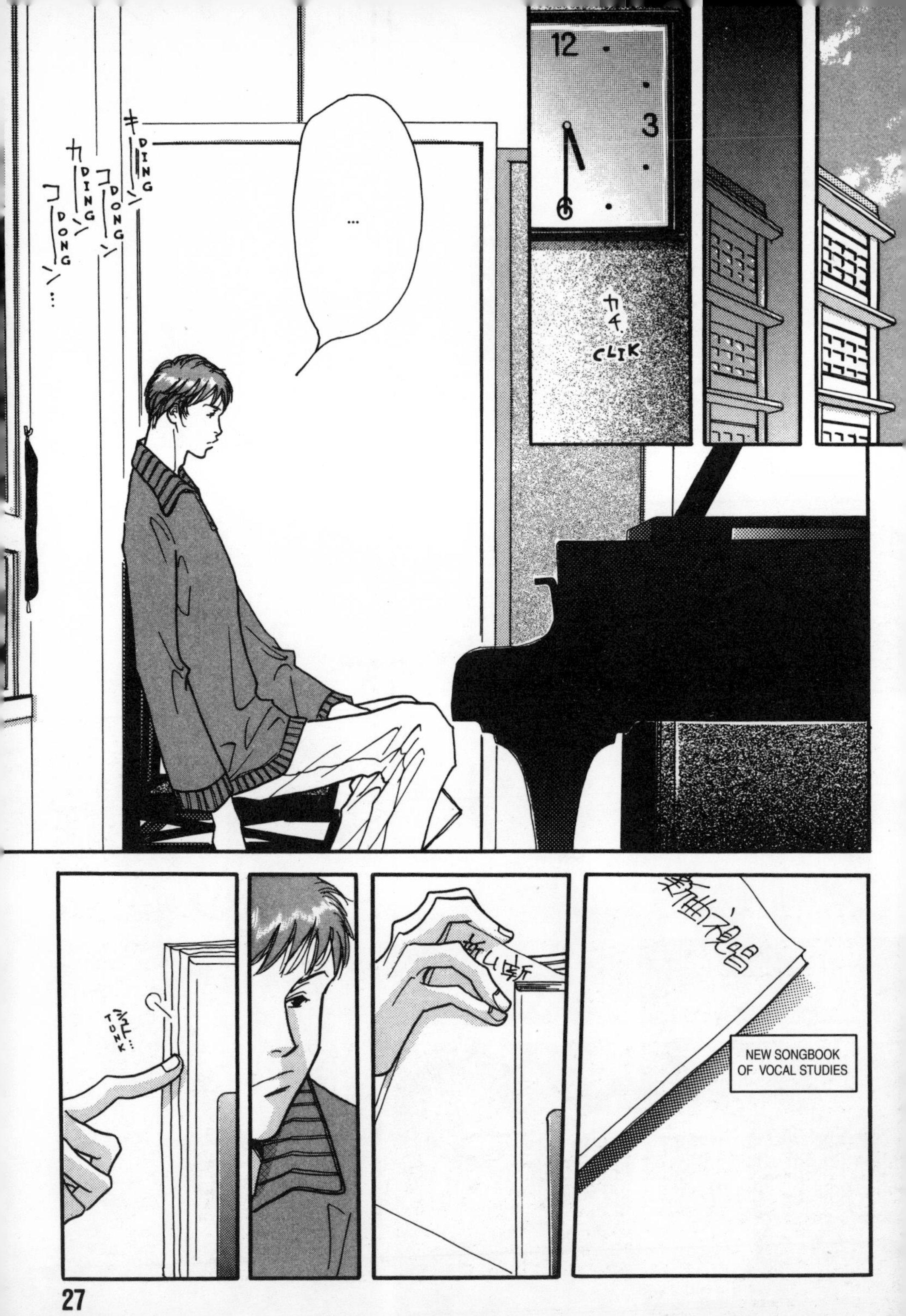

DING DONG DING DONG...
...
12
3
6
カチ
CLIK
新曲視唱
NEW SONGBOOK OF VOCAL STUDIES
TUNK

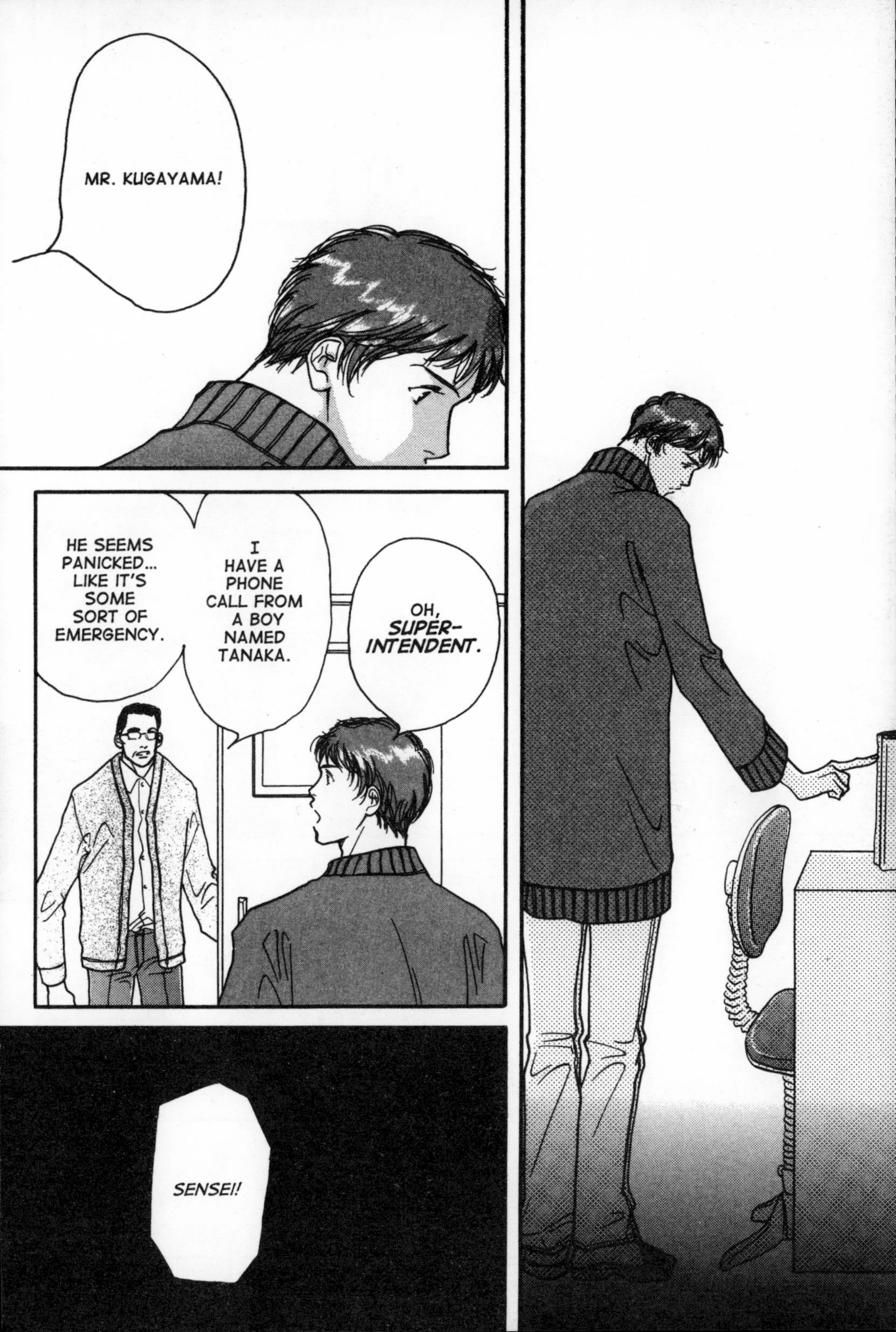
MR. KUGAYAMA!
OH, *SUPER-INTENDENT*.
I HAVE A PHONE CALL FROM A BOY NAMED TANAKA.
HE SEEMS PANICKED... LIKE IT'S SOME SORT OF EMERGENCY.
SENSEI!

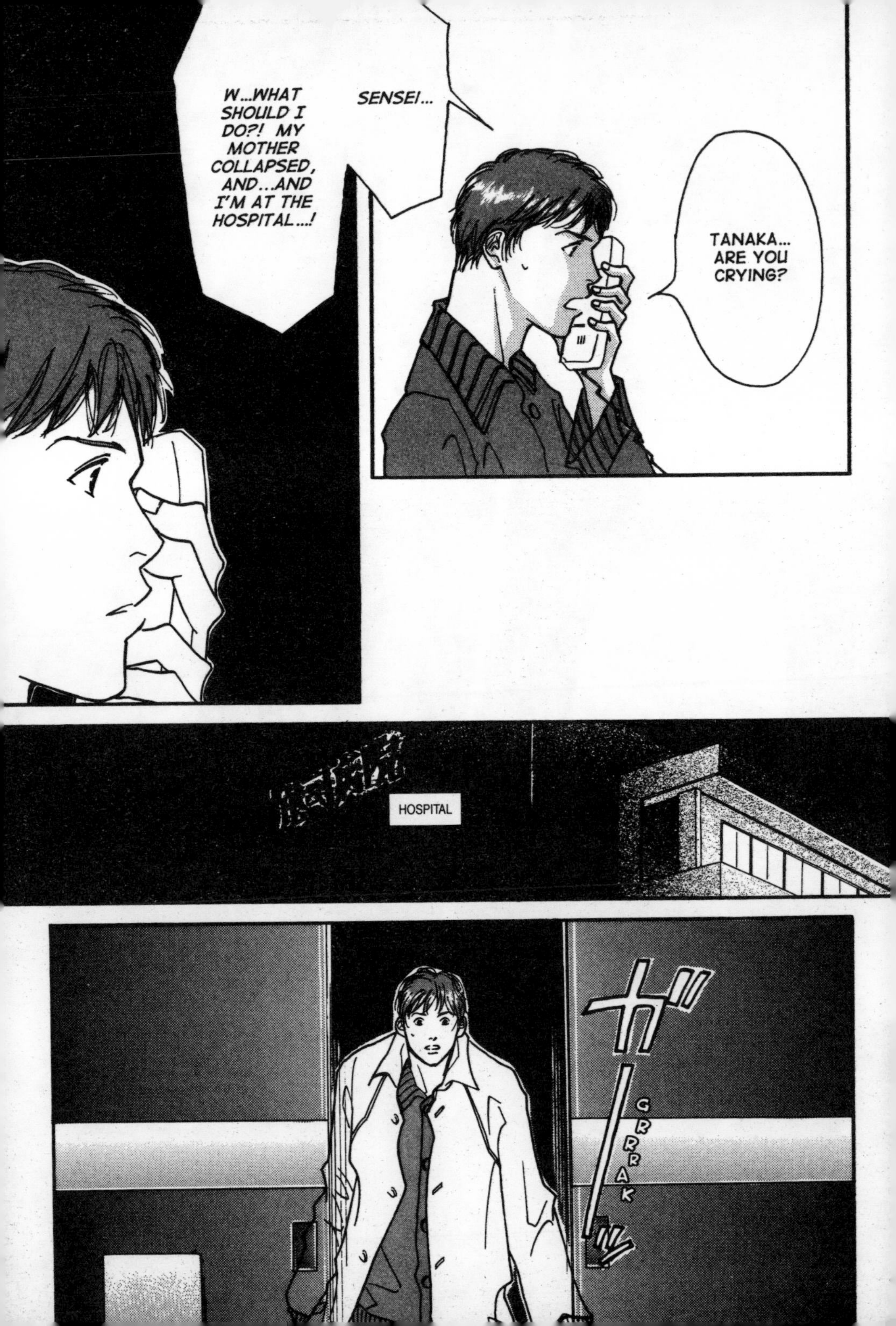
SENSEI...
W...WHAT SHOULD I DO?! MY MOTHER COLLAPSED, AND...AND I'M AT THE HOSPITAL...!
TANAKA... ARE YOU CRYING?
HOSPITAL
GRRRAK

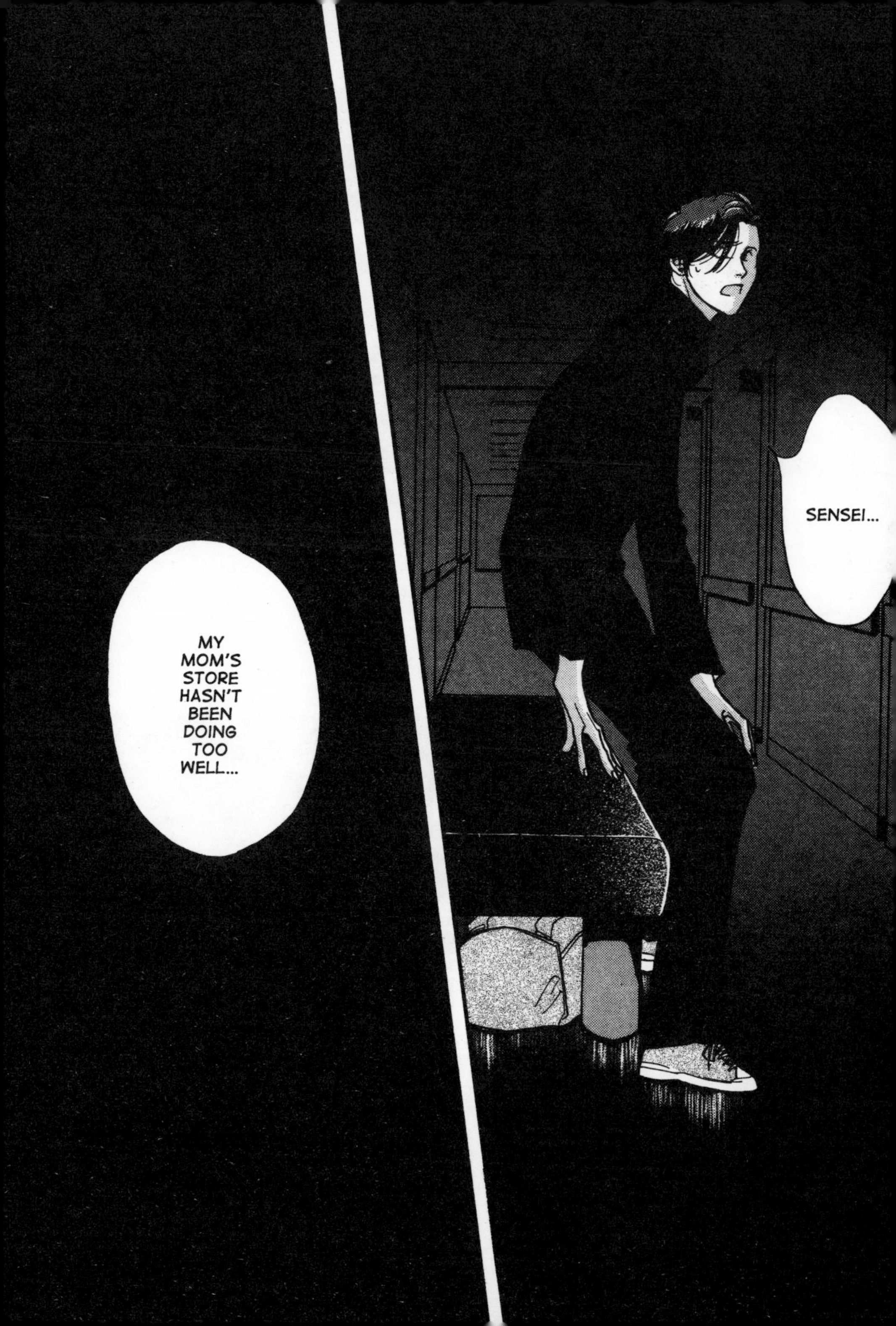
SENSEI...
MY MOM'S STORE HASN'T BEEN DOING TOO WELL...

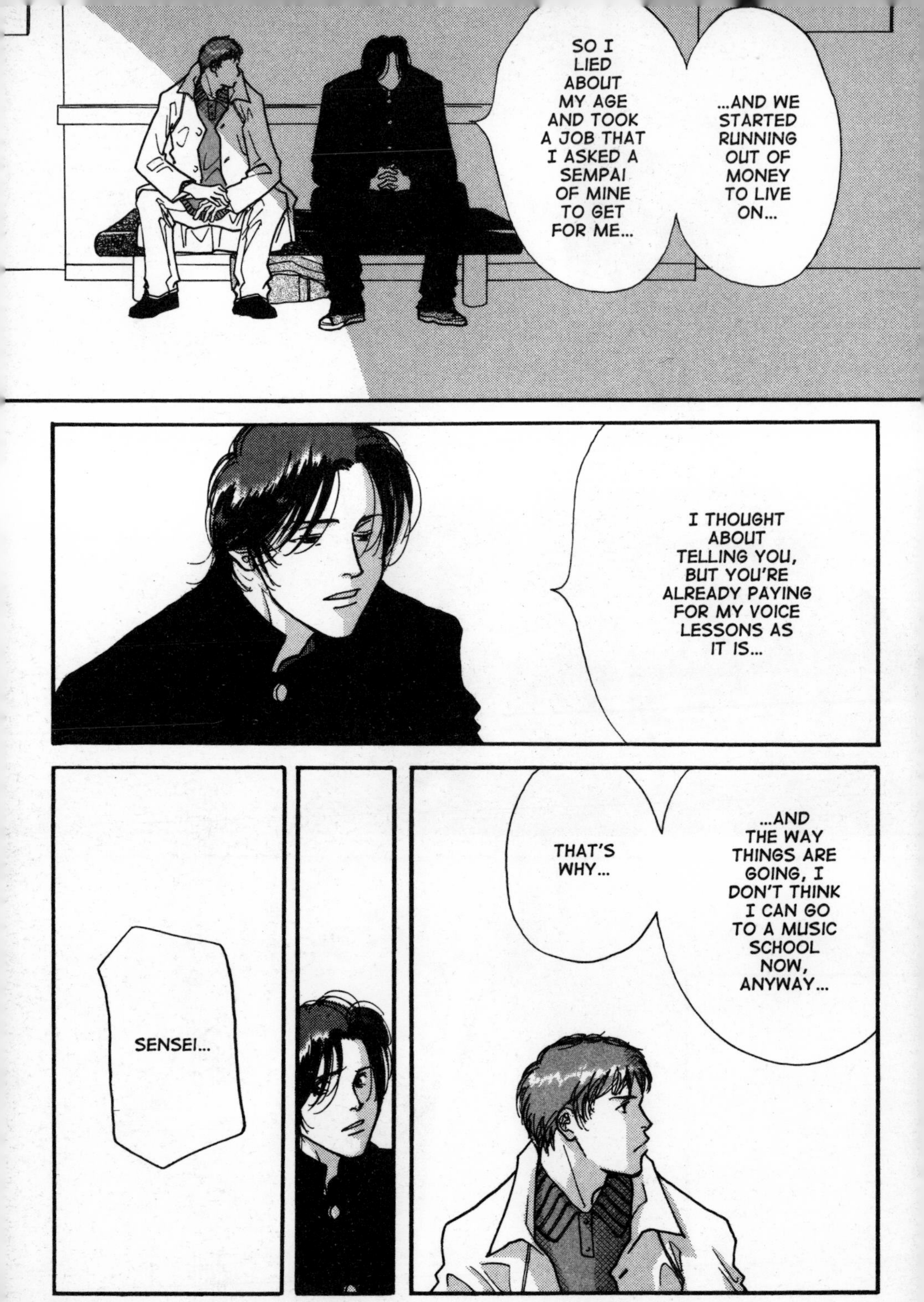
...AND WE STARTED RUNNING OUT OF MONEY TO LIVE ON...
SO I LIED ABOUT MY AGE AND TOOK A JOB THAT I ASKED A SEMPAI OF MINE TO GET FOR ME...
I THOUGHT ABOUT TELLING YOU, BUT YOU'RE ALREADY PAYING FOR MY VOICE LESSONS AS IT IS...
...AND THE WAY THINGS ARE GOING, I DON'T THINK I CAN GO TO A MUSIC SCHOOL NOW, ANYWAY...
THAT'S WHY...
SENSEI...

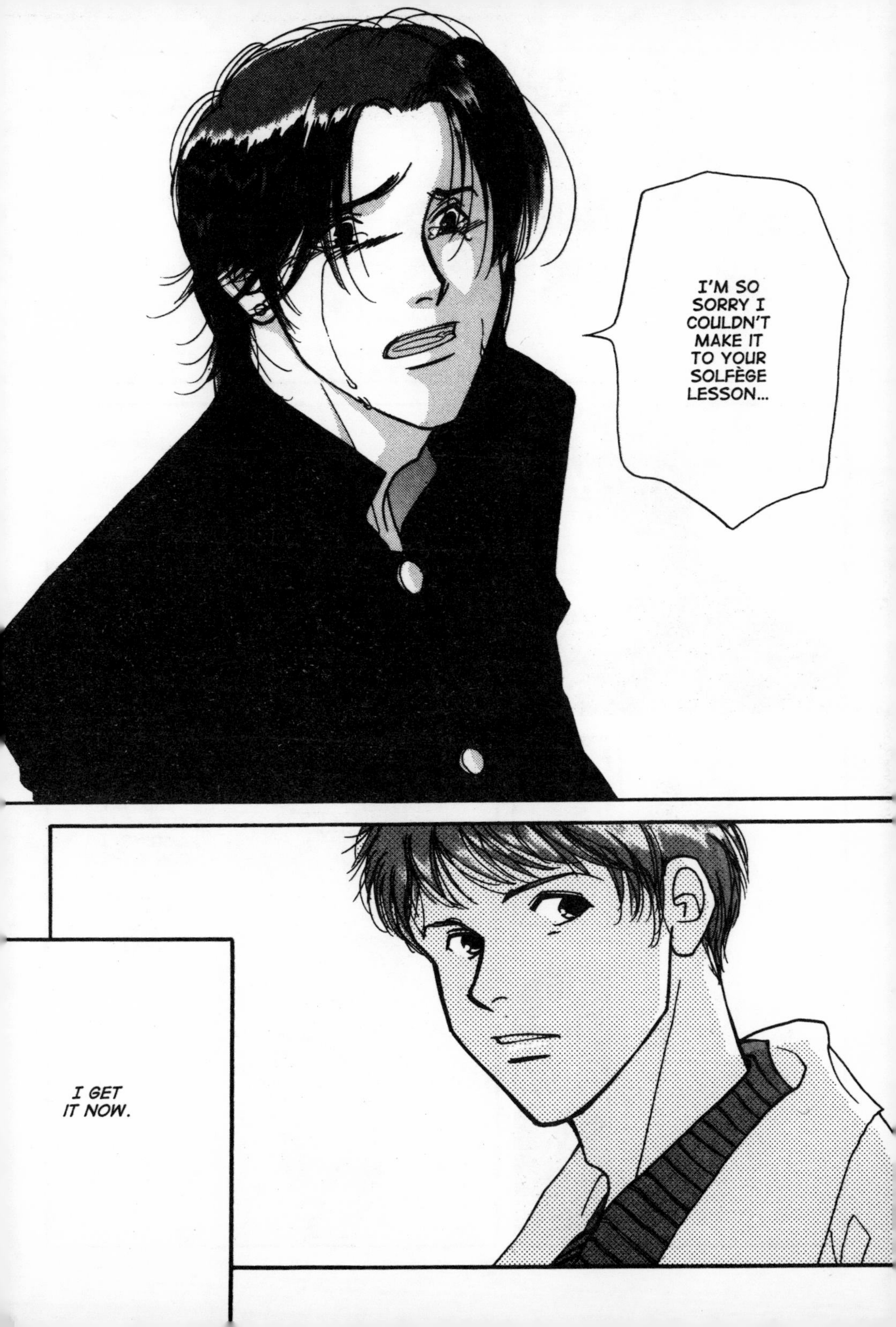
I'M SO SORRY I COULDN'T MAKE IT TO YOUR SOLFÈGE LESSON...
I GET IT NOW.

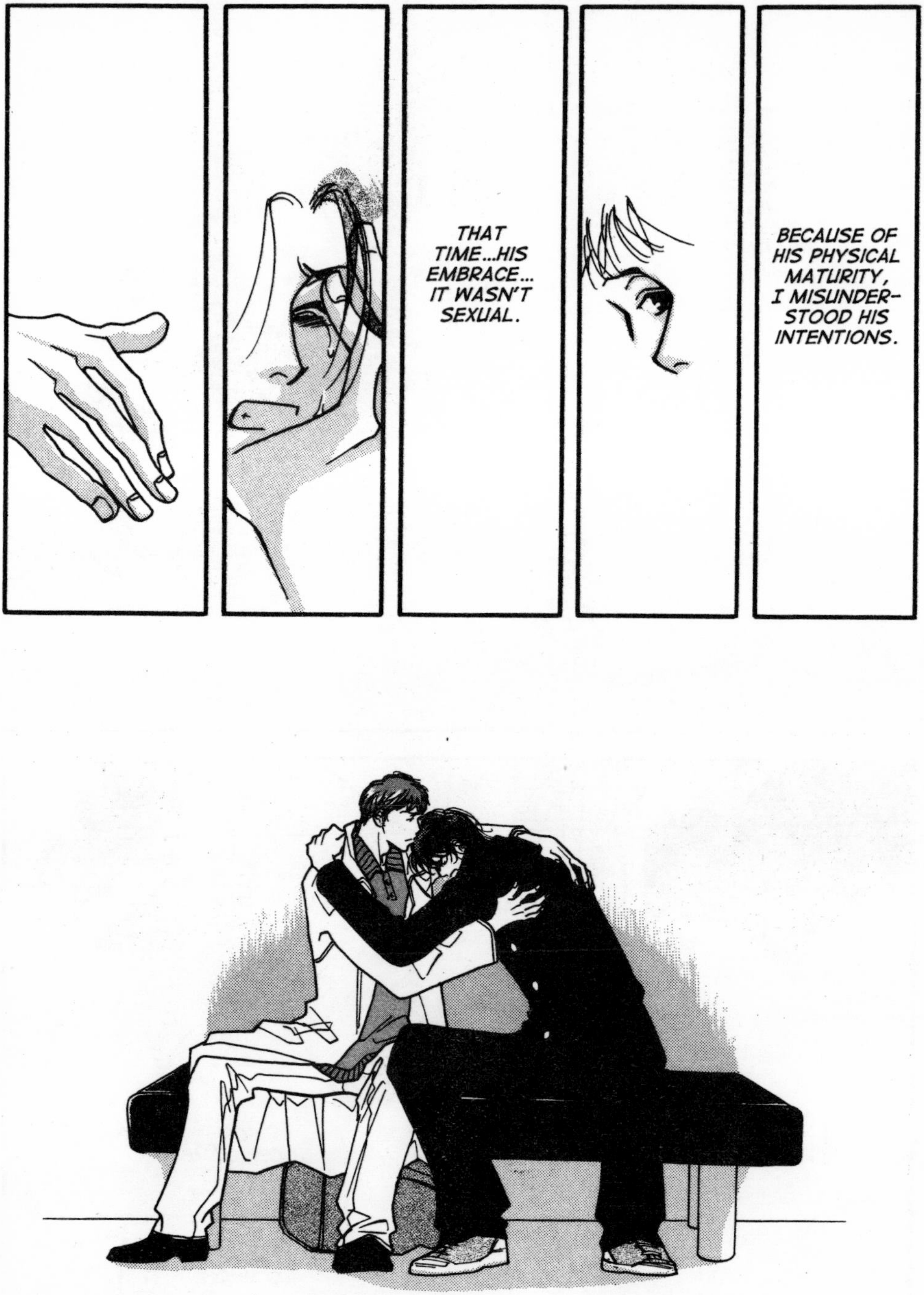
BECAUSE OF HIS PHYSICAL MATURITY, I MISUNDER-STOOD HIS INTENTIONS.
THAT TIME...HIS EMBRACE... IT WASN'T SEXUAL.

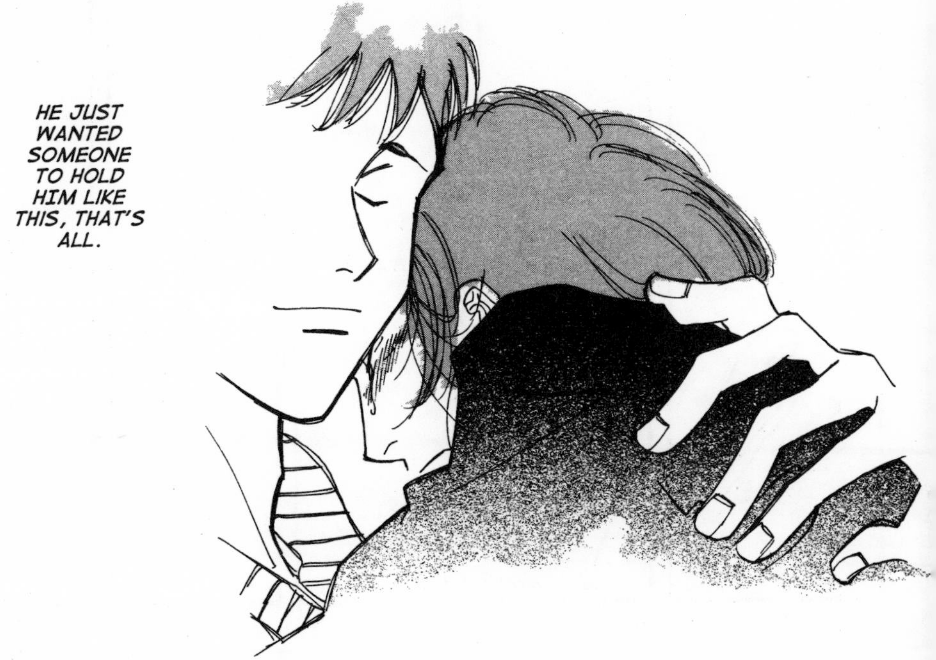
HE JUST WANTED SOMEONE TO HOLD HIM LIKE THIS, THAT'S ALL.

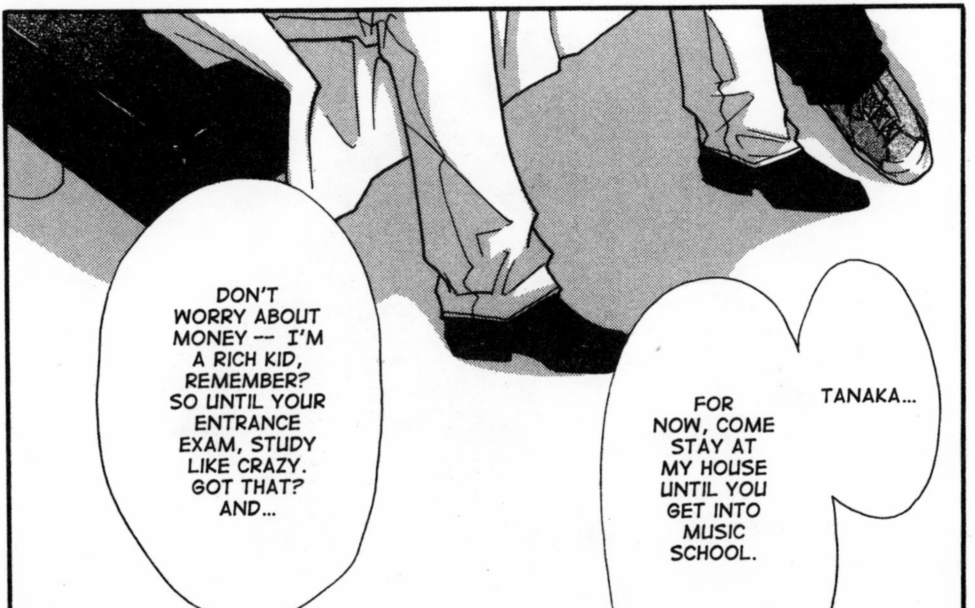
TANAKA...
FOR NOW, COME STAY AT MY HOUSE UNTIL YOU GET INTO MUSIC SCHOOL.
DON'T WORRY ABOUT MONEY -- I'M A RICH KID, REMEMBER? SO UNTIL YOUR ENTRANCE EXAM, STUDY LIKE CRAZY. GOT THAT? AND...

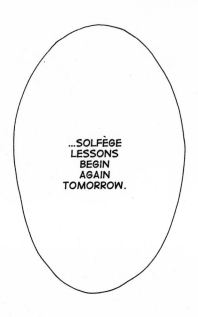

...SOLFÈGE
LESSONS
BEGIN
AGAIN
TOMORROW.

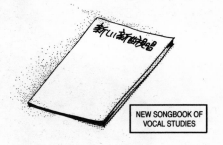

NEW SONGBOOK OF
VOCAL STUDIES

To be continued.

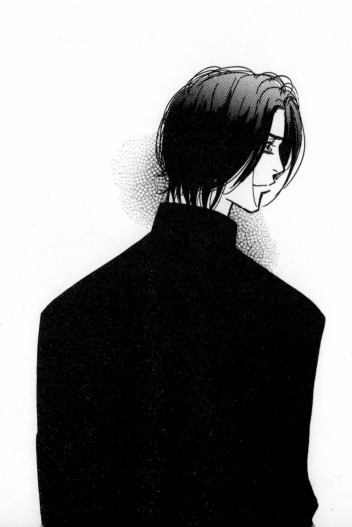

ソルフェージュ
SOLFÈGE
THE QUEEN OF THE NIGHT ARIA
★PART 1

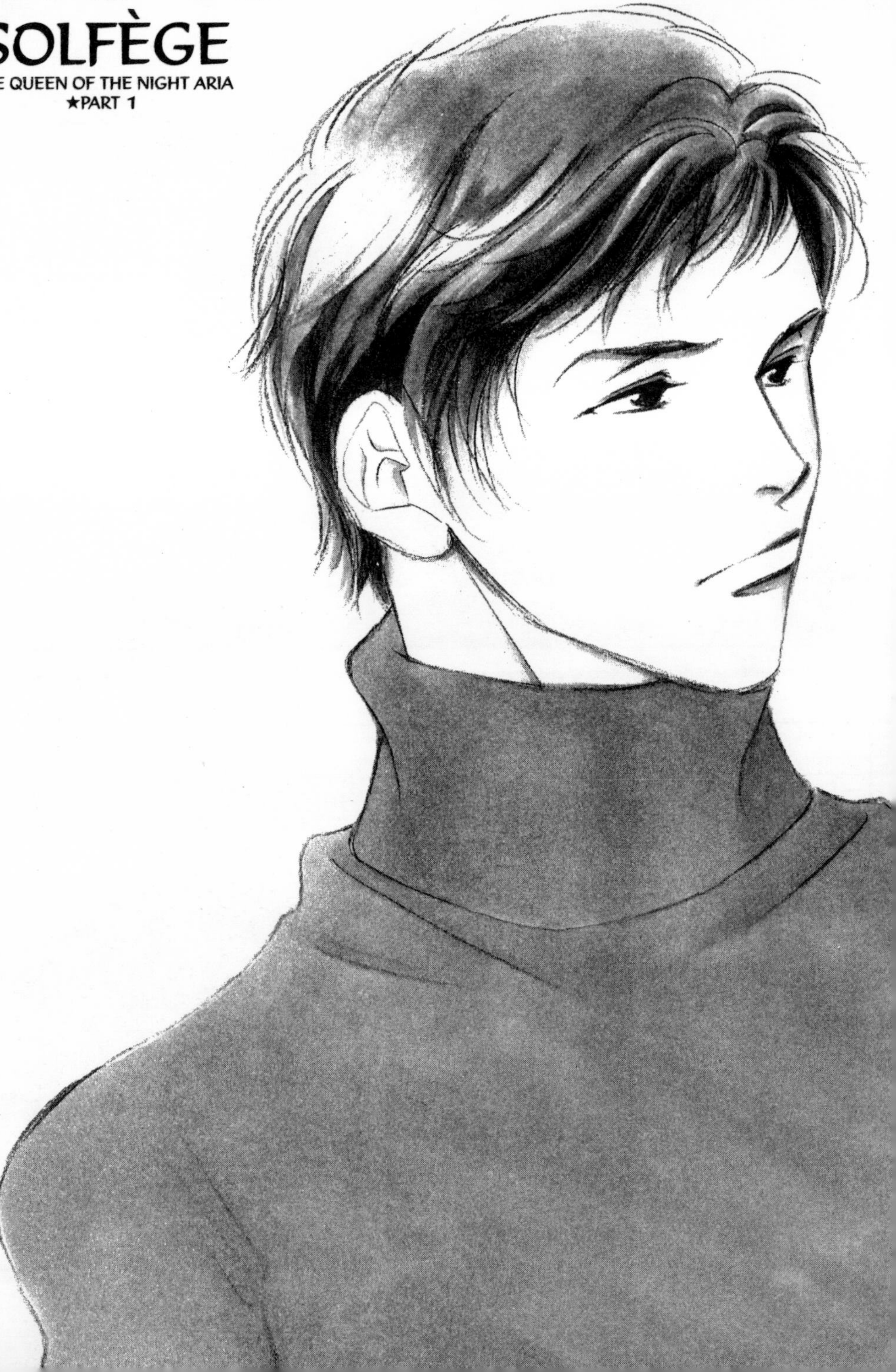

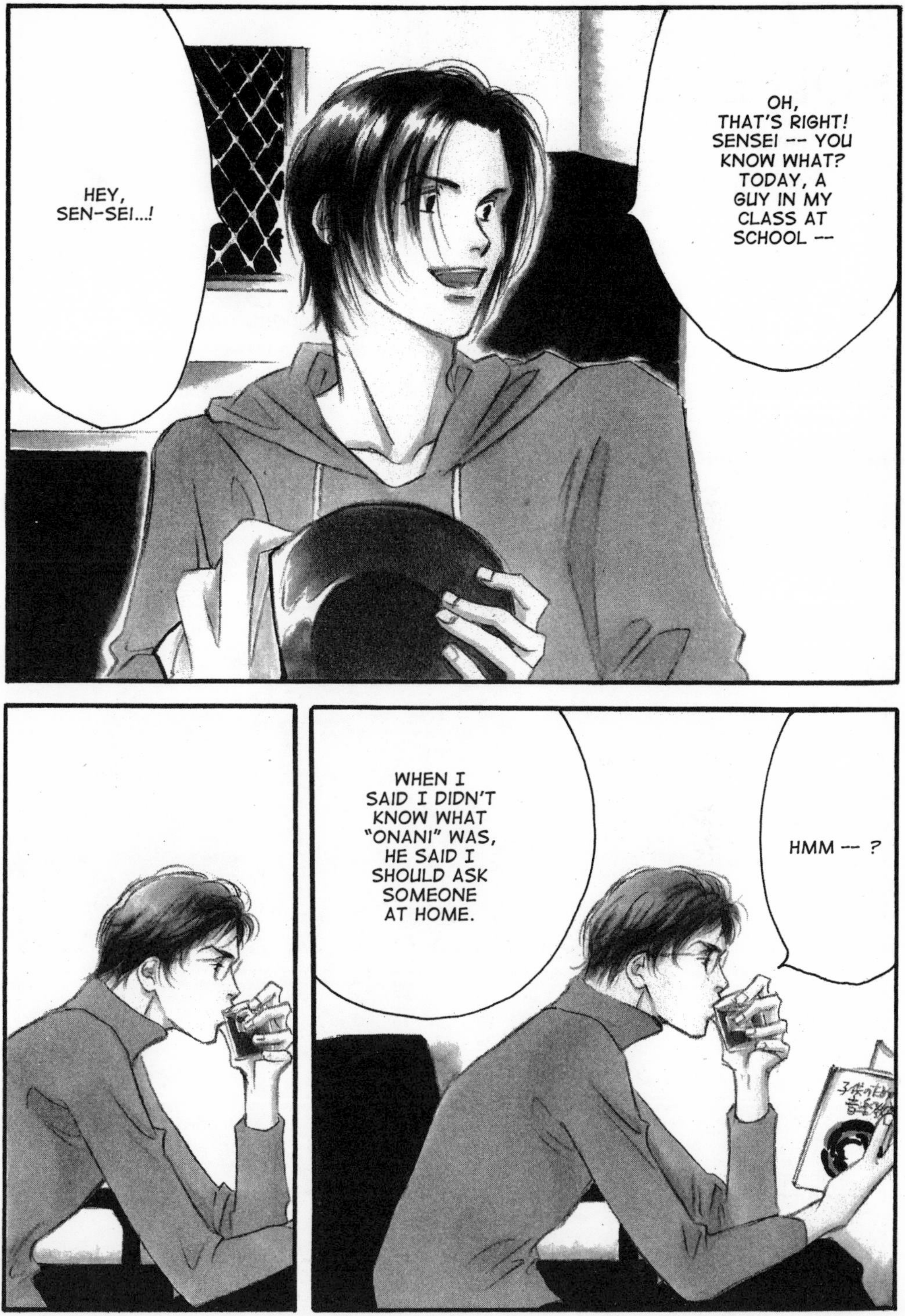
OH, THAT'S RIGHT! SENSEI -- YOU KNOW WHAT? TODAY, A GUY IN MY CLASS AT SCHOOL --
HEY, SEN-SEI...!
HMM -- ?
WHEN I SAID I DIDN'T KNOW WHAT "ONANI" WAS, HE SAID I SHOULD ASK SOMEONE AT HOME.

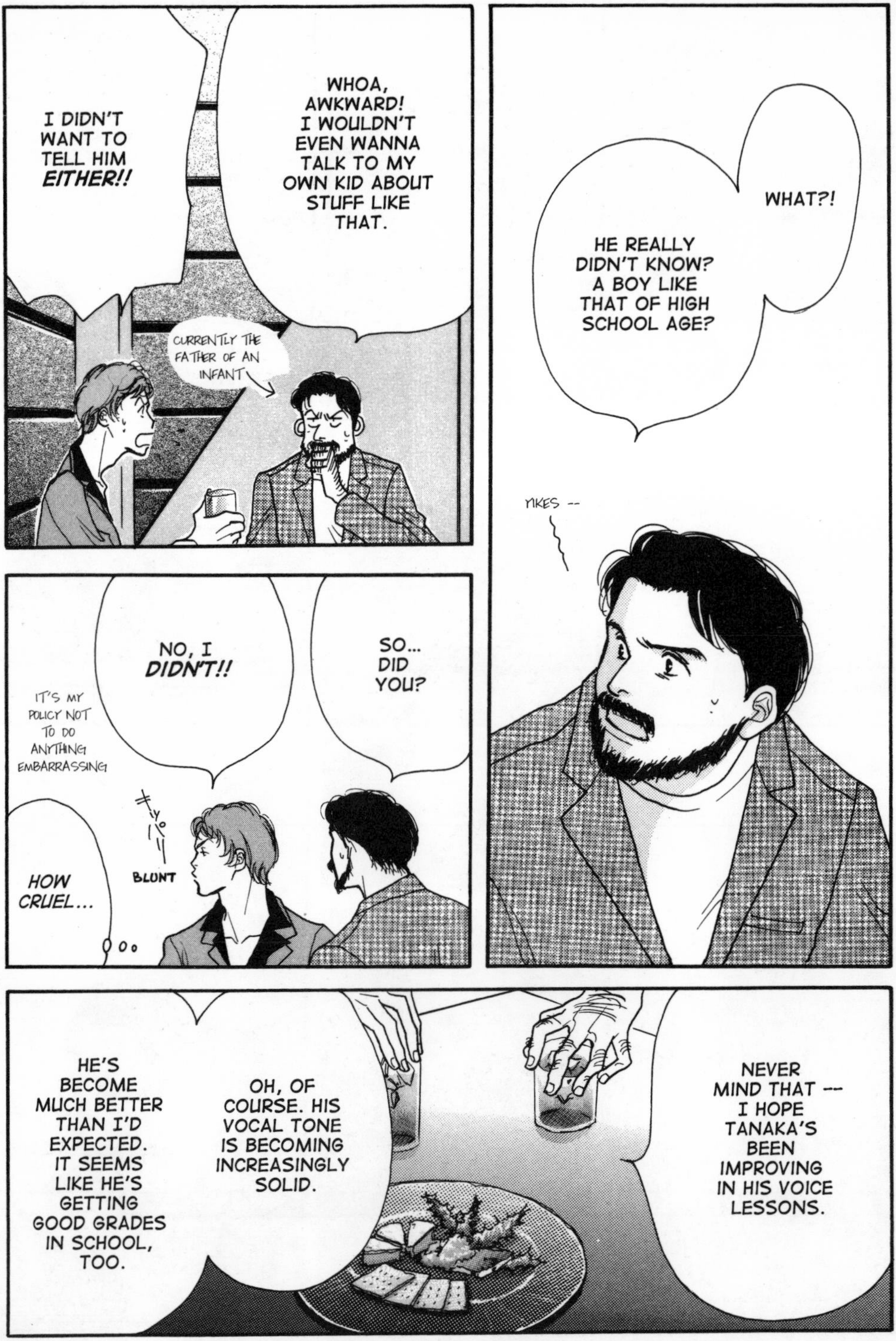
WHAT?!
HE REALLY DIDN'T KNOW? A BOY LIKE THAT OF HIGH SCHOOL AGE?
YIKES --
WHOA, AWKWARD! I WOULDN'T EVEN WANNA TALK TO MY OWN KID ABOUT STUFF LIKE THAT.
I DIDN'T WANT TO TELL HIM *EITHER!!*
CURRENTLY THE FATHER OF AN INFANT
SO... DID YOU?
NO, I *DIDN'T!!*
IT'S MY POLICY NOT TO DO ANYTHING EMBARRASSING
キッパリ
BLUNT
HOW CRUEL...
NEVER MIND THAT -- I HOPE TANAKA'S BEEN IMPROVING IN HIS VOICE LESSONS.
OH, OF COURSE. HIS VOCAL TONE IS BECOMING INCREASINGLY SOLID.
HE'S BECOME MUCH BETTER THAN I'D EXPECTED. IT SEEMS LIKE HE'S GETTING GOOD GRADES IN SCHOOL, TOO.

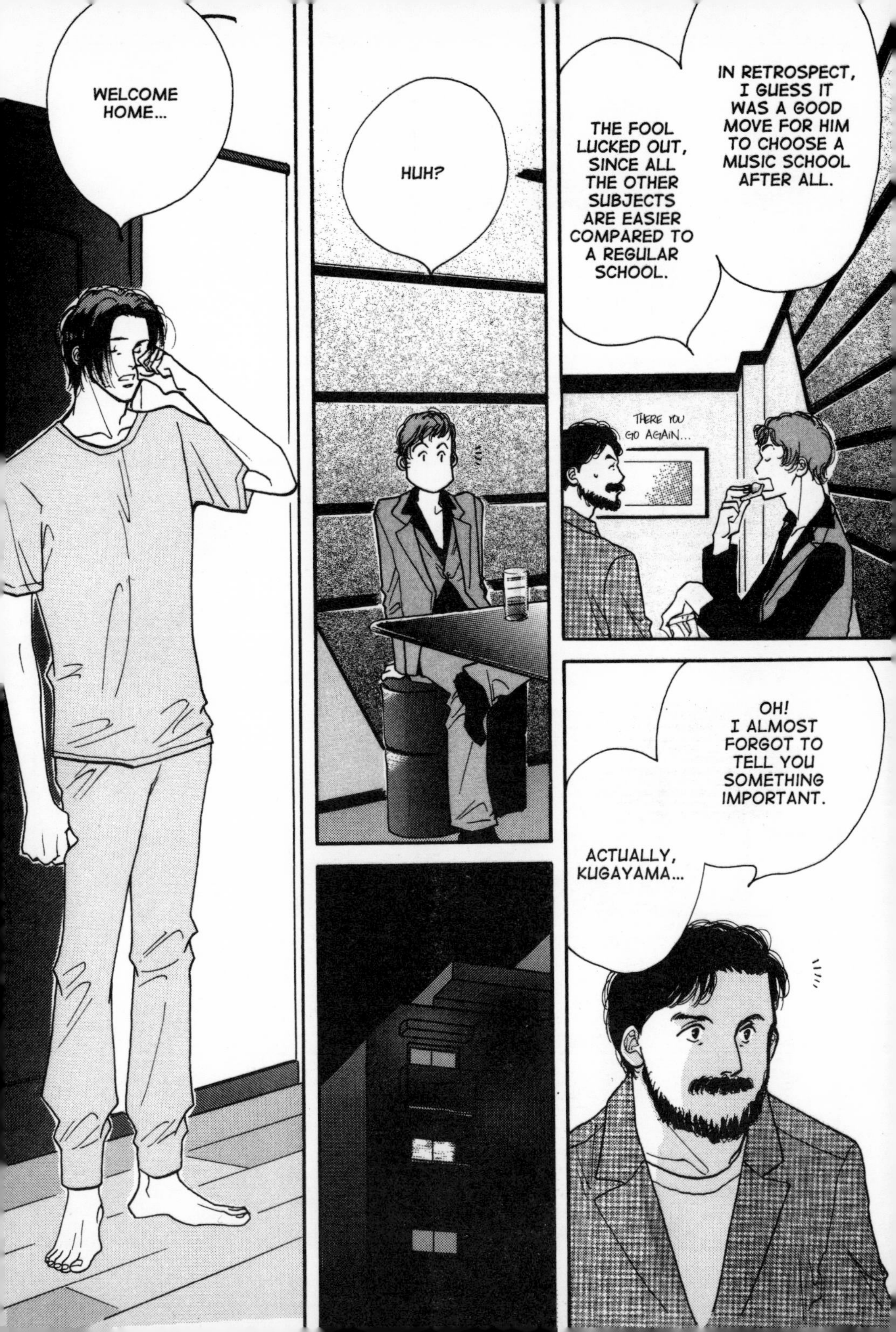
IN RETROSPECT, I GUESS IT WAS A GOOD MOVE FOR HIM TO CHOOSE A MUSIC SCHOOL AFTER ALL.
THE FOOL LUCKED OUT, SINCE ALL THE OTHER SUBJECTS ARE EASIER COMPARED TO A REGULAR SCHOOL.
THERE YOU GO AGAIN...
OH! I ALMOST FORGOT TO TELL YOU SOMETHING IMPORTANT.
ACTUALLY, KUGAYAMA...
HUH?
WELCOME HOME...

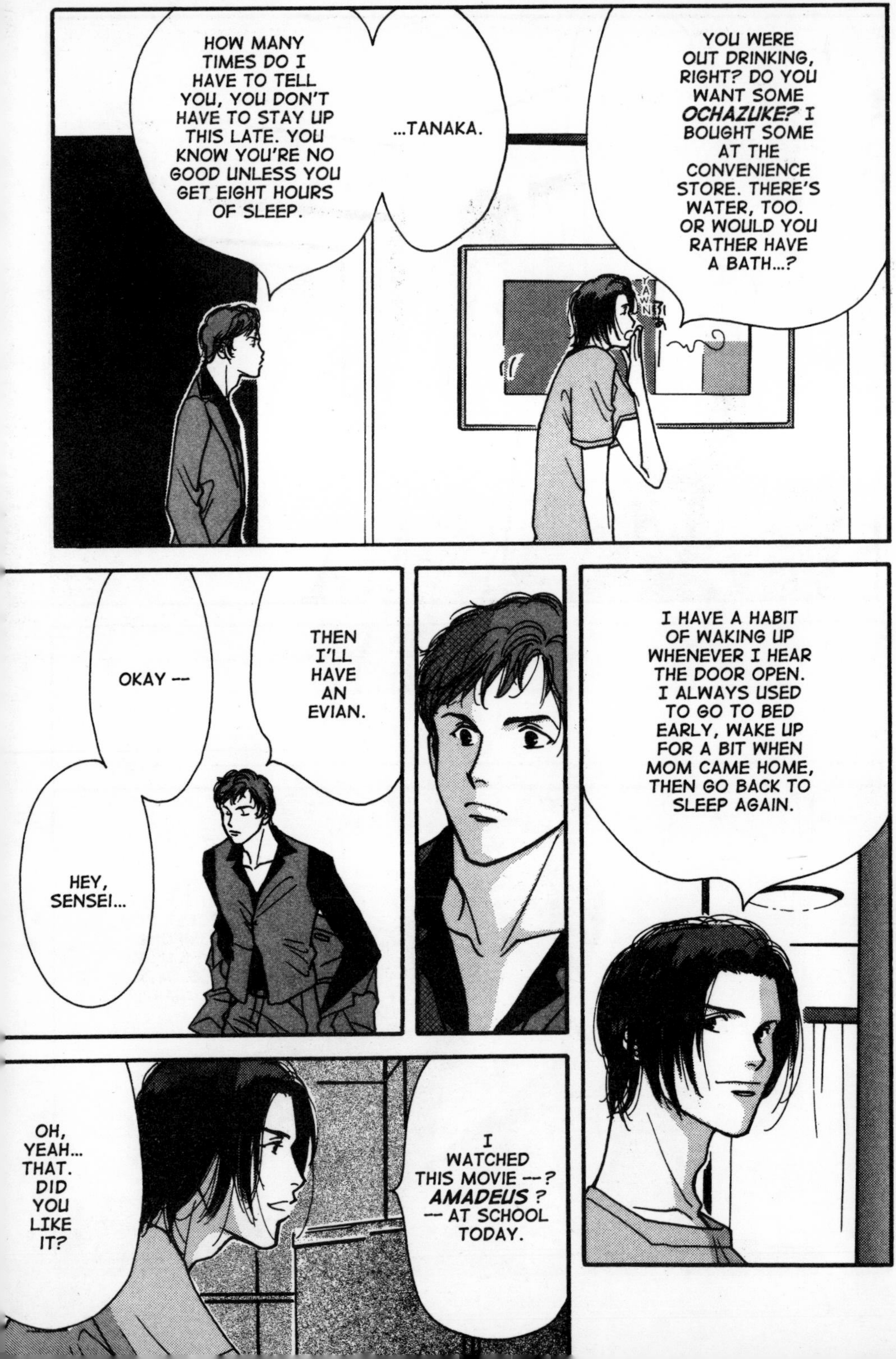
YOU WERE OUT DRINKING, RIGHT? DO YOU WANT SOME OCHAZUKE? I BOUGHT SOME AT THE CONVENIENCE STORE. THERE'S WATER, TOO. OR WOULD YOU RATHER HAVE A BATH...?
YAWN
...TANAKA.
HOW MANY TIMES DO I HAVE TO TELL YOU, YOU DON'T HAVE TO STAY UP THIS LATE. YOU KNOW YOU'RE NO GOOD UNLESS YOU GET EIGHT HOURS OF SLEEP.
I HAVE A HABIT OF WAKING UP WHENEVER I HEAR THE DOOR OPEN. I ALWAYS USED TO GO TO BED EARLY, WAKE UP FOR A BIT WHEN MOM CAME HOME, THEN GO BACK TO SLEEP AGAIN.
THEN I'LL HAVE AN EVIAN.
OKAY --
HEY, SENSEI...
I WATCHED THIS MOVIE --? AMADEUS? -- AT SCHOOL TODAY.
OH, YEAH... THAT. DID YOU LIKE IT?

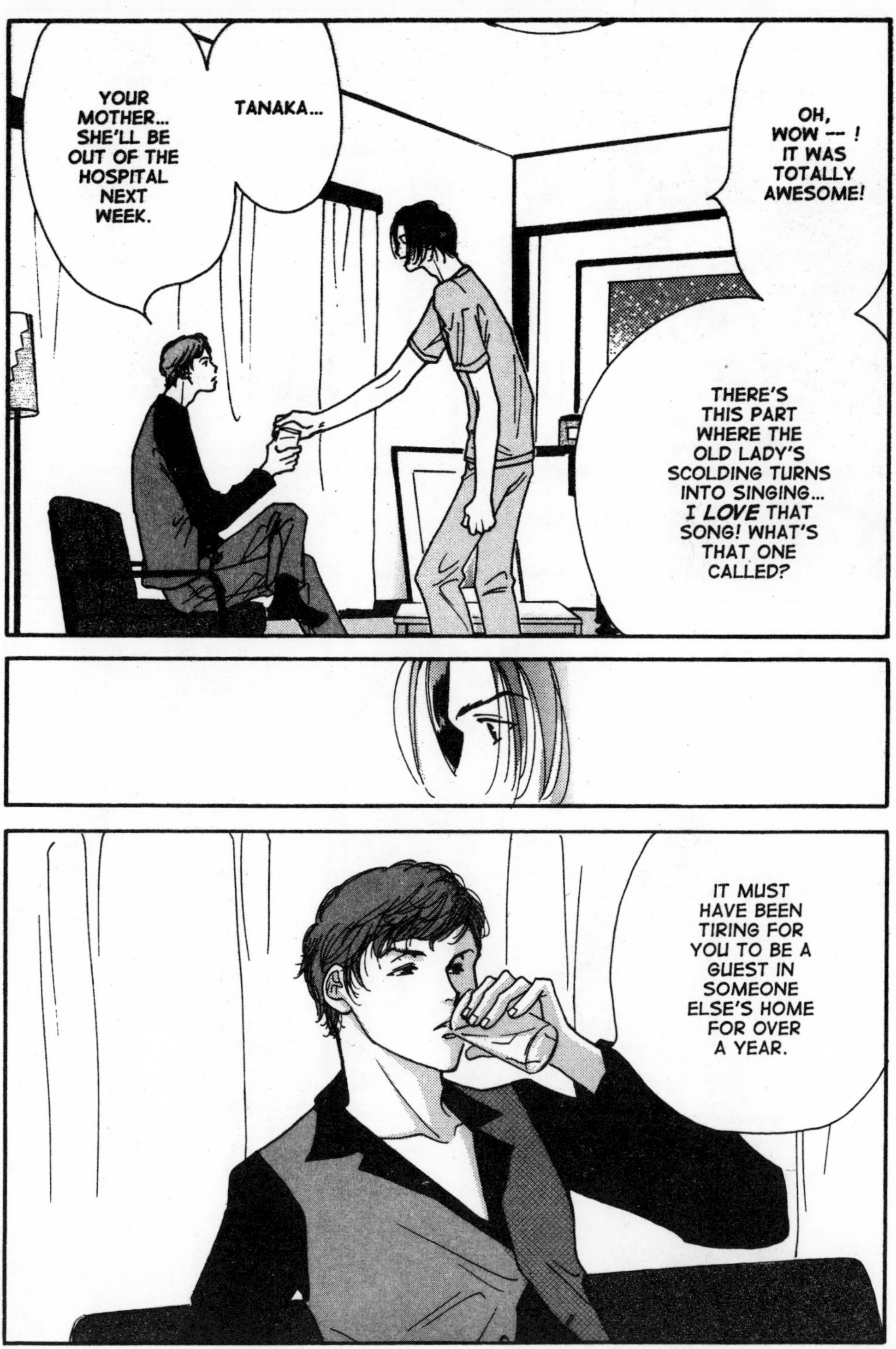
OH, WOW --- ! IT WAS TOTALLY AWESOME!
THERE'S THIS PART WHERE THE OLD LADY'S SCOLDING TURNS INTO SINGING... I *LOVE* THAT SONG! WHAT'S THAT ONE CALLED?
TANAKA...
YOUR MOTHER... SHE'LL BE OUT OF THE HOSPITAL NEXT WEEK.
IT MUST HAVE BEEN TIRING FOR YOU TO BE A GUEST IN SOMEONE ELSE'S HOME FOR OVER A YEAR.

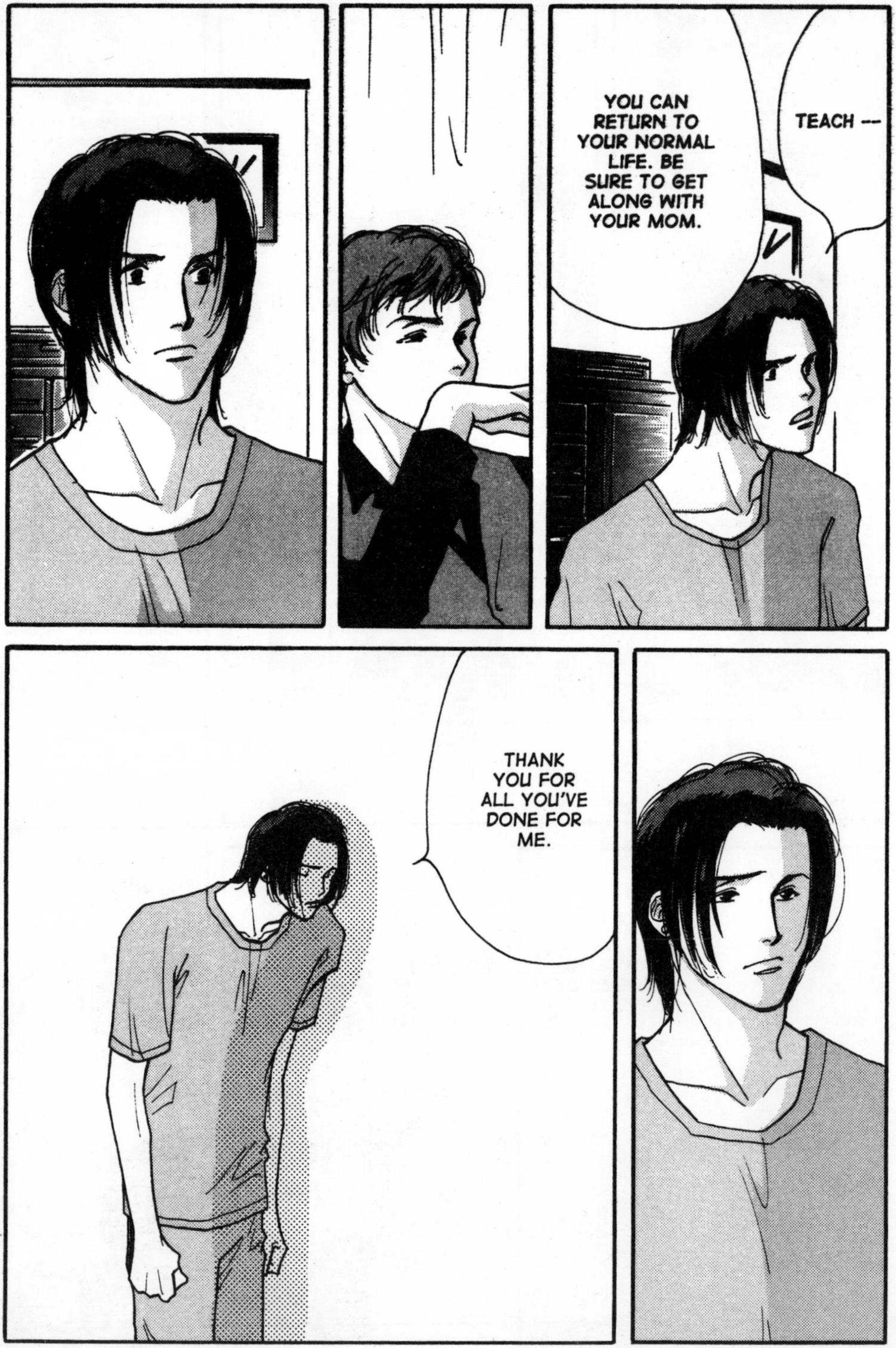
TEACH --
YOU CAN RETURN TO YOUR NORMAL LIFE. BE SURE TO GET ALONG WITH YOUR MOM.
THANK YOU FOR ALL YOU'VE DONE FOR ME.

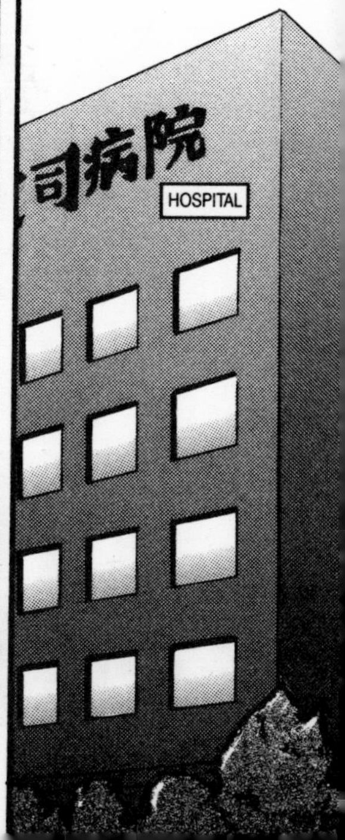
HOSPITAL

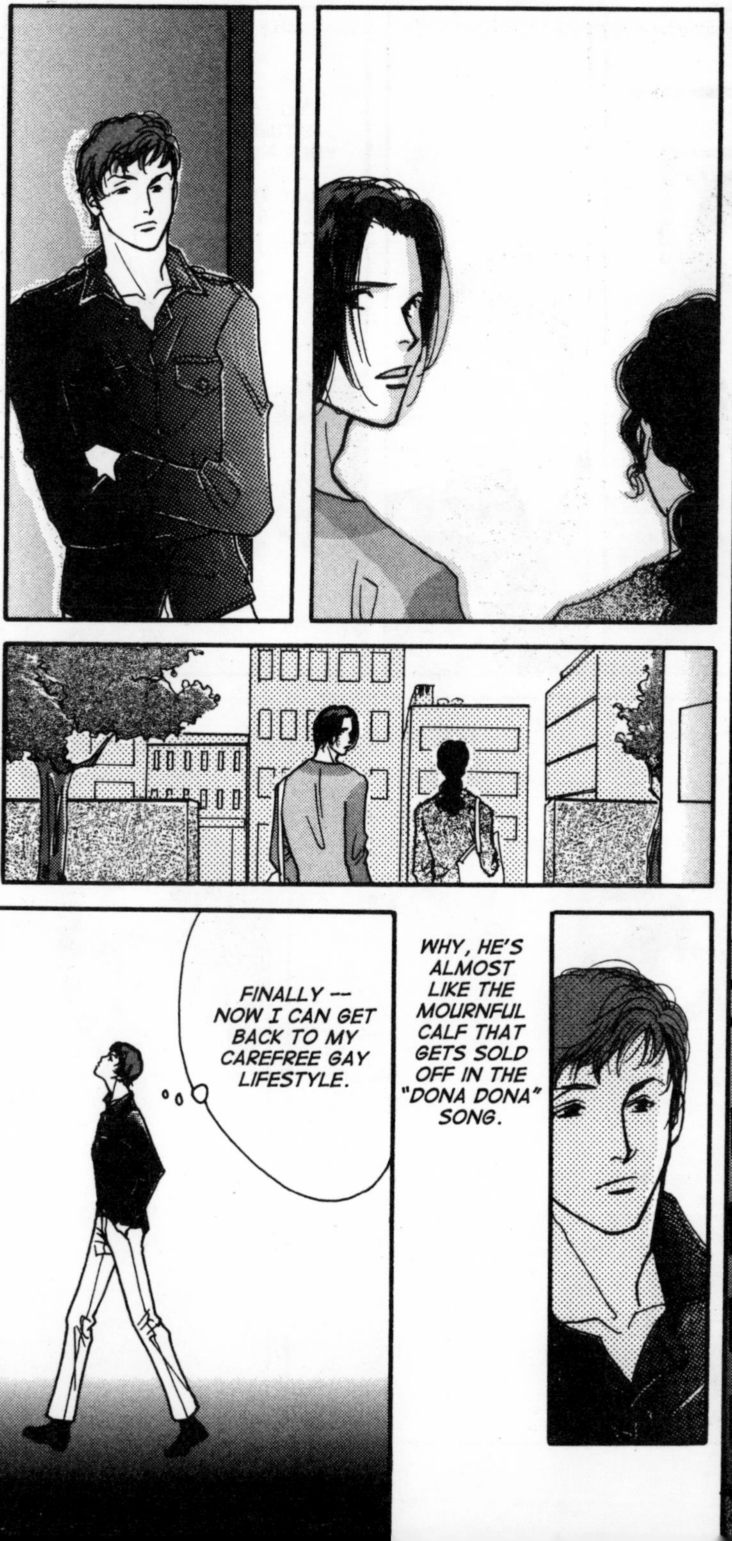
WHY, HE'S ALMOST LIKE THE MOURNFUL CALF THAT GETS SOLD OFF IN THE "DONA DONA" SONG.
FINALLY -- NOW I CAN GET BACK TO MY CAREFREE GAY LIFESTYLE.

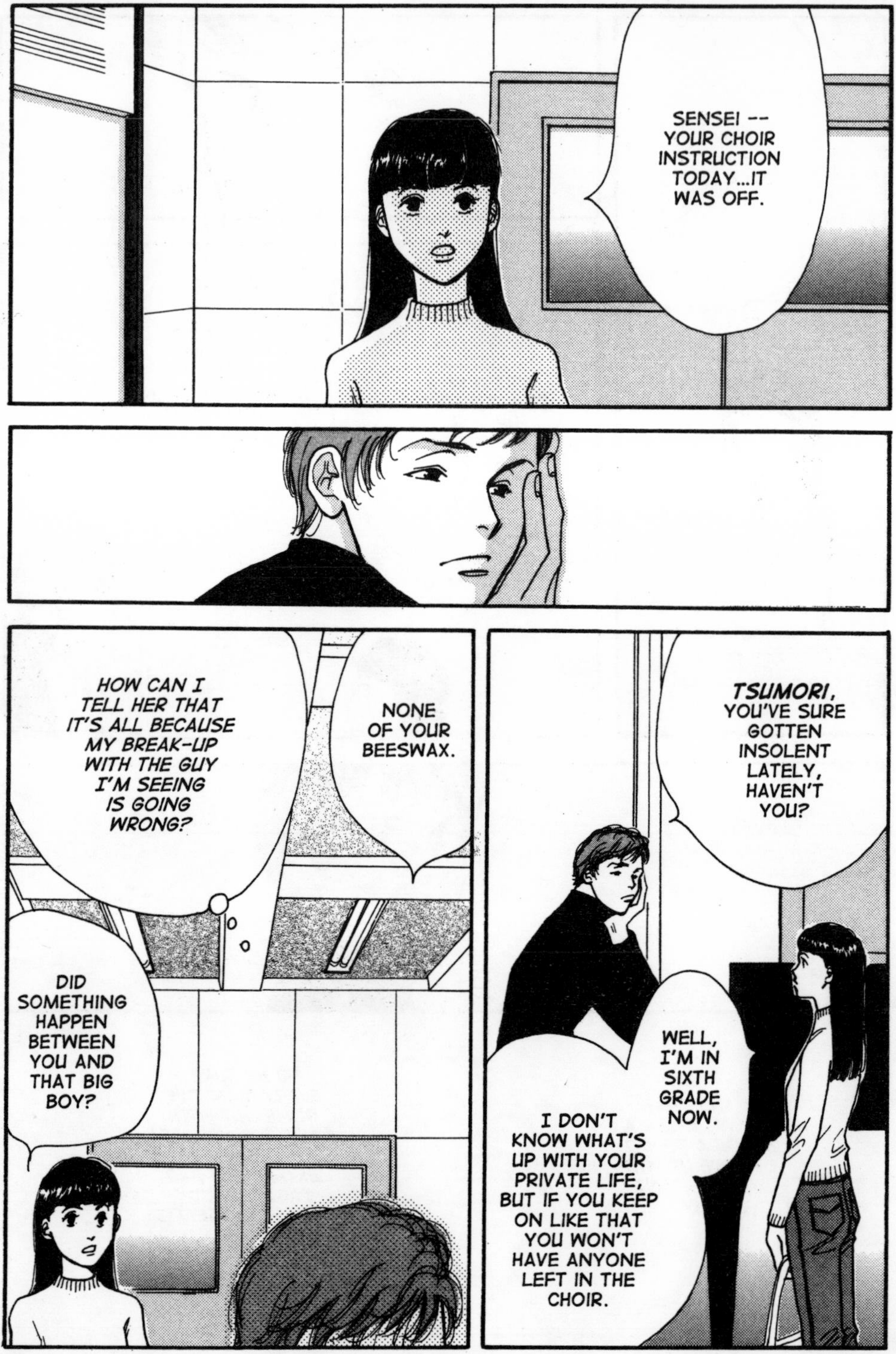
SENSEI -- YOUR CHOIR INSTRUCTION TODAY...IT WAS OFF.
TSUMORI, YOU'VE SURE GOTTEN INSOLENT LATELY, HAVEN'T YOU?
WELL, I'M IN SIXTH GRADE NOW.
I DON'T KNOW WHAT'S UP WITH YOUR PRIVATE LIFE, BUT IF YOU KEEP ON LIKE THAT YOU WON'T HAVE ANYONE LEFT IN THE CHOIR.
NONE OF YOUR BEESWAX.
HOW CAN I TELL HER THAT IT'S ALL BECAUSE MY BREAK-UP WITH THE GUY I'M SEEING IS GOING WRONG?
DID SOMETHING HAPPEN BETWEEN YOU AND THAT BIG BOY?

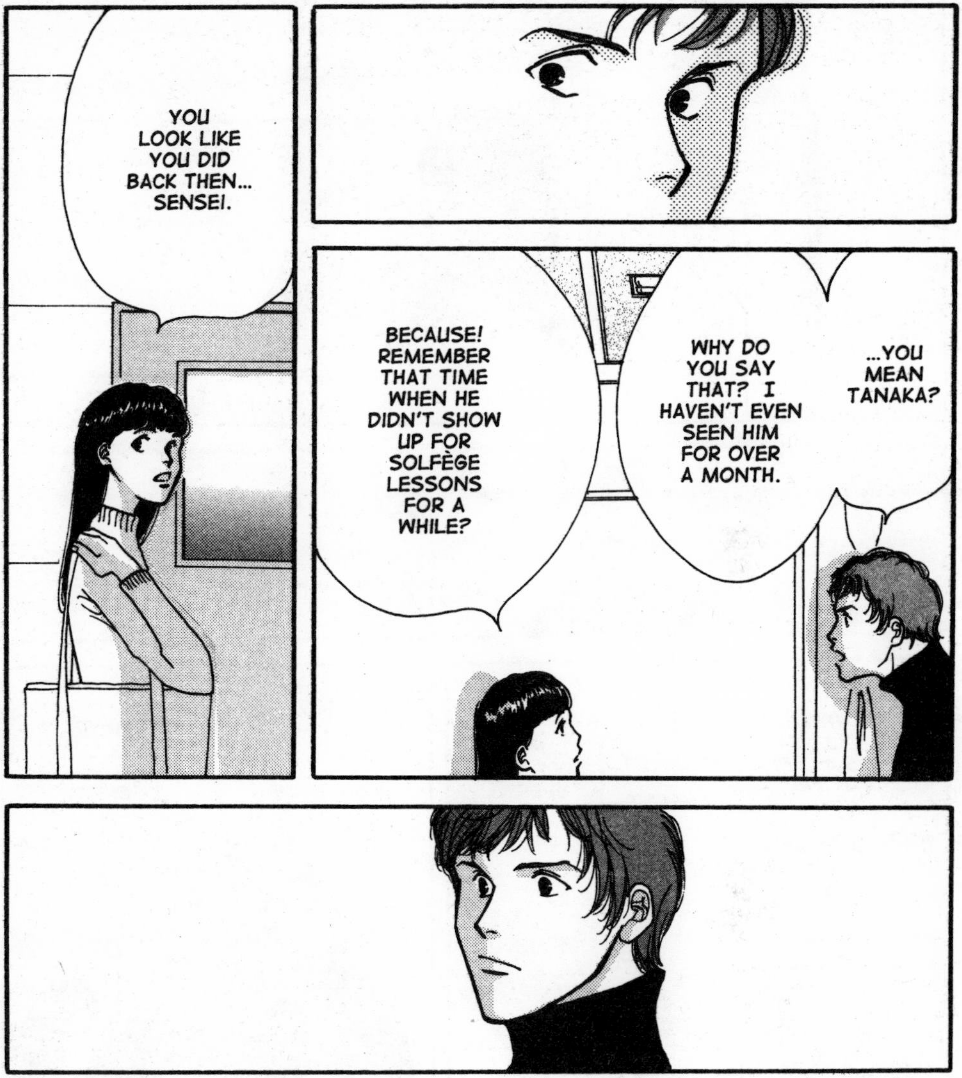
...YOU MEAN TANAKA?
WHY DO YOU SAY THAT? I HAVEN'T EVEN SEEN HIM FOR OVER A MONTH.
BECAUSE! REMEMBER THAT TIME WHEN HE DIDN'T SHOW UP FOR SOLFÈGE LESSONS FOR A WHILE?
YOU LOOK LIKE YOU DID BACK THEN... SENSEI.

TO BE SURE, EVERY MAN I'VE GONE OUT WITH SINCE TANAKA LEFT HAS BEEN IN EXTREMELY BAD TASTE, IF I DO SAY SO MYSELF...

...AND THAT NIGHT, AFTER A BIT OF A TO-DO, I BROKE UP WITH THE CURRENT GUY.

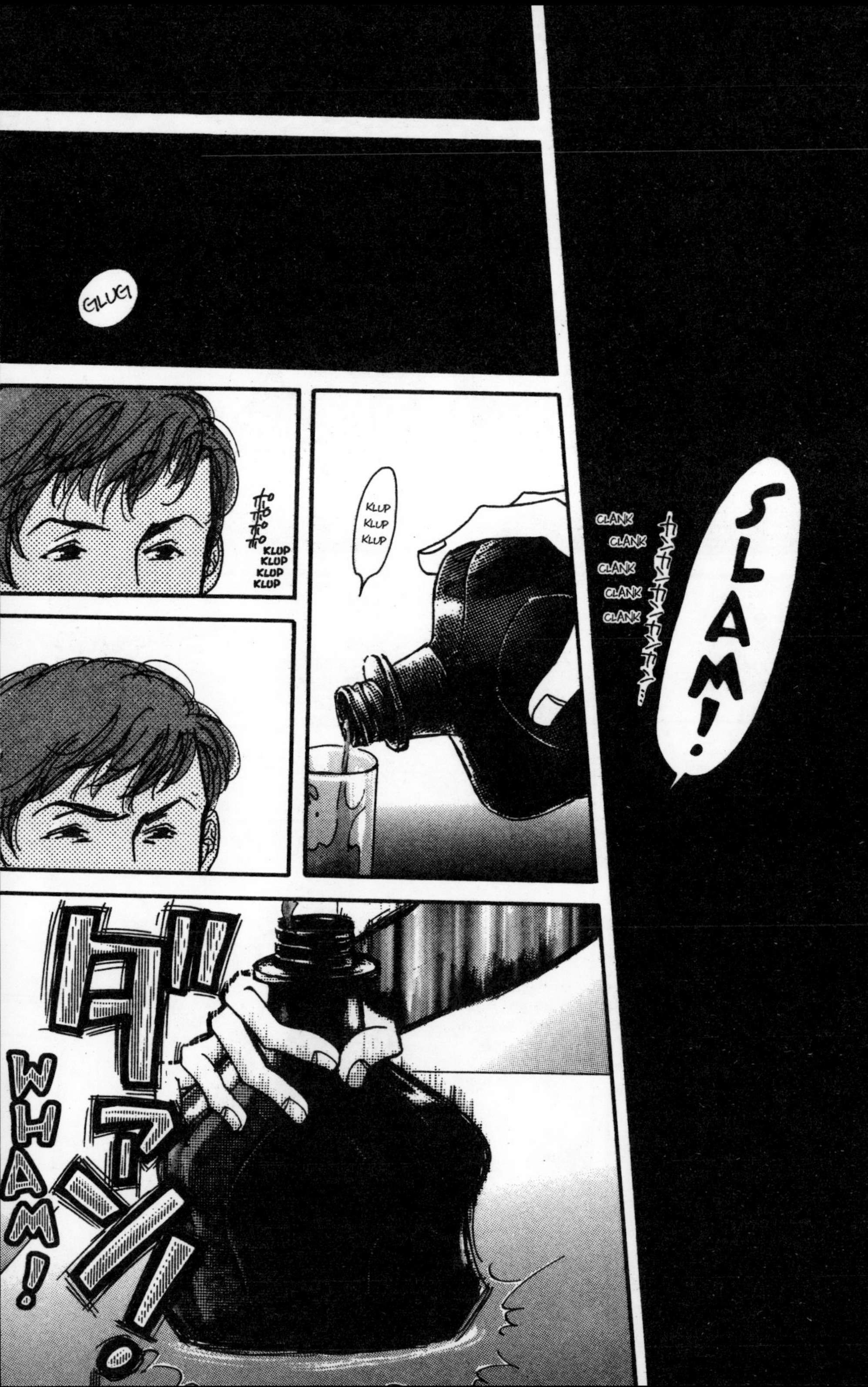
GLUG
SLAM!
CLANK CLANK CLANK CLANK CLANK
KLUP KLUP KLUP
KLUP KLUP KLUP KLUP
WHAM!

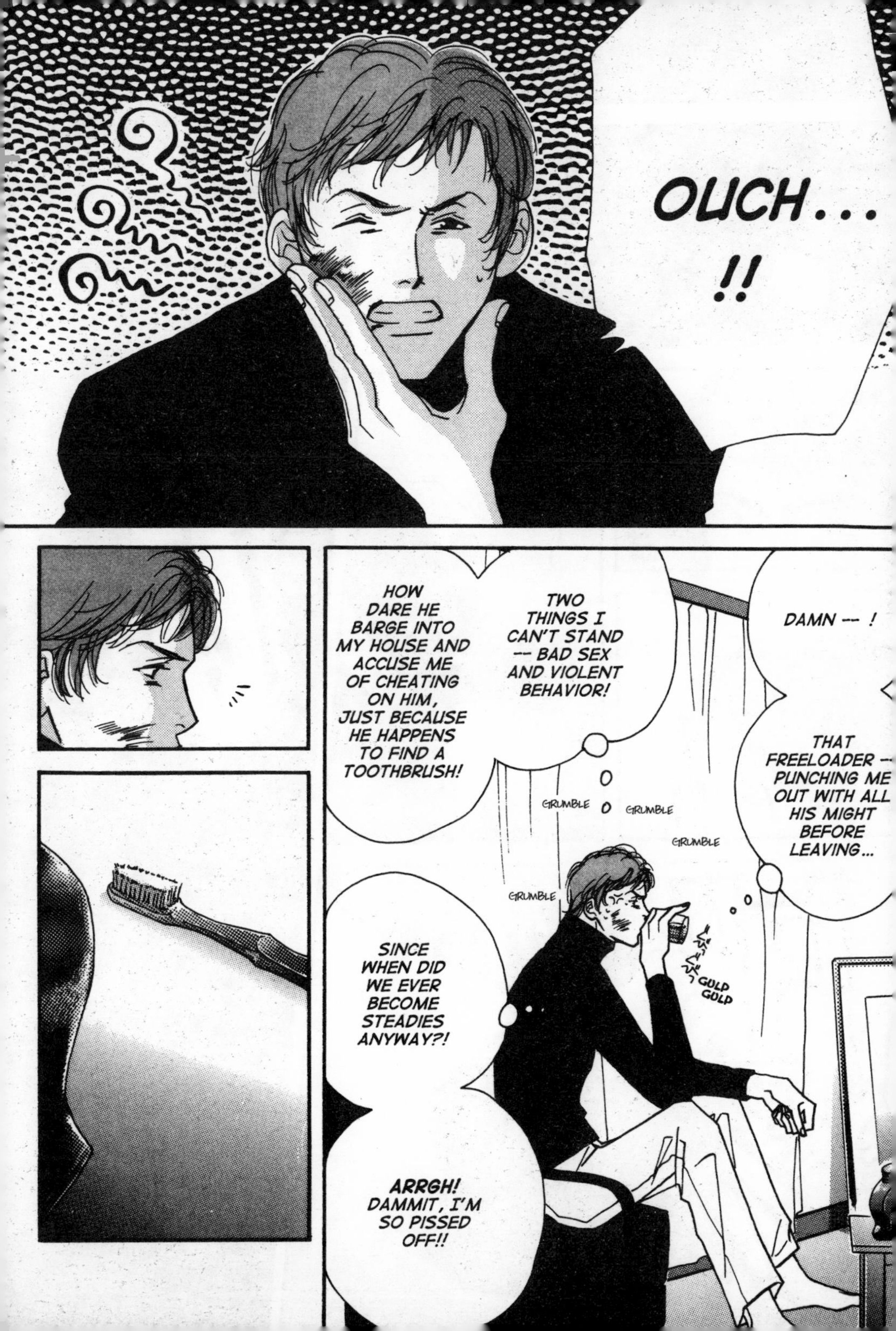
OUCH... !!
DAMN -- !
THAT FREELOADER -- PUNCHING ME OUT WITH ALL HIS MIGHT BEFORE LEAVING...
TWO THINGS I CAN'T STAND -- BAD SEX AND VIOLENT BEHAVIOR!
HOW DARE HE BARGE INTO MY HOUSE AND ACCUSE ME OF CHEATING ON HIM, JUST BECAUSE HE HAPPENS TO FIND A TOOTHBRUSH!
GRUMBLE GRUMBLE
GRUMBLE
GRUMBLE
GULP GULP
SINCE WHEN DID WE EVER BECOME STEADIES ANYWAY?!
ARRGH! DAMMIT, I'M SO PISSED OFF!!

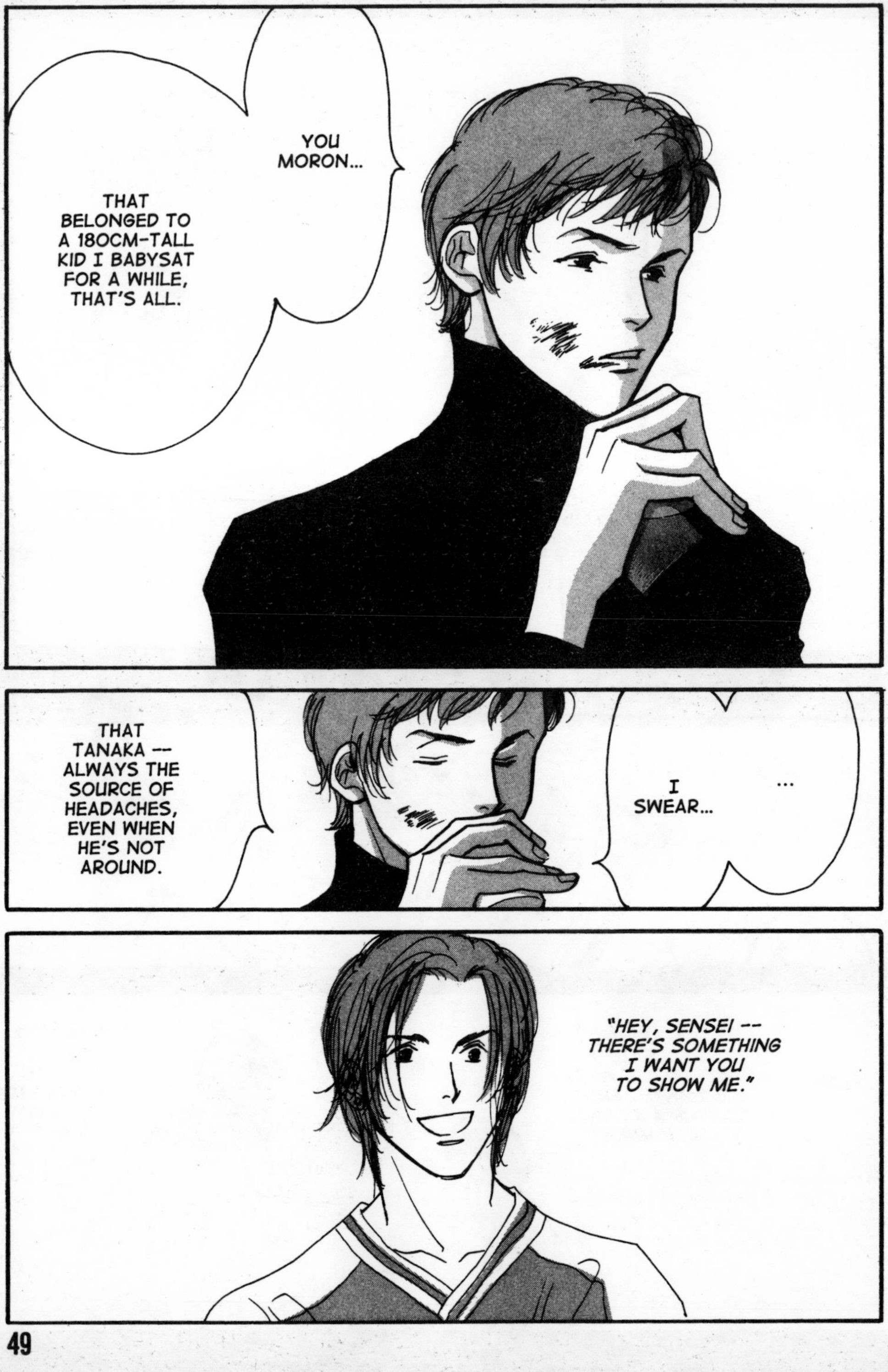
YOU MORON...
THAT BELONGED TO A 180CM-TALL KID I BABYSAT FOR A WHILE, THAT'S ALL.
...
I SWEAR...
THAT TANAKA -- ALWAYS THE SOURCE OF HEADACHES, EVEN WHEN HE'S NOT AROUND.
"HEY, SENSEI -- THERE'S SOMETHING I WANT YOU TO SHOW ME."

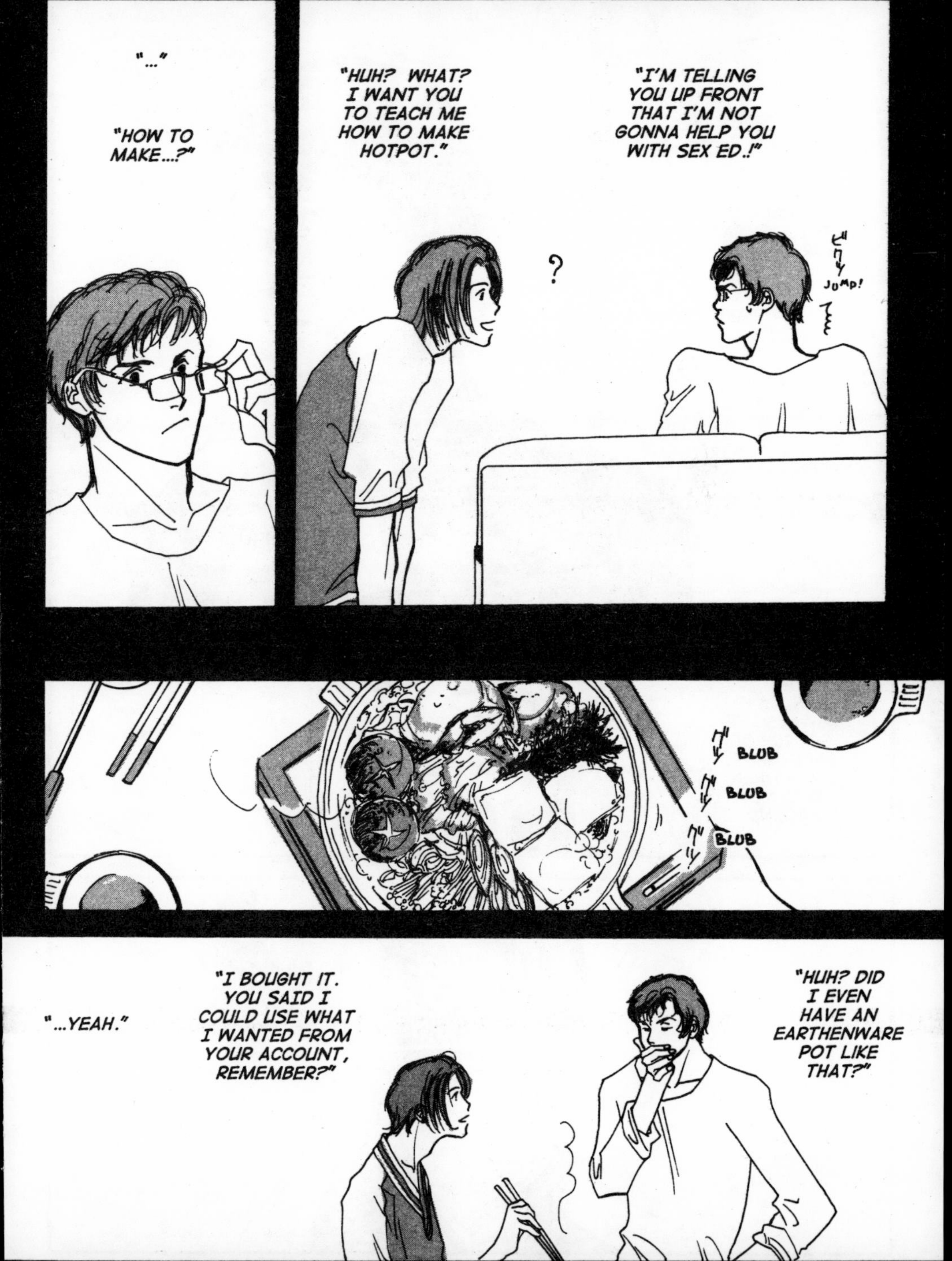
"I'M TELLING YOU UP FRONT THAT I'M NOT GONNA HELP YOU WITH SEX ED.!"
"HUH? WHAT? I WANT YOU TO TEACH ME HOW TO MAKE HOTPOT."
JUMP!
?
"..."
"HOW TO MAKE...?"
BLUB
BLUB
BLUB
"HUH? DID I EVEN HAVE AN EARTHENWARE POT LIKE THAT?"
"I BOUGHT IT. YOU SAID I COULD USE WHAT I WANTED FROM YOUR ACCOUNT, REMEMBER?"
"...YEAH."

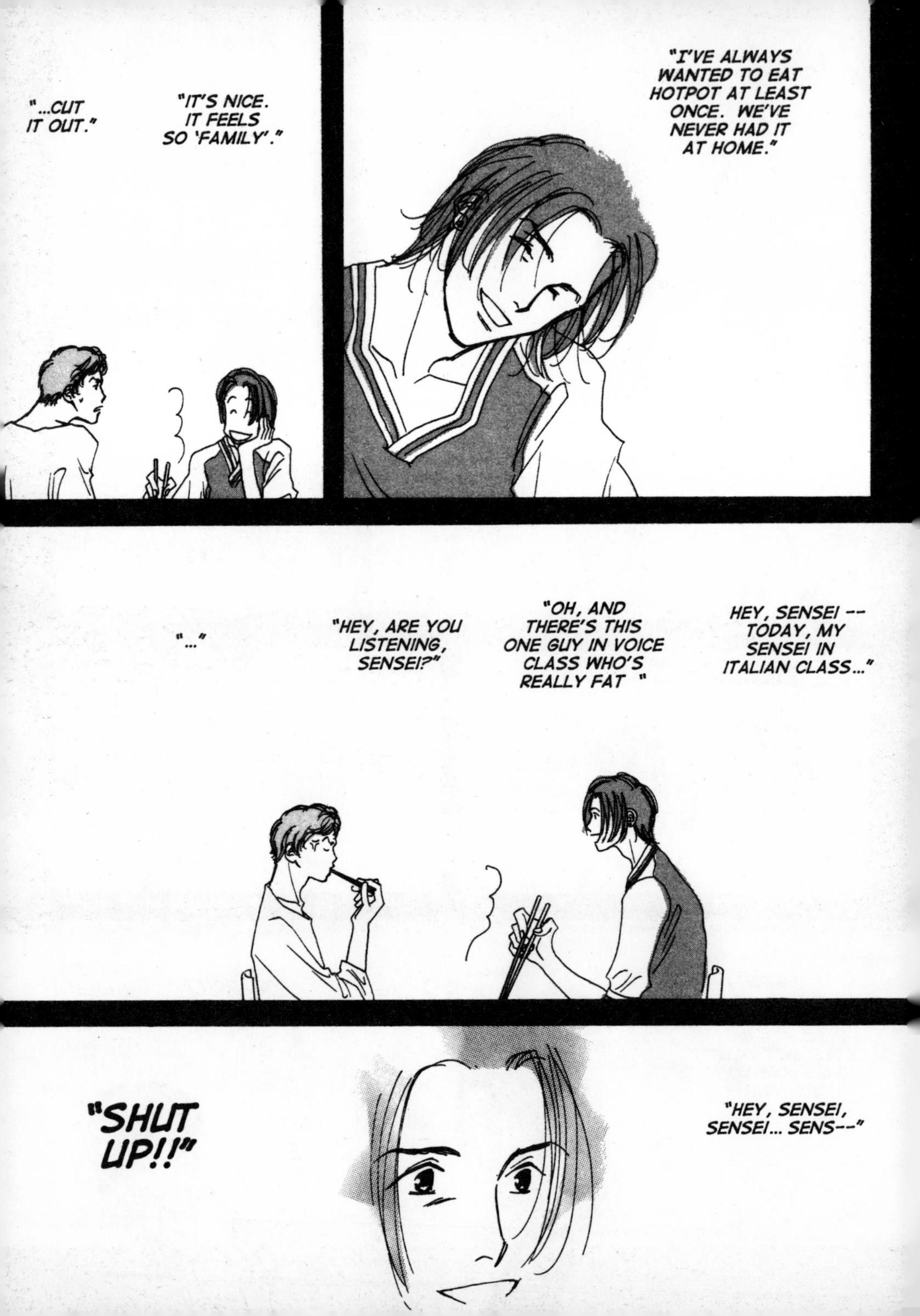
"I'VE ALWAYS WANTED TO EAT HOTPOT AT LEAST ONCE. WE'VE NEVER HAD IT AT HOME."
"IT'S NICE. IT FEELS SO 'FAMILY'."
"...CUT IT OUT."
HEY, SENSEI -- TODAY, MY SENSEI IN ITALIAN CLASS..."
"OH, AND THERE'S THIS ONE GUY IN VOICE CLASS WHO'S REALLY FAT "
"HEY, ARE YOU LISTENING, SENSEI?"
"..."
"HEY, SENSEI, SENSEI... SENS--"
"SHUT UP!!"

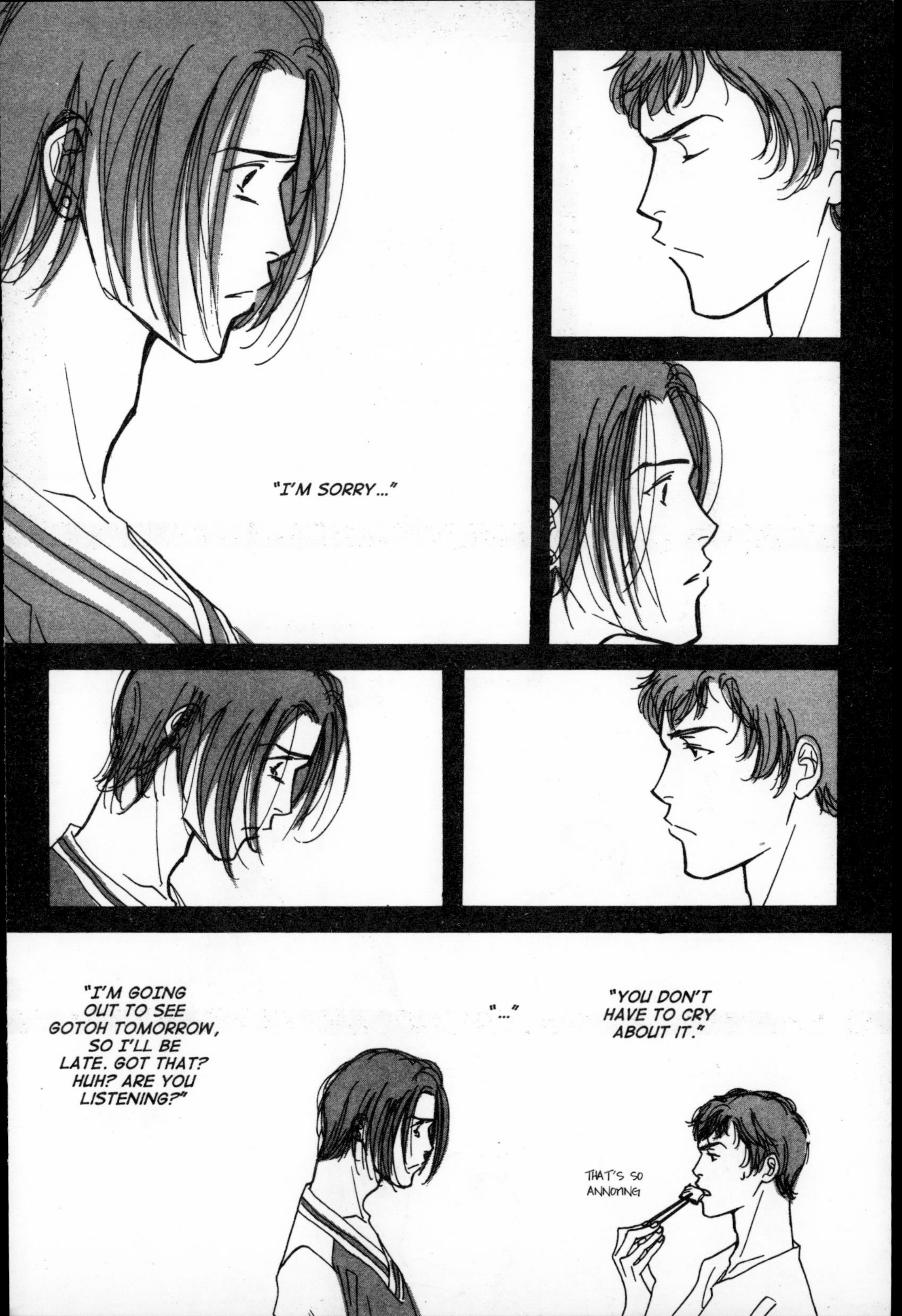
"I'M SORRY..."
"YOU DON'T HAVE TO CRY ABOUT IT."
THAT'S SO ANNOYING
"..."
"I'M GOING OUT TO SEE GOTOH TOMORROW, SO I'LL BE LATE. GOT THAT? HUH? ARE YOU LISTENING?"

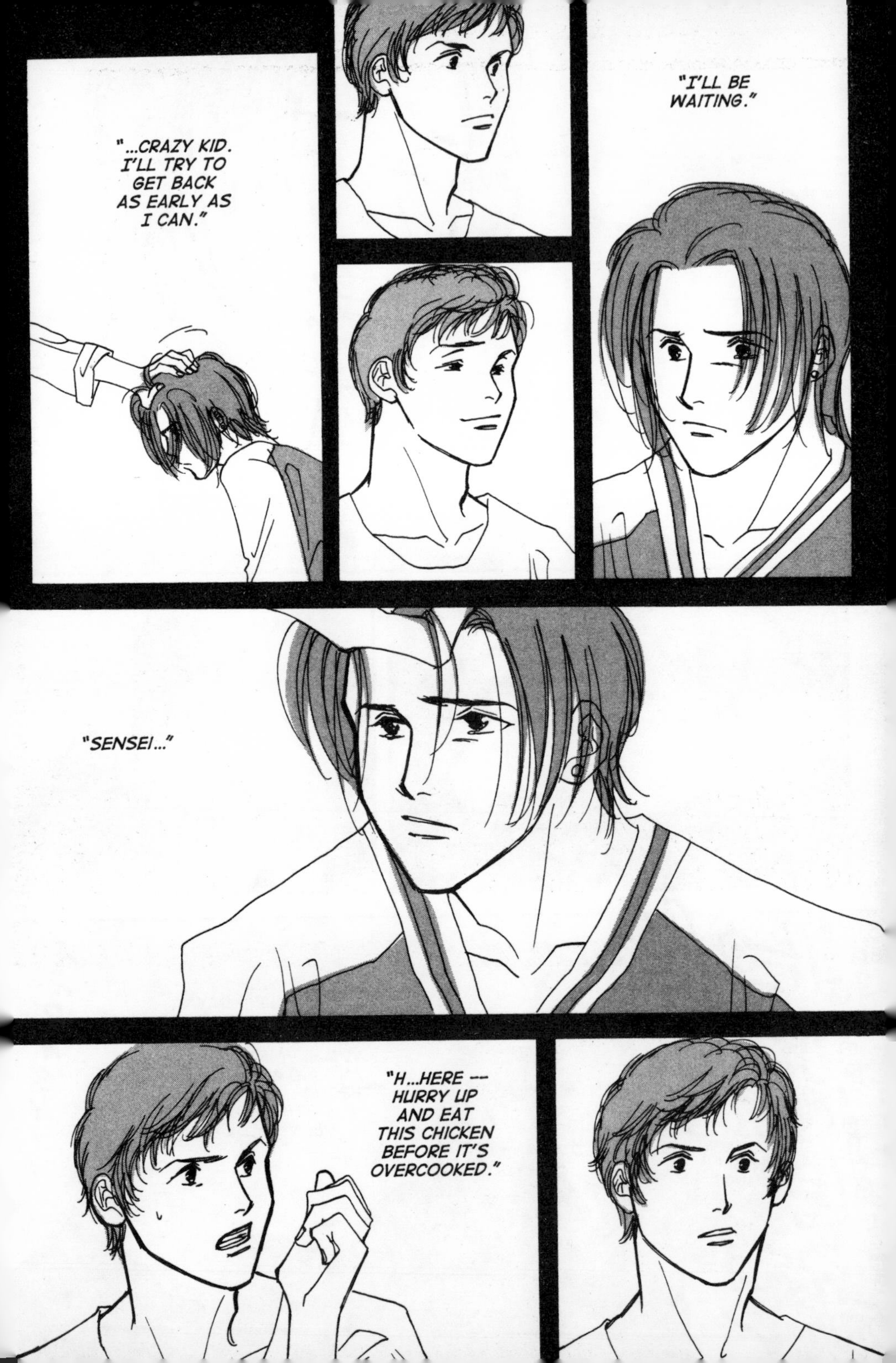
"I'LL BE WAITING."
"...CRAZY KID. I'LL TRY TO GET BACK AS EARLY AS I CAN."
"SENSEI..."
"H...HERE --- HURRY UP AND EAT THIS CHICKEN BEFORE IT'S OVERCOOKED."

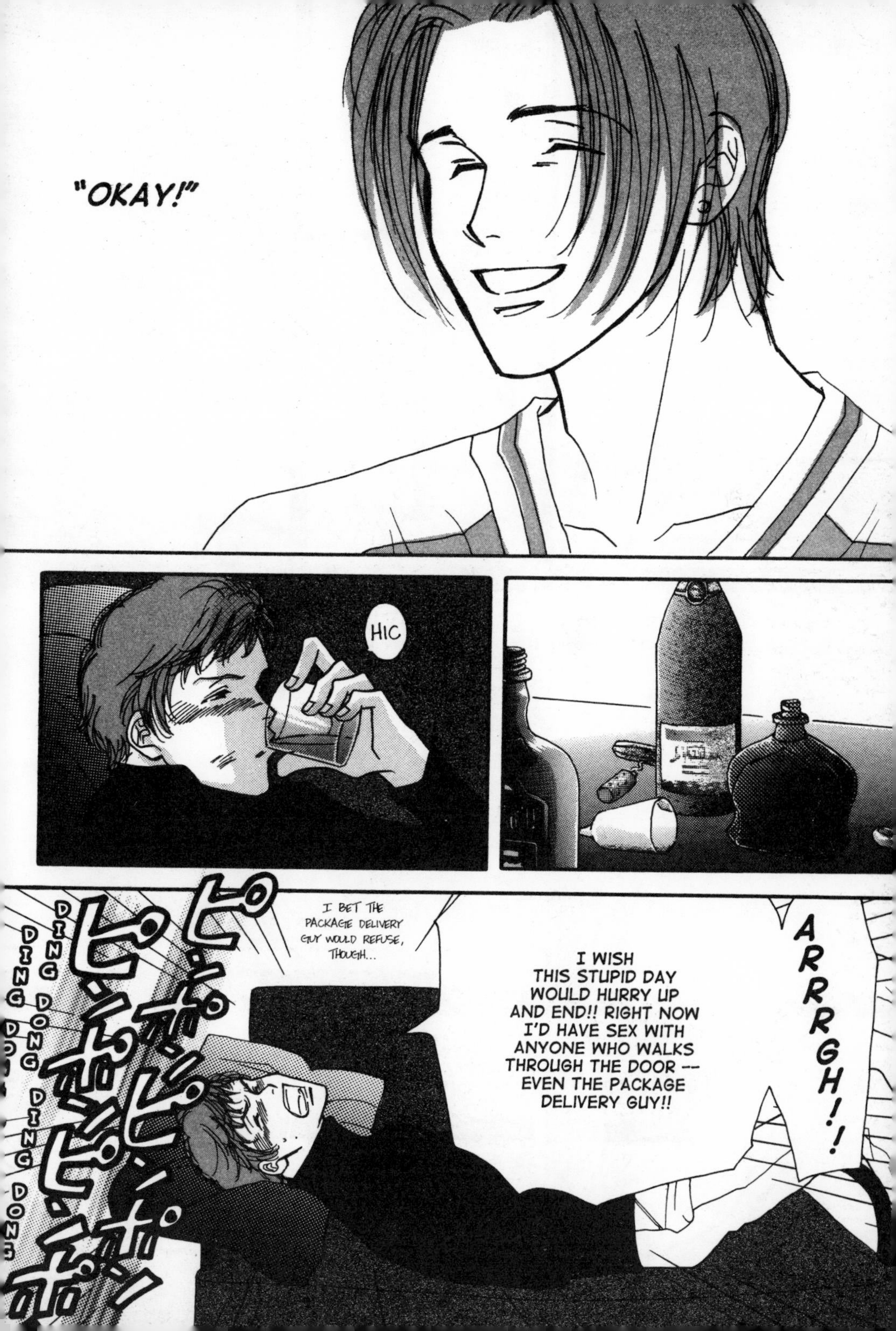
"OKAY!"
HIC
ARRRGH!!
I WISH THIS STUPID DAY WOULD HURRY UP AND END!! RIGHT NOW I'D HAVE SEX WITH ANYONE WHO WALKS THROUGH THE DOOR -- EVEN THE PACKAGE DELIVERY GUY!!
I BET THE PACKAGE DELIVERY GUY WOULD REFUSE, THOUGH...
DING DONG
DING DONG DING DONG

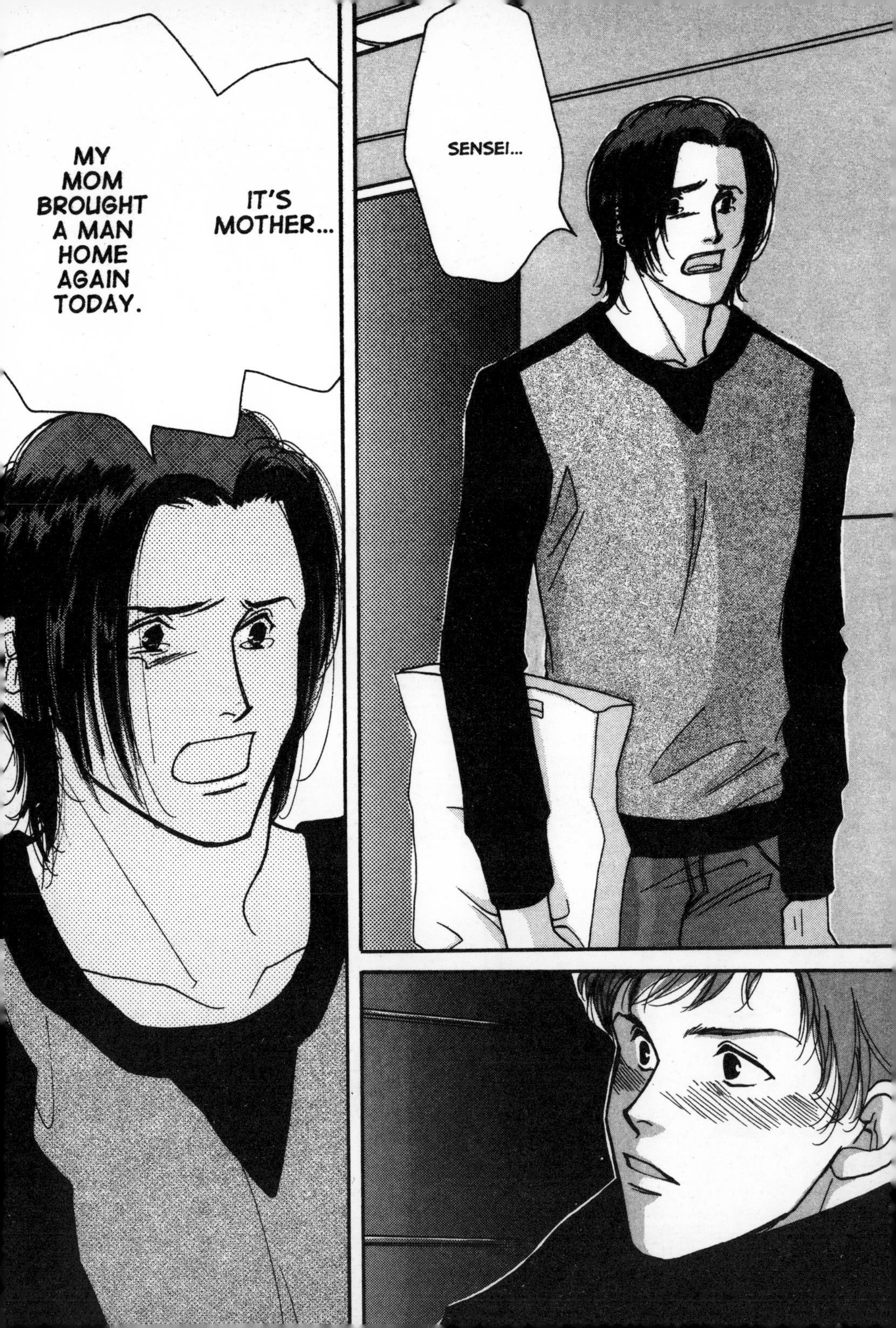
SENSEI...
IT'S MOTHER...
MY MOM BROUGHT A MAN HOME AGAIN TODAY.

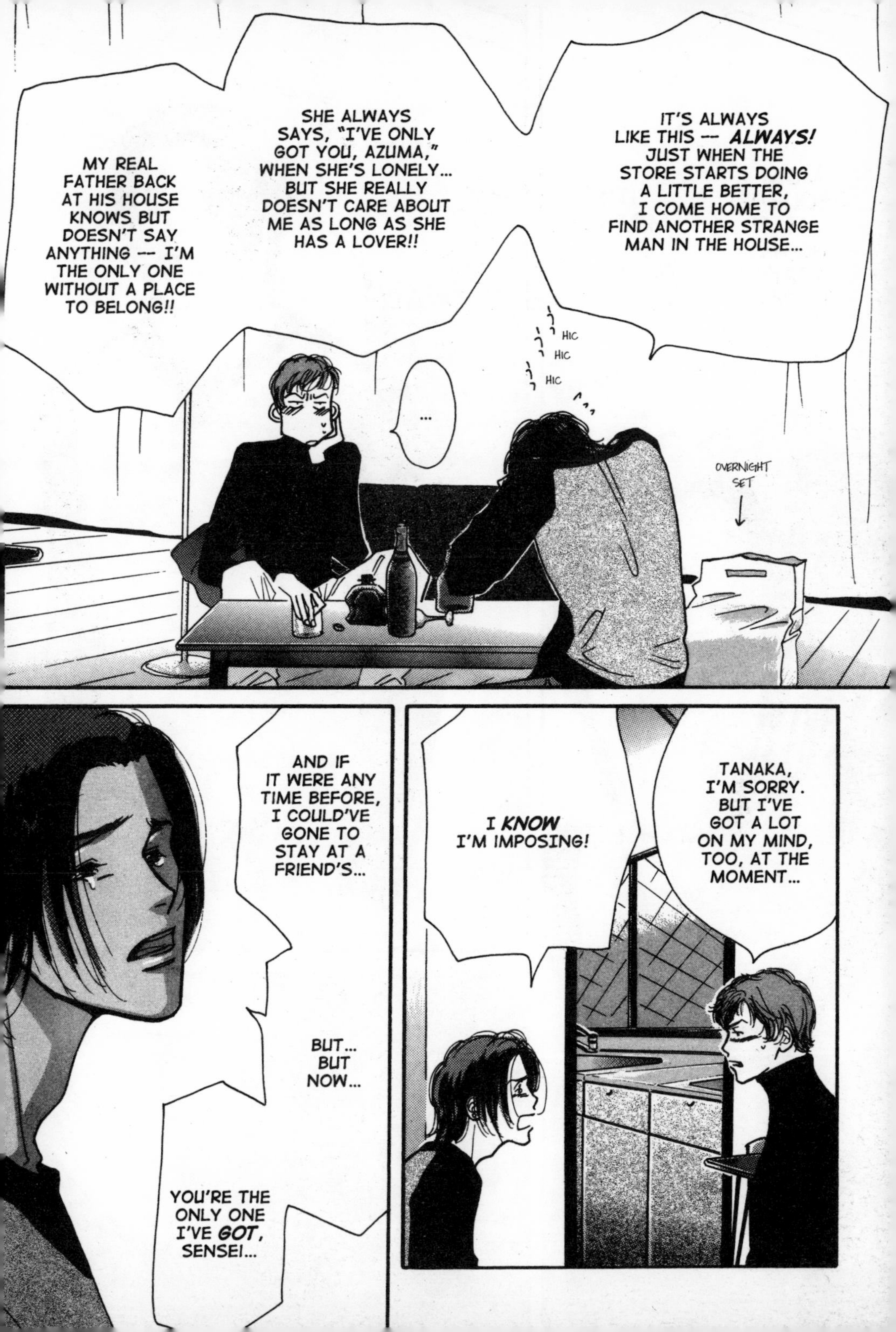
IT'S ALWAYS LIKE THIS -- ***ALWAYS!*** JUST WHEN THE STORE STARTS DOING A LITTLE BETTER, I COME HOME TO FIND ANOTHER STRANGE MAN IN THE HOUSE...
SHE ALWAYS SAYS, "I'VE ONLY GOT YOU, AZUMA," WHEN SHE'S LONELY... BUT SHE REALLY DOESN'T CARE ABOUT ME AS LONG AS SHE HAS A LOVER!!
MY REAL FATHER BACK AT HIS HOUSE KNOWS BUT DOESN'T SAY ANYTHING -- I'M THE ONLY ONE WITHOUT A PLACE TO BELONG!!
HIC
HIC
HIC
OVERNIGHT SET
...
TANAKA, I'M SORRY. BUT I'VE GOT A LOT ON MY MIND, TOO, AT THE MOMENT...
I ***KNOW*** I'M IMPOSING!
AND IF IT WERE ANY TIME BEFORE, I COULD'VE GONE TO STAY AT A FRIEND'S...
BUT... BUT NOW...
YOU'RE THE ONLY ONE I'VE ***GOT***, SENSEI...

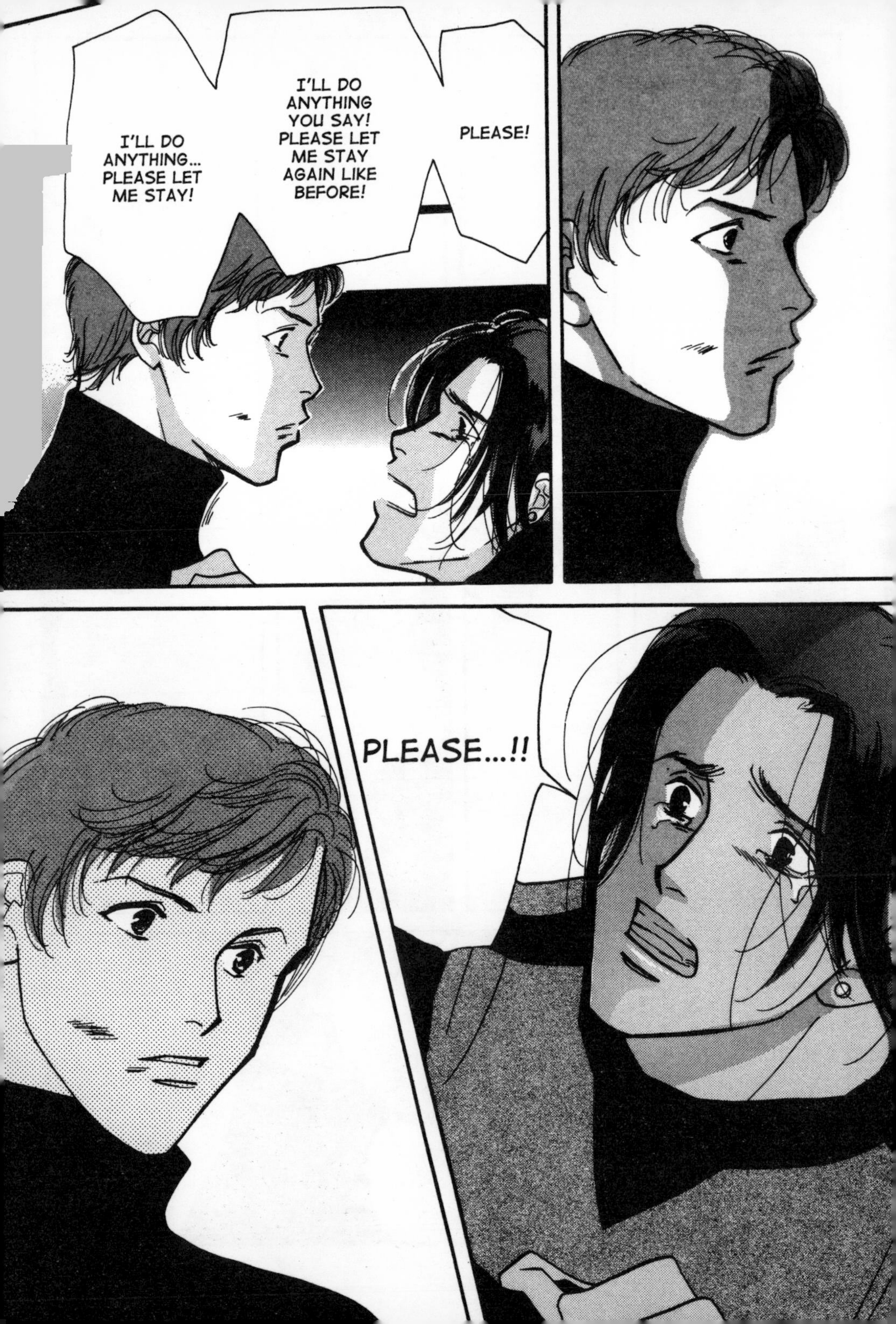
PLEASE!
I'LL DO ANYTHING YOU SAY! PLEASE LET ME STAY AGAIN LIKE BEFORE!
I'LL DO ANYTHING... PLEASE LET ME STAY!
PLEASE...!!

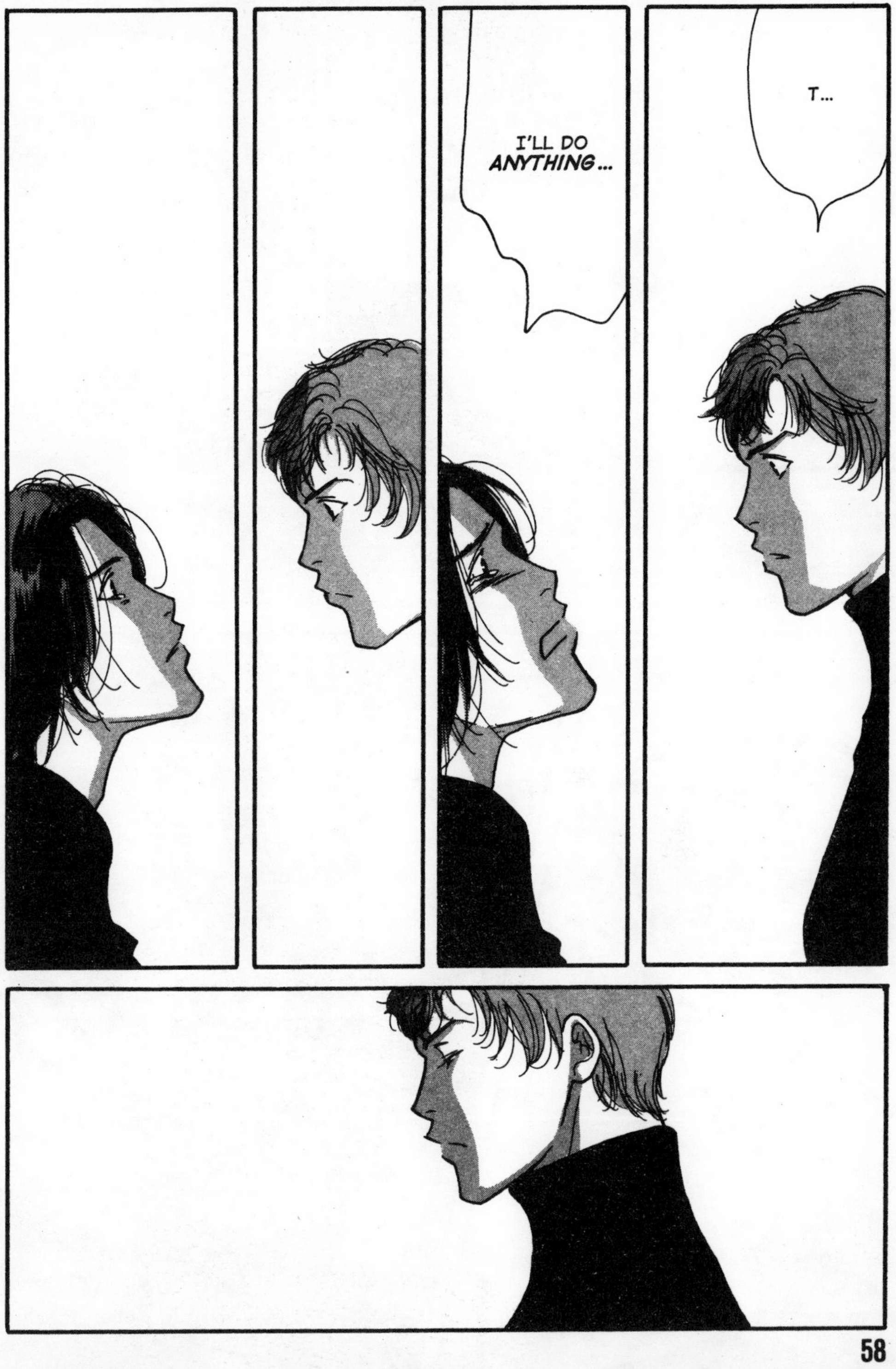
T...
I'LL DO ANYTHING...

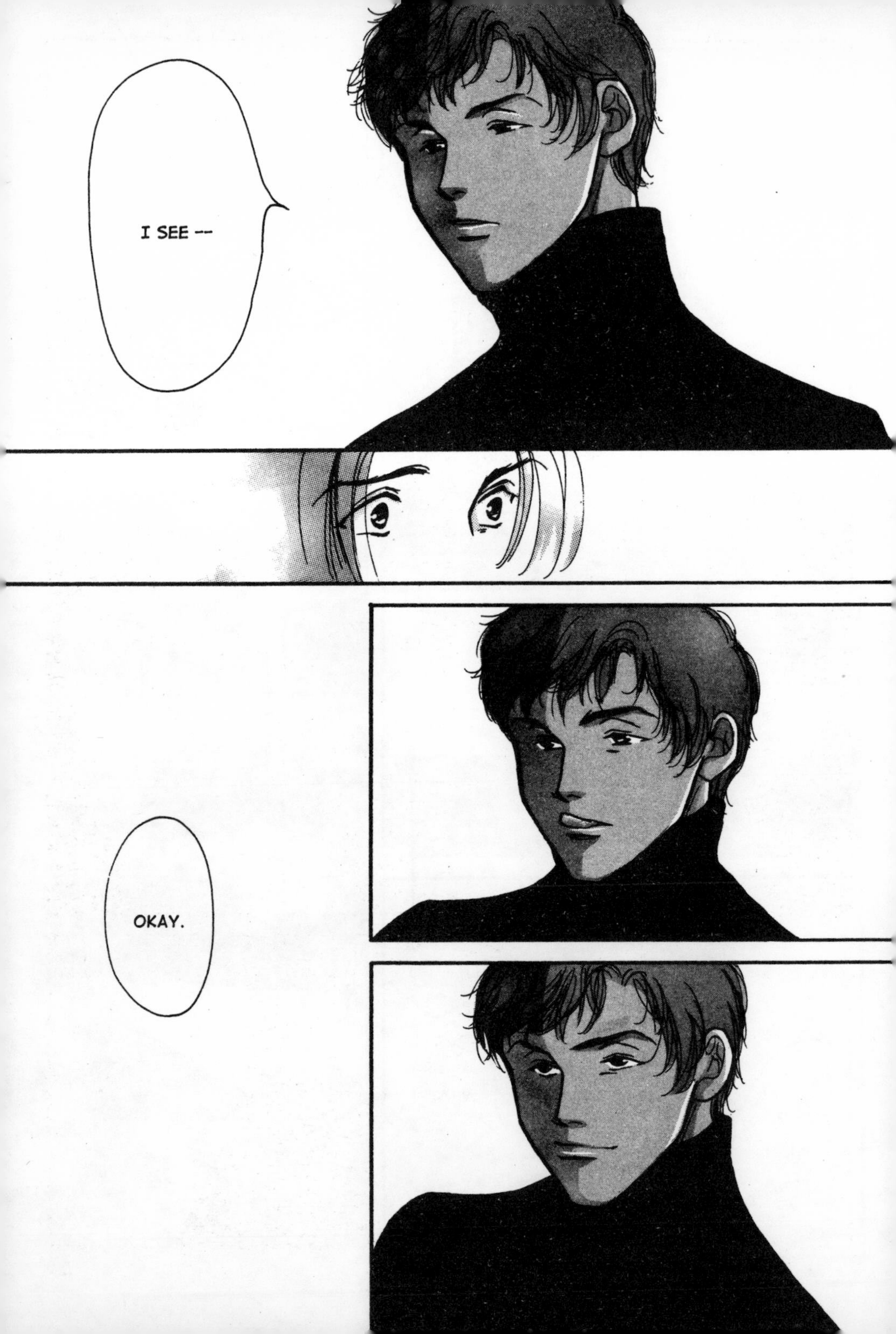
I SEE --
OKAY.

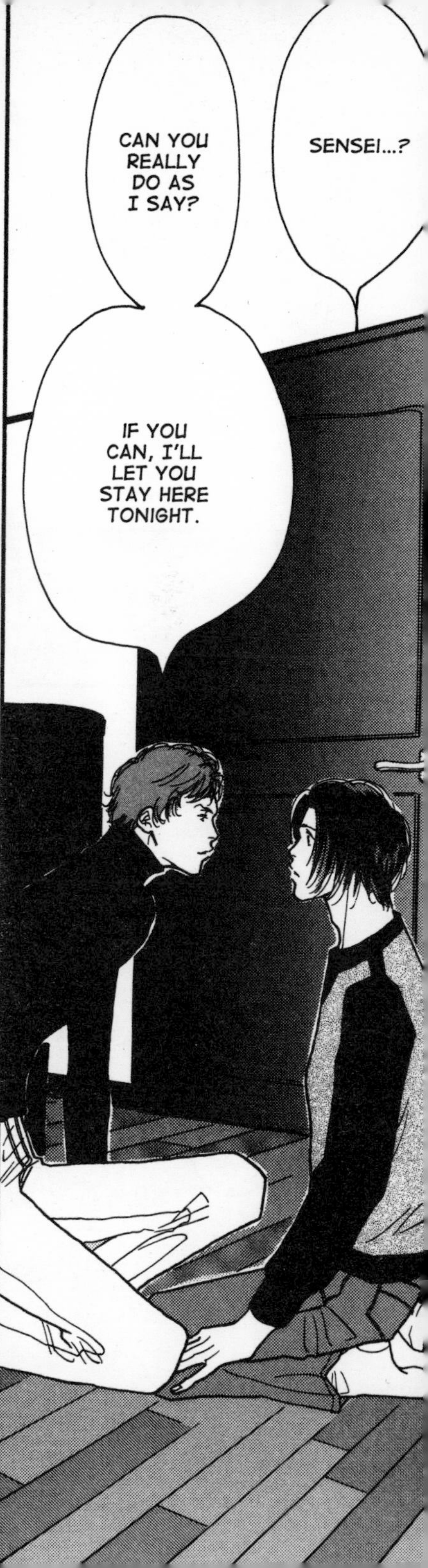
SENSEI...?
CAN YOU REALLY DO AS I SAY?
IF YOU CAN, I'LL LET YOU STAY HERE TONIGHT.

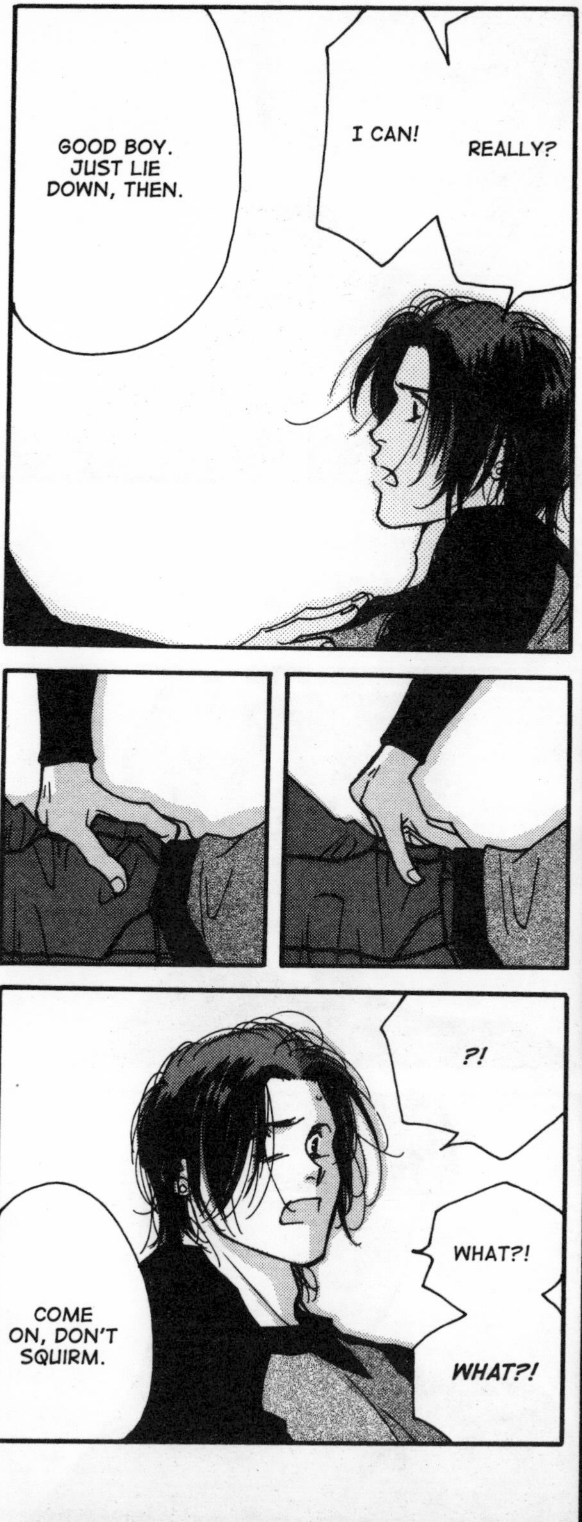
REALLY?
I CAN!
GOOD BOY. JUST LIE DOWN, THEN.
?!
WHAT?!
WHAT?!
COME ON, DON'T SQUIRM.

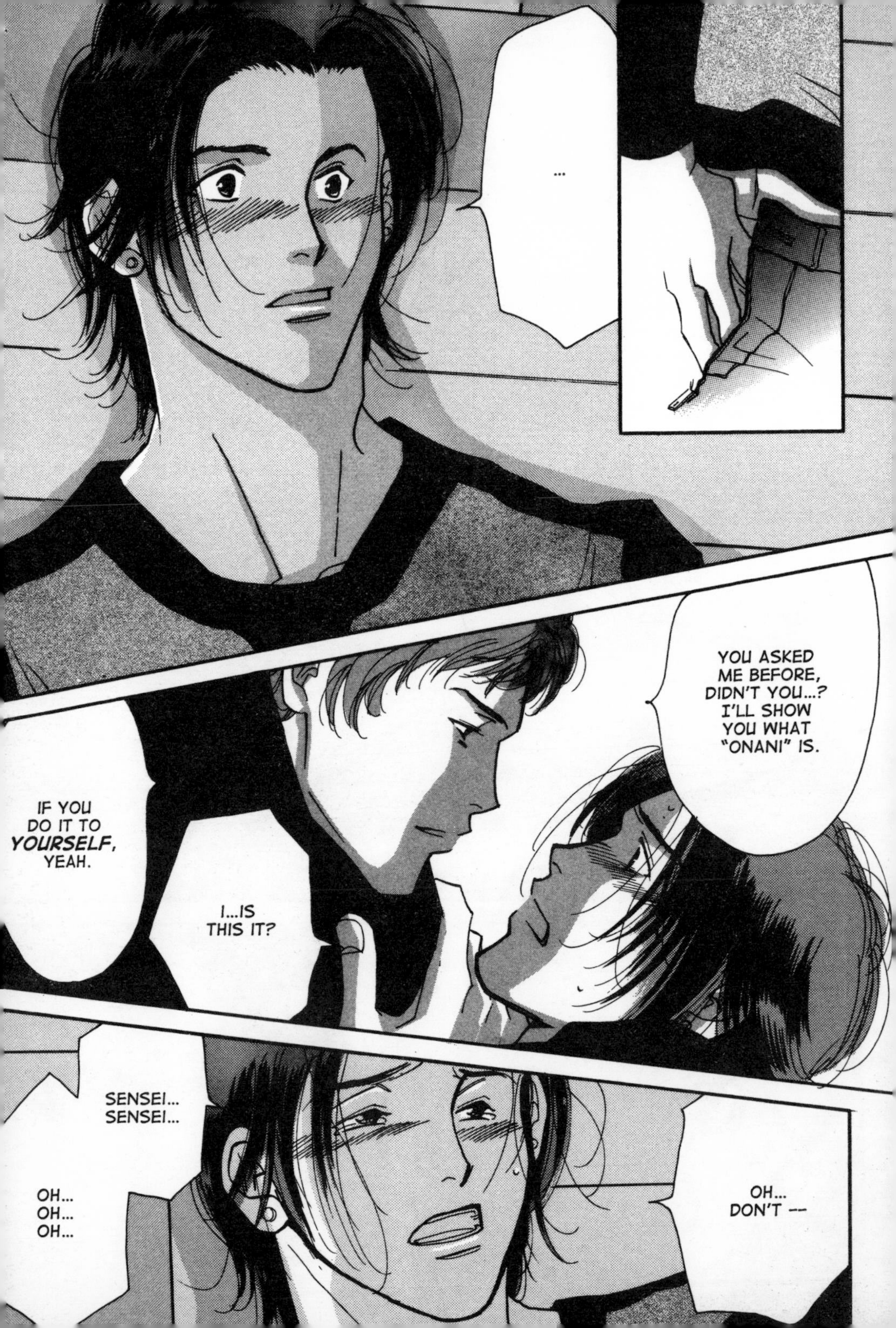
...
YOU ASKED ME BEFORE, DIDN'T YOU...? I'LL SHOW YOU WHAT "ONANI" IS.
I...IS THIS IT?
IF YOU DO IT TO ***YOURSELF***, YEAH.
OH... DON'T --
SENSEI... SENSEI...
OH... OH... OH...

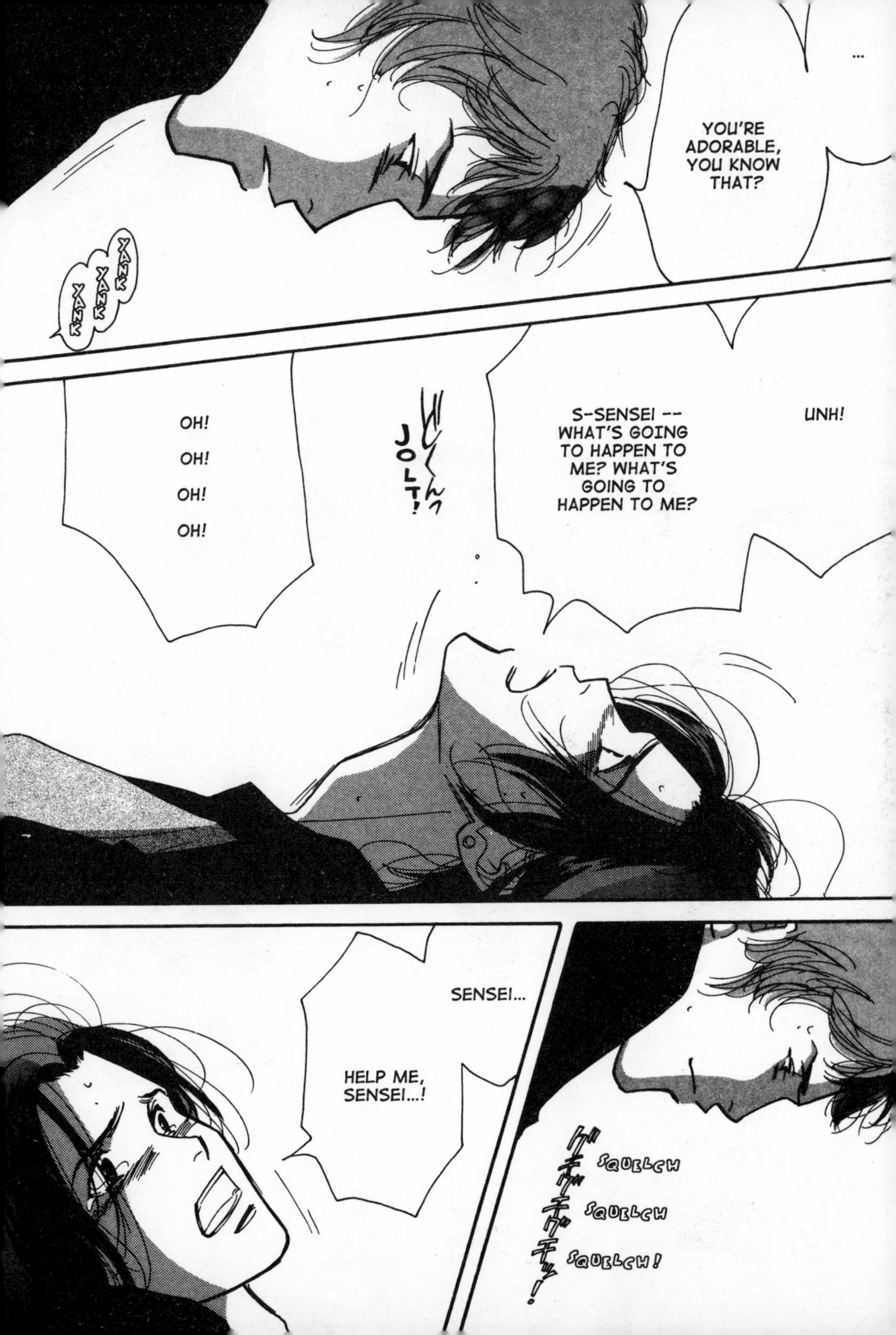
...
YOU'RE ADORABLE, YOU KNOW THAT?
YANK YANK YANK
UNH!
S-SENSEI -- WHAT'S GOING TO HAPPEN TO ME? WHAT'S GOING TO HAPPEN TO ME?
JOLT!
OH!
OH!
OH!
OH!
SQUELCH
SQUELCH
SQUELCH!
SENSEI...
HELP ME, SENSEI...!

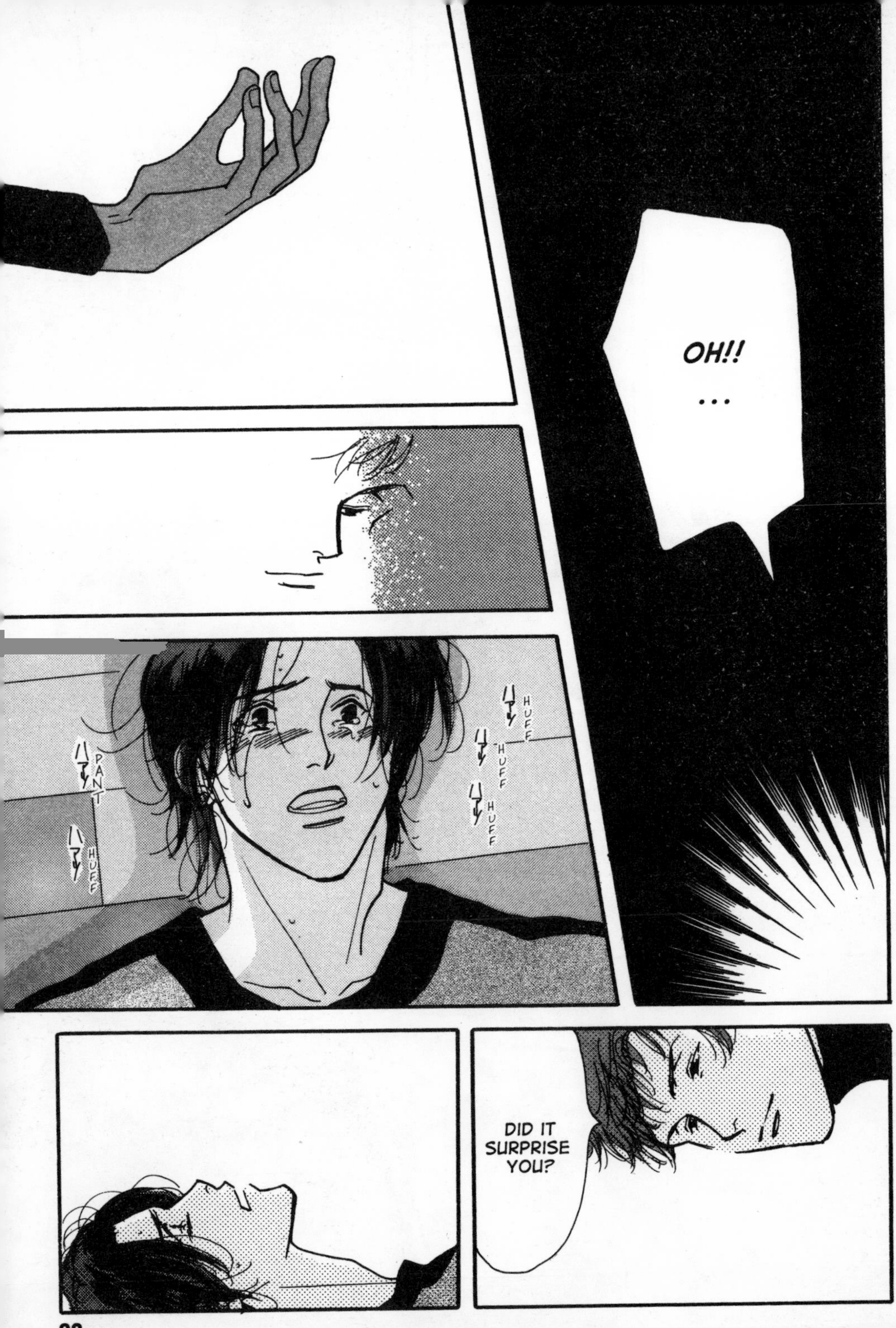
OH!!
...
ハァッ HUFF
ハァッ HUFF
ハァッ HUFF
ハァッ PANT
ハァッ HUFF
DID IT SURPRISE YOU?

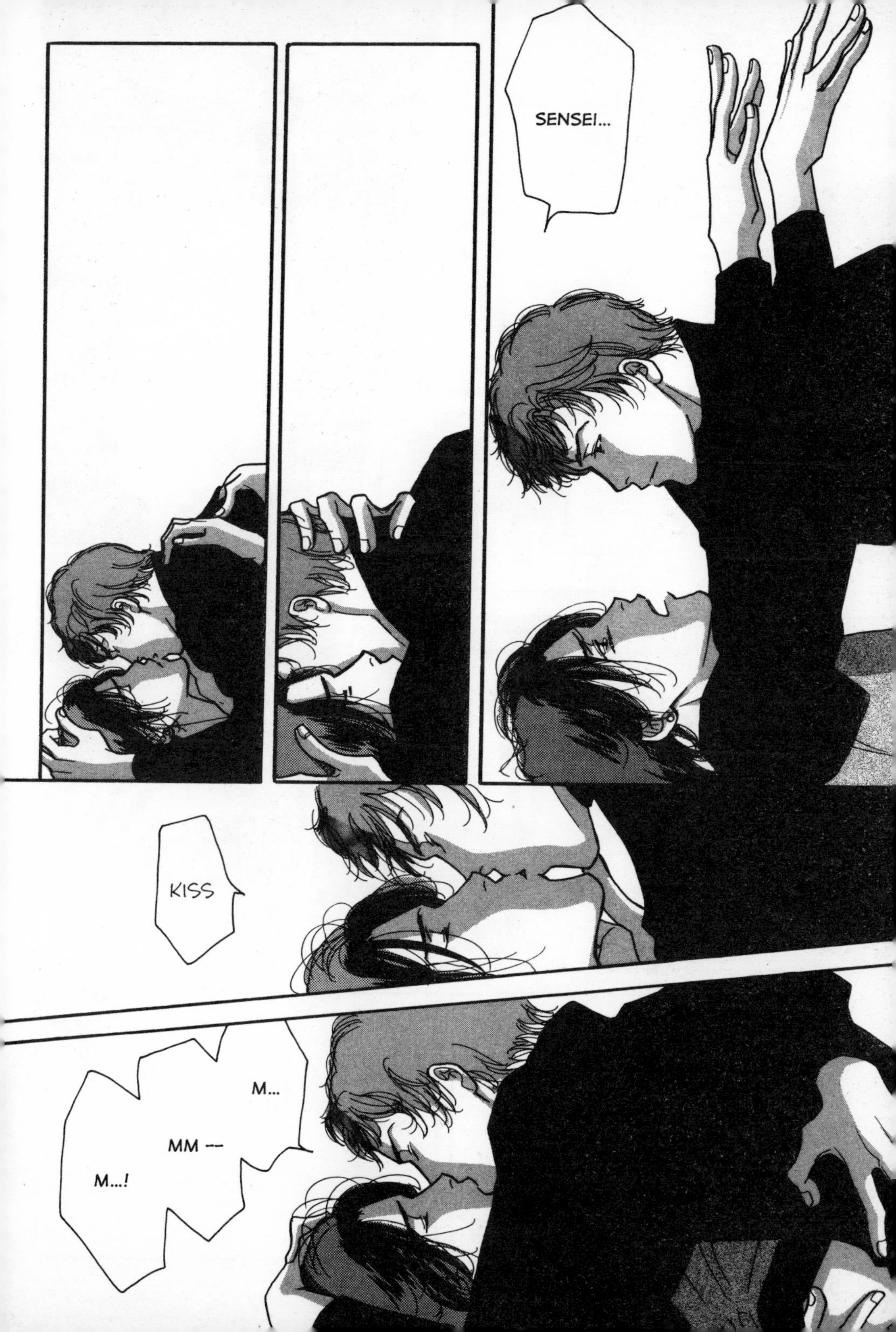
SENSEI...
KISS
M...
MM --
M...!

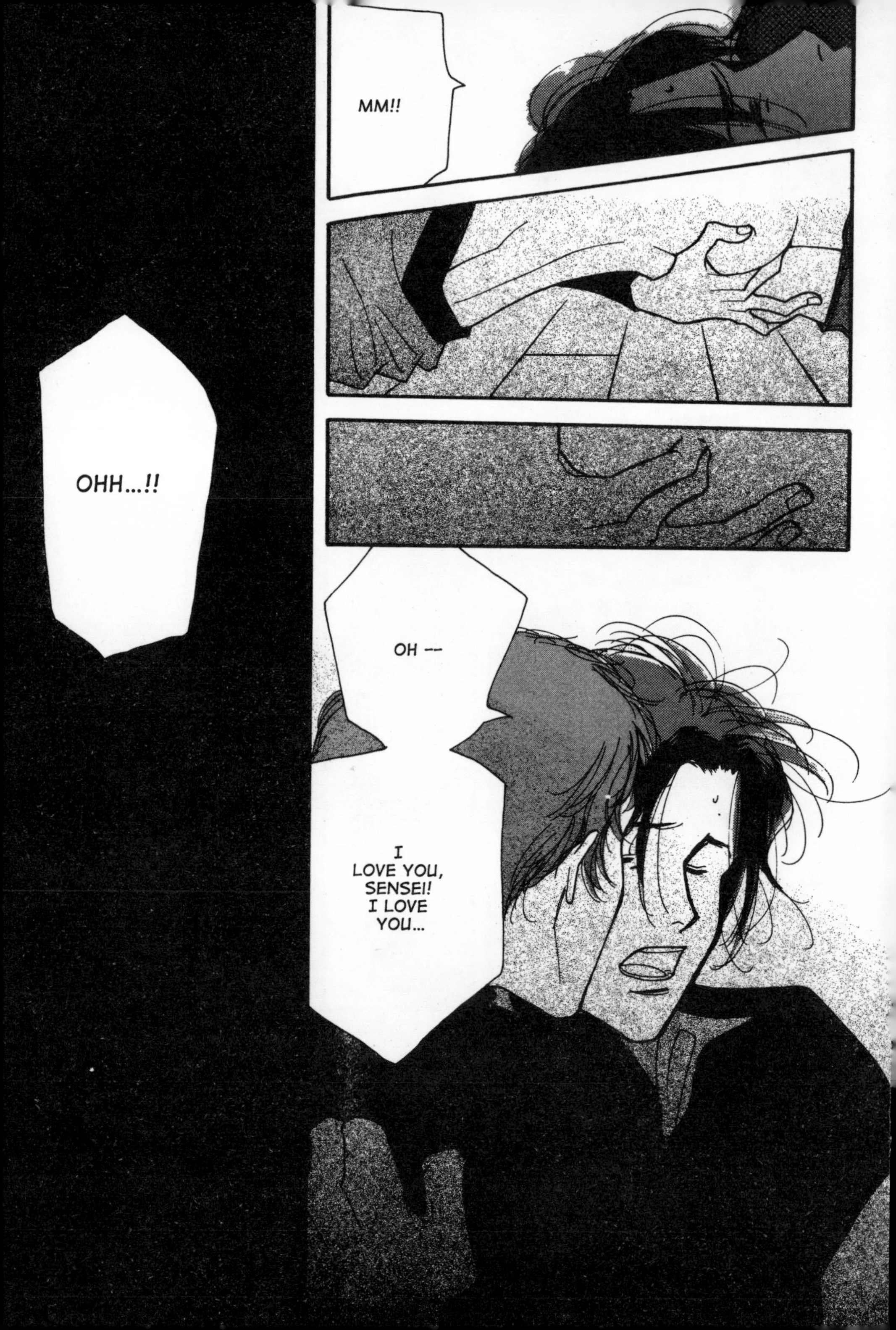
MM!!
OH --
I LOVE YOU, SENSEI! I LOVE YOU...
OHH...!!

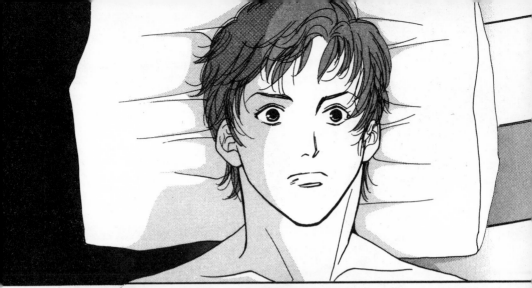

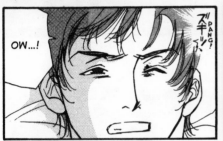

OW...!

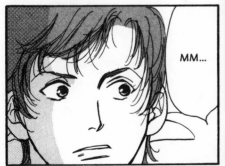

MM...

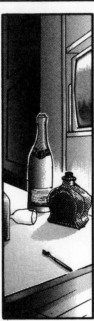

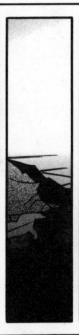

DANG!

CHEEP
CHEEP
CHEEP

CHIRP
CHIRP

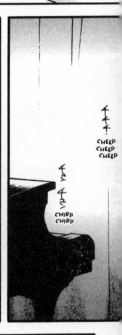

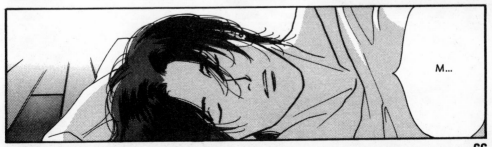

M...

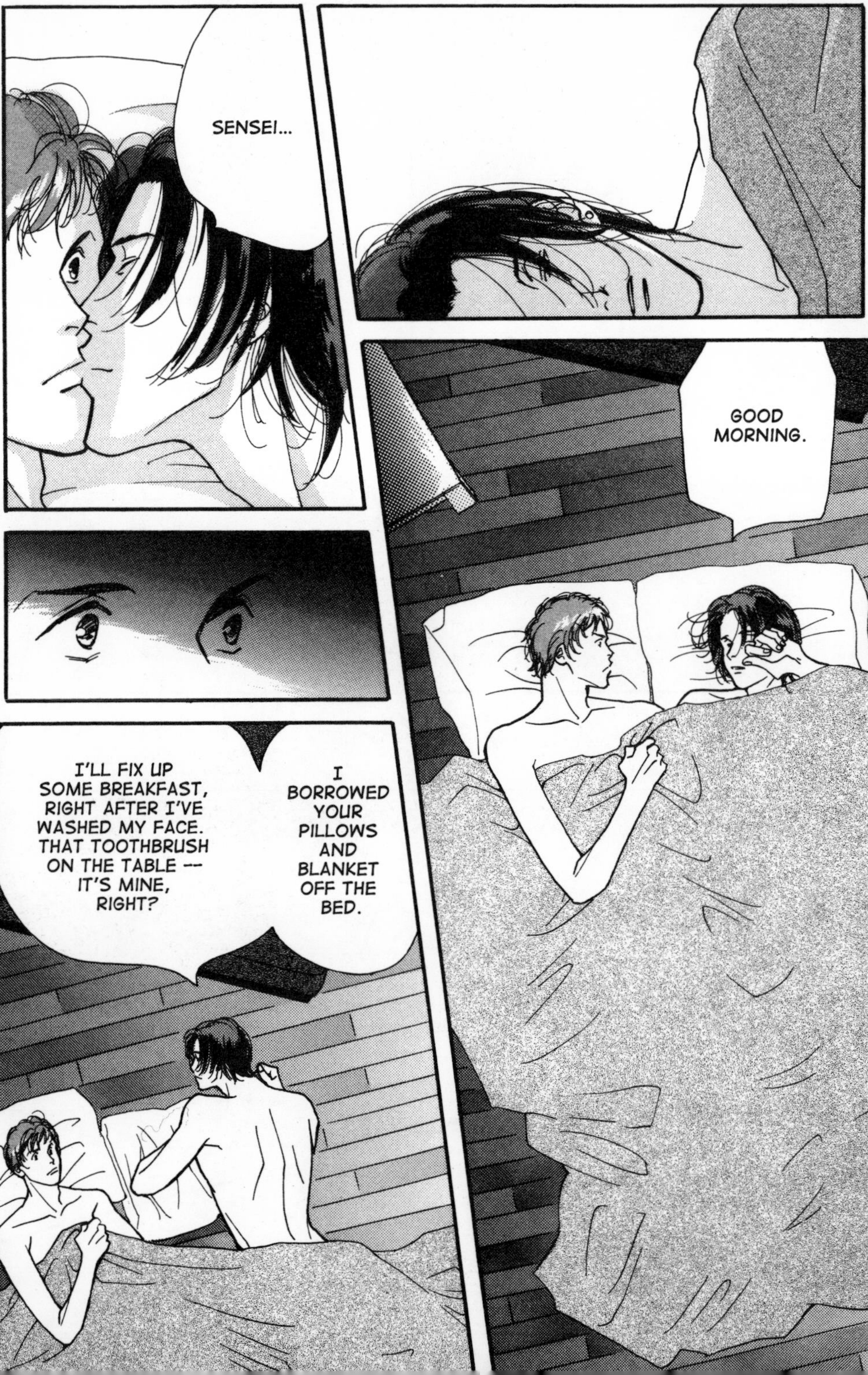
SENSEI...
GOOD MORNING.
I BORROWED YOUR PILLOWS AND BLANKET OFF THE BED.
I'LL FIX UP SOME BREAKFAST, RIGHT AFTER I'VE WASHED MY FACE. THAT TOOTHBRUSH ON THE TABLE -- IT'S MINE, RIGHT?

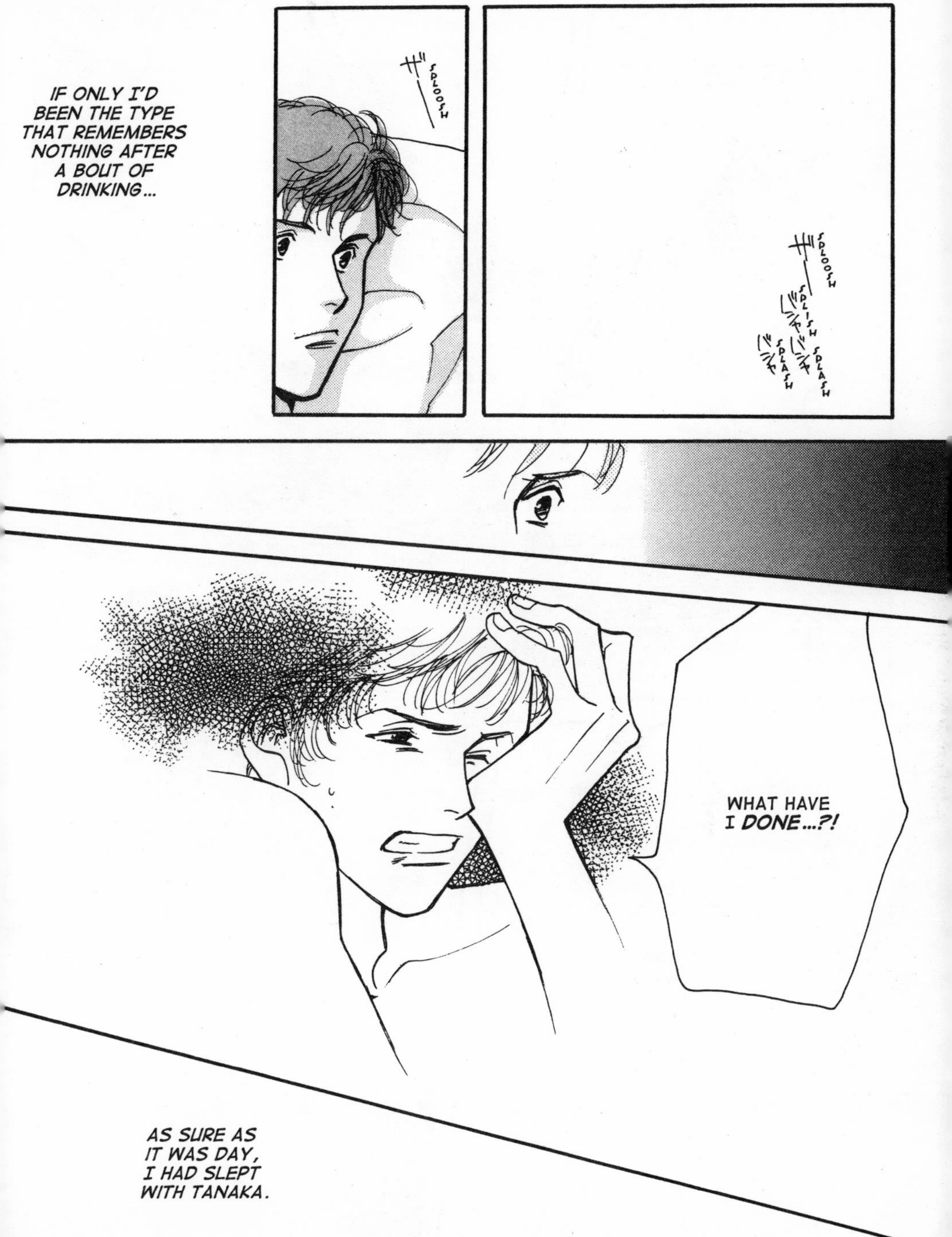
SPLOOSH
SPLISH SPLASH
SPLASH
SPLOOSH
IF ONLY I'D BEEN THE TYPE THAT REMEMBERS NOTHING AFTER A BOUT OF DRINKING...
WHAT HAVE I *DONE*...?!
AS SURE AS IT WAS DAY, I HAD SLEPT WITH TANAKA.

To be continued.

ソルフェージュ
SOLFÈGE
THE QUEEN OF THE NIGHT ARIA
★PART 2

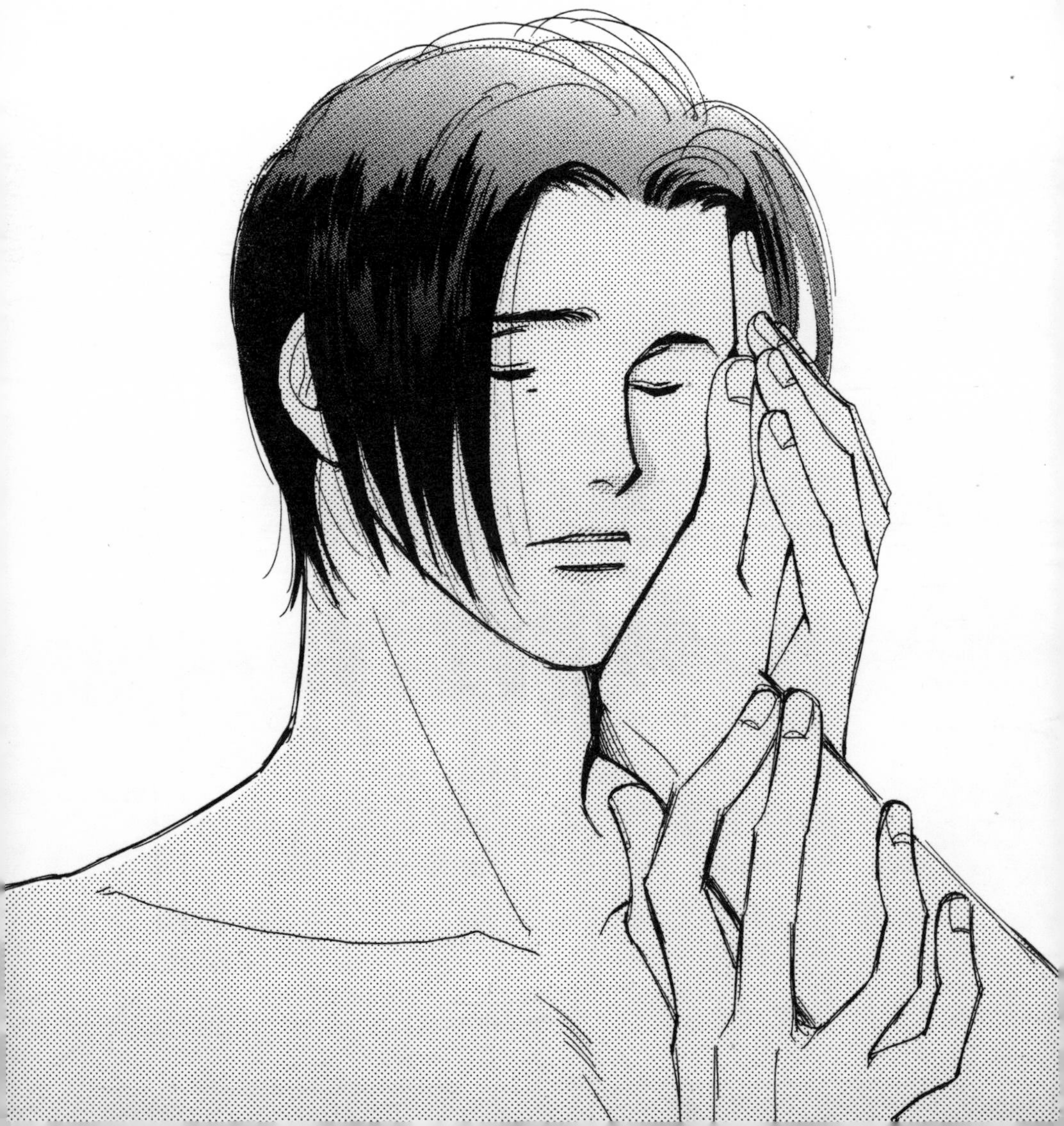

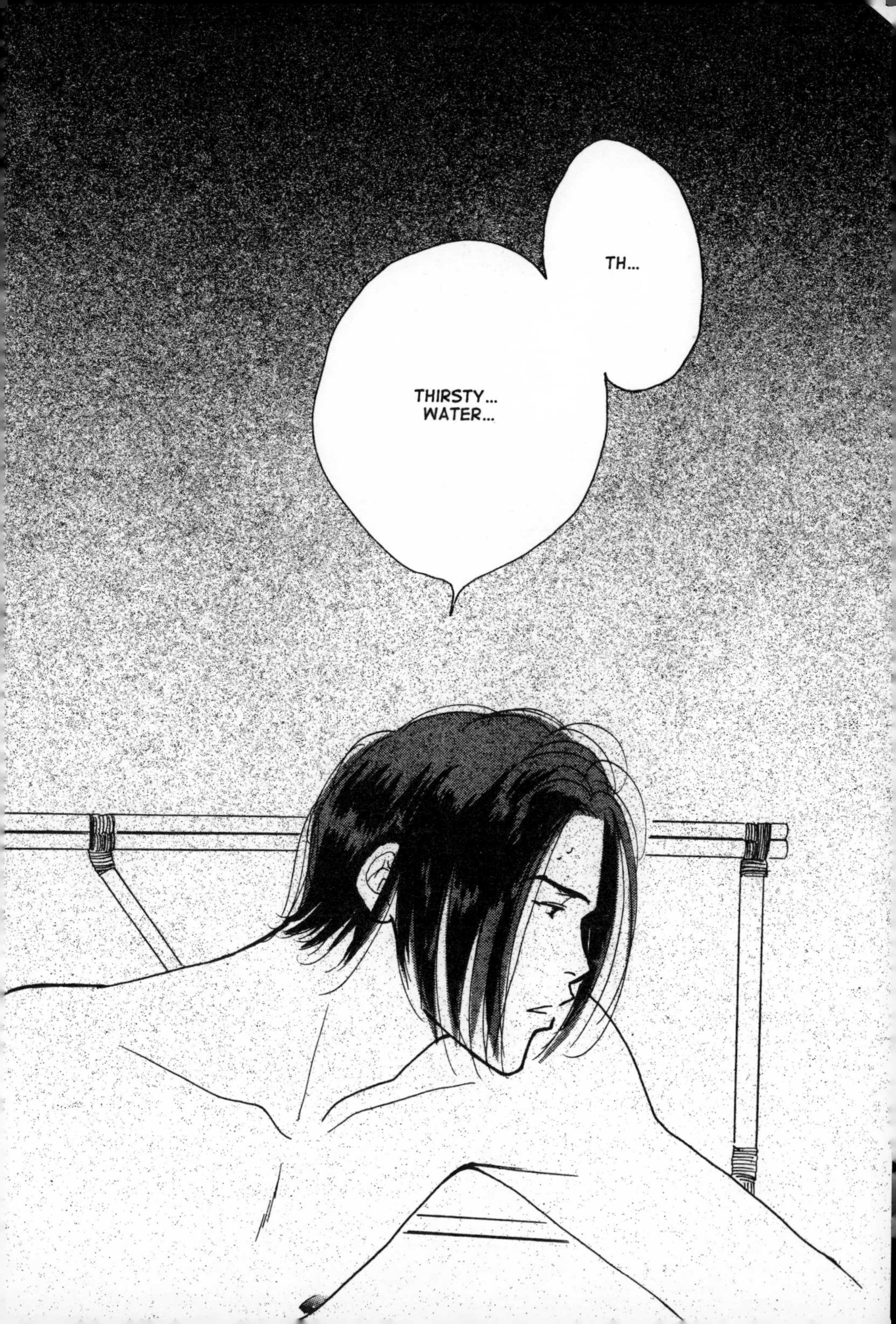
TH...
THIRSTY... WATER...

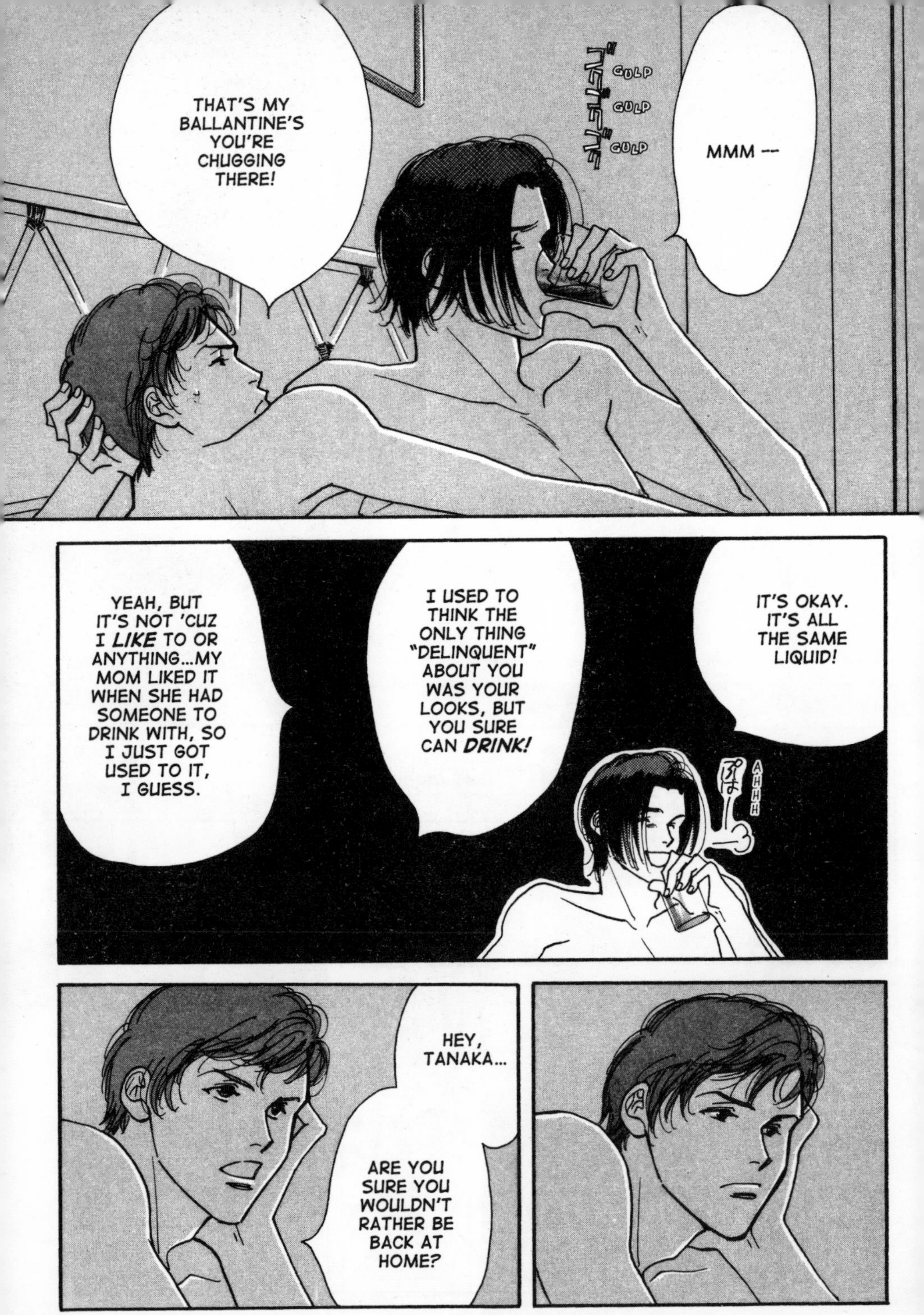
MMM --
GULP
GULP
GULP
THAT'S MY BALLANTINE'S YOU'RE CHUGGING THERE!
IT'S OKAY. IT'S ALL THE SAME LIQUID!
AHHH
I USED TO THINK THE ONLY THING "DELINQUENT" ABOUT YOU WAS YOUR LOOKS, BUT YOU SURE CAN *DRINK!*
YEAH, BUT IT'S NOT 'CUZ I *LIKE* TO OR ANYTHING...MY MOM LIKED IT WHEN SHE HAD SOMEONE TO DRINK WITH, SO I JUST GOT USED TO IT, I GUESS.
HEY, TANAKA...
ARE YOU SURE YOU WOULDN'T RATHER BE BACK AT HOME?

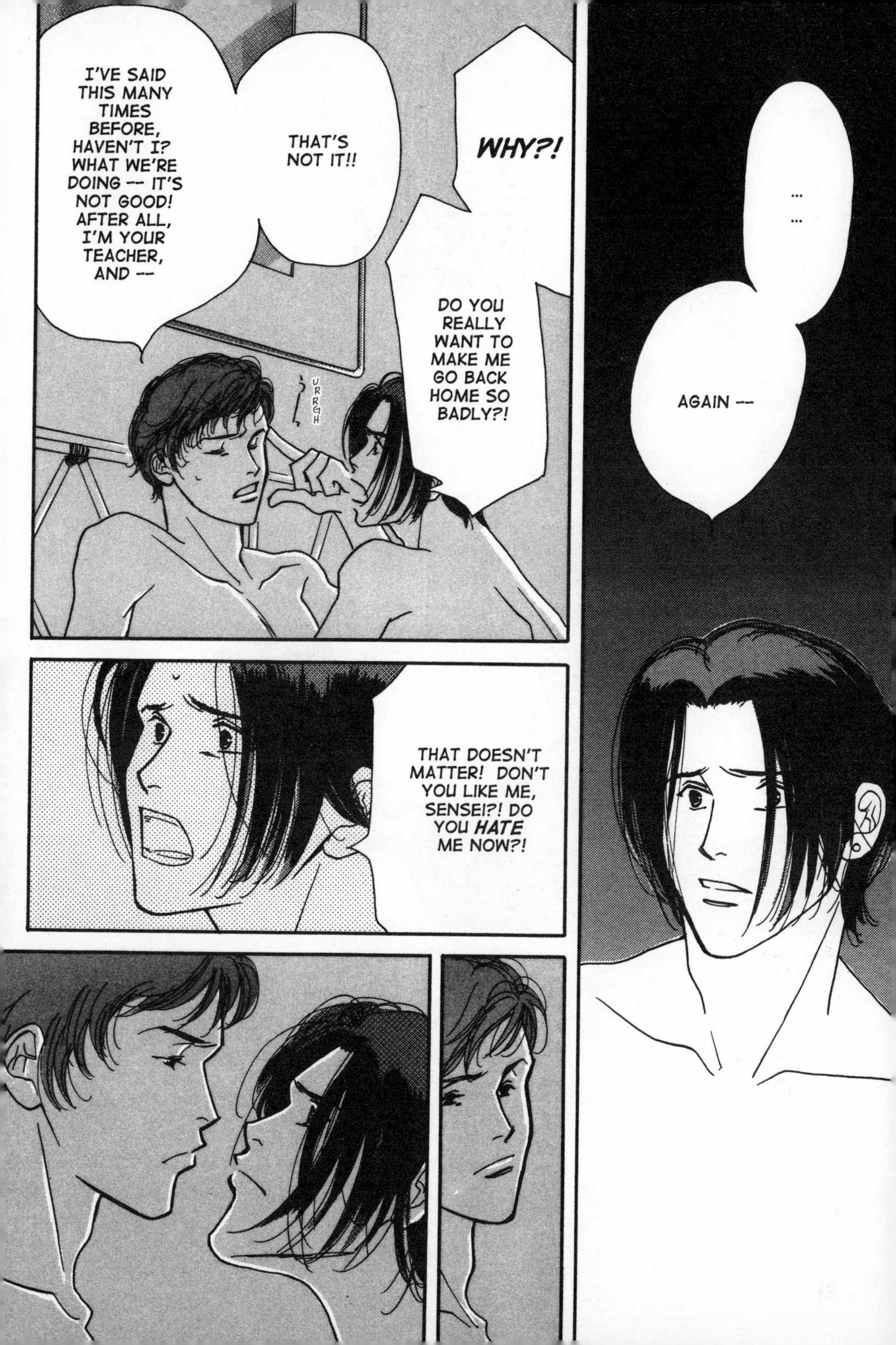

...
...
AGAIN --
WHY?!
THAT'S NOT IT!!
I'VE SAID THIS MANY TIMES BEFORE, HAVEN'T I? WHAT WE'RE DOING -- IT'S NOT GOOD! AFTER ALL, I'M YOUR TEACHER, AND --
DO YOU REALLY WANT TO MAKE ME GO BACK HOME SO BADLY?!
URRGH
THAT DOESN'T MATTER! DON'T YOU LIKE ME, SENSEI!?! DO YOU HATE ME NOW?!

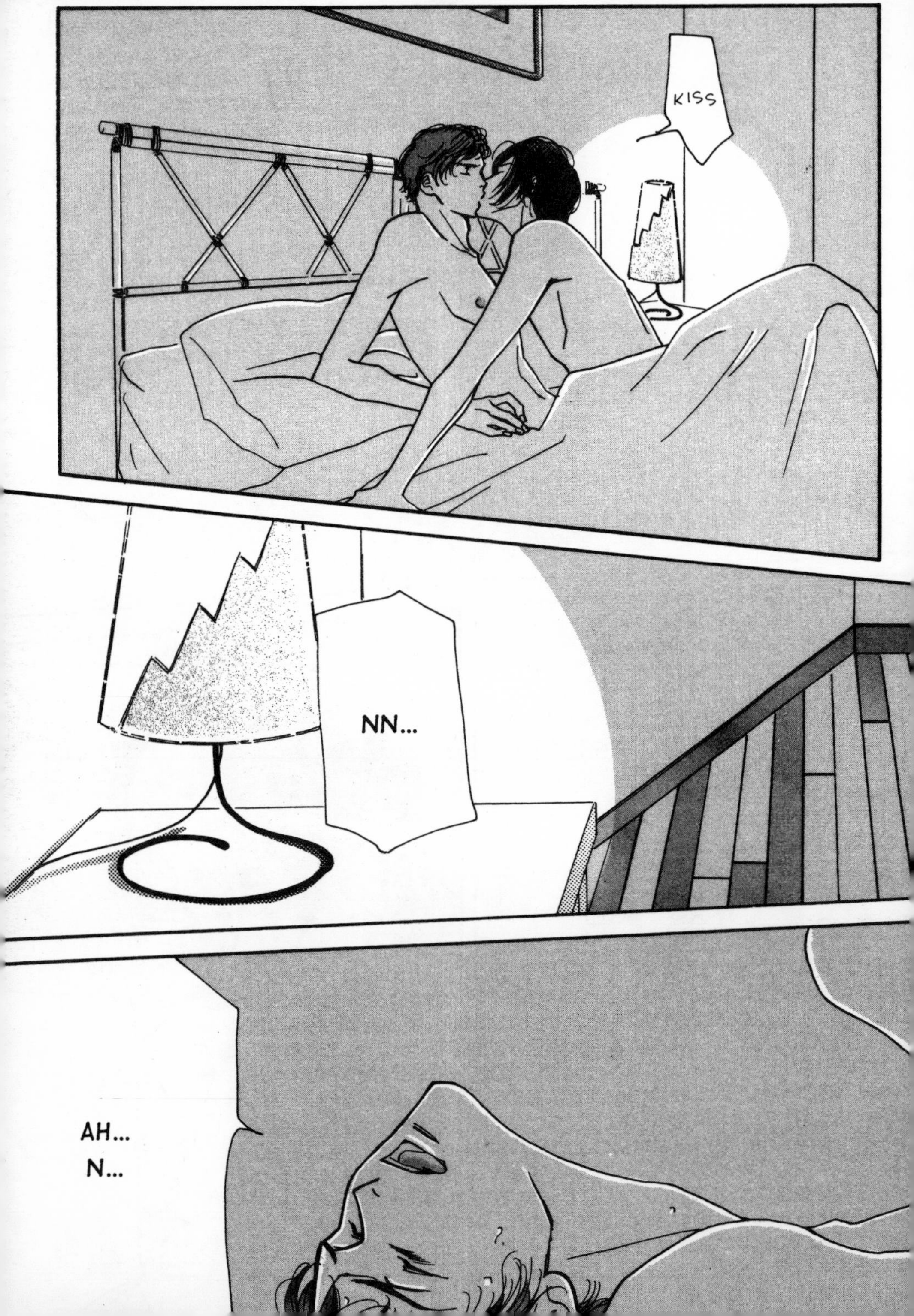
KISS
NN...
AH...
N...

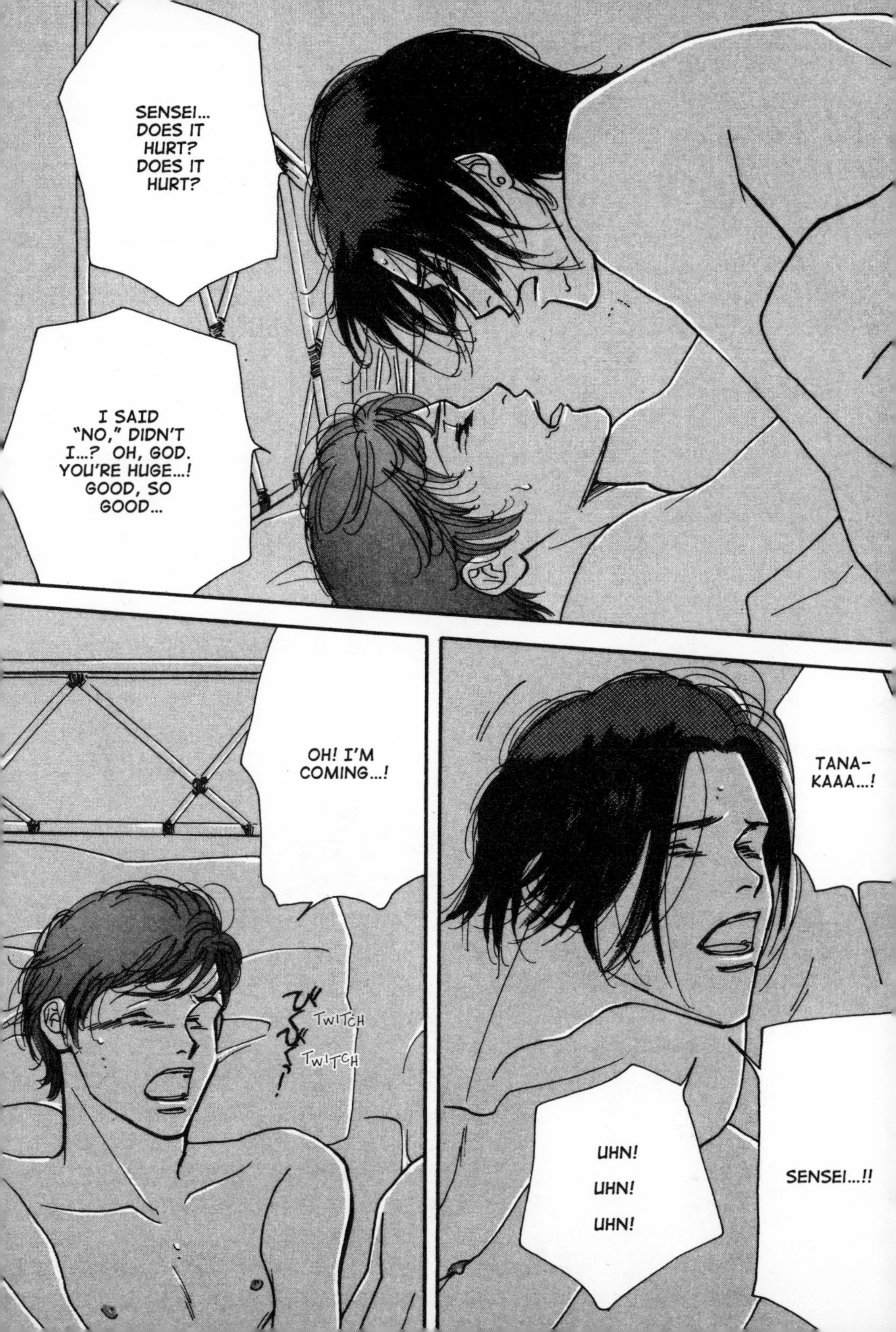
SENSEI... DOES IT HURT? DOES IT HURT?
I SAID "NO," DIDN'T I...? OH, GOD. YOU'RE HUGE...! GOOD, SO GOOD...
TANA-KAAA...!
SENSEI...!!
UHN! UHN! UHN!
OH! I'M COMING...!
TWITCH
TWITCH

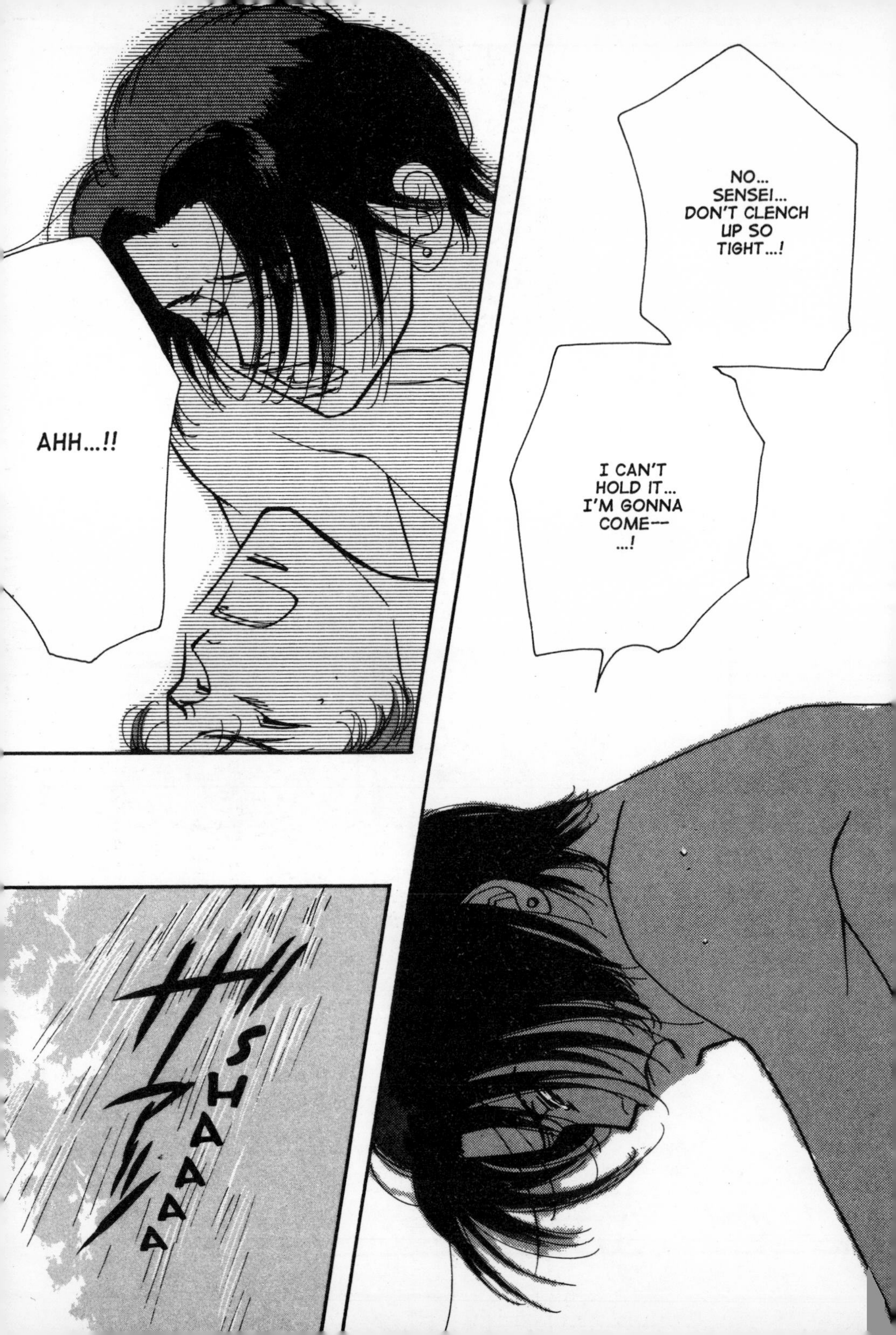
NO... SENSEI... DON'T CLENCH UP SO TIGHT...!
I CAN'T HOLD IT... I'M GONNA COME-- ...!
AHH...!!
SHAAAAA

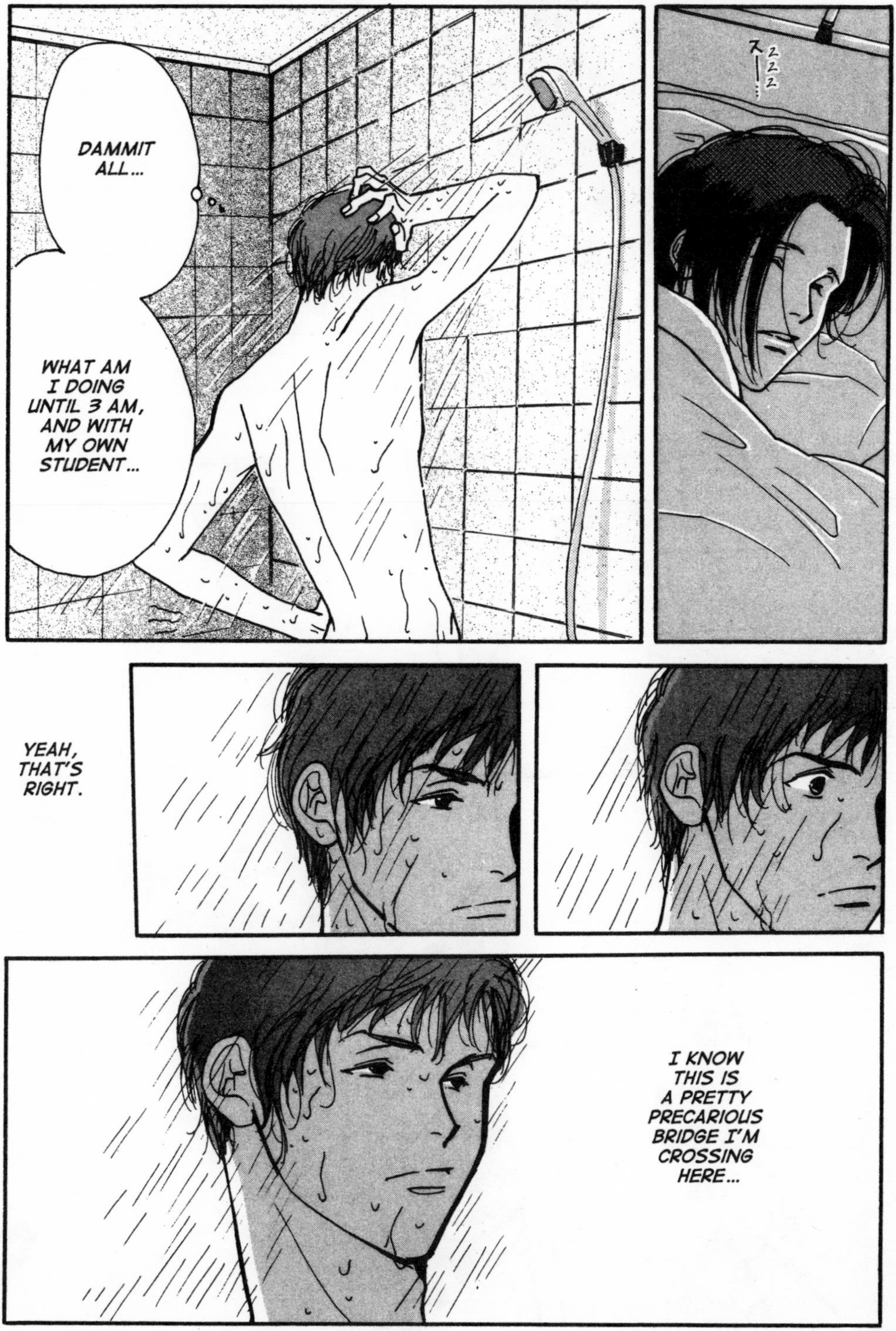
zzz
スー…
DAMMIT ALL…
WHAT AM I DOING UNTIL 3 AM, AND WITH MY OWN STUDENT…
YEAH, THAT'S RIGHT.
I KNOW THIS IS A PRETTY PRECARIOUS BRIDGE I'M CROSSING HERE…

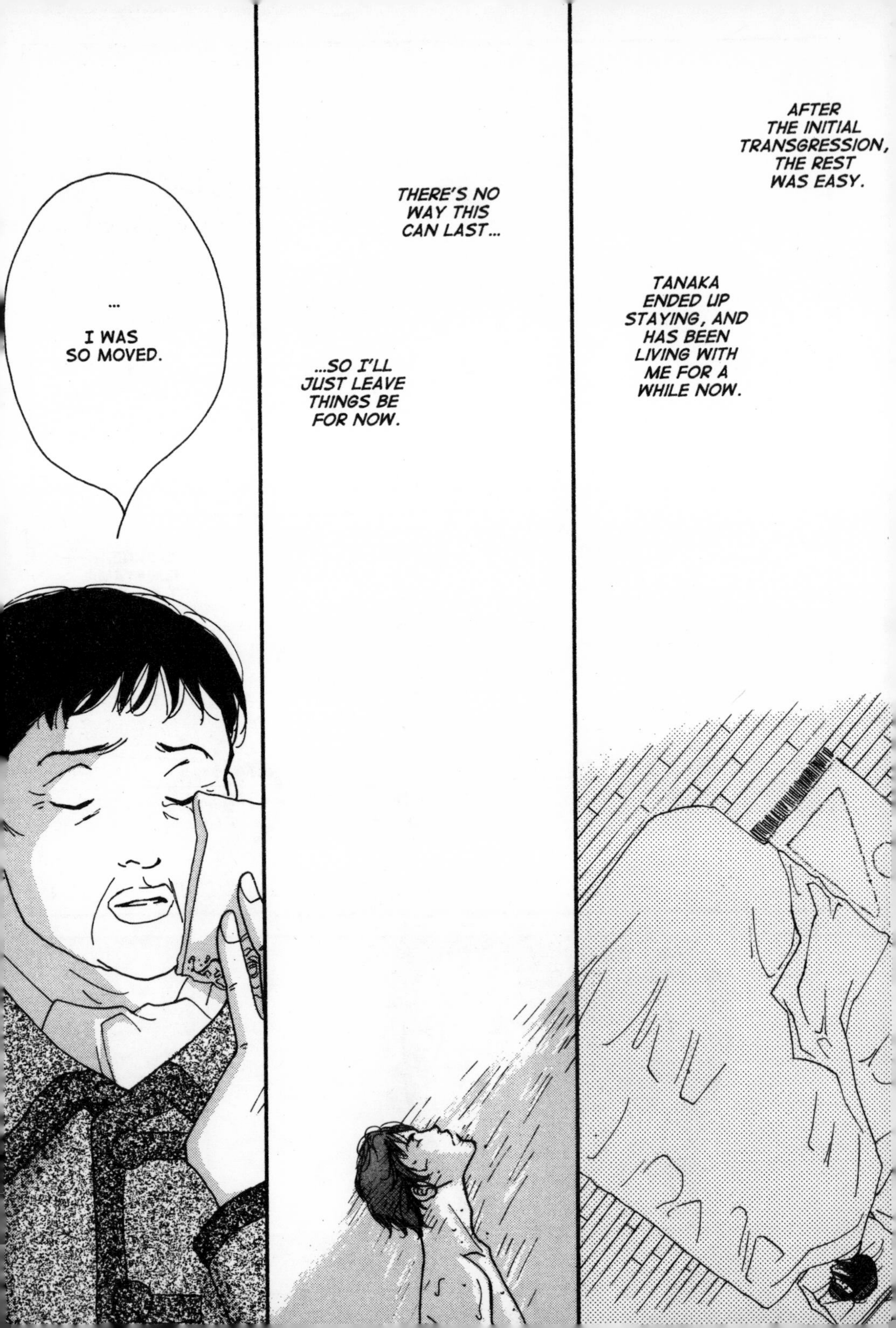
AFTER THE INITIAL TRANSGRESSION, THE REST WAS EASY.
TANAKA ENDED UP STAYING, AND HAS BEEN LIVING WITH ME FOR A WHILE NOW.
THERE'S NO WAY THIS CAN LAST...
...SO I'LL JUST LEAVE THINGS BE FOR NOW.
... I WAS SO MOVED.

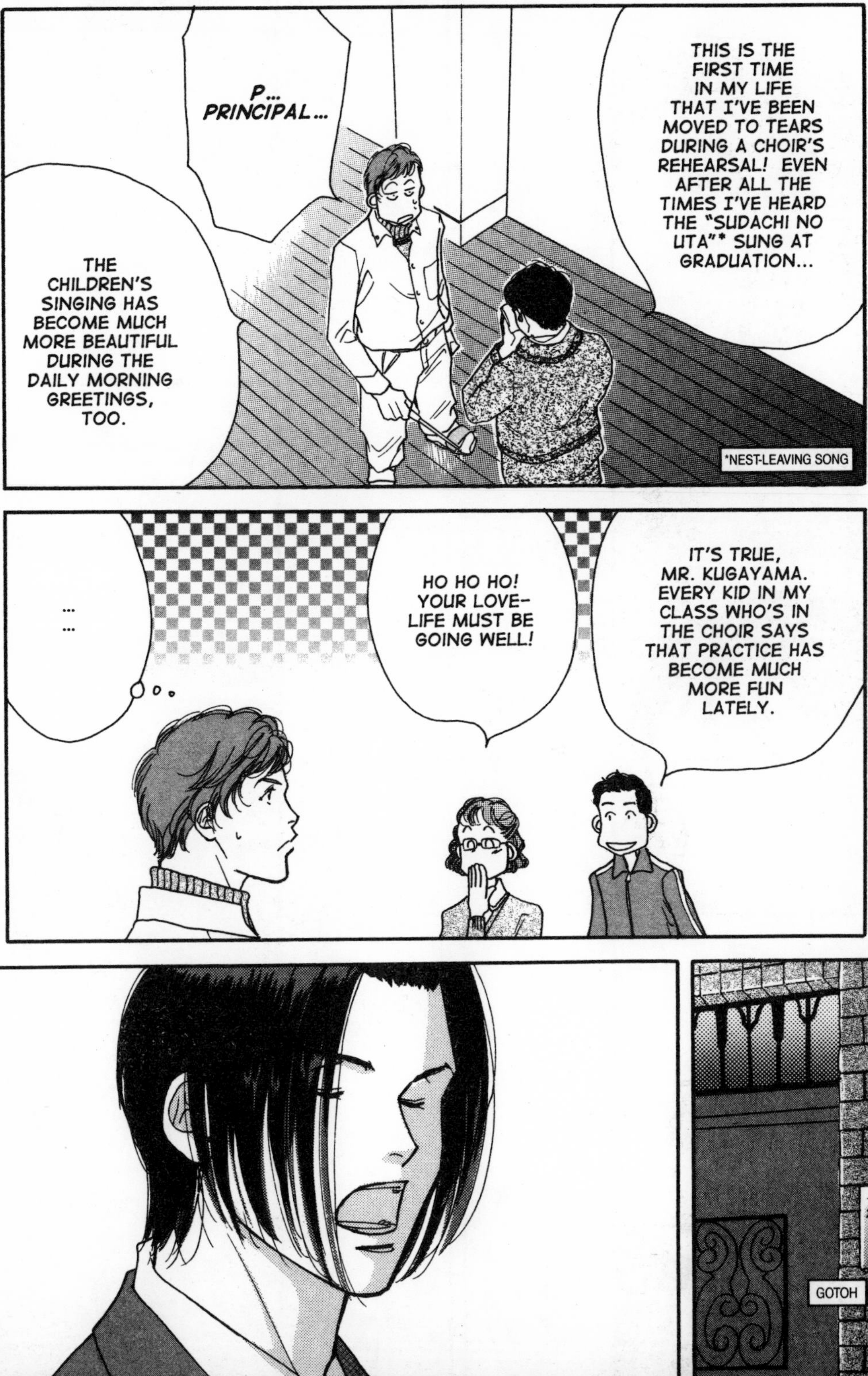
THIS IS THE FIRST TIME IN MY LIFE THAT I'VE BEEN MOVED TO TEARS DURING A CHOIR'S REHEARSAL! EVEN AFTER ALL THE TIMES I'VE HEARD THE "SUDACHI NO UTA"* SUNG AT GRADUATION...
P... PRINCIPAL...
THE CHILDREN'S SINGING HAS BECOME MUCH MORE BEAUTIFUL DURING THE DAILY MORNING GREETINGS, TOO.
*NEST-LEAVING SONG
IT'S TRUE, MR. KUGAYAMA. EVERY KID IN MY CLASS WHO'S IN THE CHOIR SAYS THAT PRACTICE HAS BECOME MUCH MORE FUN LATELY.
HO HO HO! YOUR LOVE-LIFE MUST BE GOING WELL!
... ...
GOTOH

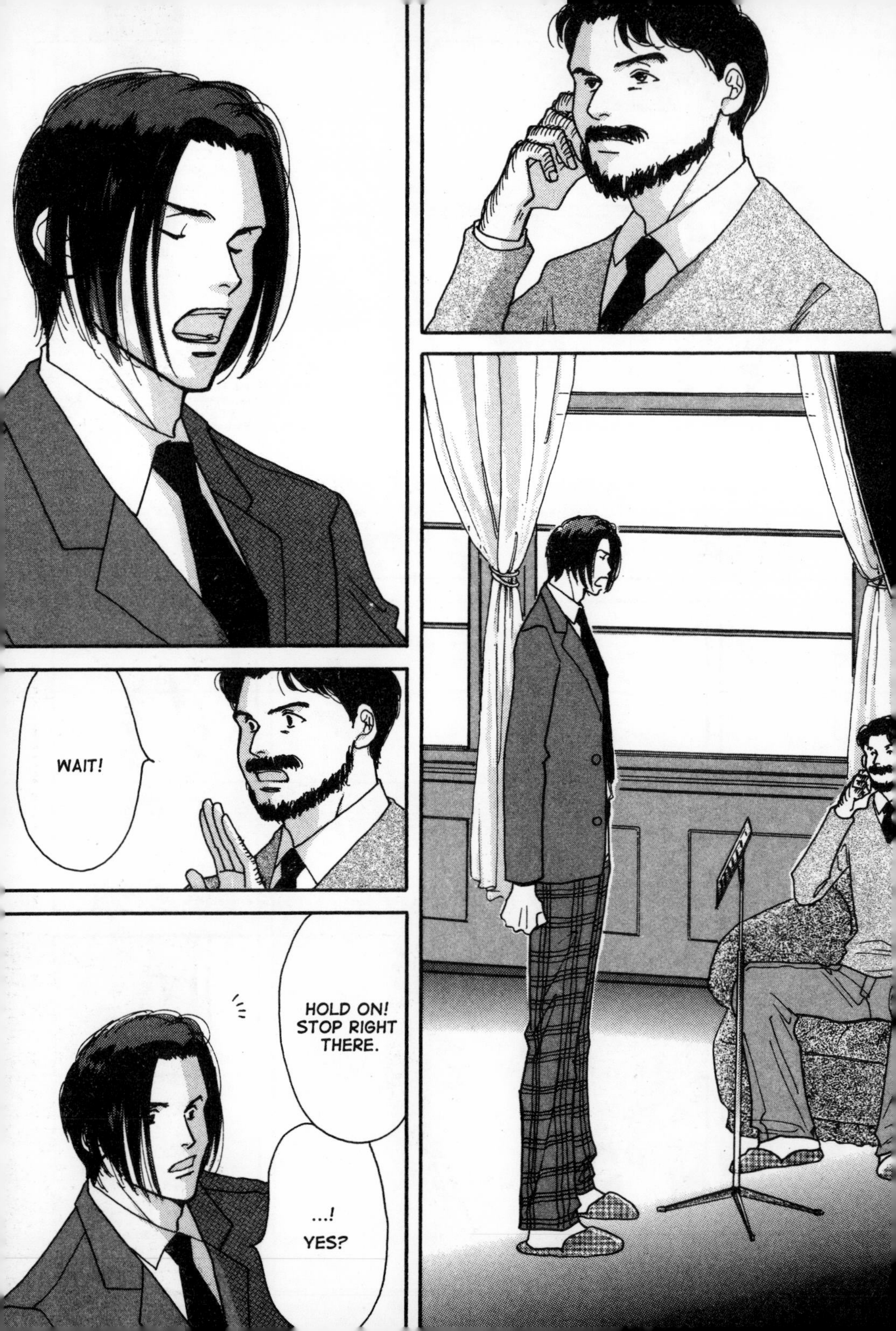
WAIT!
HOLD ON! STOP RIGHT THERE.
...! YES?

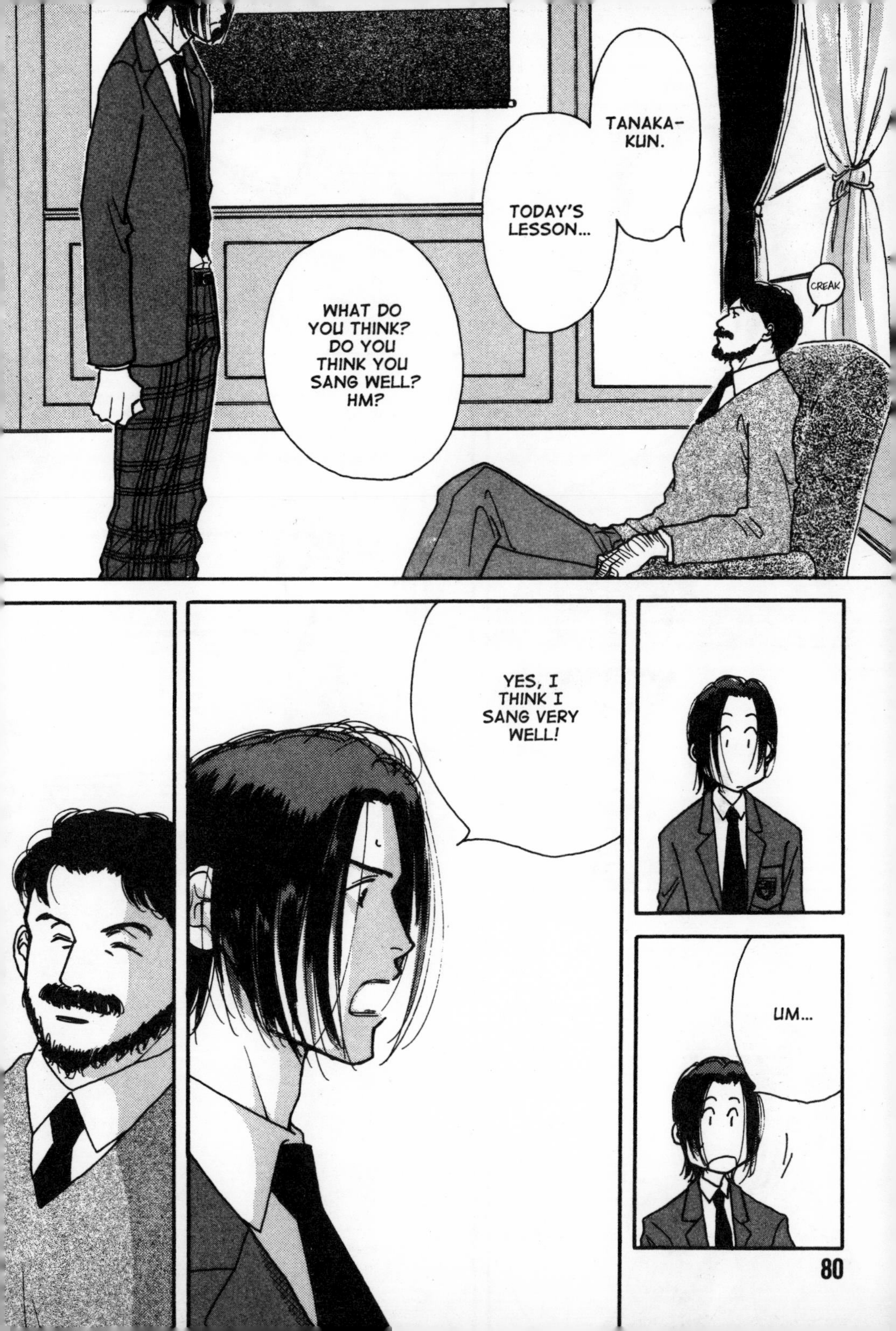
TANAKA-KUN.
TODAY'S LESSON...
CREAK
WHAT DO YOU THINK? DO YOU THINK YOU SANG WELL? HM?
UM...
YES, I THINK I SANG VERY WELL!

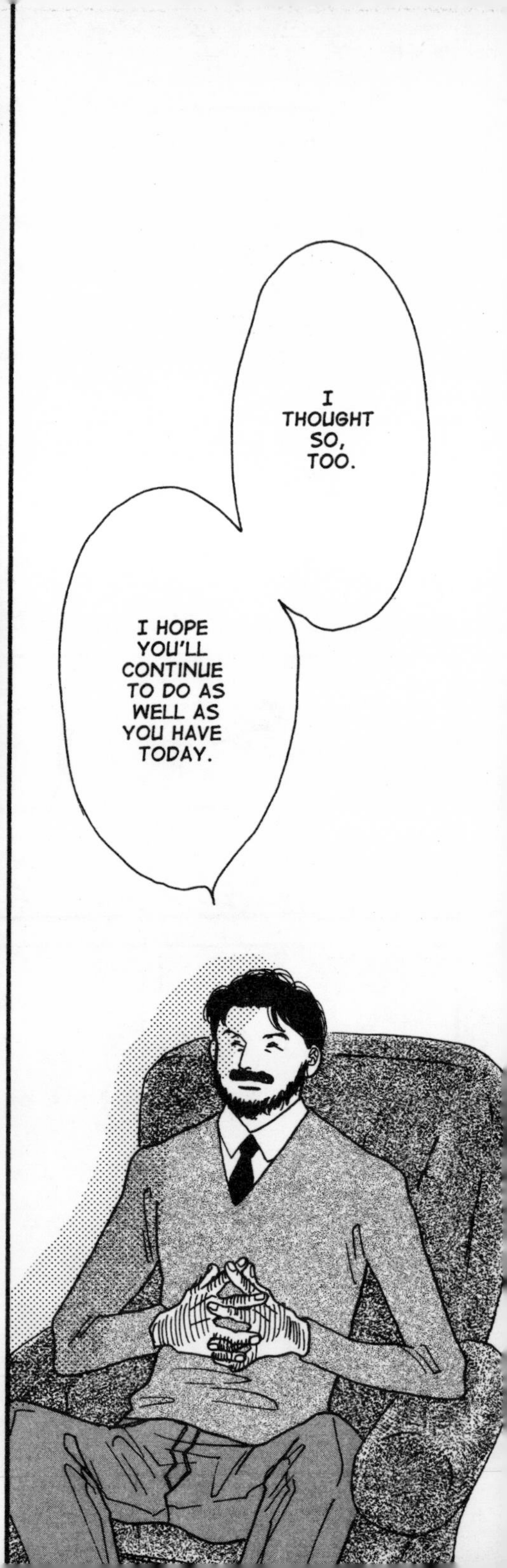
I THOUGHT SO, TOO.
I HOPE YOU'LL CONTINUE TO DO AS WELL AS YOU HAVE TODAY.
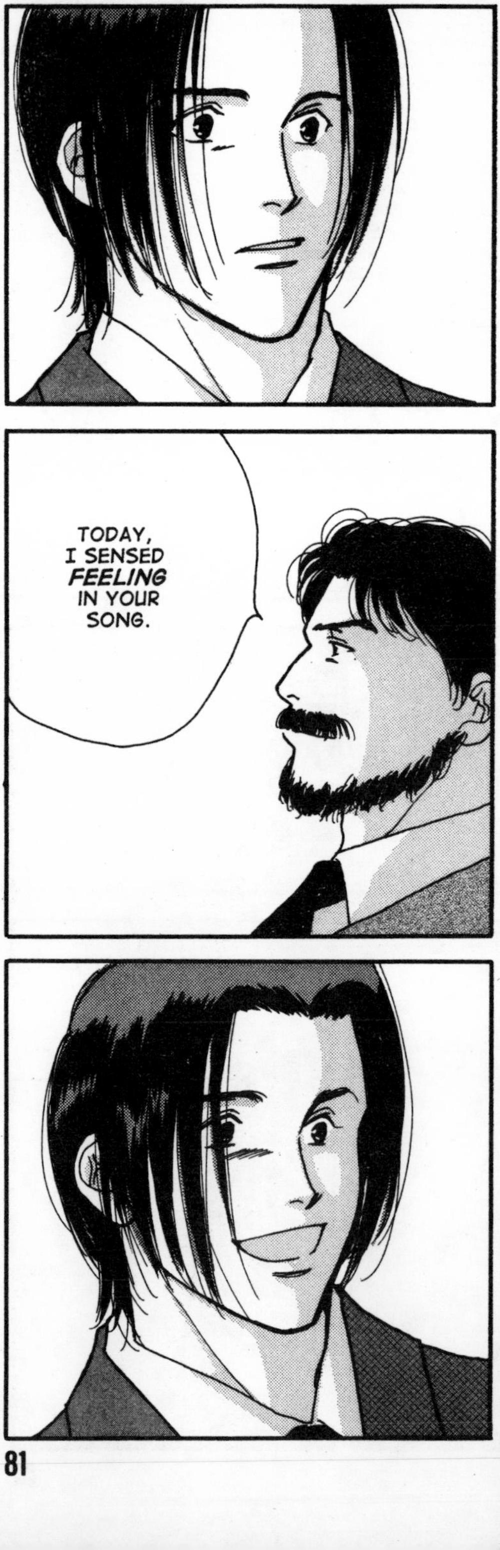
TODAY, I SENSED *FEELING* IN YOUR SONG.

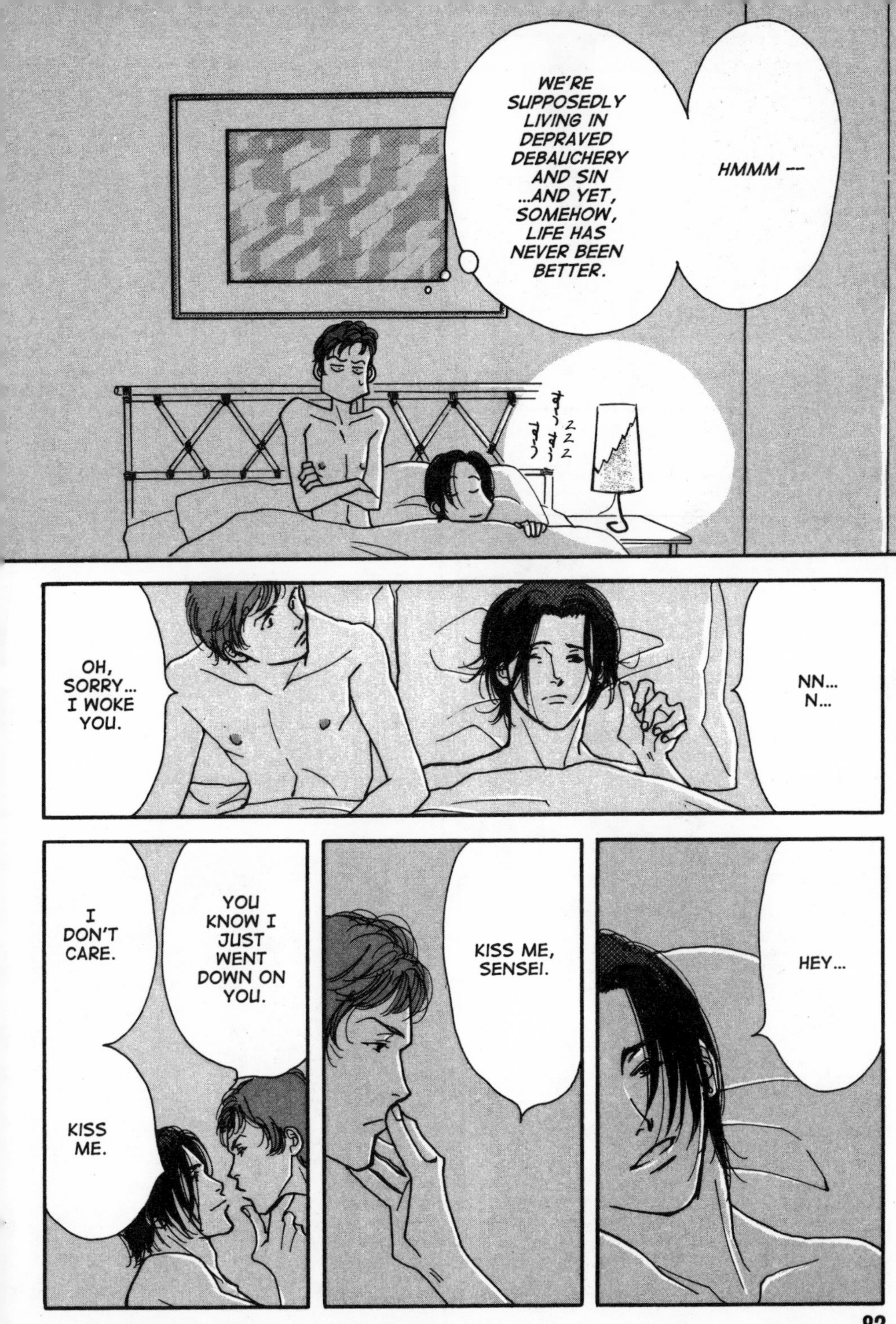
HMMM --
WE'RE SUPPOSEDLY LIVING IN DEPRAVED DEBAUCHERY AND SIN ...AND YET, SOMEHOW, LIFE HAS NEVER BEEN BETTER.
ZZZ
NN... N...
OH, SORRY... I WOKE YOU.
HEY...
KISS ME, SENSEI.
YOU KNOW I JUST WENT DOWN ON YOU.
I DON'T CARE.
KISS ME.

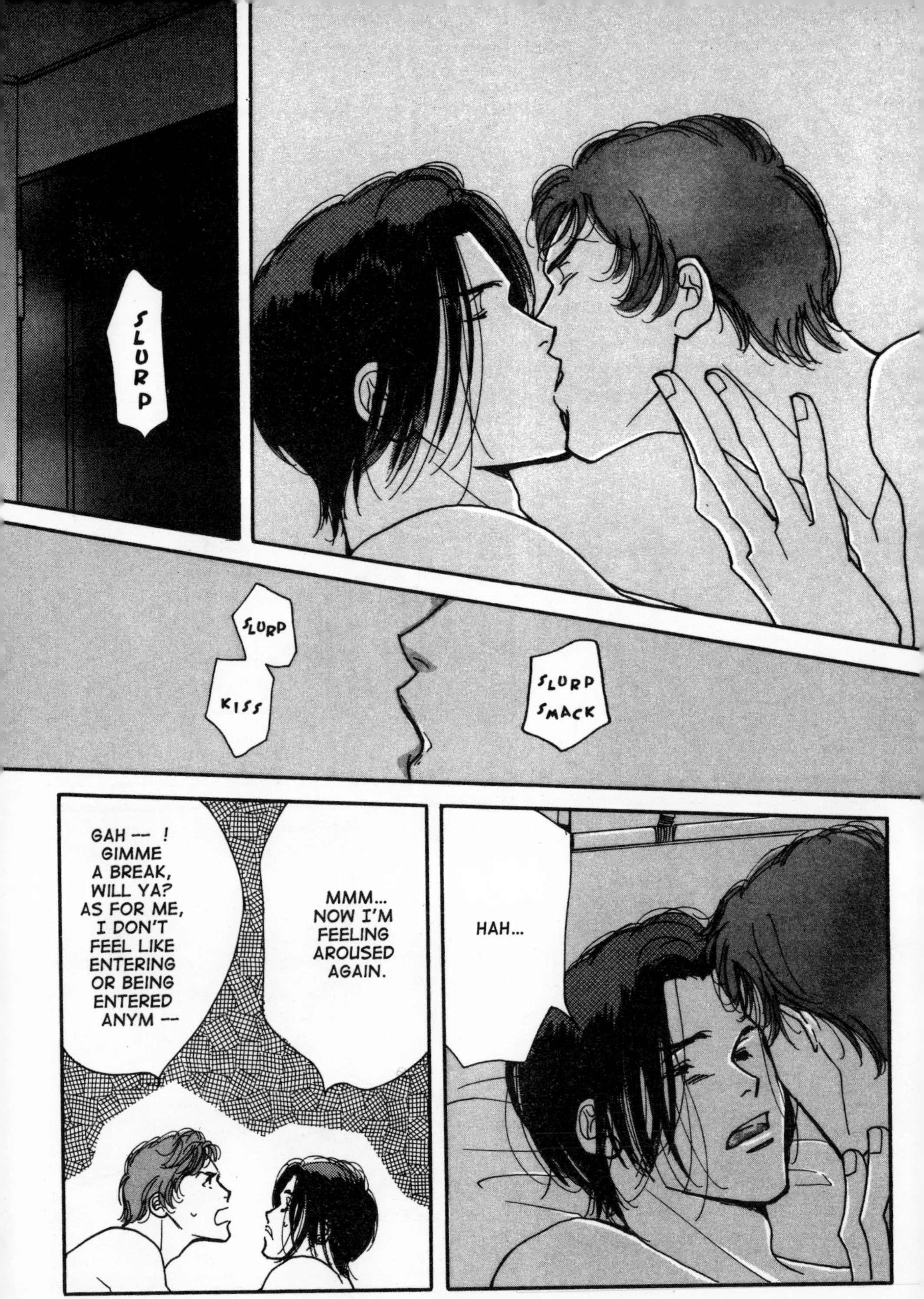
SLURP
SLURP SMACK
SLURP
KISS
HAH...
MMM... NOW I'M FEELING AROUSED AGAIN.
GAH -- ! GIMME A BREAK, WILL YA? AS FOR ME, I DON'T FEEL LIKE ENTERING OR BEING ENTERED ANYM --

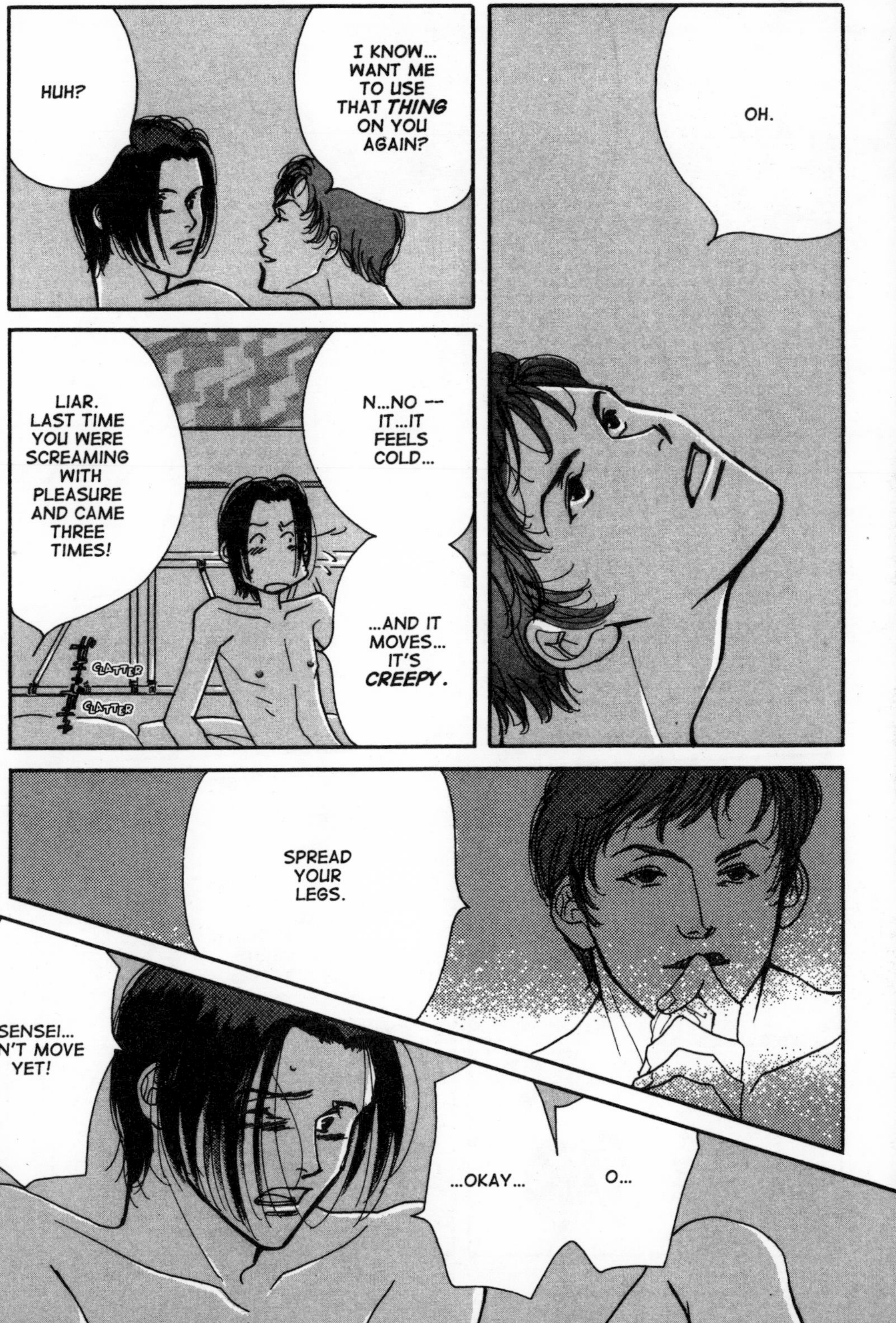
OH.
I KNOW... WANT ME TO USE THAT *THING* ON YOU AGAIN?
HUH?
N...NO --- IT...IT FEELS COLD...
...AND IT MOVES... IT'S *CREEPY*.
LIAR. LAST TIME YOU WERE SCREAMING WITH PLEASURE AND CAME THREE TIMES!
CLATTER
CLATTER
SPREAD YOUR LEGS.
O...
...OKAY...
SENSEI... ON'T MOVE YET!

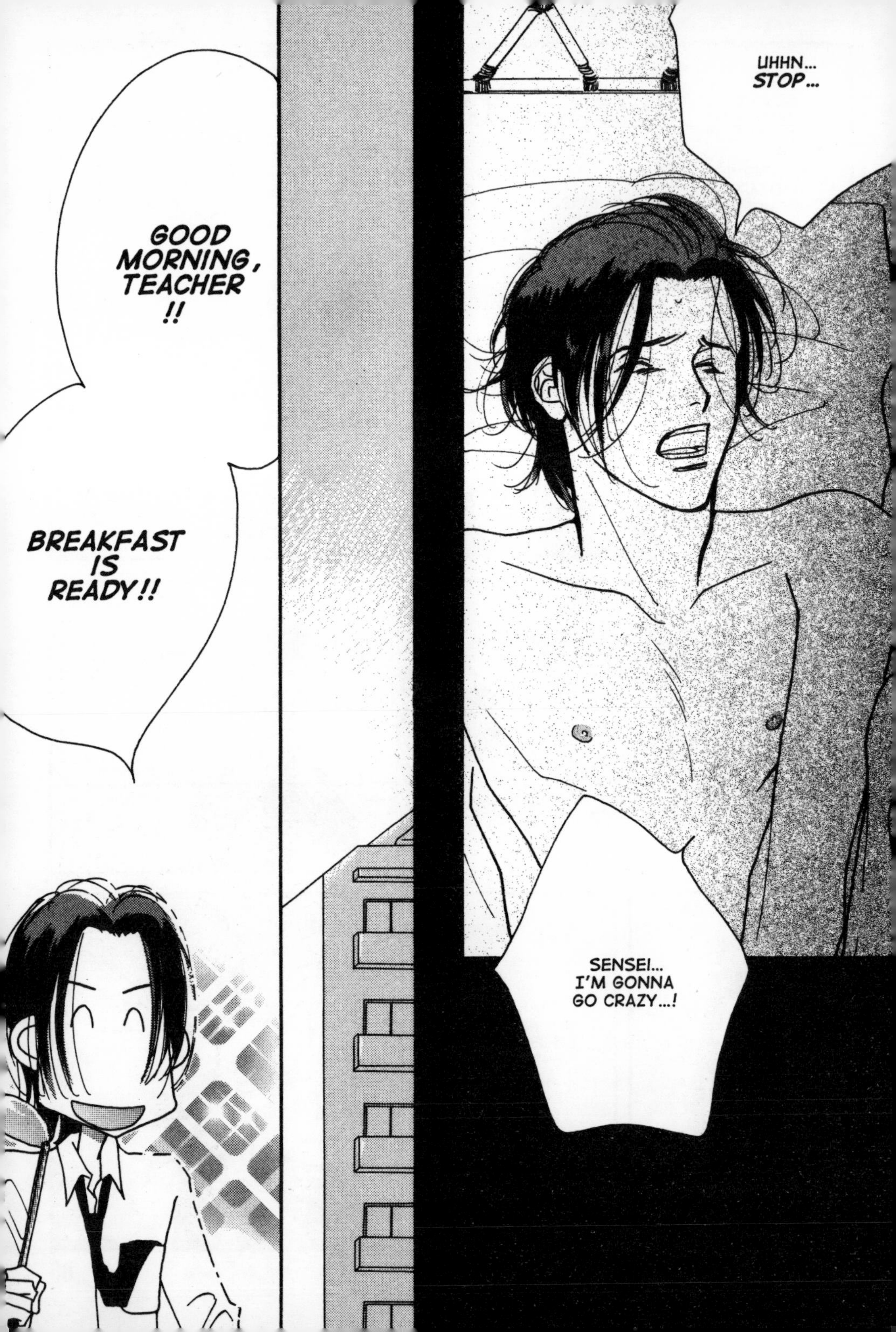
UHHN... STOP...
SENSEI... I'M GONNA GO CRAZY...!
GOOD MORNING, TEACHER!!
BREAKFAST IS READY!!

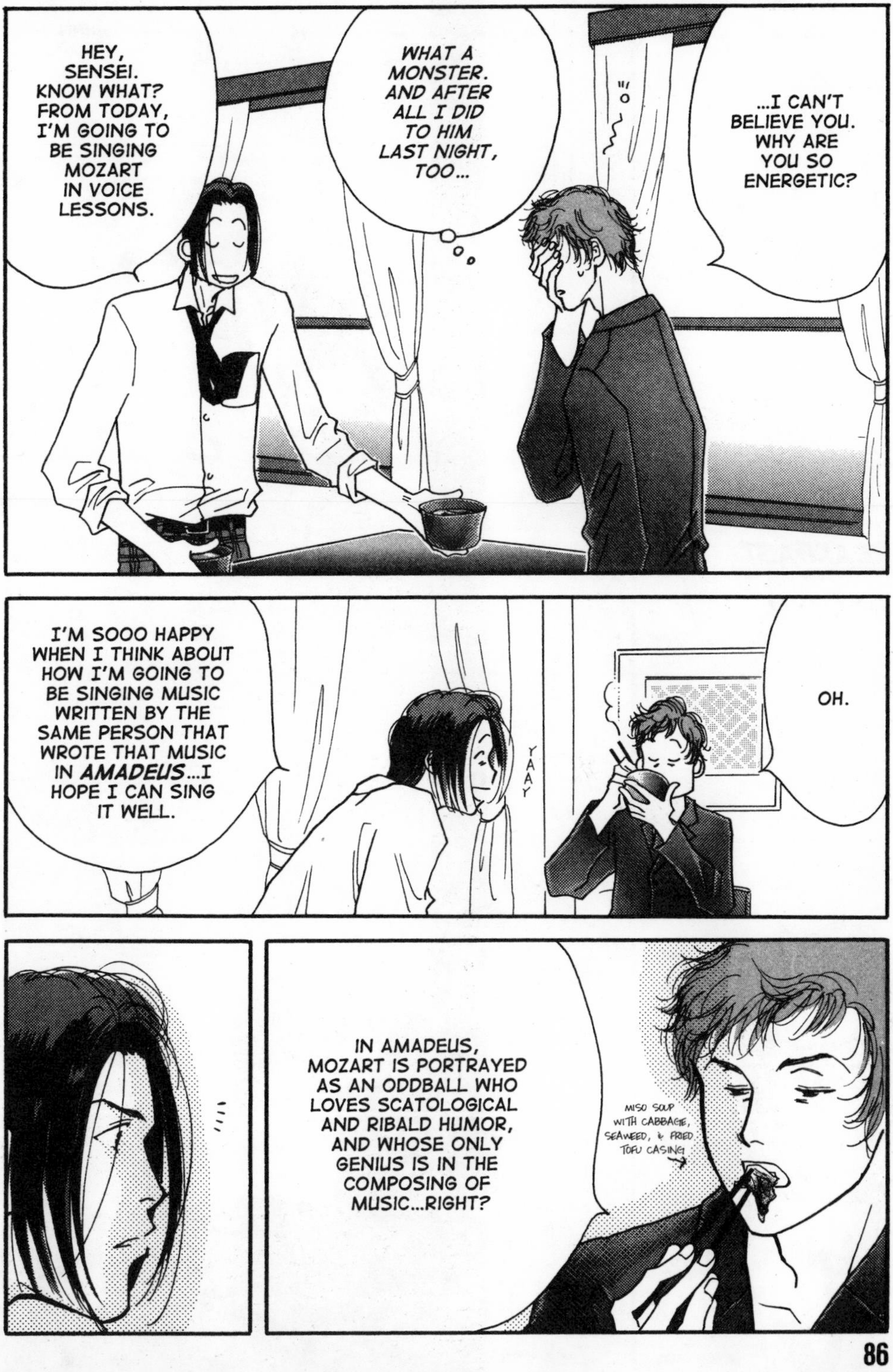
...I CAN'T BELIEVE YOU. WHY ARE YOU SO ENERGETIC?
WHAT A MONSTER. AND AFTER ALL I DID TO HIM LAST NIGHT, TOO...
HEY, SENSEI. KNOW WHAT? FROM TODAY, I'M GOING TO BE SINGING MOZART IN VOICE LESSONS.
OH.
YAAY
I'M SOOO HAPPY WHEN I THINK ABOUT HOW I'M GOING TO BE SINGING MUSIC WRITTEN BY THE SAME PERSON THAT WROTE THAT MUSIC IN **AMADEUS**...I HOPE I CAN SING IT WELL.
IN AMADEUS, MOZART IS PORTRAYED AS AN ODDBALL WHO LOVES SCATOLOGICAL AND RIBALD HUMOR, AND WHOSE ONLY GENIUS IS IN THE COMPOSING OF MUSIC...RIGHT?
MISO SOUP WITH CABBAGE, SEAWEED, & FRIED TOFU CASING

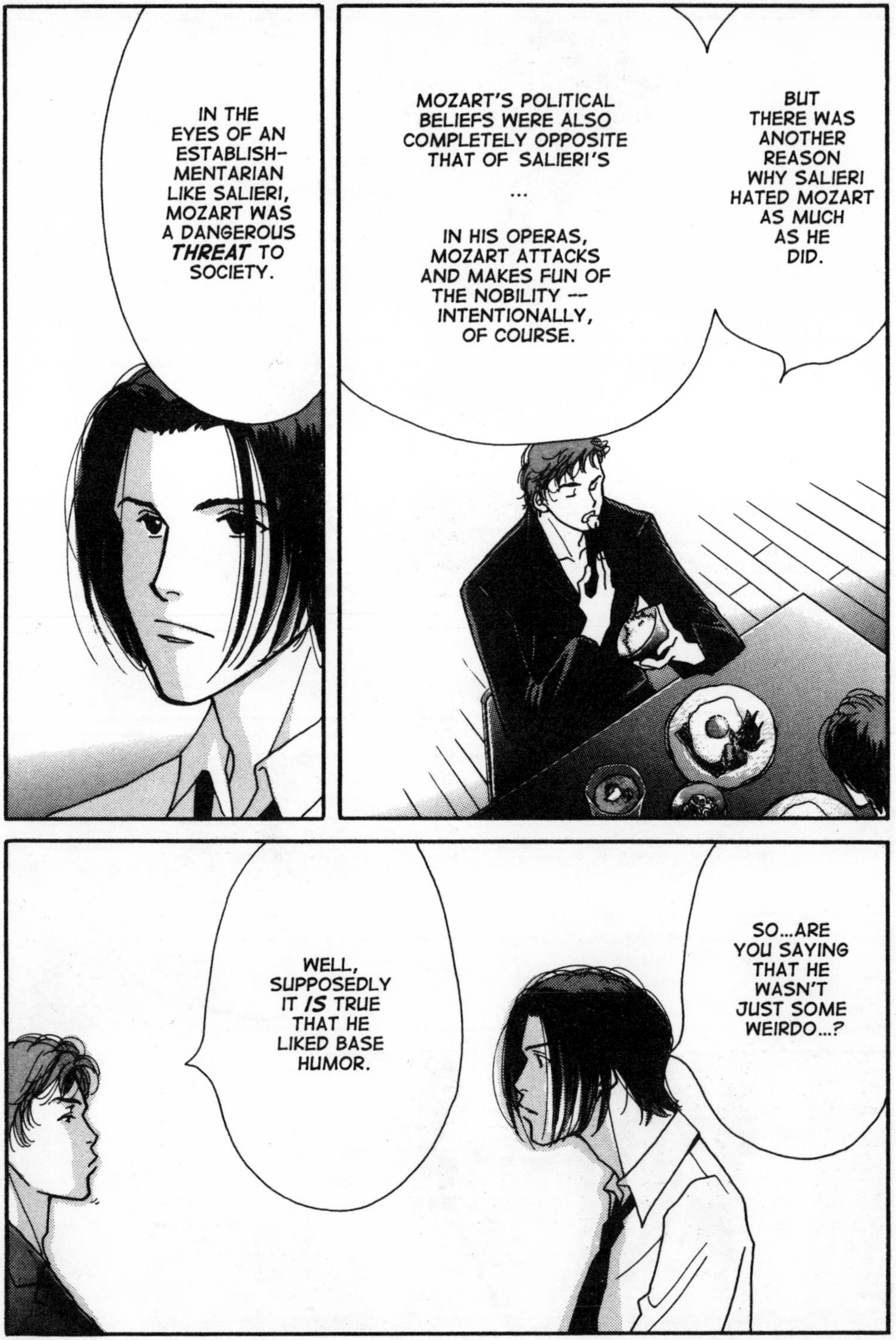
BUT THERE WAS ANOTHER REASON WHY SALIERI HATED MOZART AS MUCH AS HE DID.
MOZART'S POLITICAL BELIEFS WERE ALSO COMPLETELY OPPOSITE THAT OF SALIERI'S ...
IN HIS OPERAS, MOZART ATTACKS AND MAKES FUN OF THE NOBILITY -- INTENTIONALLY, OF COURSE.
IN THE EYES OF AN ESTABLISH-MENTARIAN LIKE SALIERI, MOZART WAS A DANGEROUS *THREAT* TO SOCIETY.
SO...ARE YOU SAYING THAT HE WASN'T JUST SOME WEIRDO...?
WELL, SUPPOSEDLY IT *IS* TRUE THAT HE LIKED BASE HUMOR.

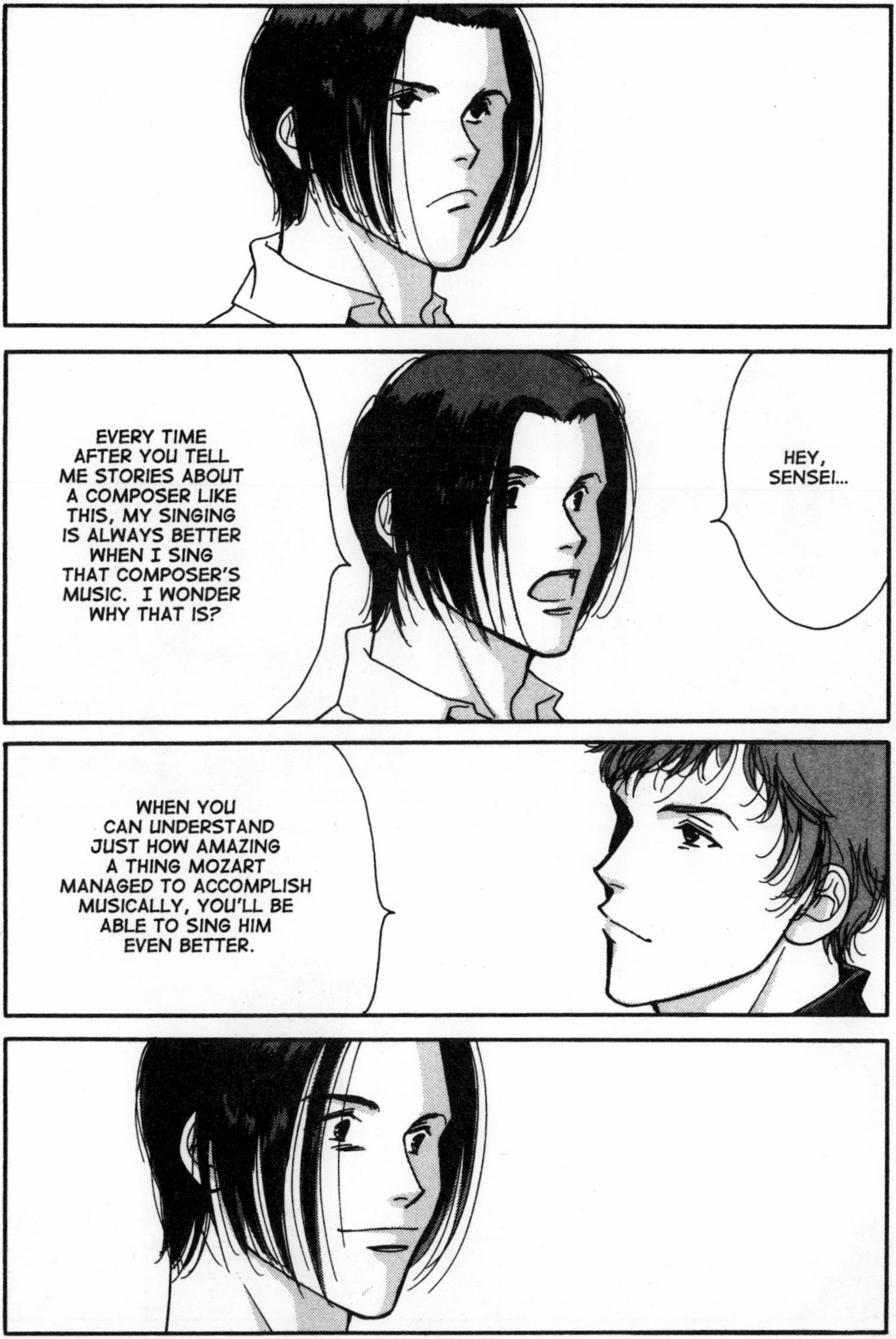
HEY, SENSEI...
EVERY TIME AFTER YOU TELL ME STORIES ABOUT A COMPOSER LIKE THIS, MY SINGING IS ALWAYS BETTER WHEN I SING THAT COMPOSER'S MUSIC. I WONDER WHY THAT IS?
WHEN YOU CAN UNDERSTAND JUST HOW AMAZING A THING MOZART MANAGED TO ACCOMPLISH MUSICALLY, YOU'LL BE ABLE TO SING HIM EVEN BETTER.

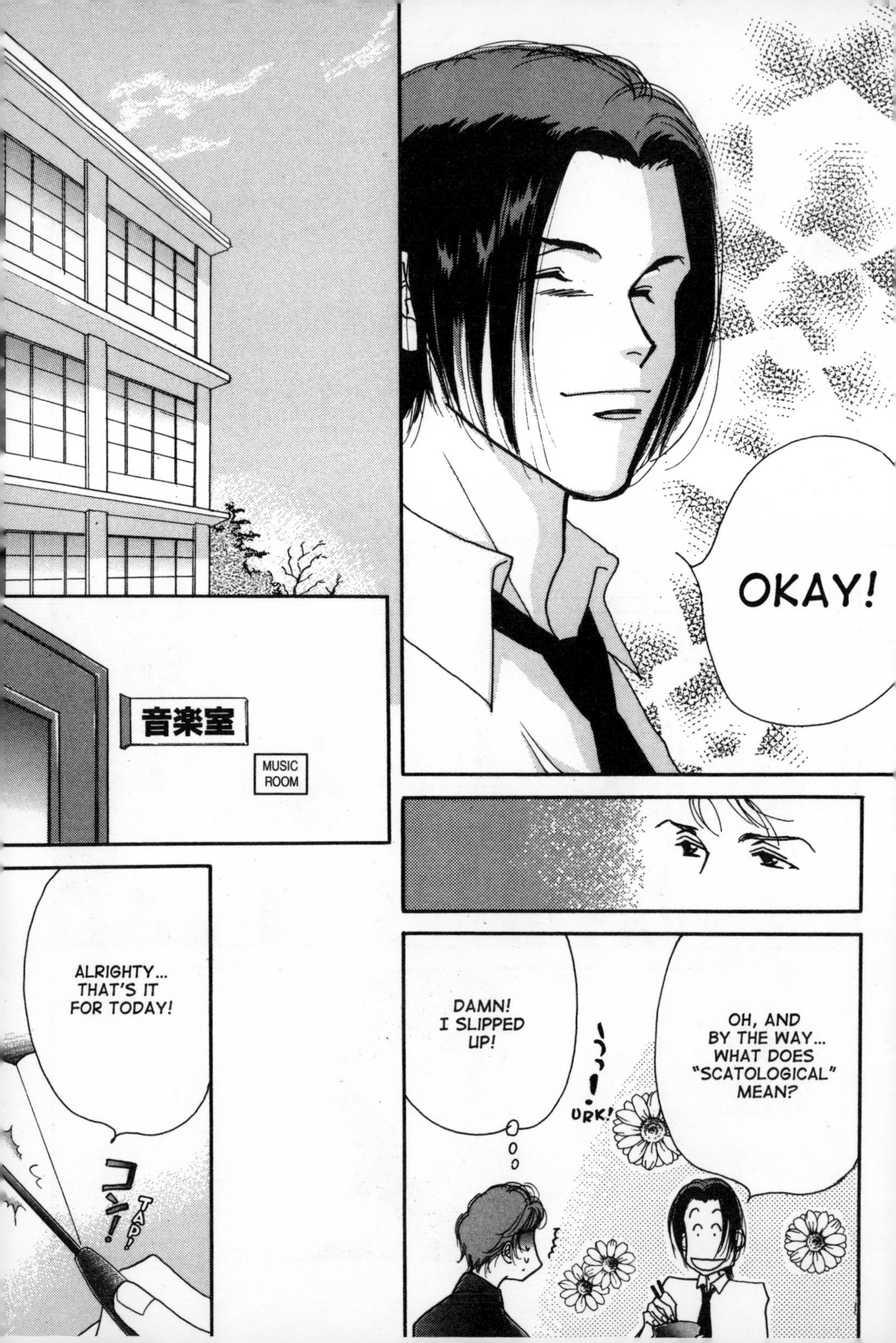
OKAY!
音楽室
MUSIC ROOM
OH, AND BY THE WAY... WHAT DOES "SCATOLOGICAL" MEAN?
URK!
DAMN! I SLIPPED UP!
ALRIGHTY... THAT'S IT FOR TODAY!
TAP!

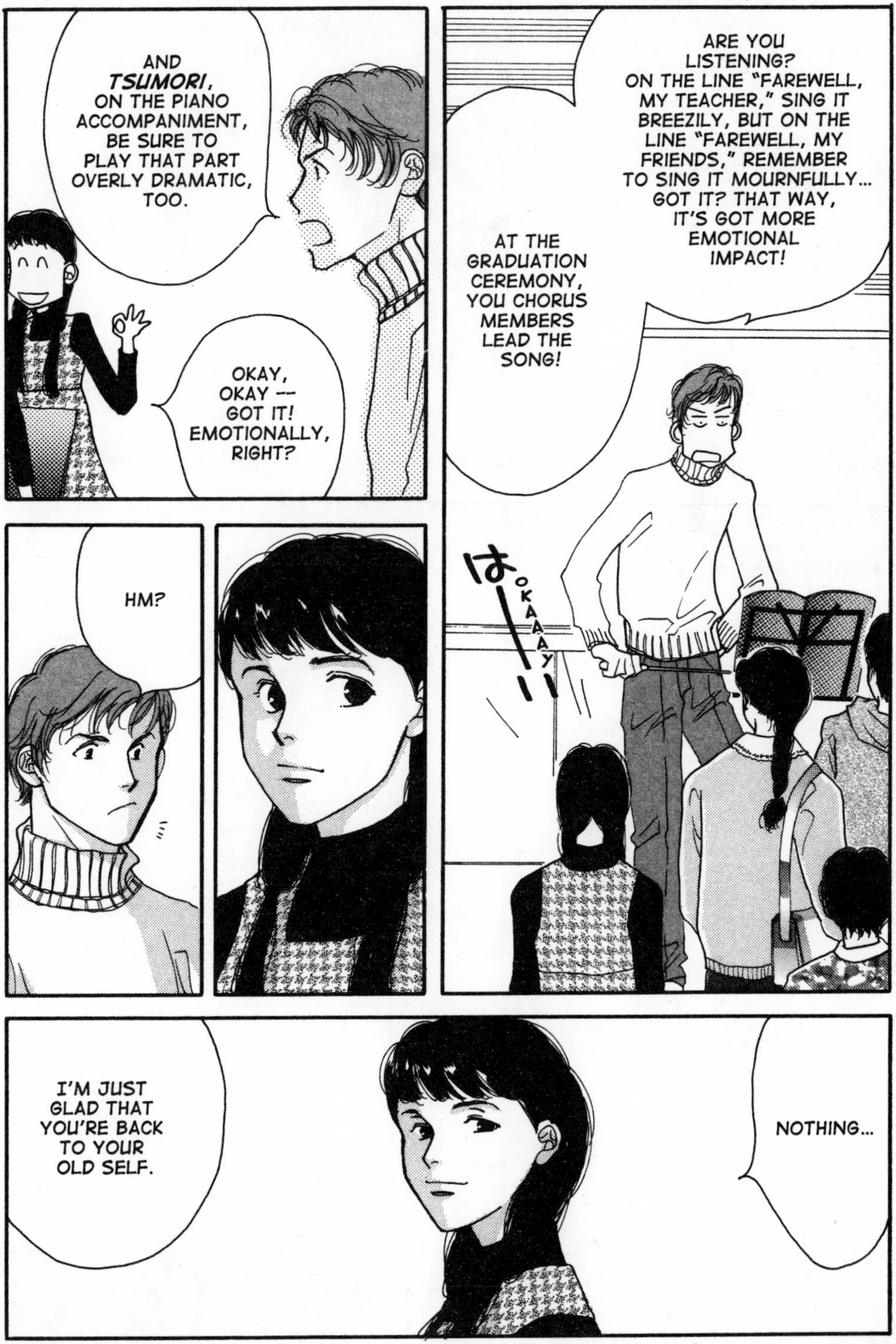
ARE YOU LISTENING? ON THE LINE "FAREWELL, MY TEACHER," SING IT BREEZILY, BUT ON THE LINE "FAREWELL, MY FRIENDS," REMEMBER TO SING IT MOURNFULLY... GOT IT? THAT WAY, IT'S GOT MORE EMOTIONAL IMPACT!
AT THE GRADUATION CEREMONY, YOU CHORUS MEMBERS LEAD THE SONG!
は——
OKAAAY
AND TSUMORI, ON THE PIANO ACCOMPANIMENT, BE SURE TO PLAY THAT PART OVERLY DRAMATIC, TOO.
OKAY, OKAY -- GOT IT! EMOTIONALLY, RIGHT?
HM?
NOTHING...
I'M JUST GLAD THAT YOU'RE BACK TO YOUR OLD SELF.

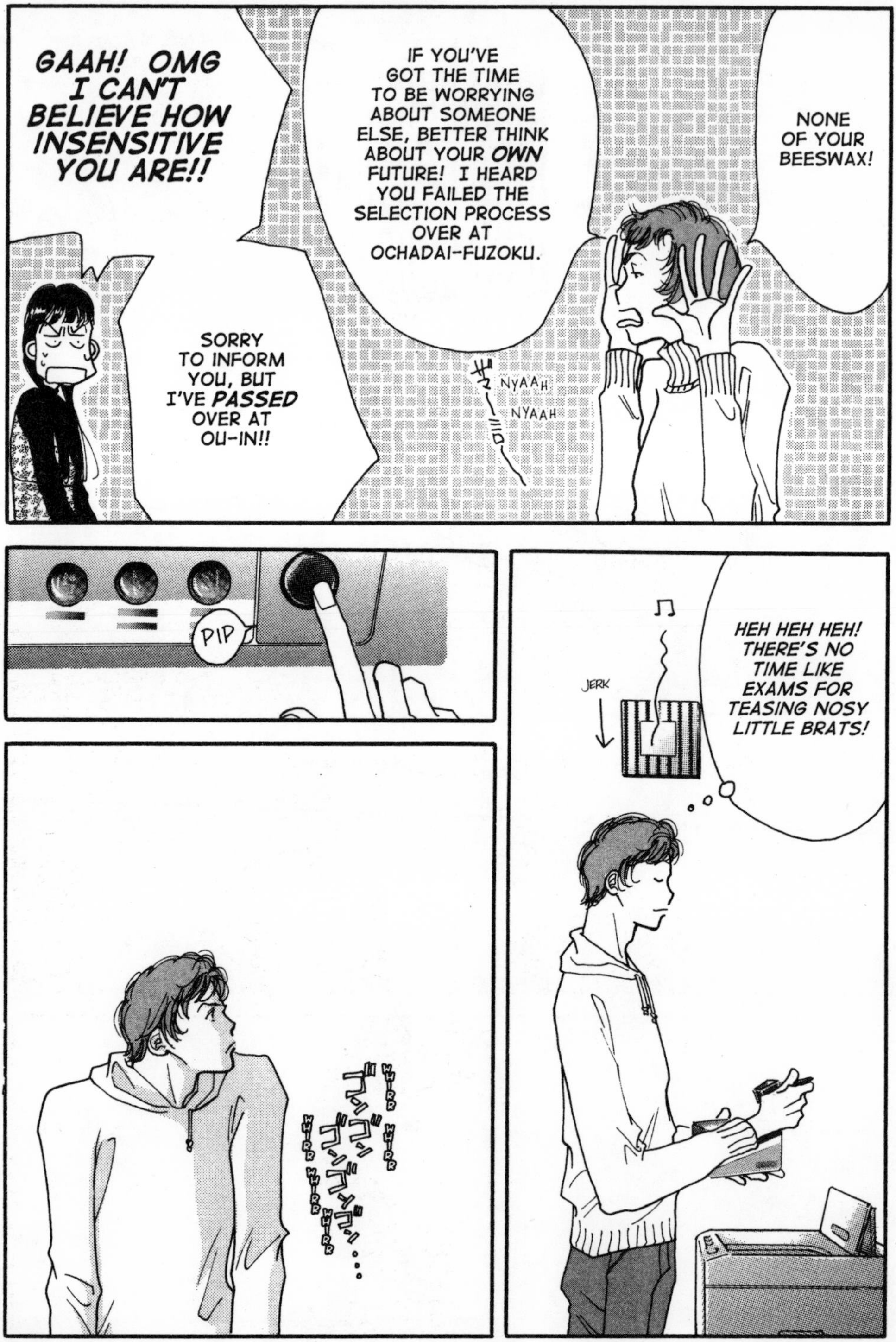
NONE OF YOUR BEESWAX!
IF YOU'VE GOT THE TIME TO BE WORRYING ABOUT SOMEONE ELSE, BETTER THINK ABOUT YOUR *OWN* FUTURE! I HEARD YOU FAILED THE SELECTION PROCESS OVER AT OCHADAI-FUZOKU.
GAAH! OMG I CAN'T BELIEVE HOW INSENSITIVE YOU ARE!!
NYAAH NYAAH
SORRY TO INFORM YOU, BUT I'VE *PASSED* OVER AT OU-IN!!
HEH HEH HEH! THERE'S NO TIME LIKE EXAMS FOR TEASING NOSY LITTLE BRATS!
JERK
PIP
WHIRR WHIRR WHIRR WHIRR WHIRR

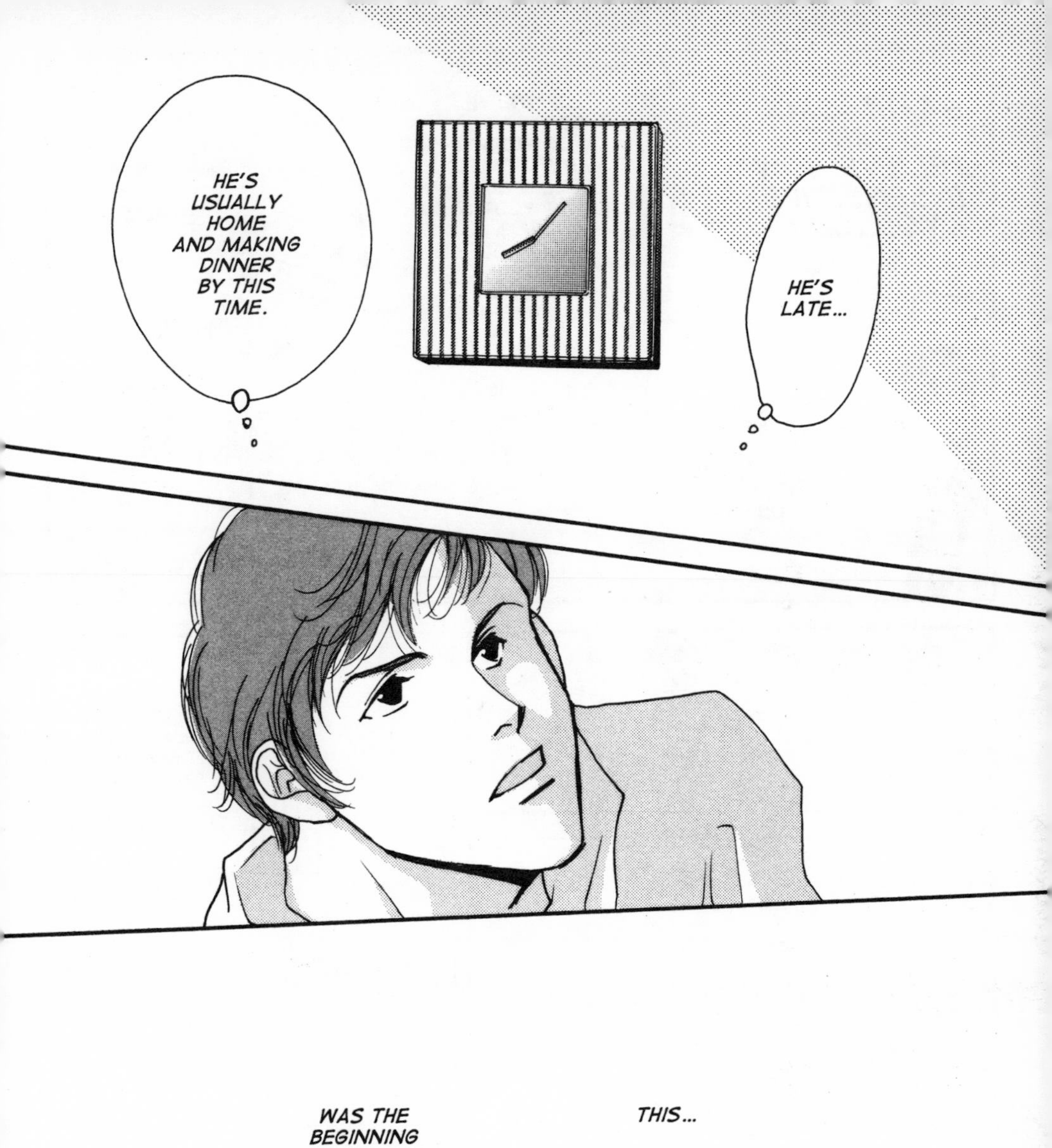
HE'S LATE...
HE'S USUALLY HOME AND MAKING DINNER BY THIS TIME.
THIS...
WAS THE BEGINNING OF THE END.

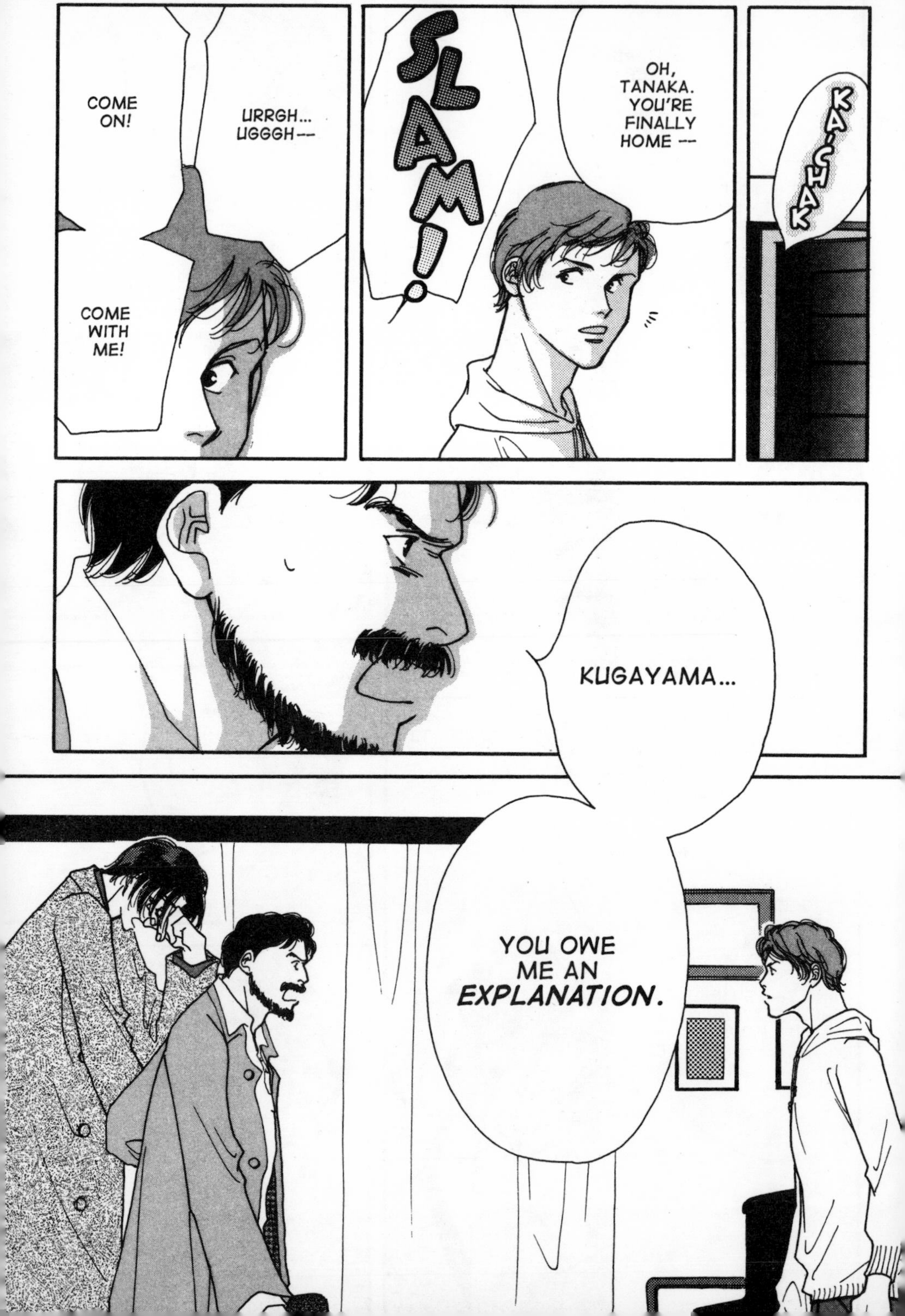
KA-CHAK
OH, TANAKA. YOU'RE FINALLY HOME --
SLAM!
URRGH... UGGGH --
COME ON!
COME WITH ME!
KUGAYAMA...
YOU OWE ME AN *EXPLANATION*.

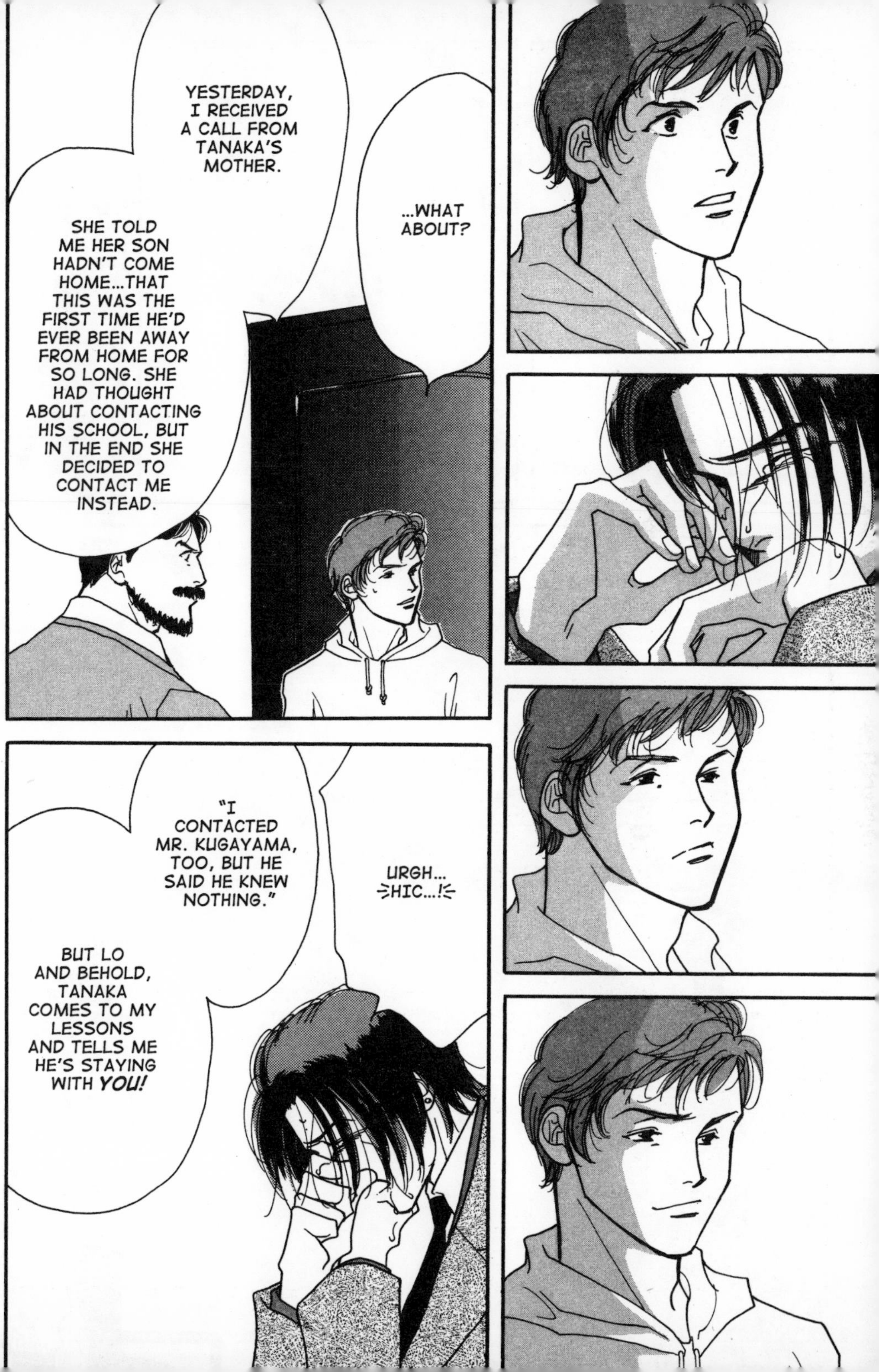
YESTERDAY, I RECEIVED A CALL FROM TANAKA'S MOTHER.
...WHAT ABOUT?
SHE TOLD ME HER SON HADN'T COME HOME...THAT THIS WAS THE FIRST TIME HE'D EVER BEEN AWAY FROM HOME FOR SO LONG. SHE HAD THOUGHT ABOUT CONTACTING HIS SCHOOL, BUT IN THE END SHE DECIDED TO CONTACT ME INSTEAD.
"I CONTACTED MR. KUGAYAMA, TOO, BUT HE SAID HE KNEW NOTHING."
URGH... HIC...!
BUT LO AND BEHOLD, TANAKA COMES TO MY LESSONS AND TELLS ME HE'S STAYING WITH *YOU!*

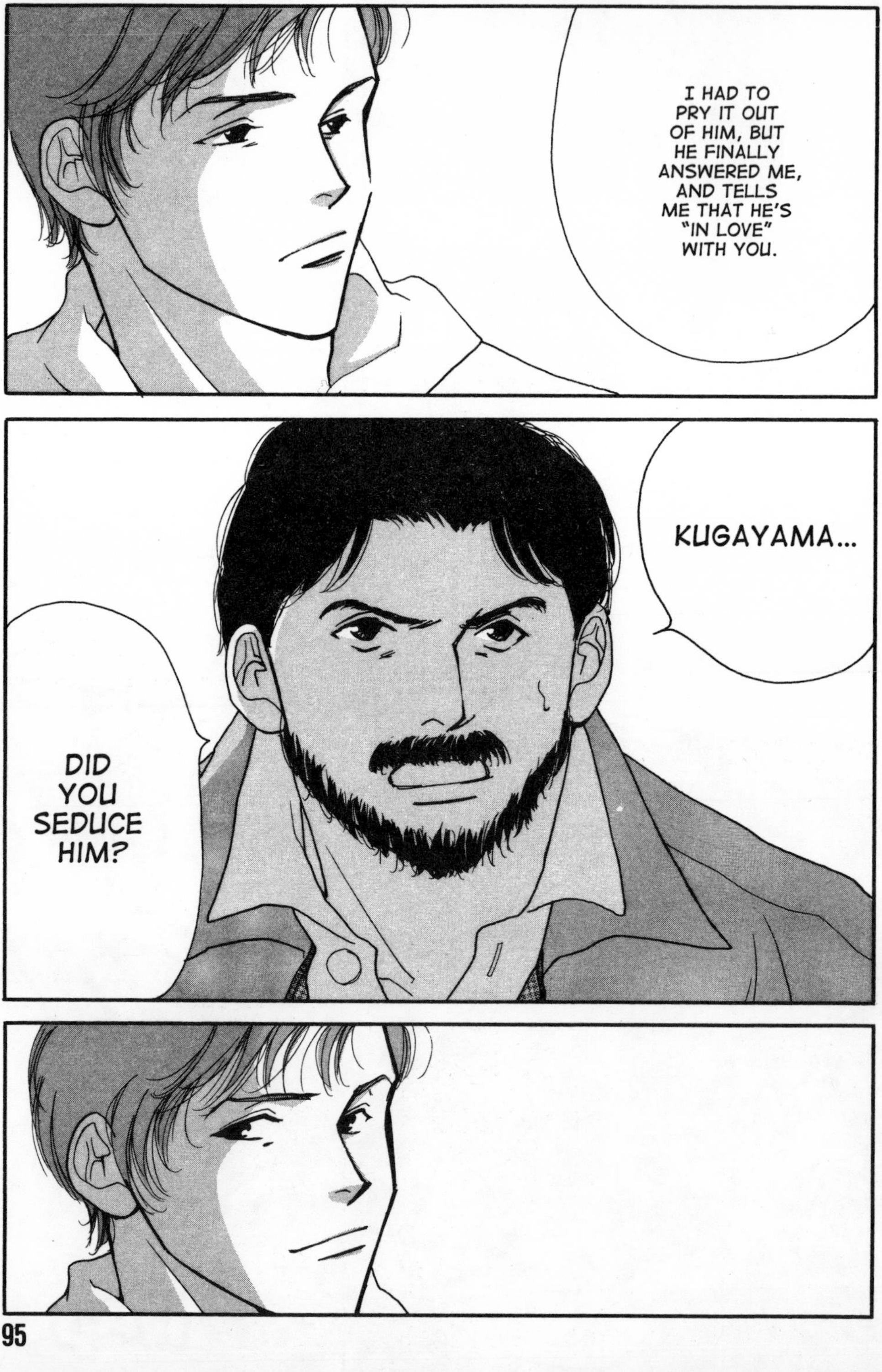
I HAD TO PRY IT OUT OF HIM, BUT HE FINALLY ANSWERED ME, AND TELLS ME THAT HE'S "IN LOVE" WITH YOU.
KUGAYAMA...
DID YOU SEDUCE HIM?

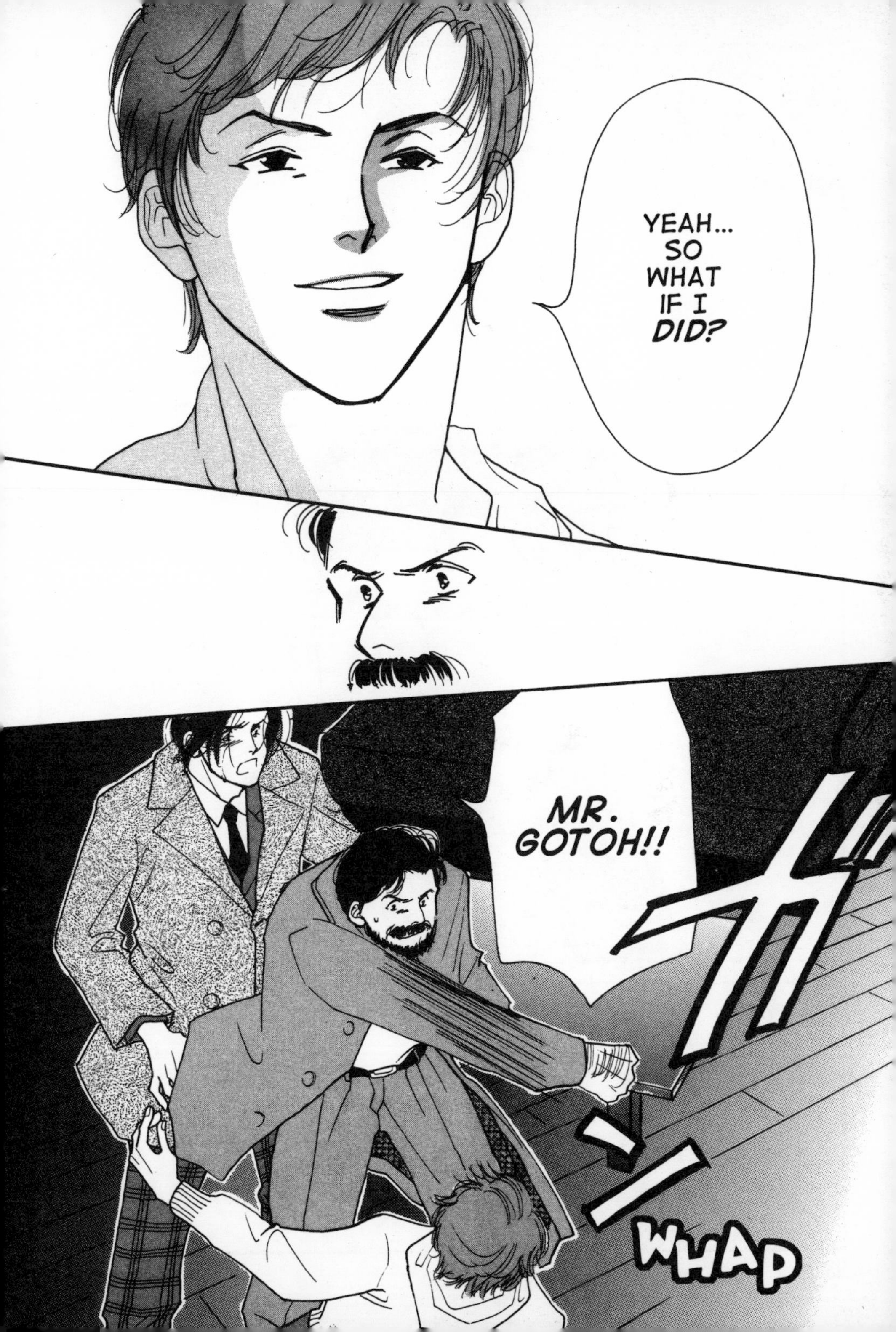
YEAH... SO WHAT IF I DID?
MR. GOTOH!!
WHAP

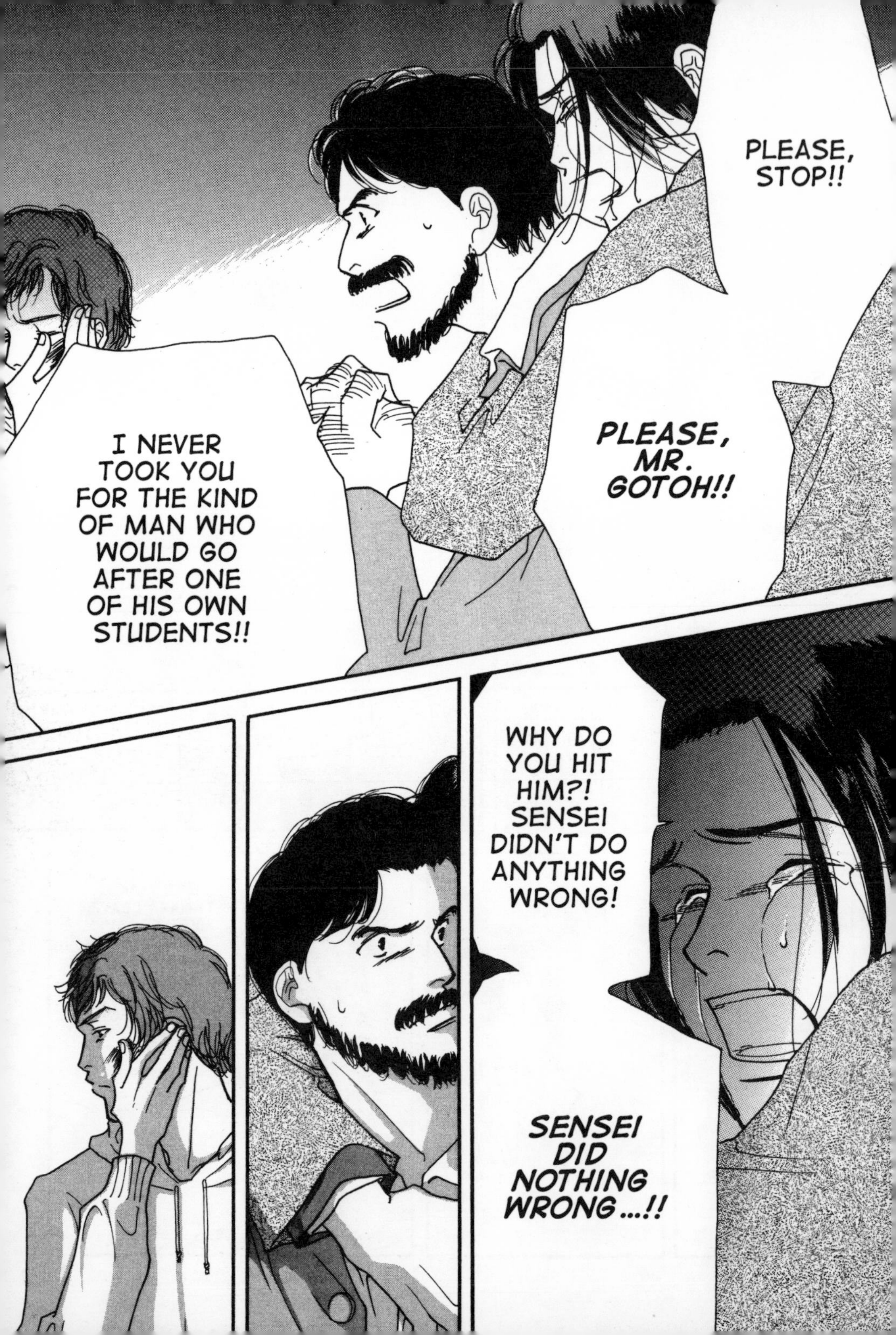
PLEASE, STOP!!
PLEASE, MR. GOTOH!!
I NEVER TOOK YOU FOR THE KIND OF MAN WHO WOULD GO AFTER ONE OF HIS OWN STUDENTS!!
WHY DO YOU HIT HIM?! SENSEI DIDN'T DO ANYTHING WRONG!
SENSEI DID NOTHING WRONG...!!

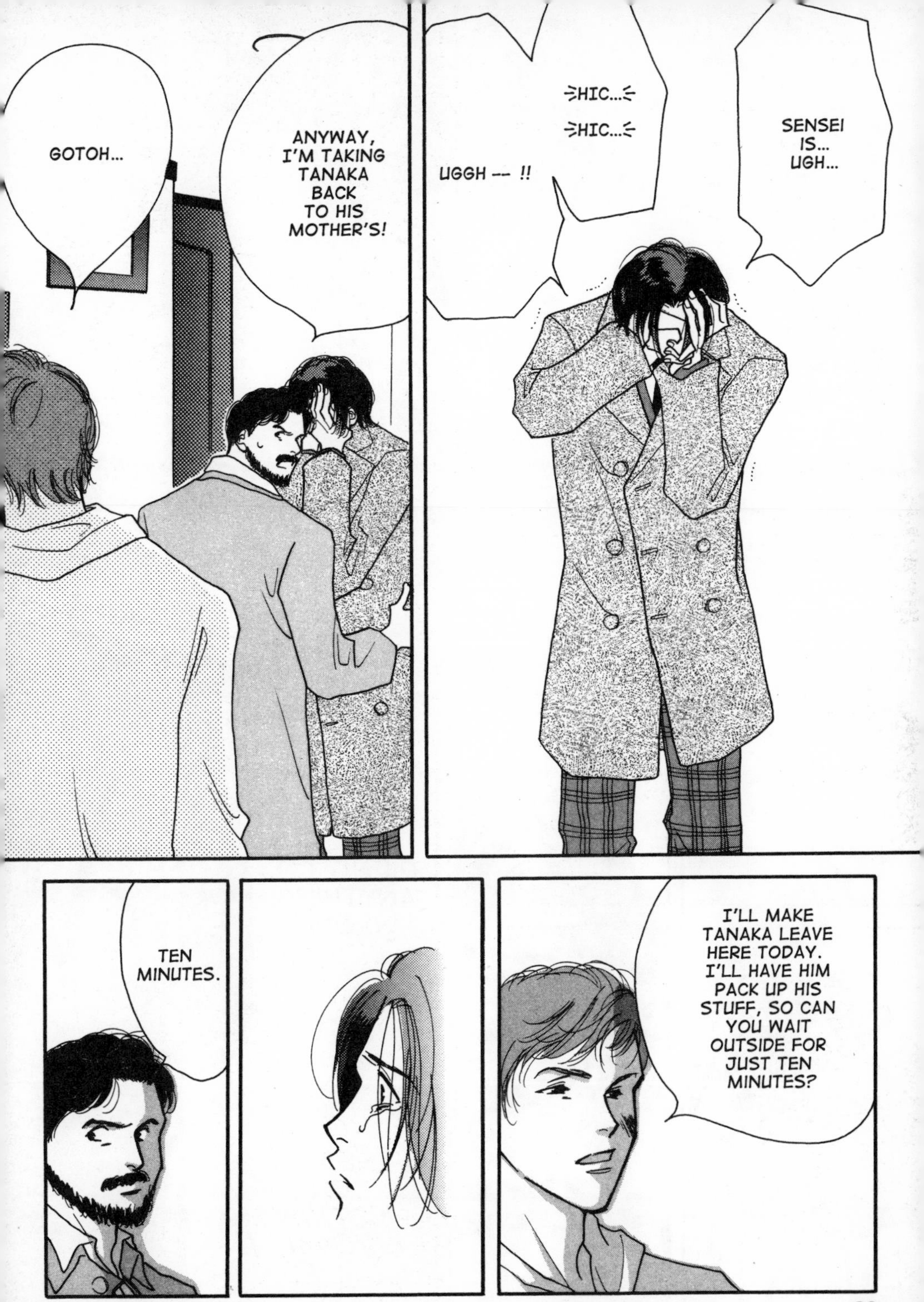
SENSEI IS... UGH...
HIC... HIC...
UGGH -- !!
ANYWAY, I'M TAKING TANAKA BACK TO HIS MOTHER'S!
GOTOH...
I'LL MAKE TANAKA LEAVE HERE TODAY. I'LL HAVE HIM PACK UP HIS STUFF, SO CAN YOU WAIT OUTSIDE FOR JUST TEN MINUTES?
TEN MINUTES.

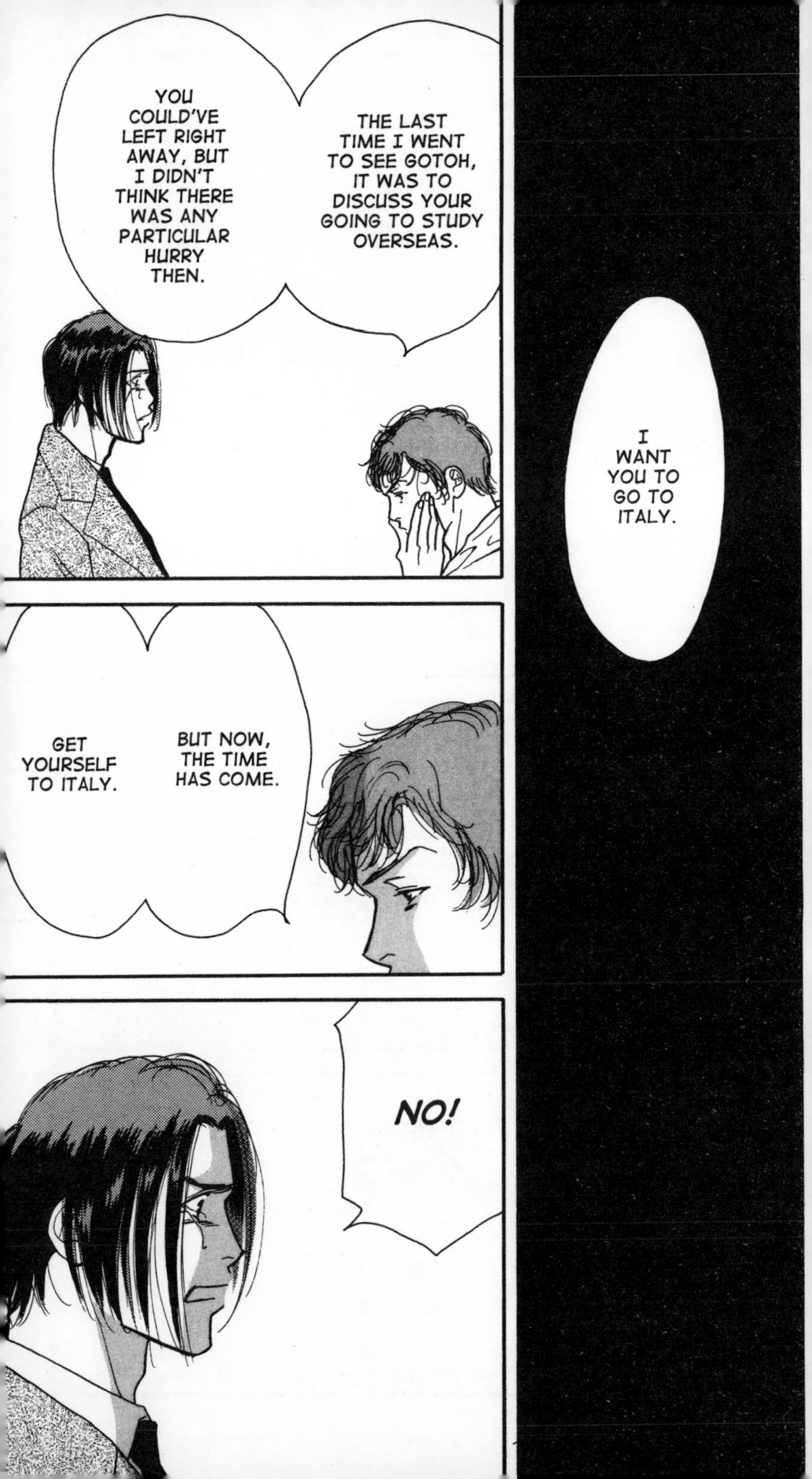
I WANT YOU TO GO TO ITALY.
THE LAST TIME I WENT TO SEE GOTOH, IT WAS TO DISCUSS YOUR GOING TO STUDY OVERSEAS.
YOU COULD'VE LEFT RIGHT AWAY, BUT I DIDN'T THINK THERE WAS ANY PARTICULAR HURRY THEN.
BUT NOW, THE TIME HAS COME.
GET YOURSELF TO ITALY.
NO!

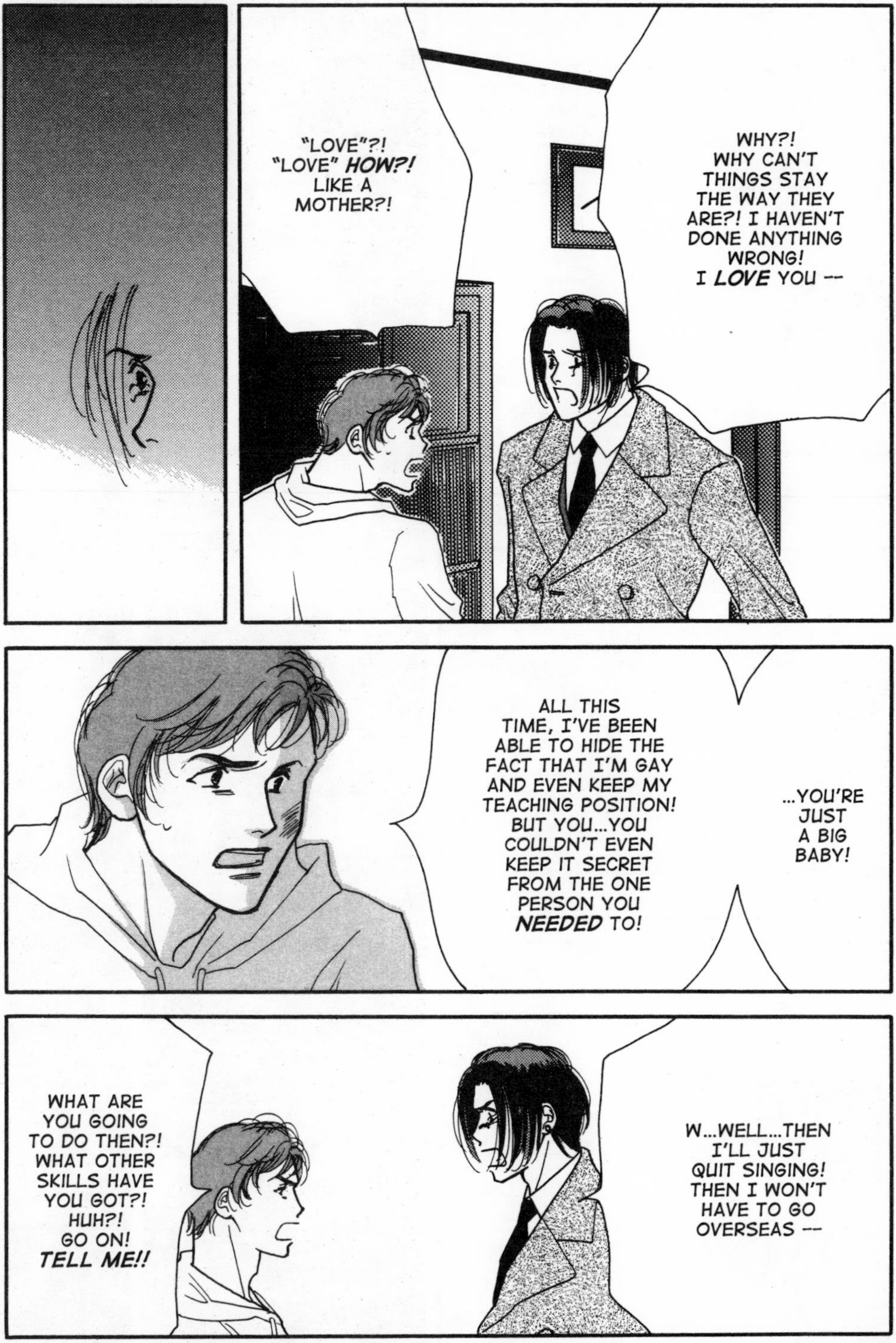
WHY?! WHY CAN'T THINGS STAY THE WAY THEY ARE?! I HAVEN'T DONE ANYTHING WRONG! I *LOVE* YOU --
"LOVE"?! "LOVE" *HOW?!* LIKE A MOTHER?!
ALL THIS TIME, I'VE BEEN ABLE TO HIDE THE FACT THAT I'M GAY AND EVEN KEEP MY TEACHING POSITION! BUT YOU...YOU COULDN'T EVEN KEEP IT SECRET FROM THE ONE PERSON YOU *NEEDED* TO!
...YOU'RE JUST A BIG BABY!
W...WELL...THEN I'LL JUST QUIT SINGING! THEN I WON'T HAVE TO GO OVERSEAS --
WHAT ARE YOU GOING TO DO THEN?! WHAT OTHER SKILLS HAVE YOU GOT?! HUH?! GO ON! *TELL ME!!*

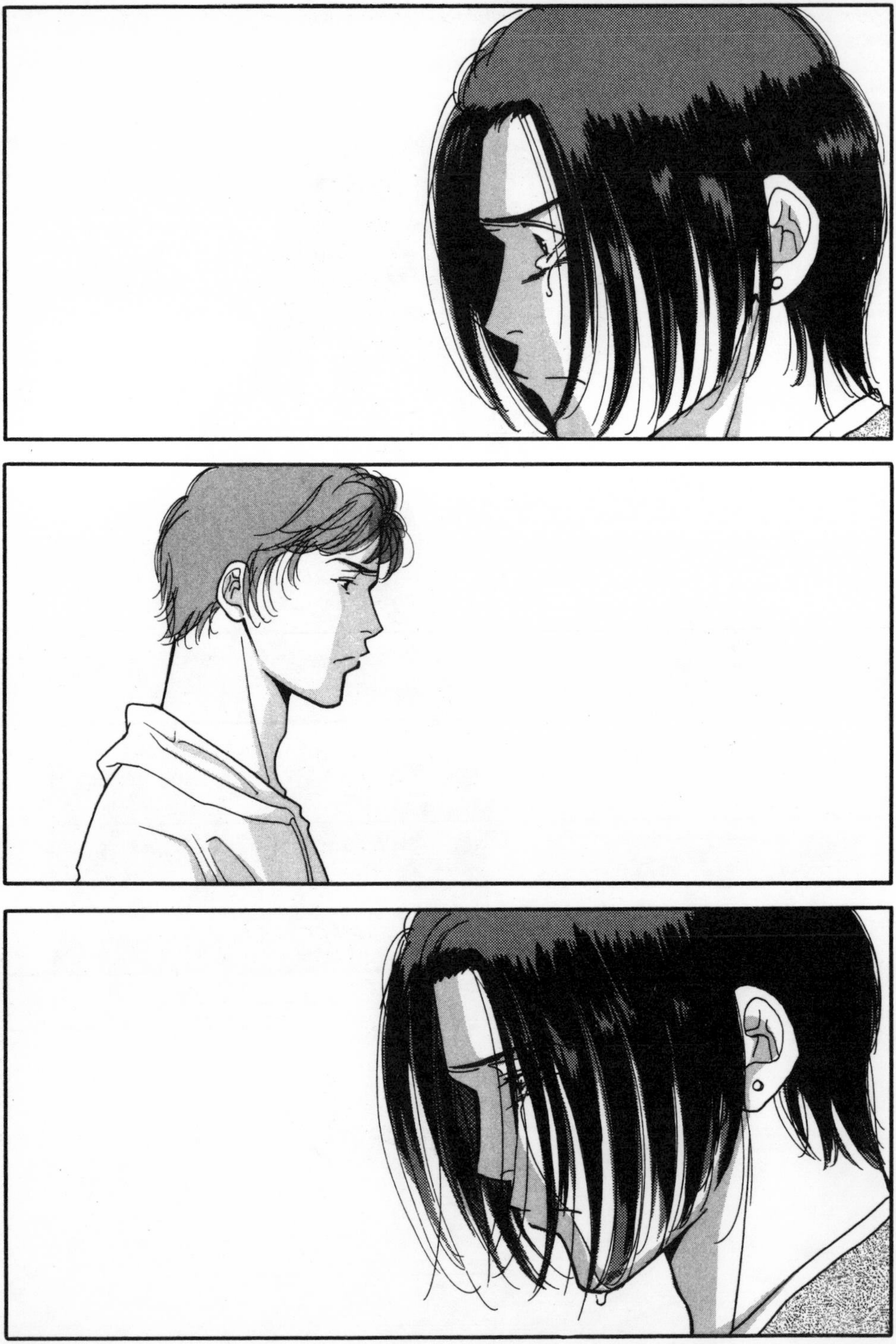

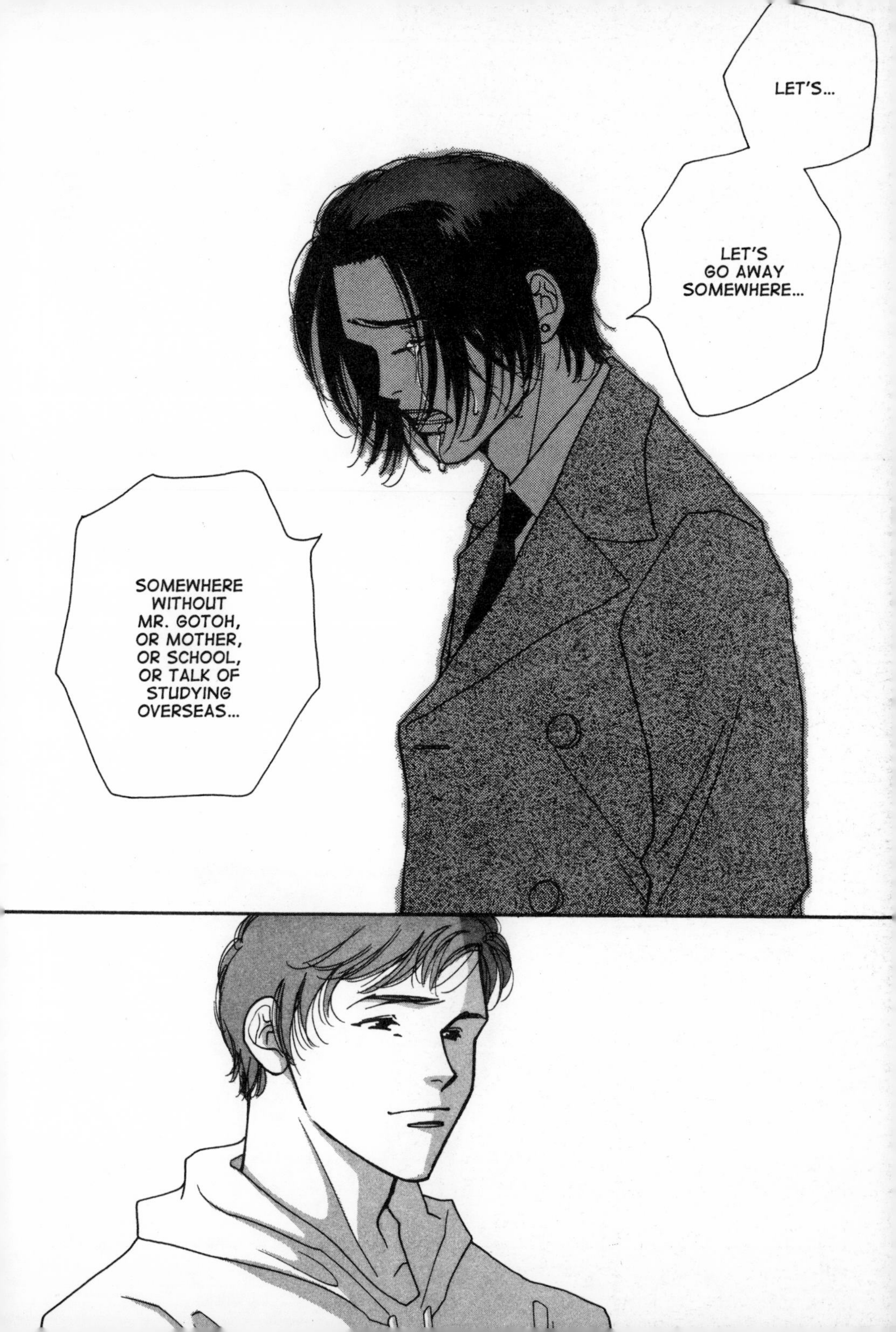
LET'S...
LET'S GO AWAY SOMEWHERE...
SOMEWHERE WITHOUT MR. GOTOH, OR MOTHER, OR SCHOOL, OR TALK OF STUDYING OVERSEAS...

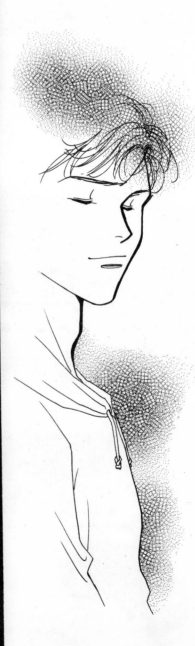

THAT'S
IMPOSSIBLE.

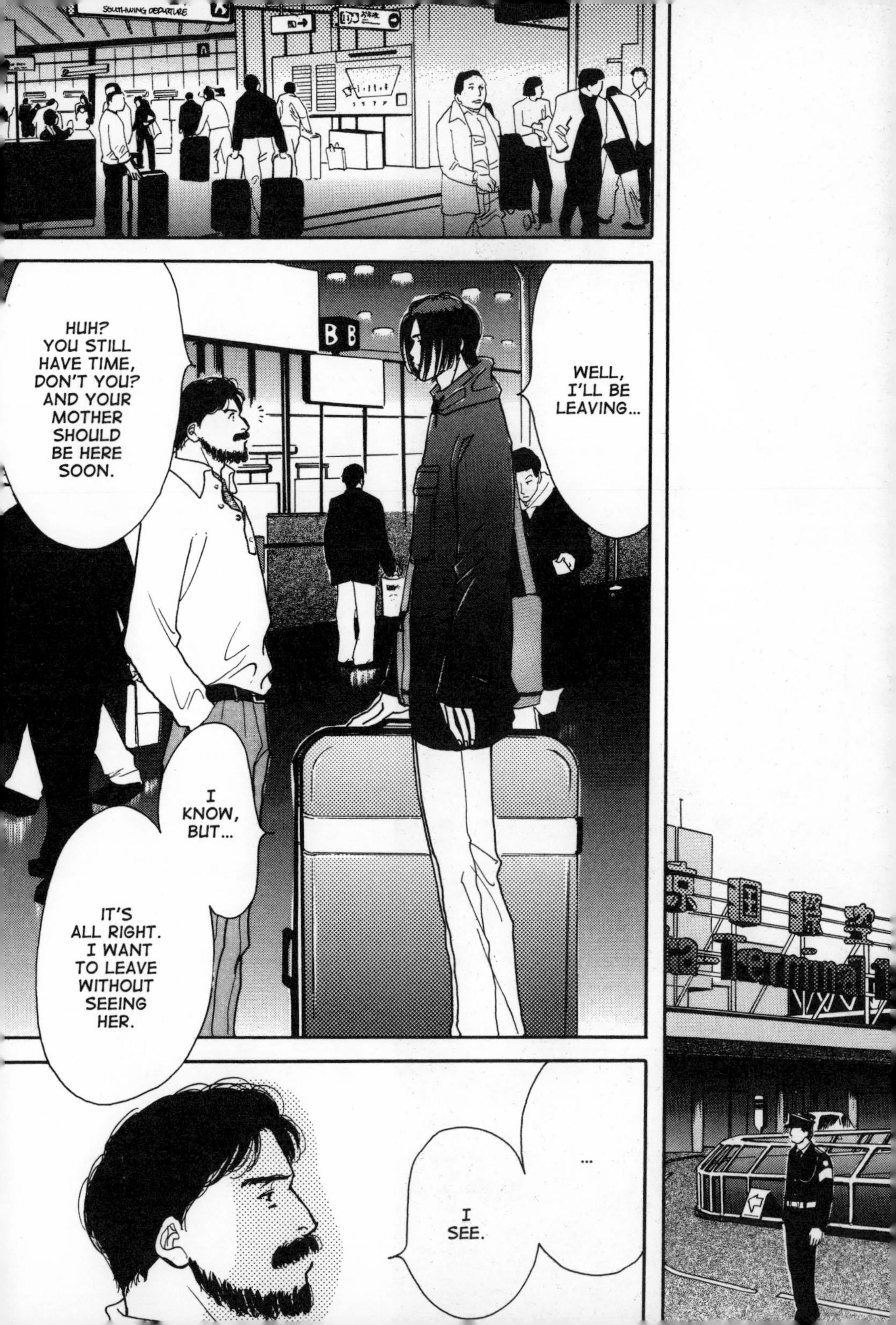
SOUTHWING DEPARTURE
B B
WELL, I'LL BE LEAVING...
HUH? YOU STILL HAVE TIME, DON'T YOU? AND YOUR MOTHER SHOULD BE HERE SOON.
I KNOW, BUT...
IT'S ALL RIGHT. I WANT TO LEAVE WITHOUT SEEING HER.
...
I SEE.

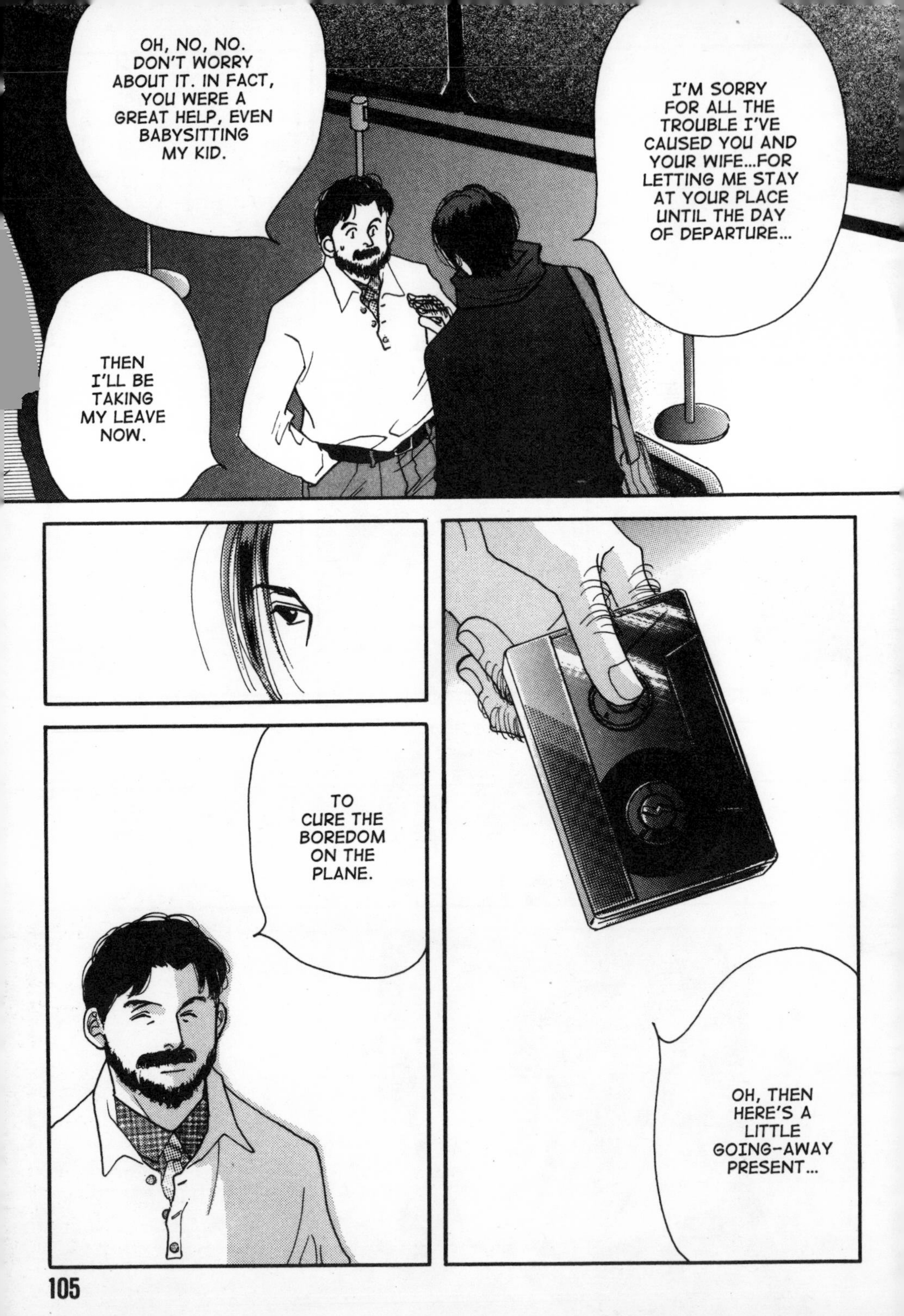
I'M SORRY FOR ALL THE TROUBLE I'VE CAUSED YOU AND YOUR WIFE...FOR LETTING ME STAY AT YOUR PLACE UNTIL THE DAY OF DEPARTURE...
OH, NO, NO. DON'T WORRY ABOUT IT. IN FACT, YOU WERE A GREAT HELP, EVEN BABYSITTING MY KID.
THEN I'LL BE TAKING MY LEAVE NOW.
OH, THEN HERE'S A LITTLE GOING-AWAY PRESENT...
TO CURE THE BOREDOM ON THE PLANE.

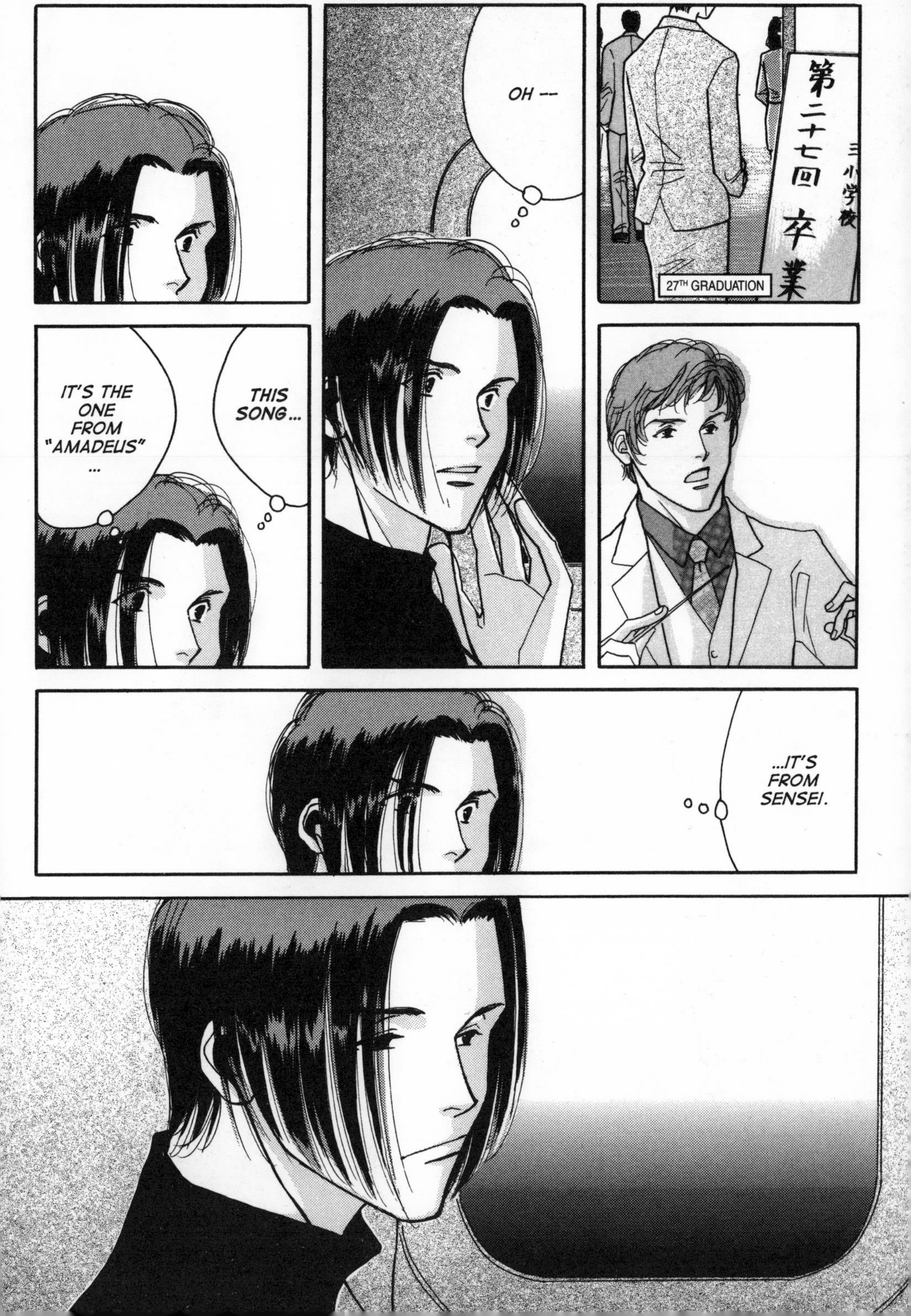

第二十七回
卒業
三小学校
27TH GRADUATION
OH --
THIS SONG...
IT'S THE ONE FROM "AMADEUS" ...
...IT'S FROM SENSEI.

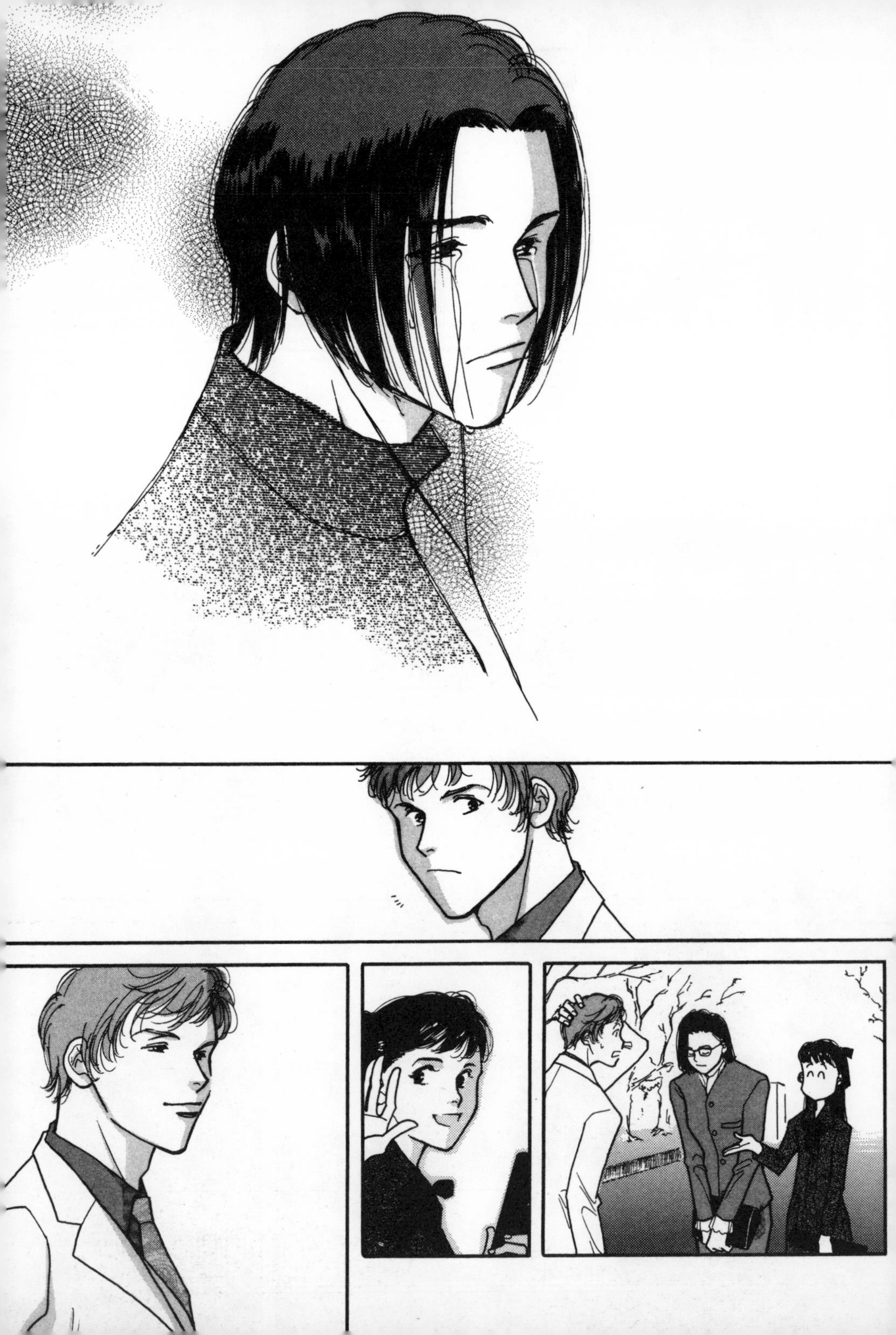

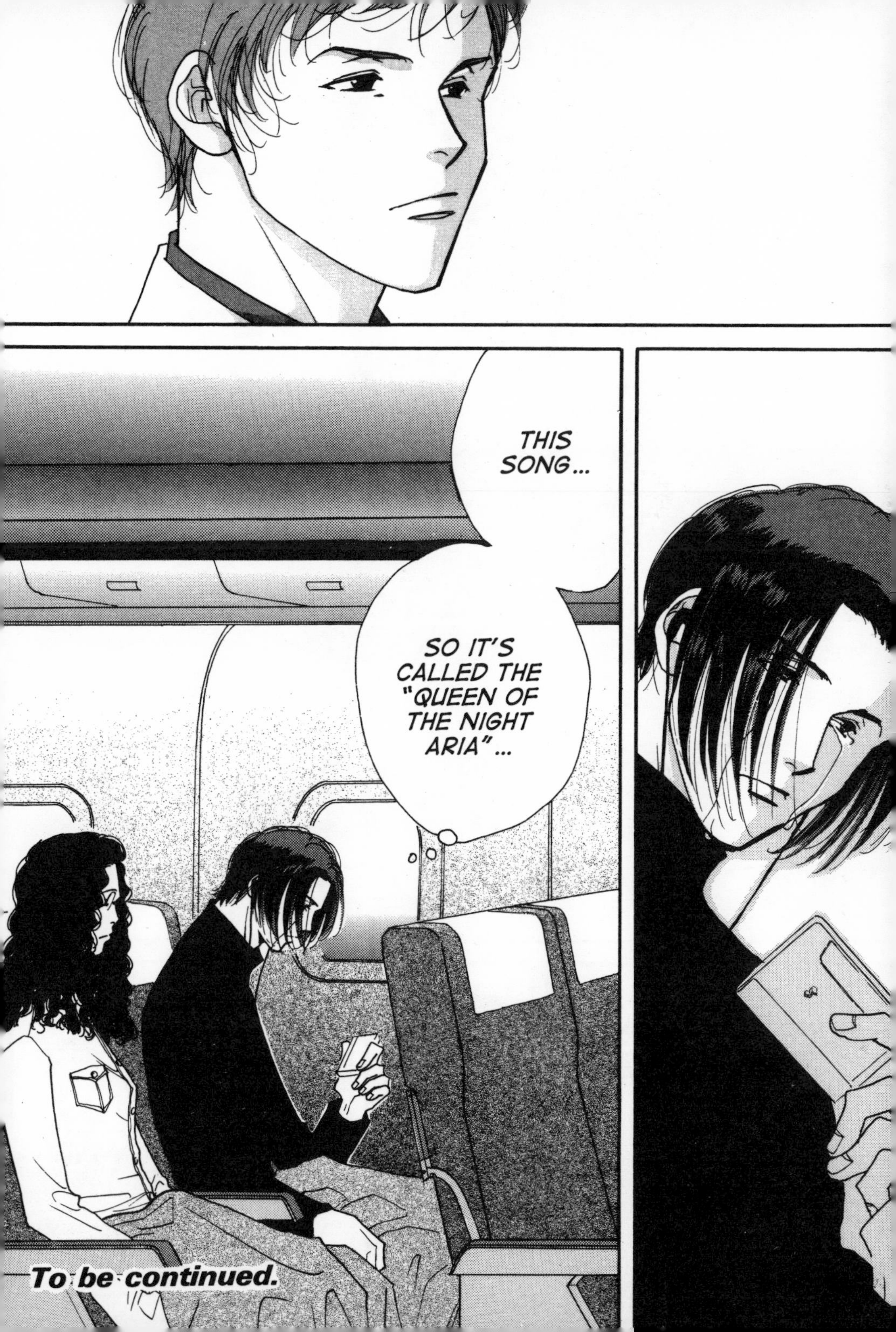
THIS SONG...
SO IT'S CALLED THE "QUEEN OF THE NIGHT ARIA"...
To be continued.

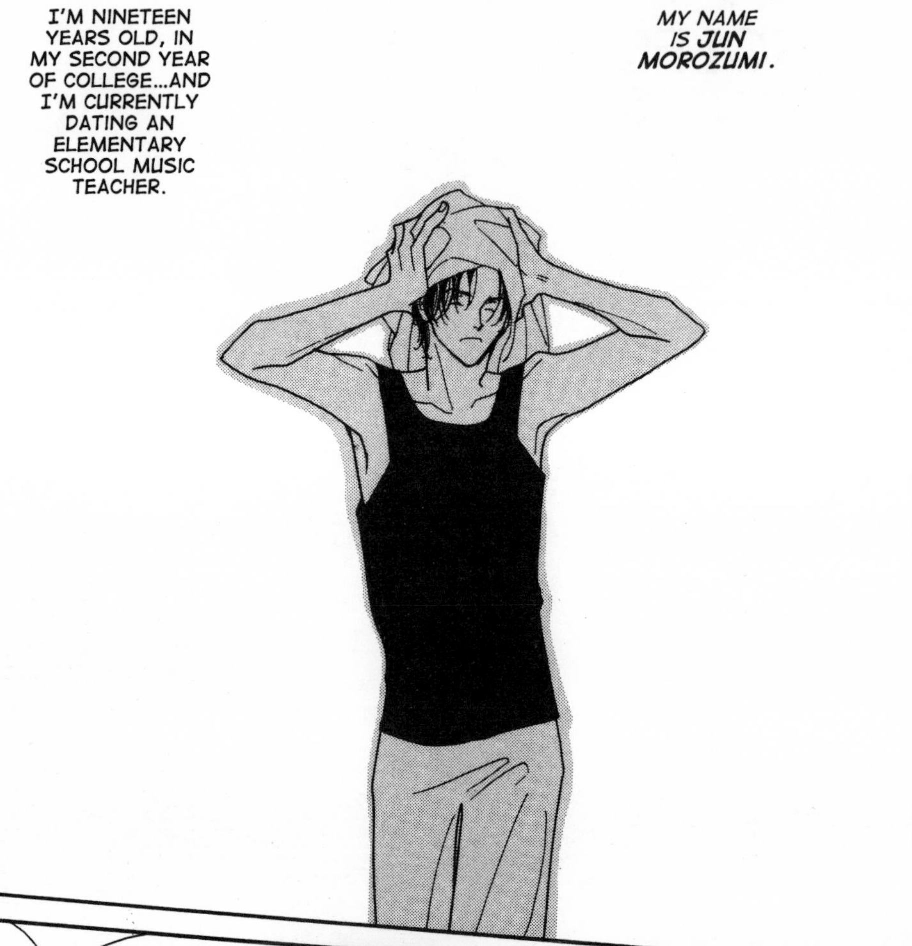
MY NAME IS JUN MOROZUMI.
I'M NINETEEN YEARS OLD, IN MY SECOND YEAR OF COLLEGE...AND I'M CURRENTLY DATING AN ELEMENTARY SCHOOL MUSIC TEACHER.
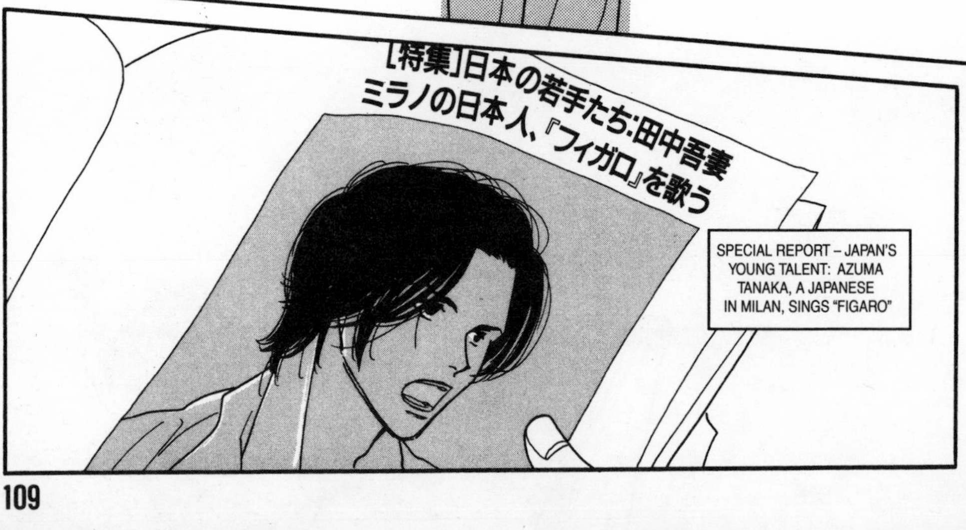
[特集]日本の若手たち:田中吾妻
ミラノの日本人、『フィガロ』を歌う
SPECIAL REPORT – JAPAN'S YOUNG TALENT: AZUMA TANAKA, A JAPANESE IN MILAN, SINGS "FIGARO"

ソルフェージュ
SOLFÈGE
NO MORE SHALL YOU FLUTTER,
O BUTTERFLY

"IN YOUTH, ONE TENDS
TO SING OVERZEALOUSLY, IN
AN EFFORT TO MAKE EVERY
NOTE AS INTERESTING AS
POSSIBLE; THIS CAUSES AN
OPPOSITE EFFECT ON
THE LISTENER, WHO IS
INEVITABLY BORED..."

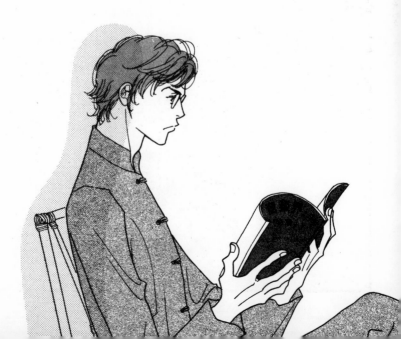

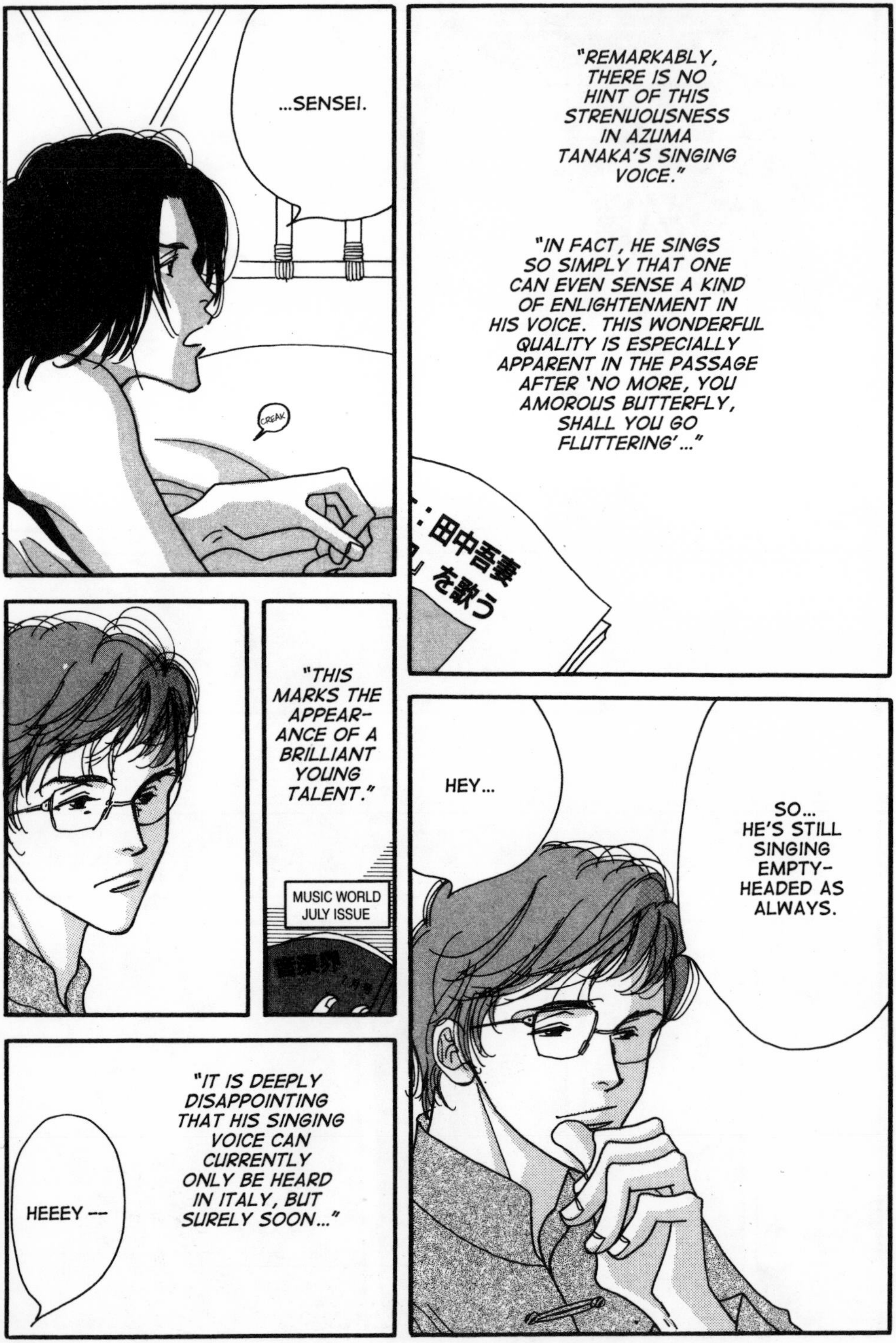
"REMARKABLY, THERE IS NO HINT OF THIS STRENUOUSNESS IN AZUMA TANAKA'S SINGING VOICE."
"IN FACT, HE SINGS SO SIMPLY THAT ONE CAN EVEN SENSE A KIND OF ENLIGHTENMENT IN HIS VOICE. THIS WONDERFUL QUALITY IS ESPECIALLY APPARENT IN THE PASSAGE AFTER 'NO MORE, YOU AMOROUS BUTTERFLY, SHALL YOU GO FLUTTERING'..."
：田中吾妻
」を歌う
...SENSEI.
CREAK
HEY...
SO... HE'S STILL SINGING EMPTY-HEADED AS ALWAYS.
"THIS MARKS THE APPEAR-ANCE OF A BRILLIANT YOUNG TALENT."
MUSIC WORLD JULY ISSUE
"IT IS DEEPLY DISAPPOINTING THAT HIS SINGING VOICE CAN CURRENTLY ONLY BE HEARD IN ITALY, BUT SURELY SOON..."
HEEEY --

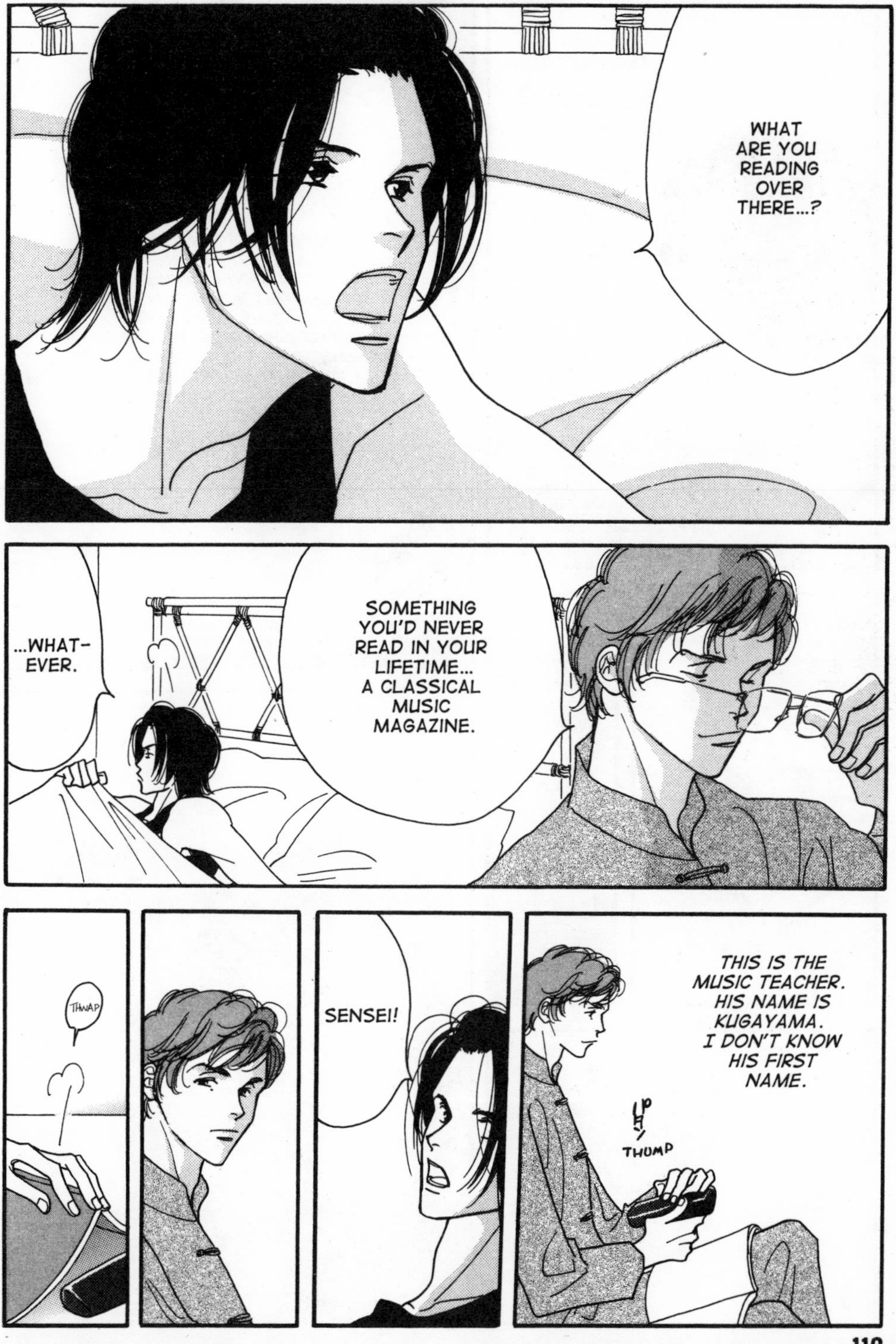
WHAT ARE YOU READING OVER THERE...?
SOMETHING YOU'D NEVER READ IN YOUR LIFETIME... A CLASSICAL MUSIC MAGAZINE.
...WHAT-EVER.
THIS IS THE MUSIC TEACHER. HIS NAME IS KUGAYAMA. I DON'T KNOW HIS FIRST NAME.
THUMP
SENSEI!
THWAP

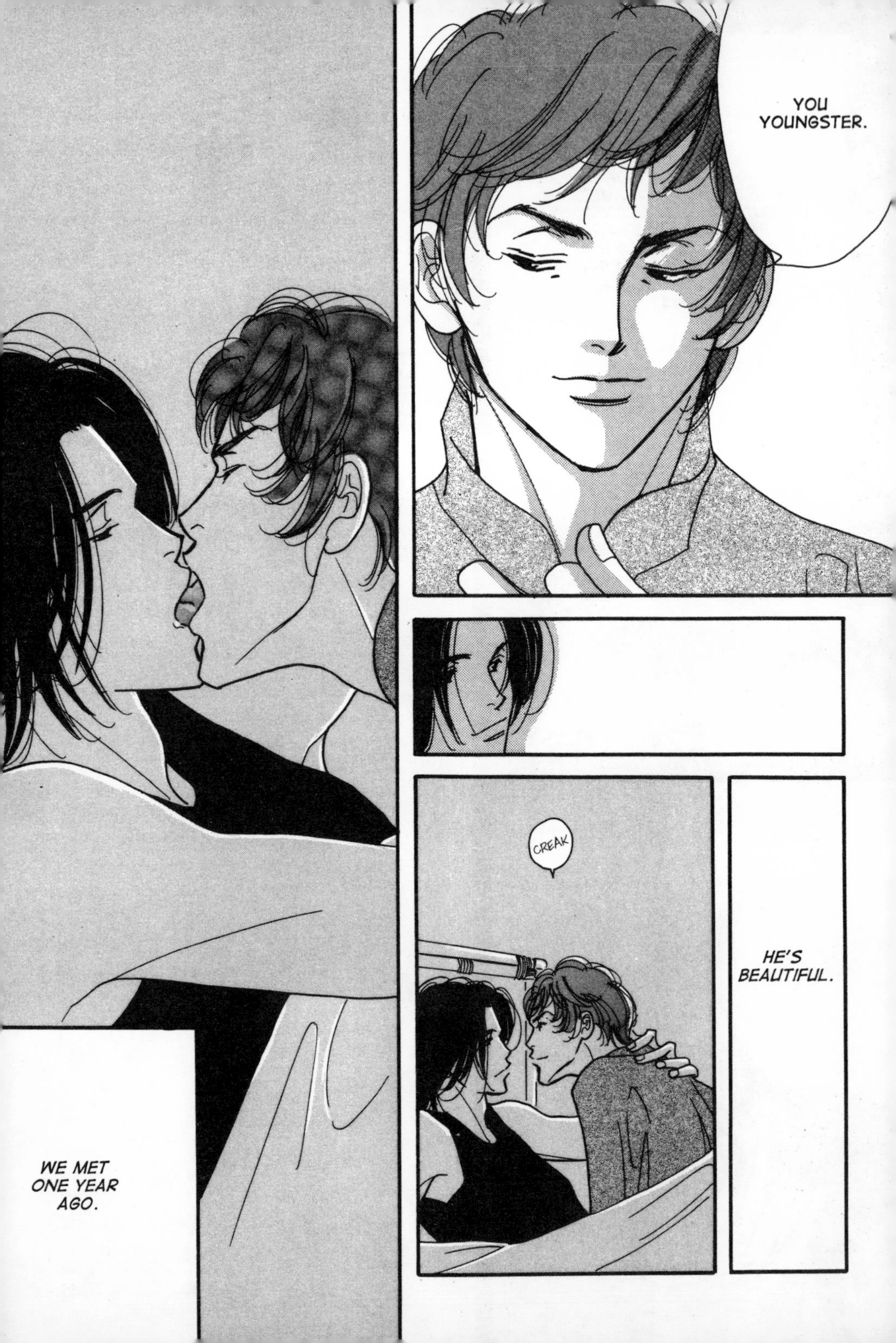
YOU YOUNGSTER.
HE'S BEAUTIFUL.
CREAK
WE MET ONE YEAR AGO.

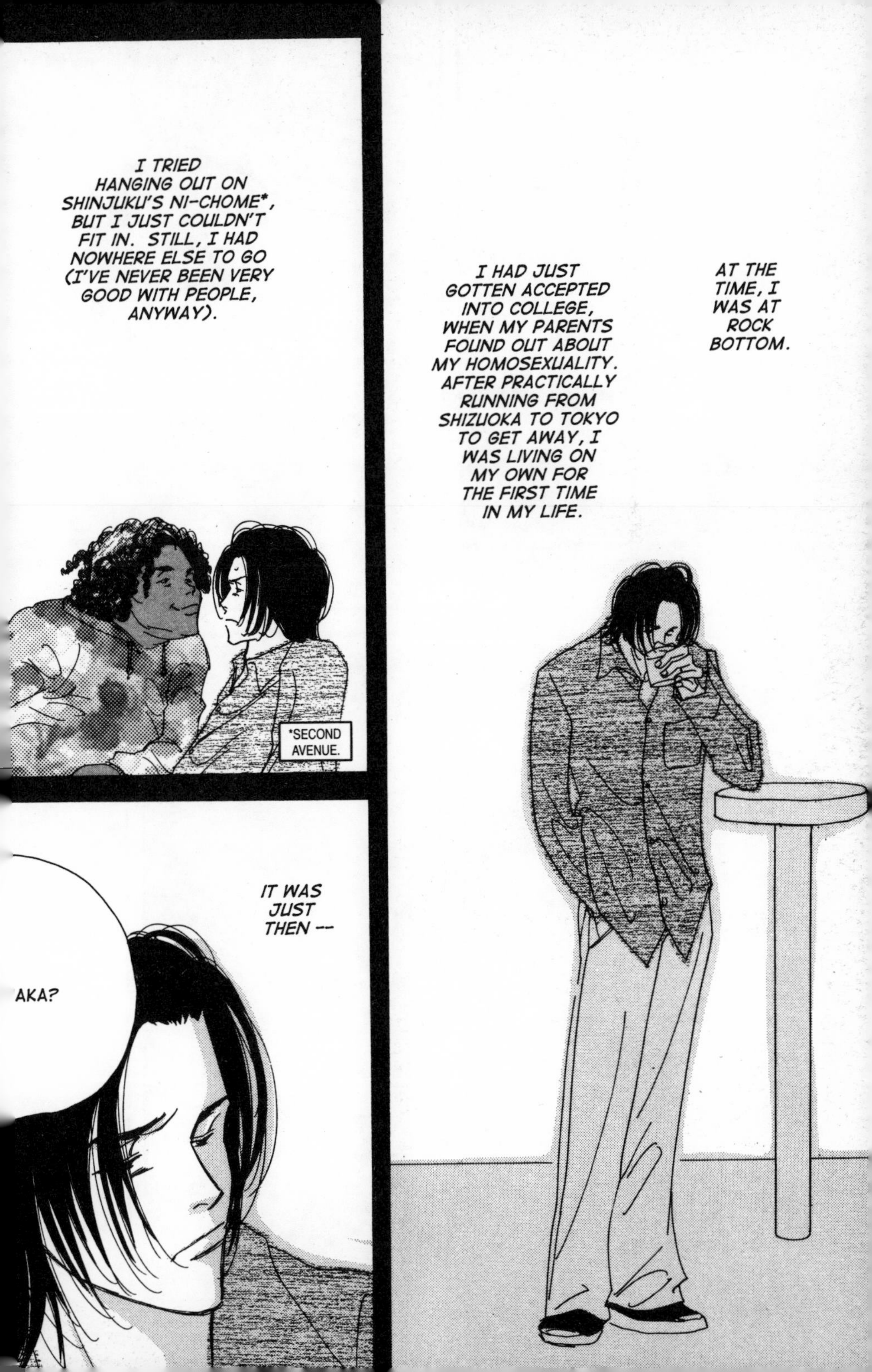
AT THE TIME, I WAS AT ROCK BOTTOM.
I HAD JUST GOTTEN ACCEPTED INTO COLLEGE, WHEN MY PARENTS FOUND OUT ABOUT MY HOMOSEXUALITY. AFTER PRACTICALLY RUNNING FROM SHIZUOKA TO TOKYO TO GET AWAY, I WAS LIVING ON MY OWN FOR THE FIRST TIME IN MY LIFE.
I TRIED HANGING OUT ON SHINJUKU'S NI-CHOME*, BUT I JUST COULDN'T FIT IN. STILL, I HAD NOWHERE ELSE TO GO (I'VE NEVER BEEN VERY GOOD WITH PEOPLE, ANYWAY).
*SECOND AVENUE.
IT WAS JUST THEN --
AKA?

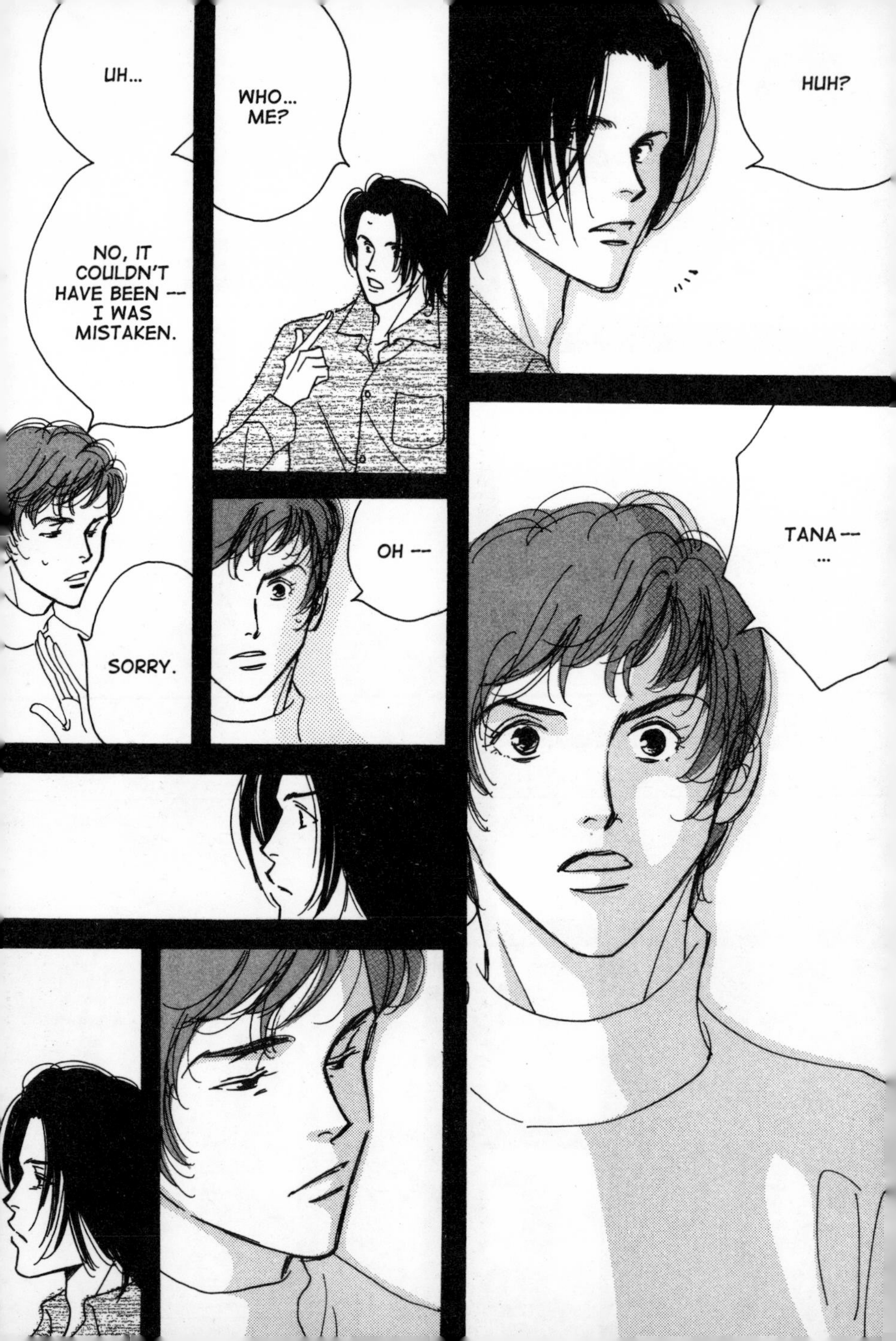
HUH?
WHO... ME?
UH...
NO, IT COULDN'T HAVE BEEN -- I WAS MISTAKEN.
SORRY.
OH --
TANA-- ...

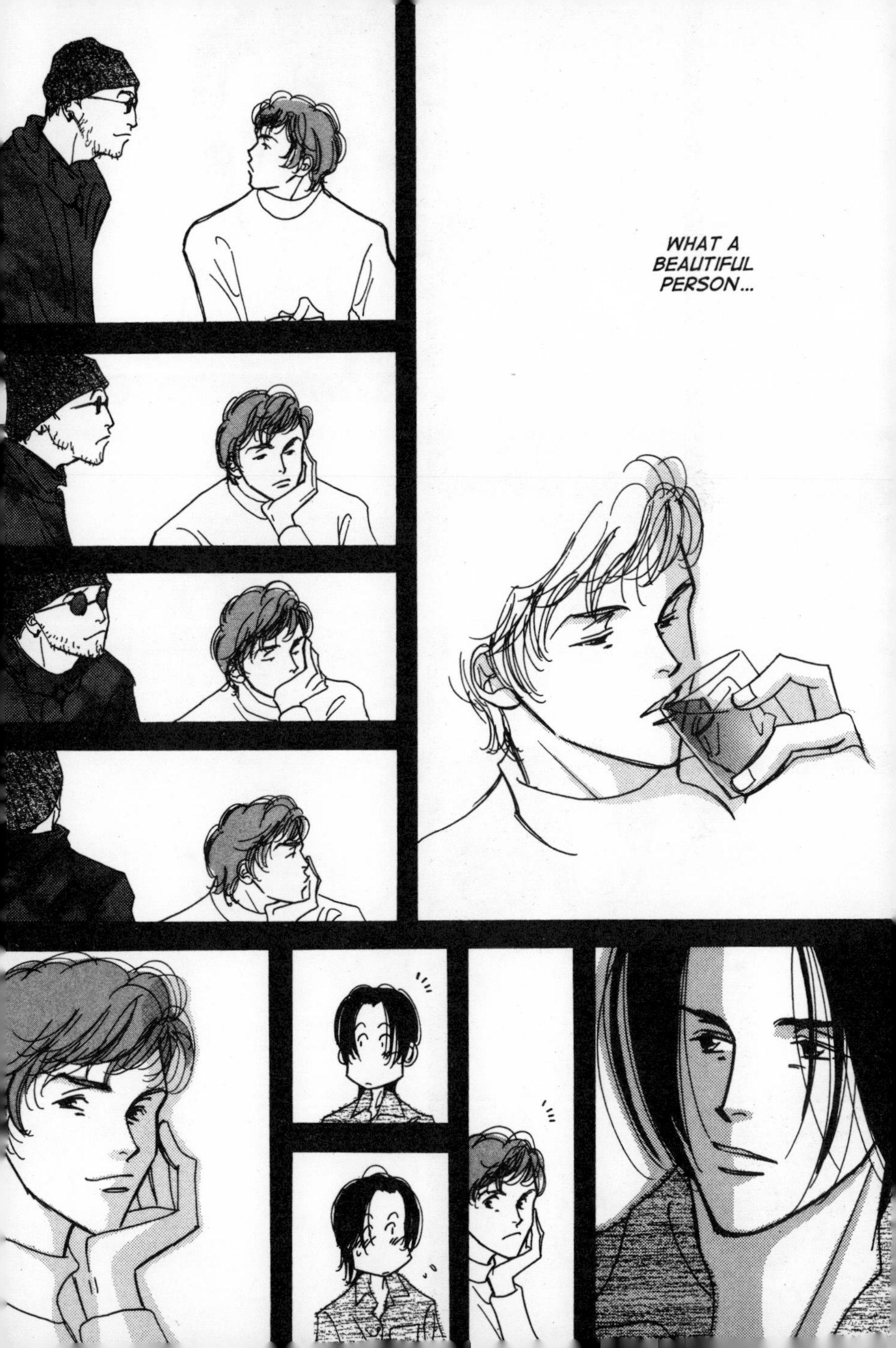
WHAT A BEAUTIFUL PERSON...

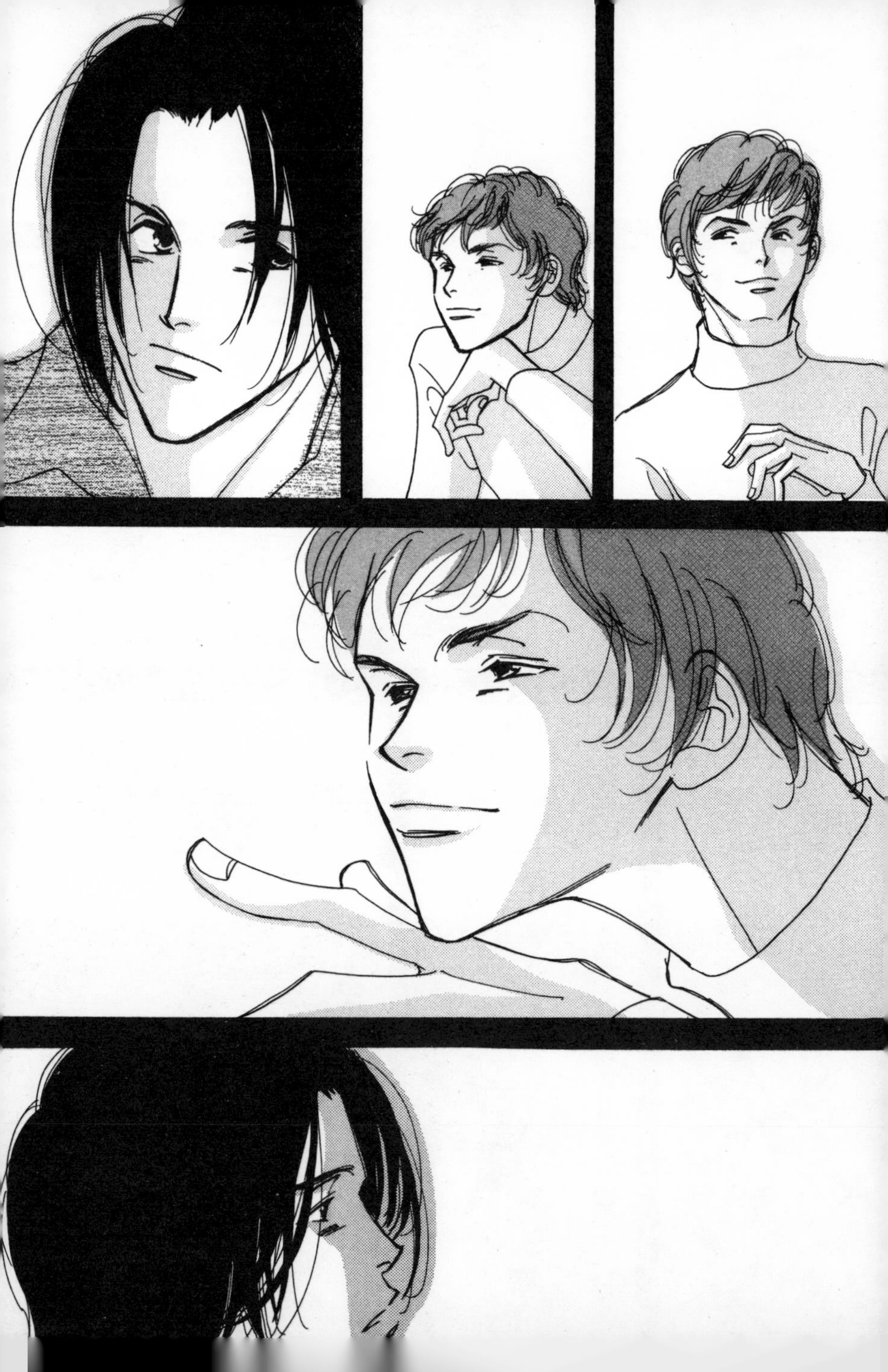

WE HEADED STRAIGHT
TO A HOTEL. IT WAS AN
EXPENSIVE-LOOKING,
HIGH-CLASS ONE,
SOMEWHERE IN
WEST SHINJUKU.

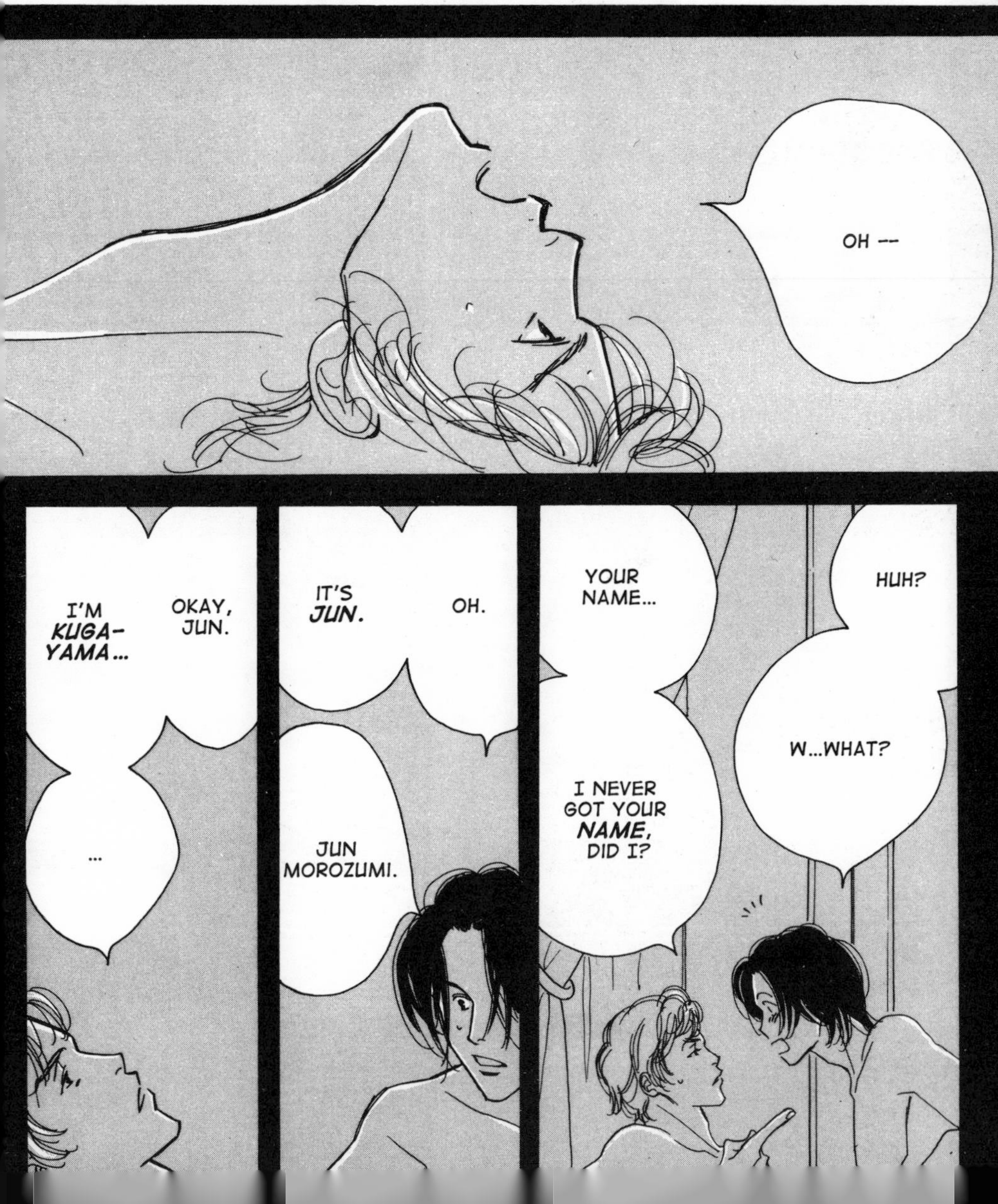
OH --
HUH?
YOUR NAME...
W...WHAT?
I NEVER GOT YOUR NAME, DID I?
OH.
IT'S JUN.
JUN MOROZUMI.
OKAY, JUN.
I'M KUGA-YAMA...
...

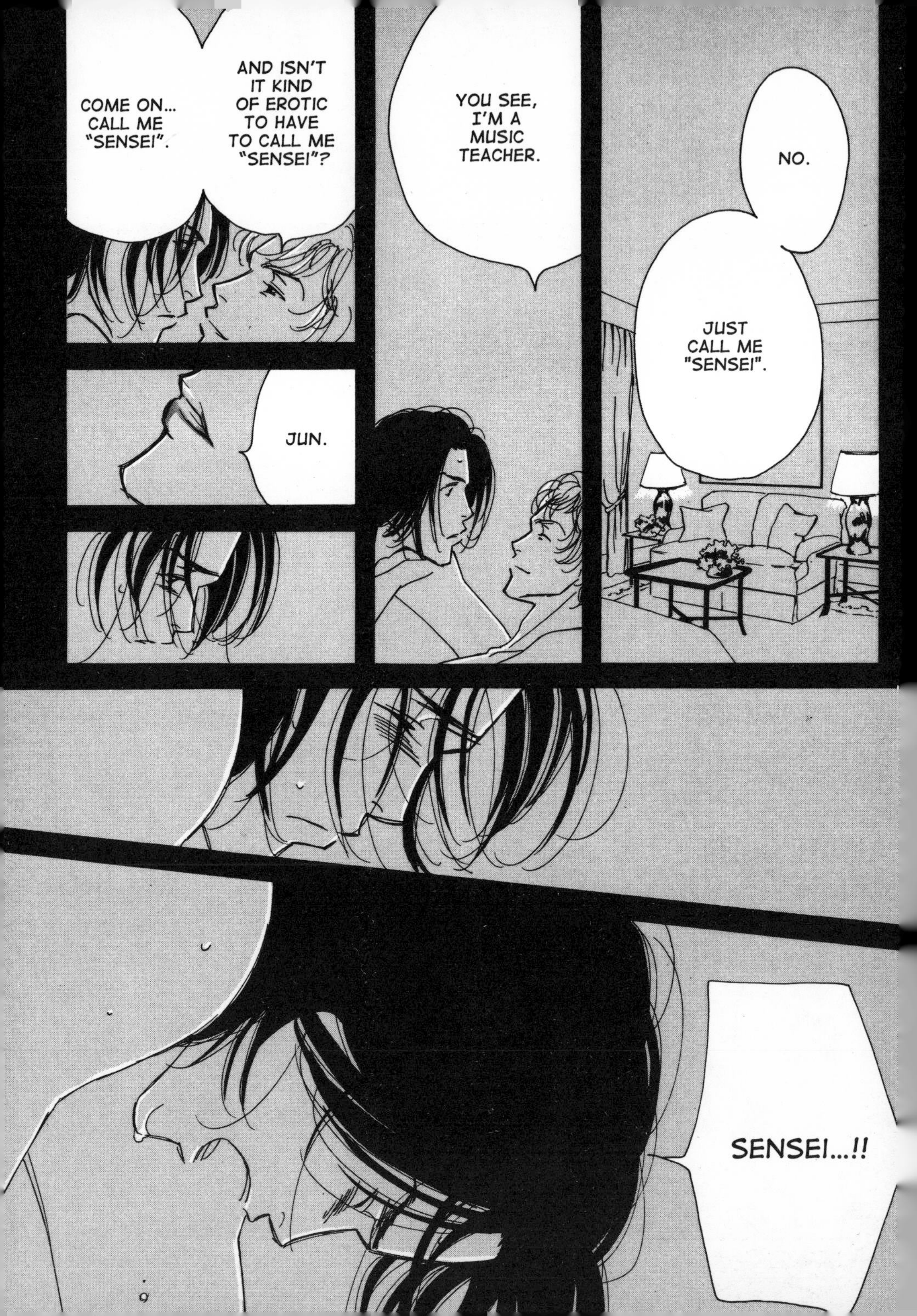
NO.
JUST CALL ME "SENSEI".
YOU SEE, I'M A MUSIC TEACHER.
AND ISN'T IT KIND OF EROTIC TO HAVE TO CALL ME "SENSEI"?
COME ON... CALL ME "SENSEI".
JUN.
SENSEI...!!

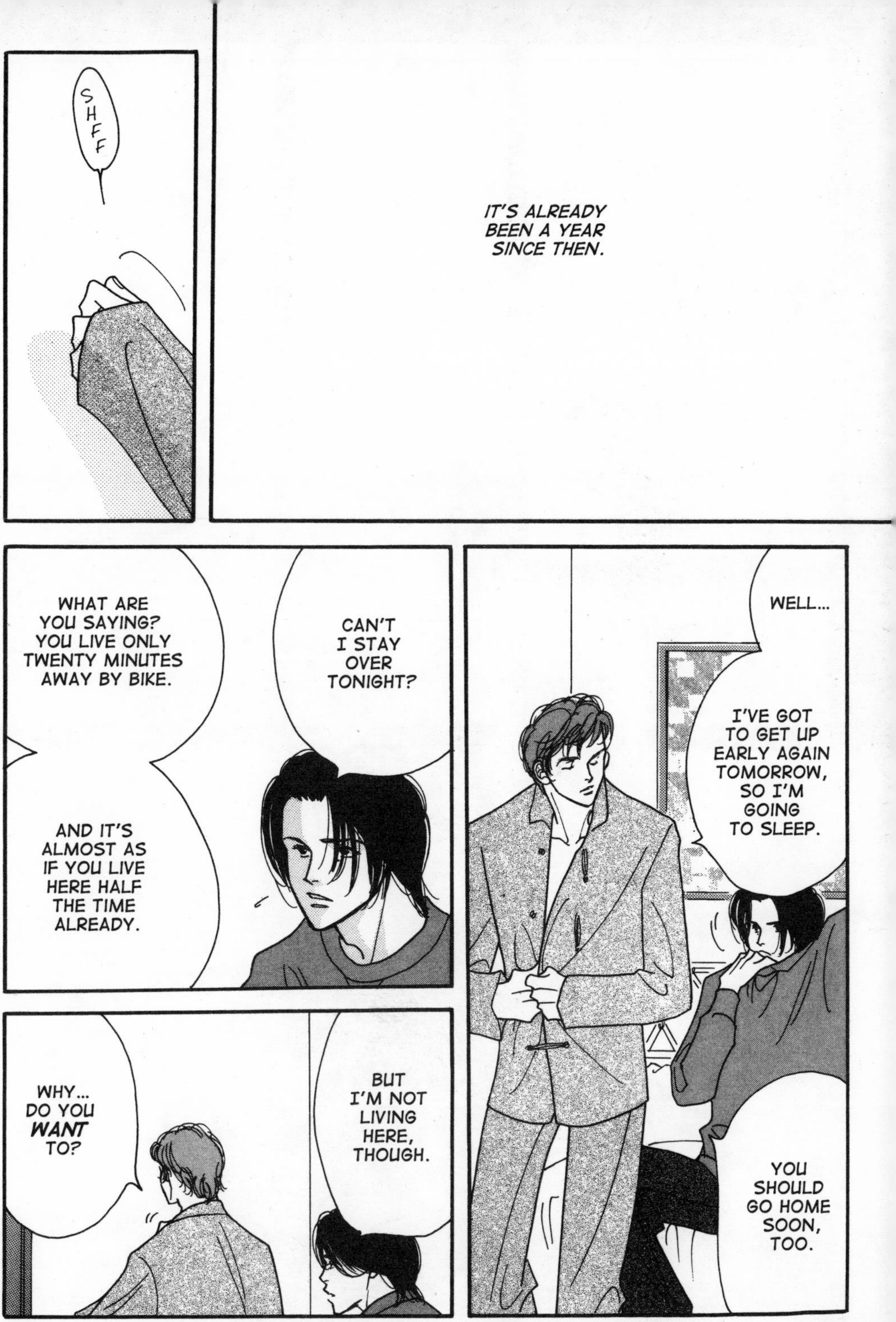
IT'S ALREADY BEEN A YEAR SINCE THEN.
SHFF
WELL...
I'VE GOT TO GET UP EARLY AGAIN TOMORROW, SO I'M GOING TO SLEEP.
YOU SHOULD GO HOME SOON, TOO.
CAN'T I STAY OVER TONIGHT?
WHAT ARE YOU SAYING? YOU LIVE ONLY TWENTY MINUTES AWAY BY BIKE.
AND IT'S ALMOST AS IF YOU LIVE HERE HALF THE TIME ALREADY.
BUT I'M NOT LIVING HERE, THOUGH.
WHY... DO YOU ***WANT*** TO?

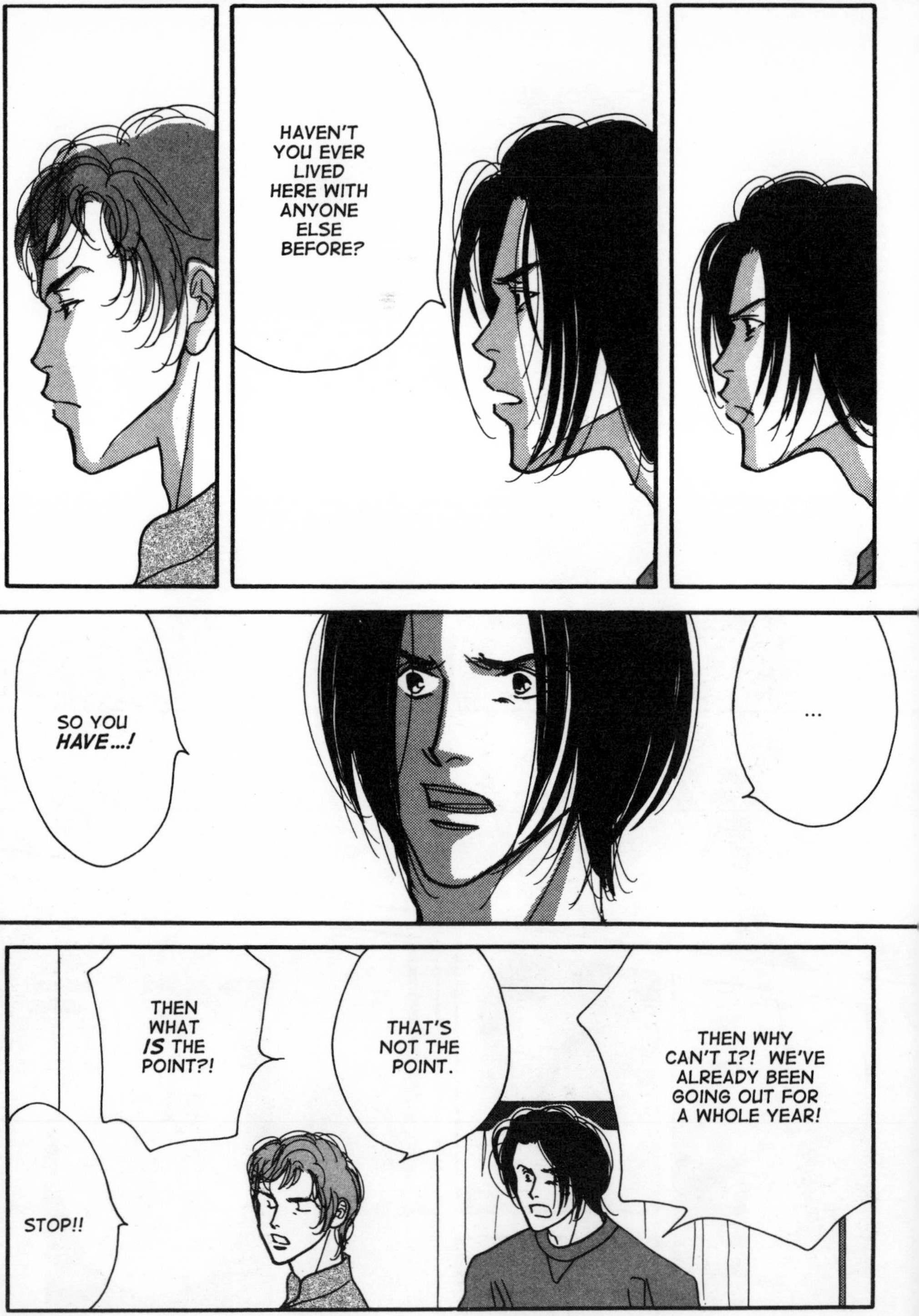
HAVEN'T YOU EVER LIVED HERE WITH ANYONE ELSE BEFORE?
...
SO YOU *HAVE*...!
THEN WHY CAN'T I?! WE'VE ALREADY BEEN GOING OUT FOR A WHOLE YEAR!
THAT'S NOT THE POINT.
THEN WHAT *IS* THE POINT?!
STOP!!

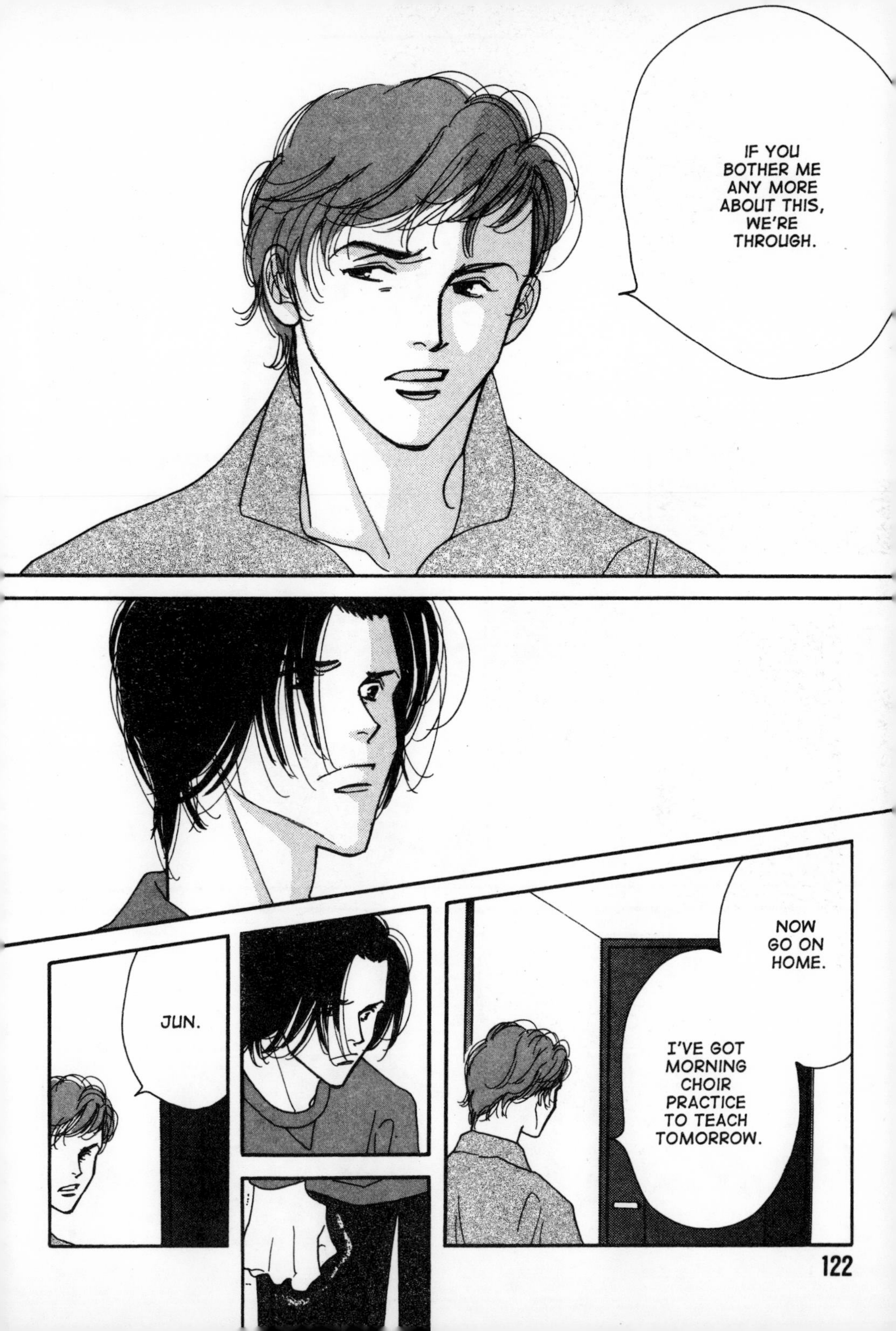
IF YOU BOTHER ME ANY MORE ABOUT THIS, WE'RE THROUGH.
NOW GO ON HOME.
I'VE GOT MORNING CHOIR PRACTICE TO TEACH TOMORROW.
JUN.

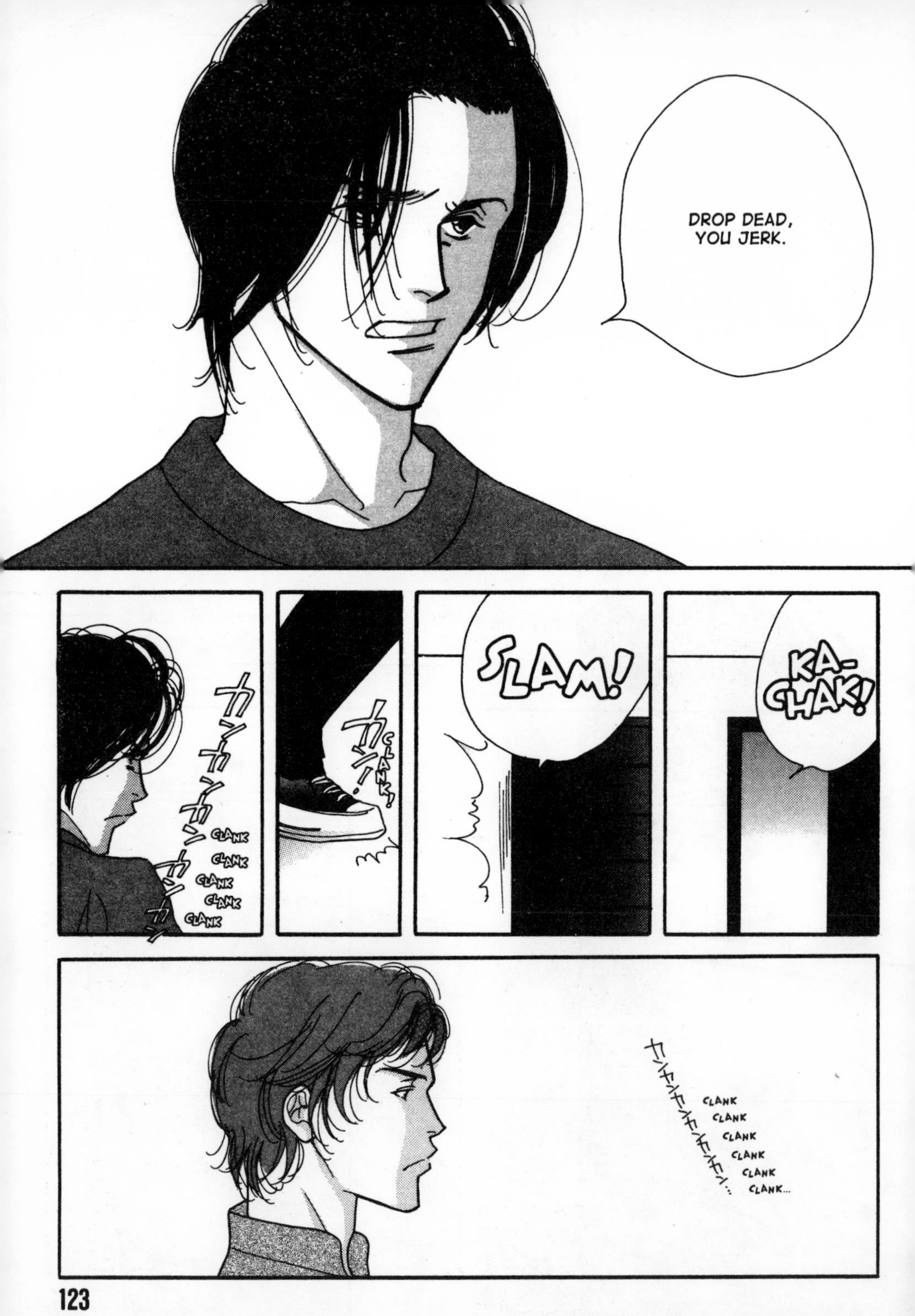
DROP DEAD, YOU JERK.
KA-CHAK!
SLAM!
CLANK!
CLANK
CLANK
CLANK
CLANK
CLANK
CLANK
CLANK
CLANK
CLANK
CLANK
CLANK...

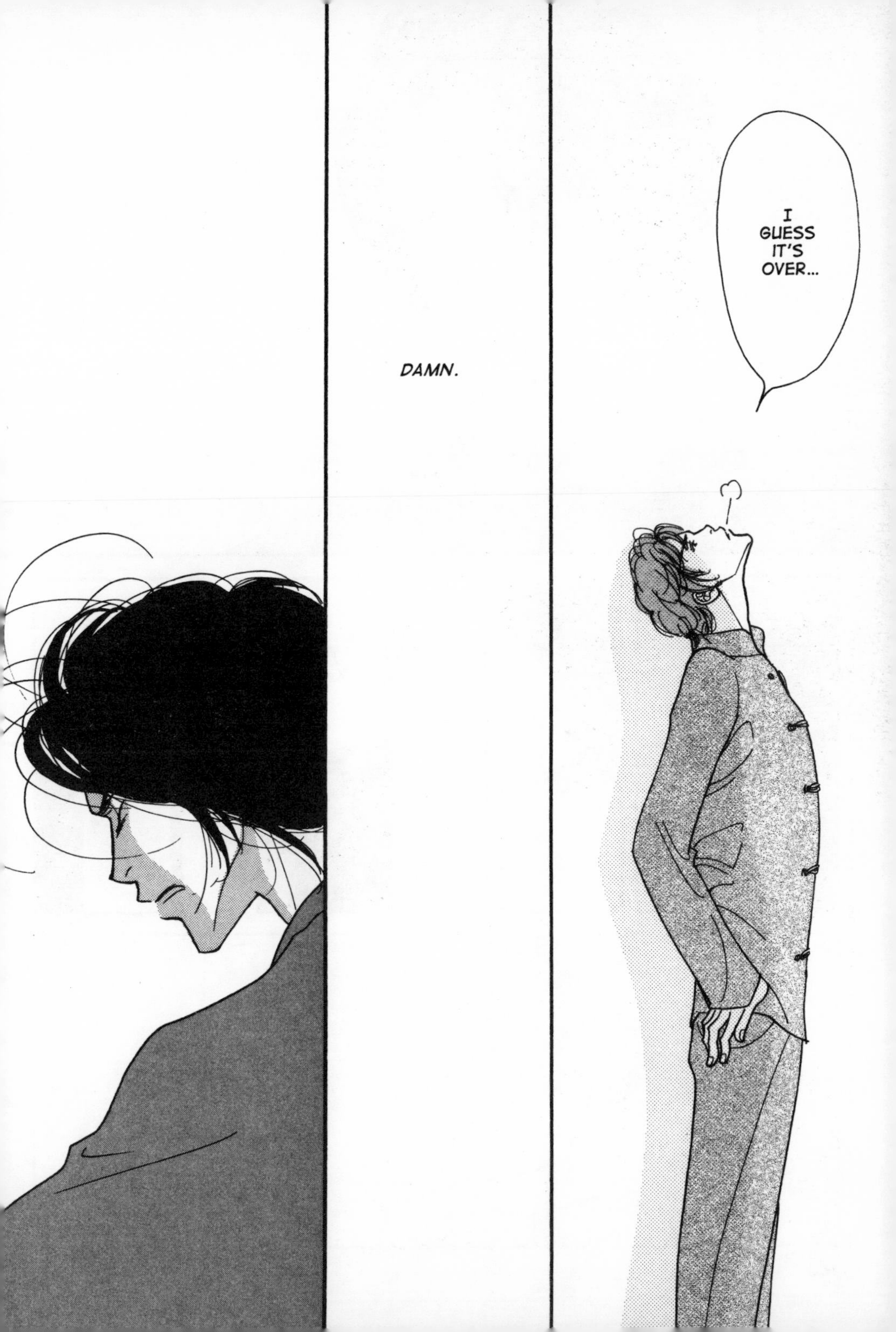
I GUESS IT'S OVER...
DAMN.

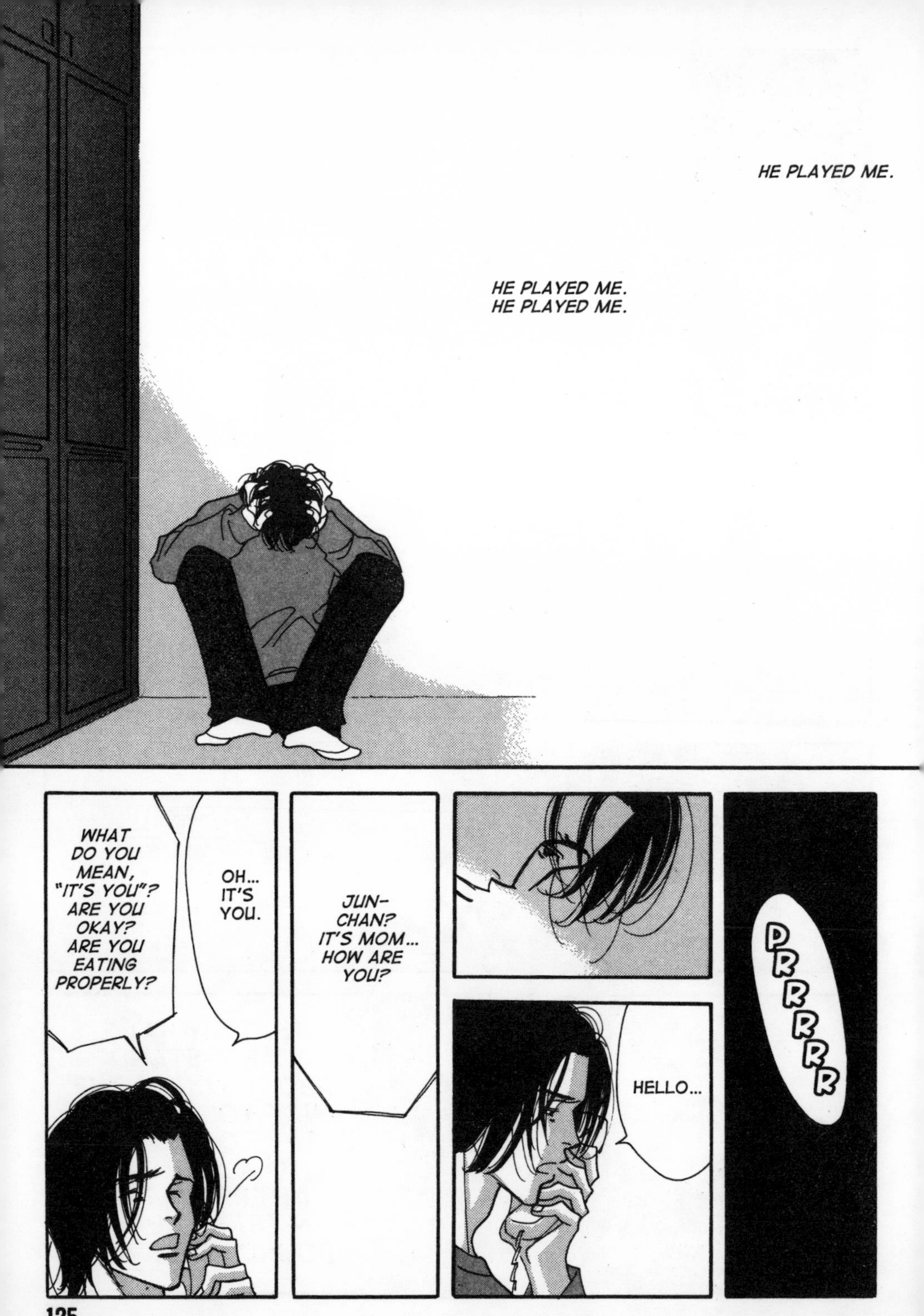
HE PLAYED ME.
HE PLAYED ME.
HE PLAYED ME.
PRRRRR
HELLO...
JUN-CHAN? IT'S MOM... HOW ARE YOU?
OH... IT'S YOU.
WHAT DO YOU MEAN, "IT'S YOU"? ARE YOU OKAY? ARE YOU EATING PROPERLY?

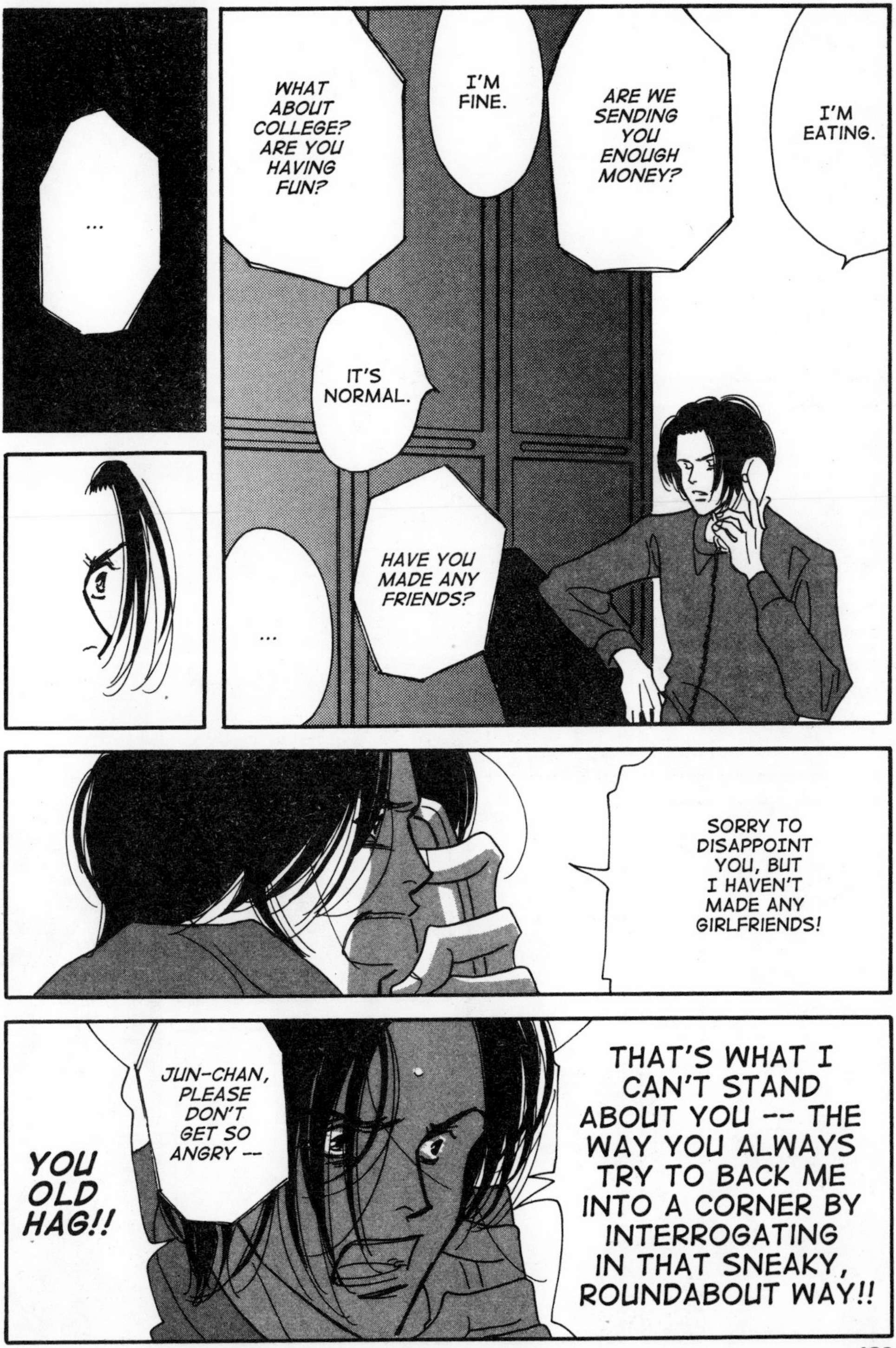
I'M EATING.
ARE WE SENDING YOU ENOUGH MONEY?
I'M FINE.
WHAT ABOUT COLLEGE? ARE YOU HAVING FUN?
IT'S NORMAL.
HAVE YOU MADE ANY FRIENDS?
...
...
SORRY TO DISAPPOINT YOU, BUT I HAVEN'T MADE ANY GIRLFRIENDS!
THAT'S WHAT I CAN'T STAND ABOUT YOU -- THE WAY YOU ALWAYS TRY TO BACK ME INTO A CORNER BY INTERROGATING IN THAT SNEAKY, ROUNDABOUT WAY!!
JUN-CHAN, PLEASE DON'T GET SO ANGRY --
YOU OLD HAG!!

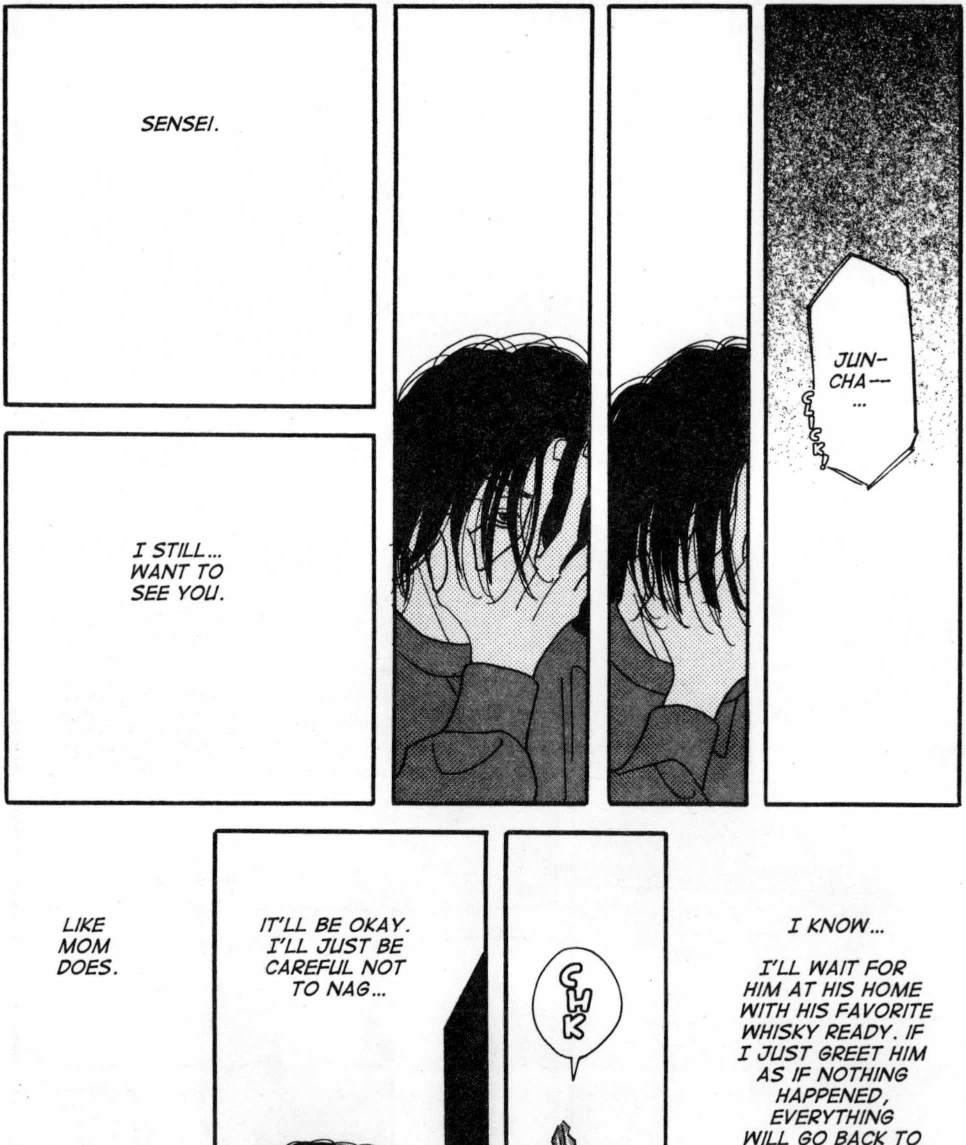
JUN-
CHA---
...
CLICK!
SENSEI.
I STILL... WANT TO SEE YOU.
I KNOW...
I'LL WAIT FOR HIM AT HIS HOME WITH HIS FAVORITE WHISKY READY. IF I JUST GREET HIM AS IF NOTHING HAPPENED, EVERYTHING WILL GO BACK TO THE WAY IT WAS.
CHK
IT'LL BE OKAY. I'LL JUST BE CAREFUL NOT TO NAG...
CLICK!
LIKE MOM DOES.

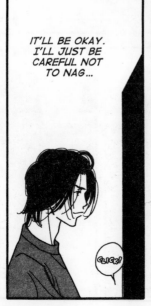

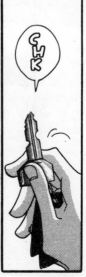

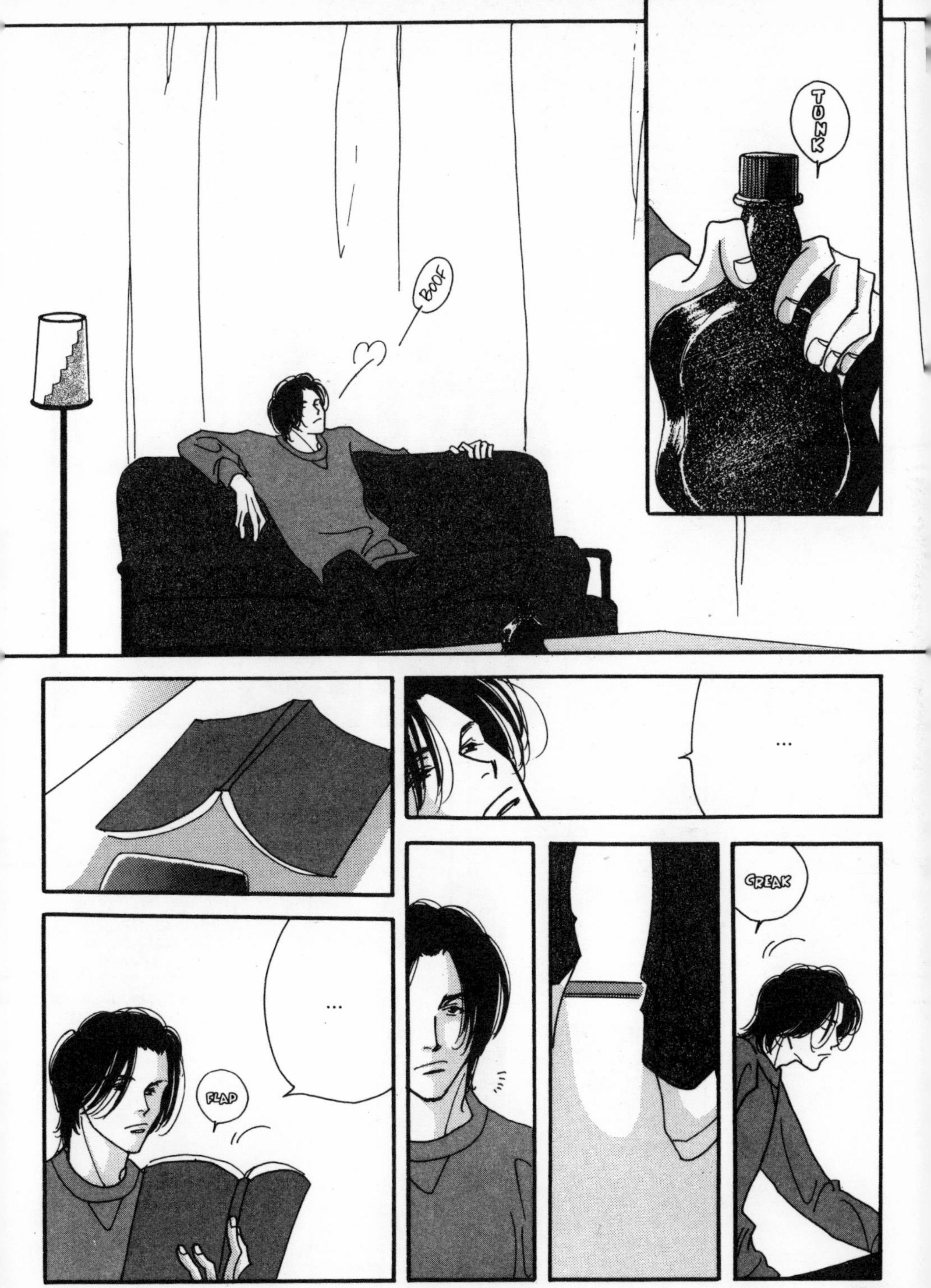
TUNK
BOOF
...
CREAK
...
FLAP

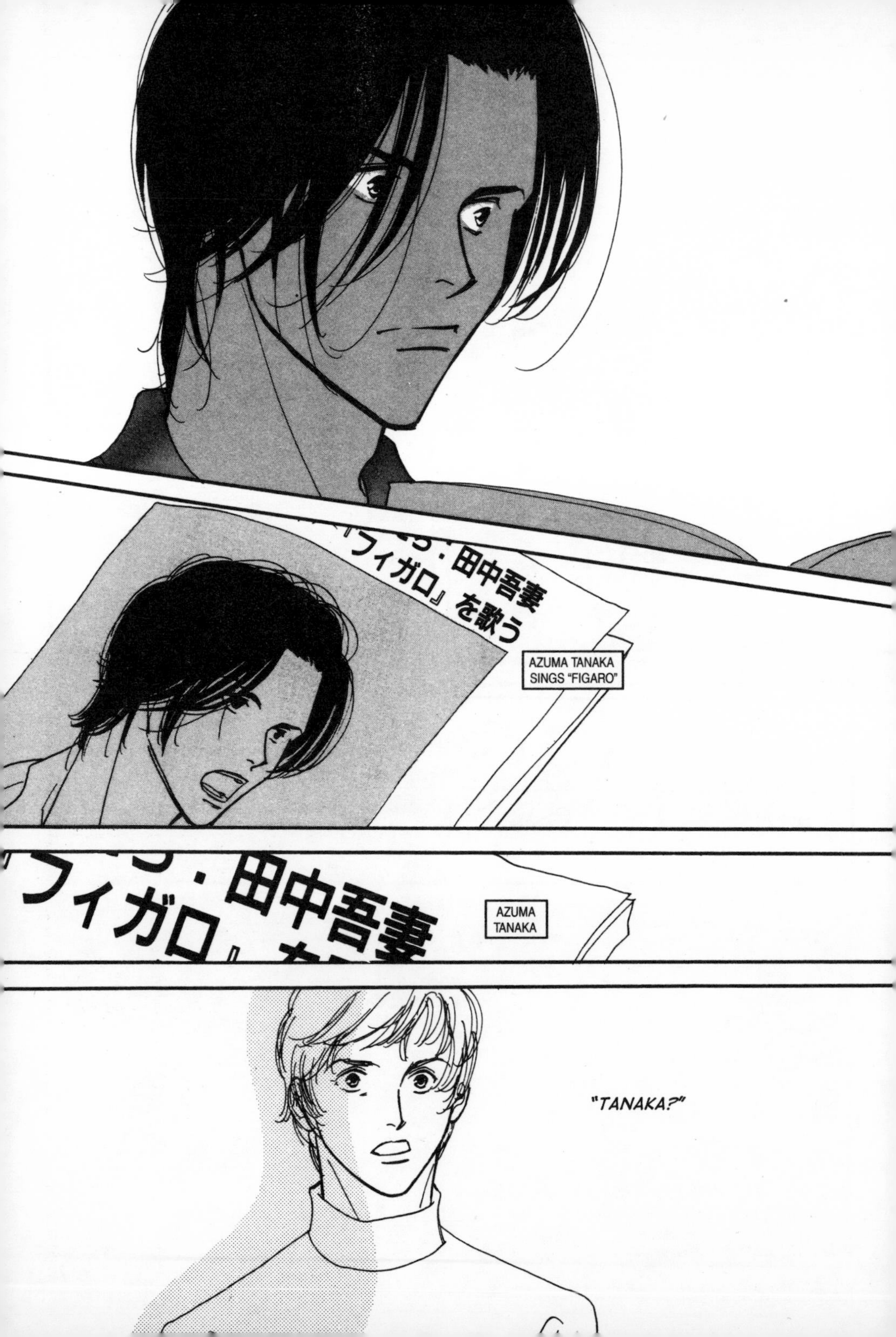
田中吾妻
『フィガロ』を歌う
AZUMA TANAKA SINGS "FIGARO"
田中吾妻
AZUMA TANAKA
"TANAKA?"

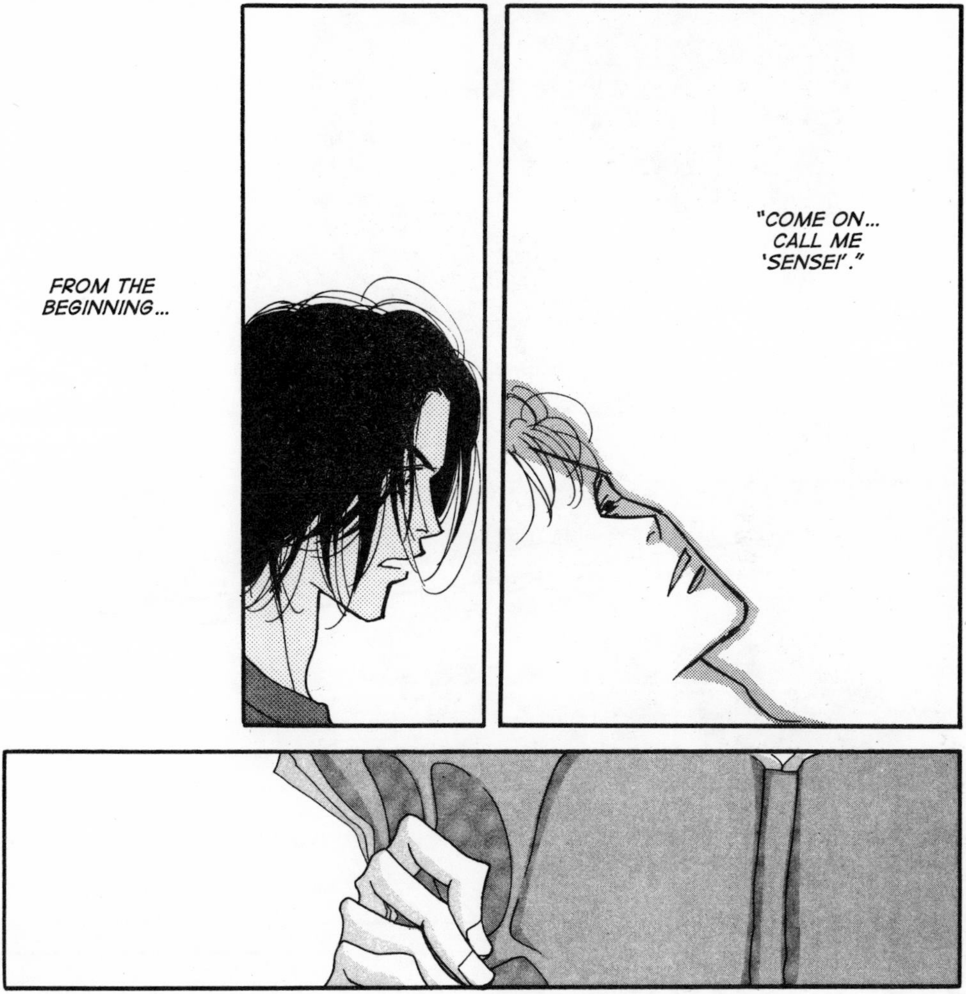
"COME ON... CALL ME 'SENSEI'."

FROM THE BEGINNING...

FROM THE VERY BEGINNING... IT WAS ONLY BECAUSE I LOOKED LIKE THIS GUY.

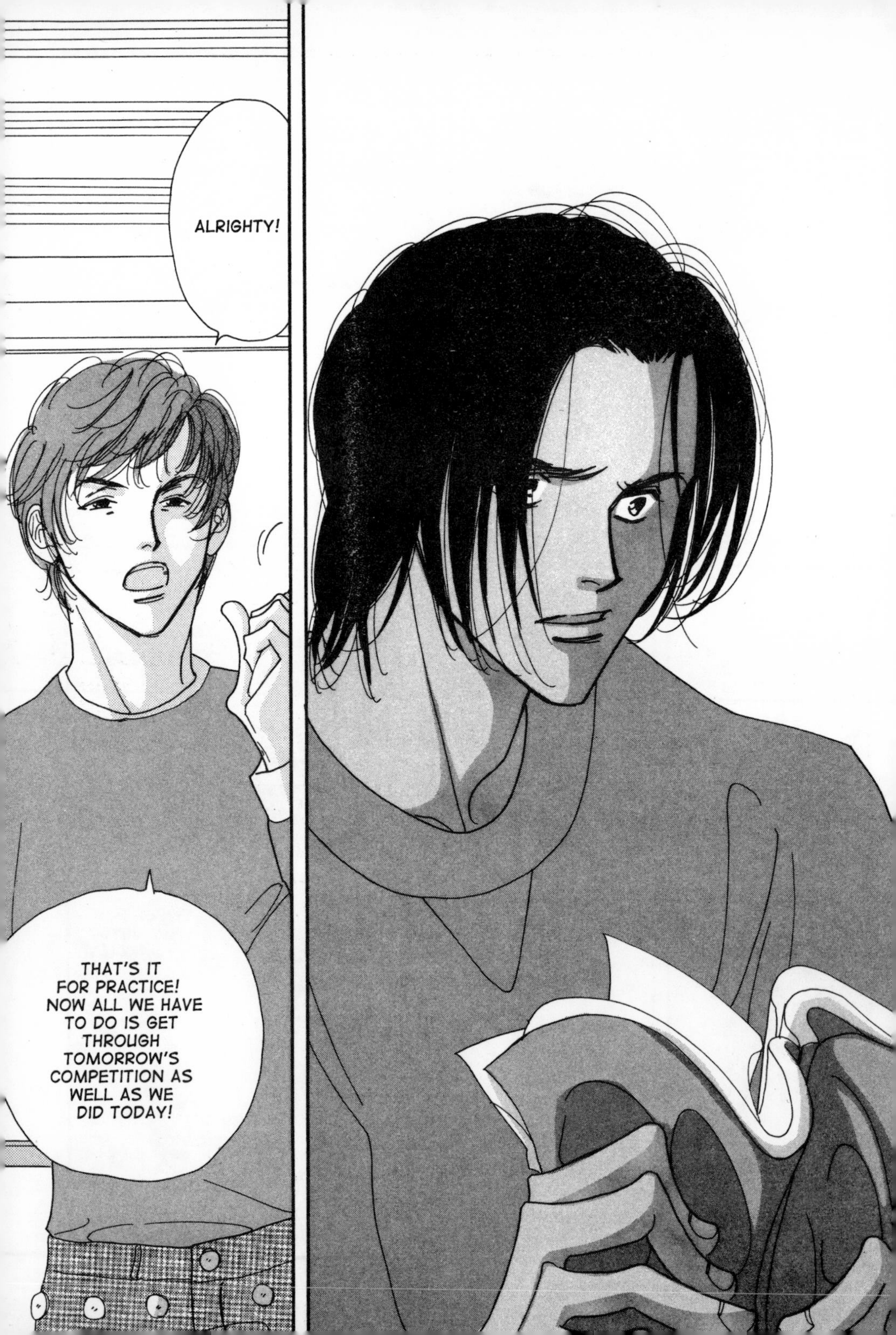
ALRIGHTY!
THAT'S IT FOR PRACTICE! NOW ALL WE HAVE TO DO IS GET THROUGH TOMORROW'S COMPETITION AS WELL AS WE DID TODAY!

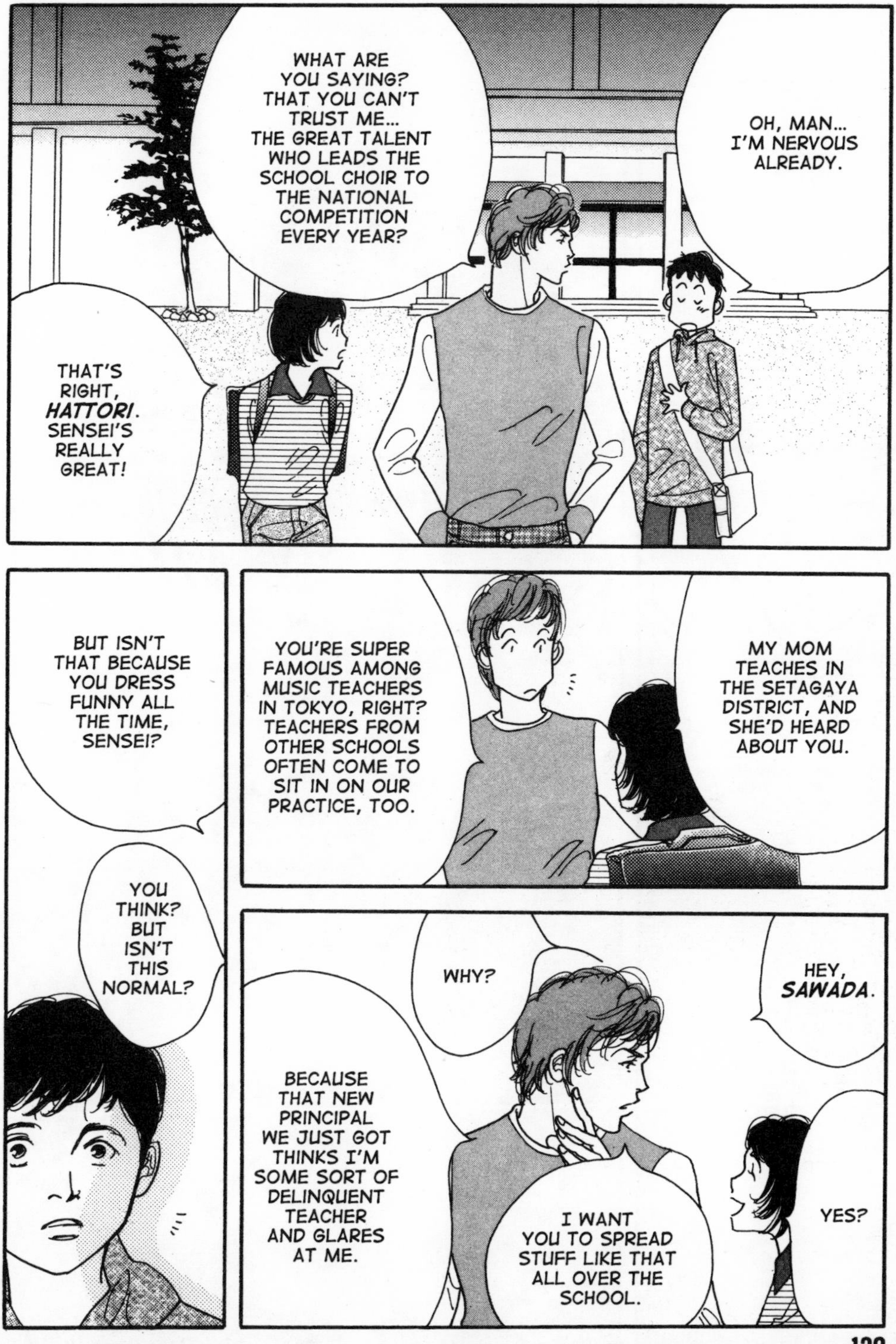
OH, MAN... I'M NERVOUS ALREADY.
WHAT ARE YOU SAYING? THAT YOU CAN'T TRUST ME... THE GREAT TALENT WHO LEADS THE SCHOOL CHOIR TO THE NATIONAL COMPETITION EVERY YEAR?
THAT'S RIGHT, ***HATTORI***. SENSEI'S REALLY GREAT!
MY MOM TEACHES IN THE SETAGAYA DISTRICT, AND SHE'D HEARD ABOUT YOU.
YOU'RE SUPER FAMOUS AMONG MUSIC TEACHERS IN TOKYO, RIGHT? TEACHERS FROM OTHER SCHOOLS OFTEN COME TO SIT IN ON OUR PRACTICE, TOO.
HEY, ***SAWADA***.
YES?
I WANT YOU TO SPREAD STUFF LIKE THAT ALL OVER THE SCHOOL.
WHY?
BECAUSE THAT NEW PRINCIPAL WE JUST GOT THINKS I'M SOME SORT OF DELINQUENT TEACHER AND GLARES AT ME.
BUT ISN'T THAT BECAUSE YOU DRESS FUNNY ALL THE TIME, SENSEI?
YOU THINK? BUT ISN'T THIS NORMAL?

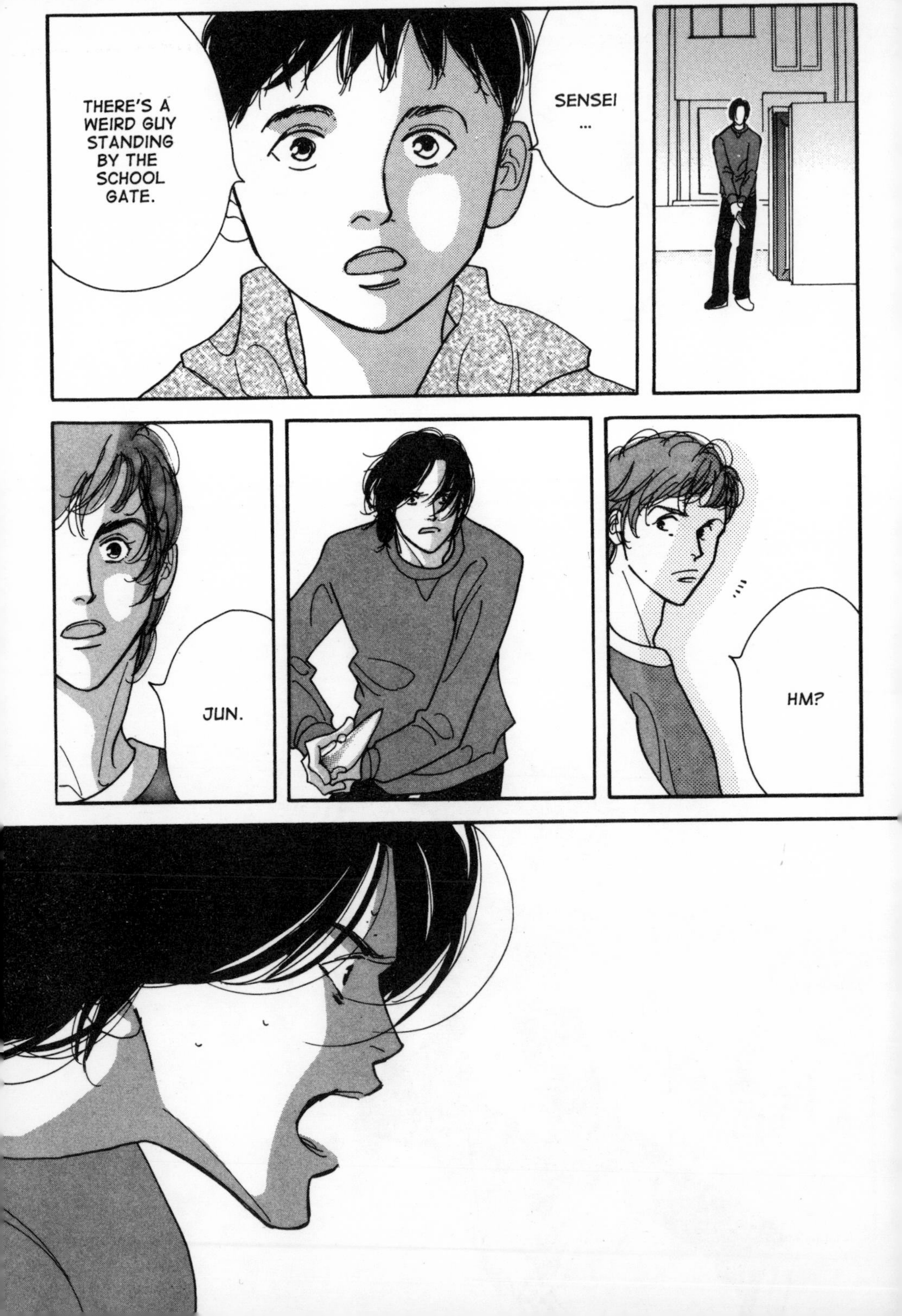
SENSEI ...
THERE'S A WEIRD GUY STANDING BY THE SCHOOL GATE.
HM?
JUN.

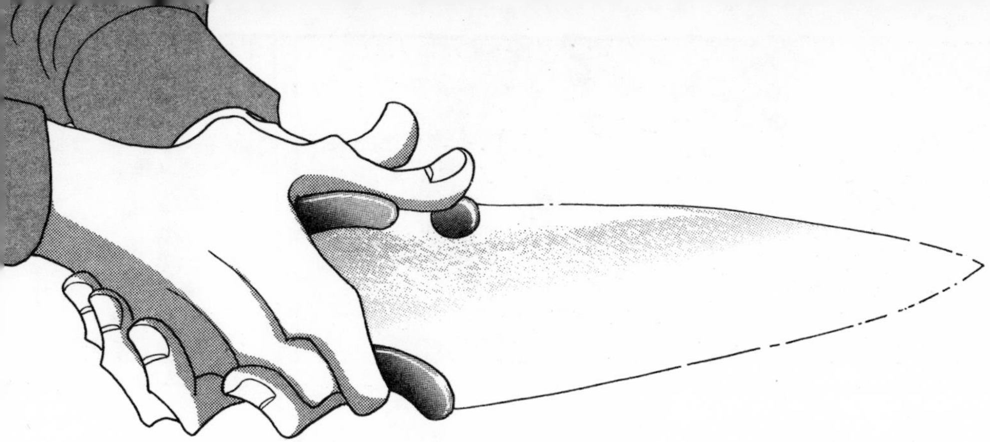
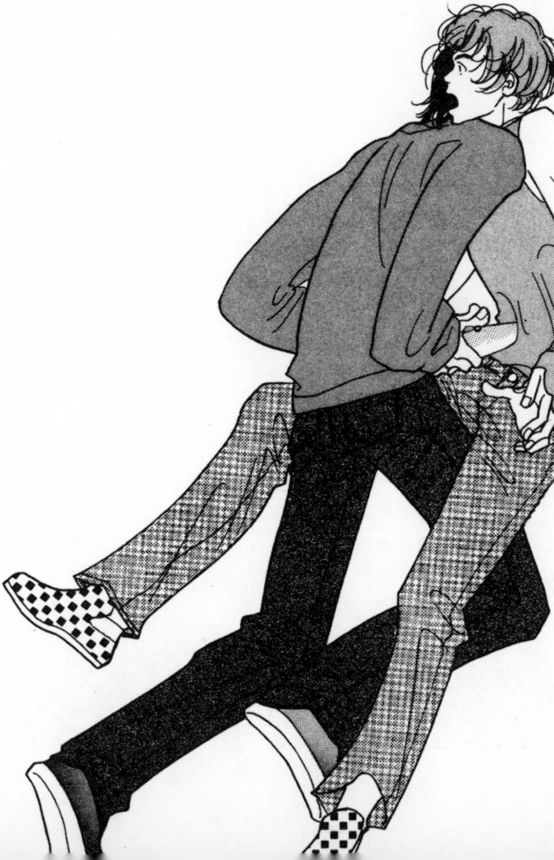

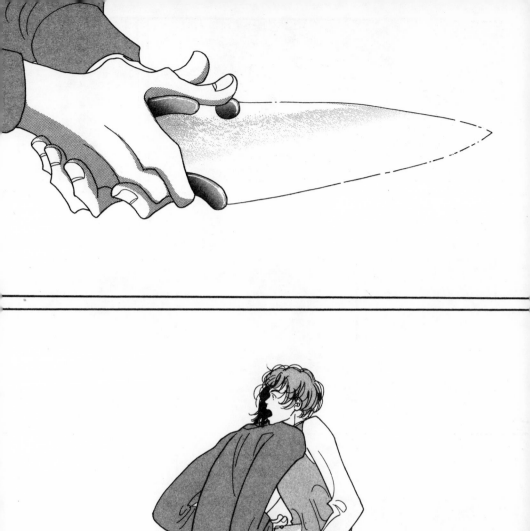

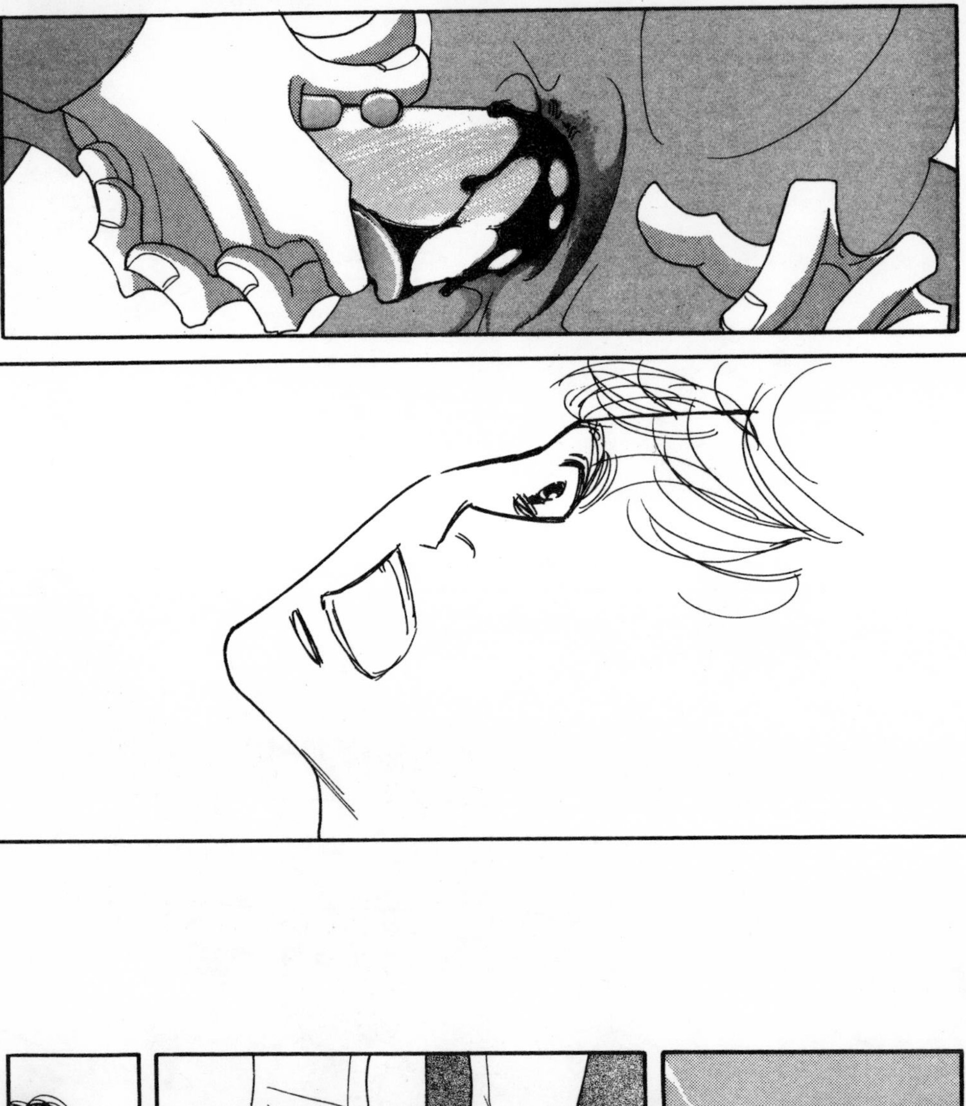
WHOOOSH
Narita Terminal
TAP

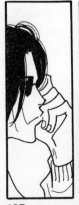

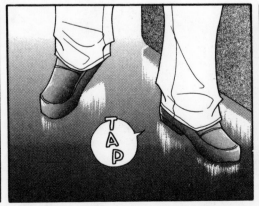

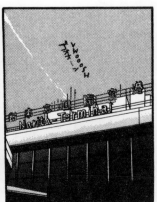

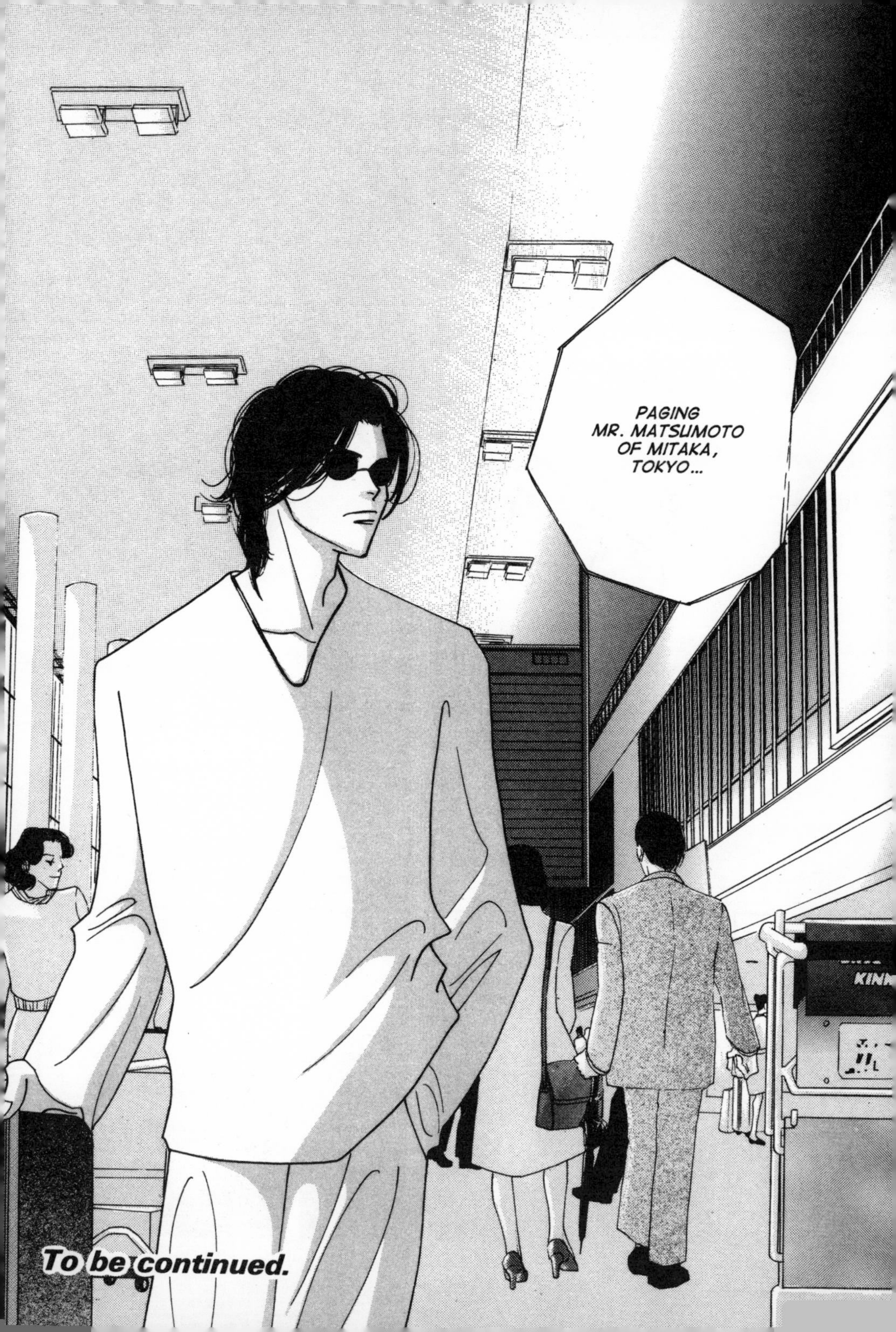
PAGING MR. MATSUMOTO OF MITAKA, TOKYO...
KINK
To be continued.

ソルフェージュ
SOLFÈGE
CURTAIN CALL

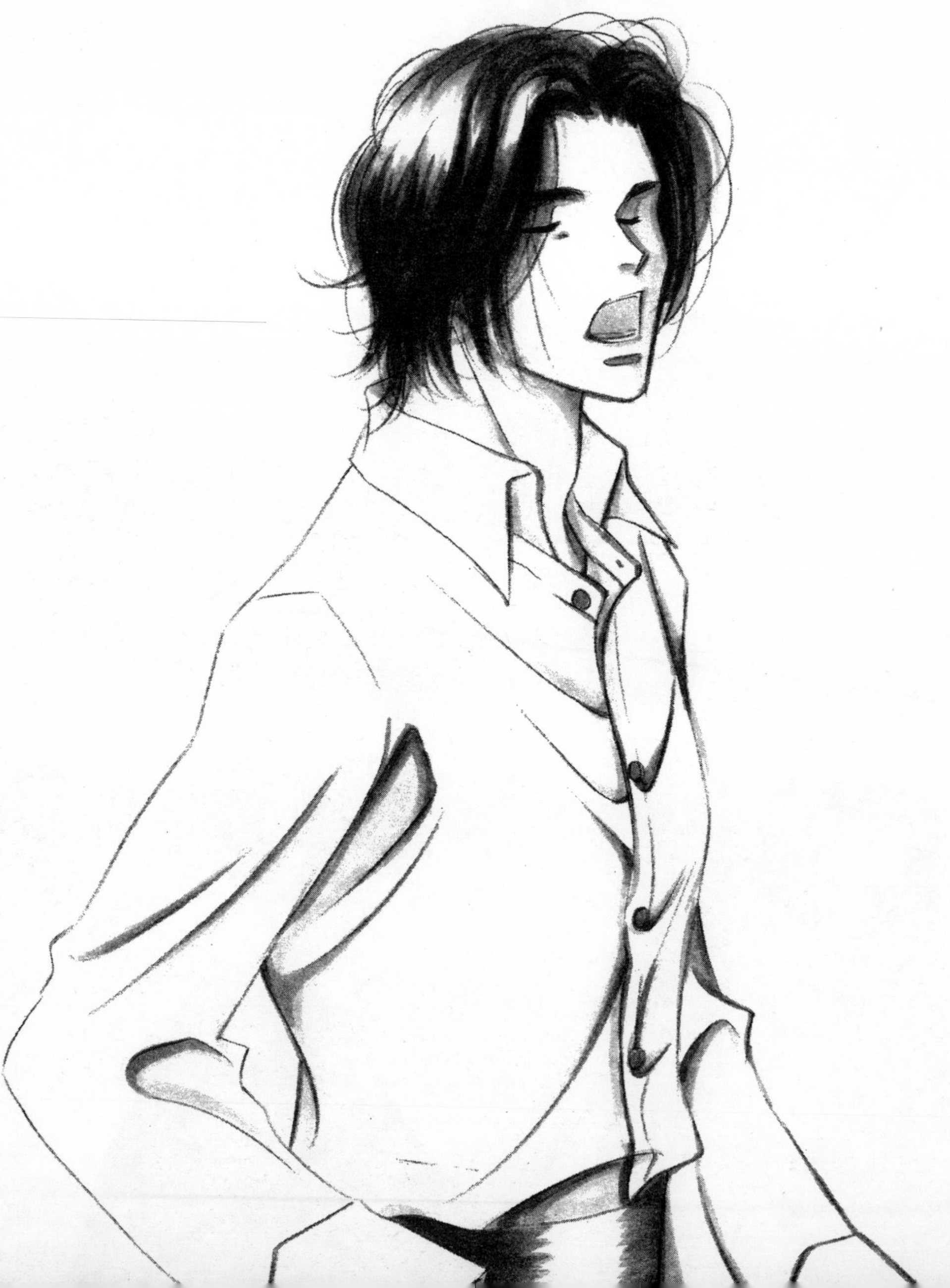

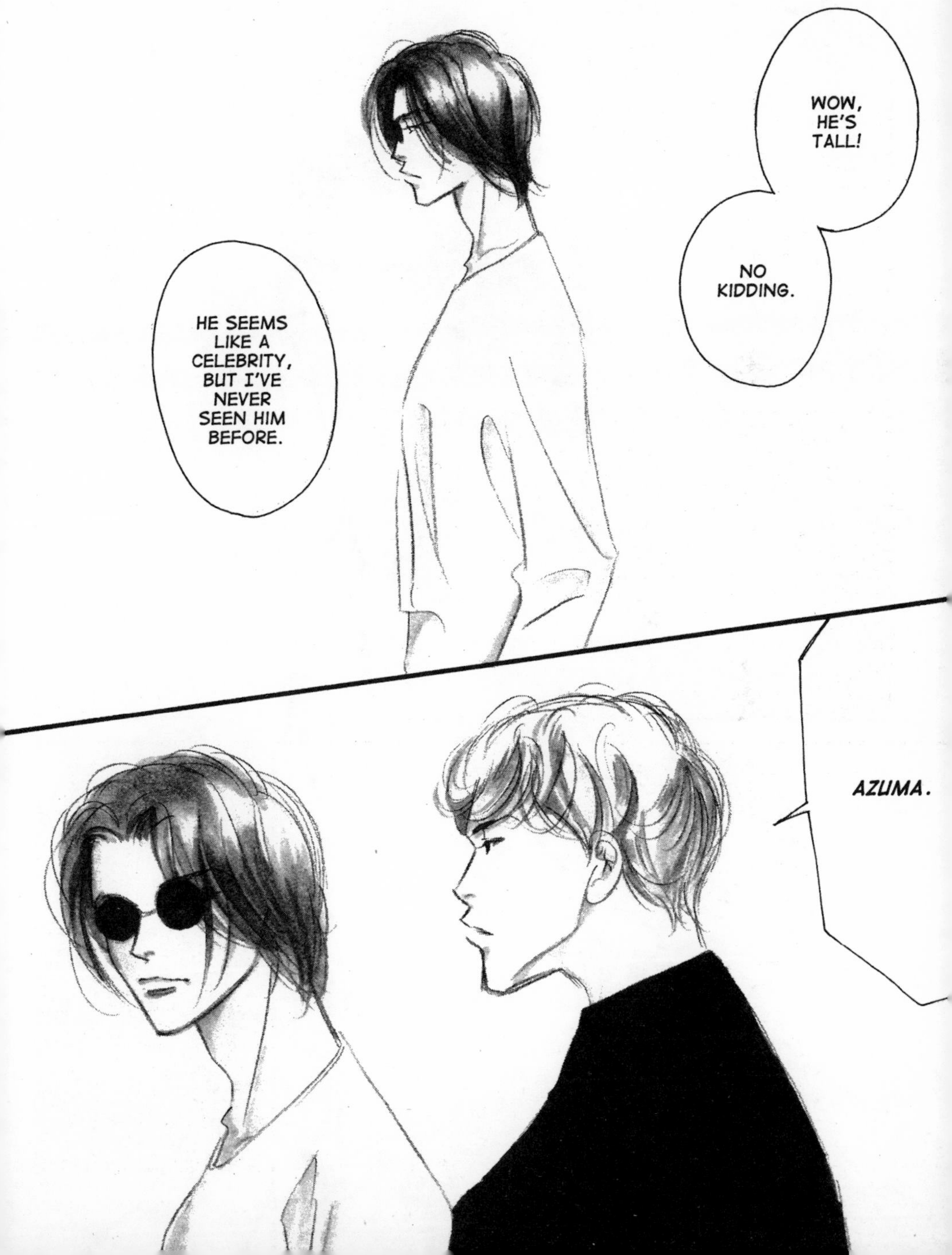
WOW, HE'S TALL!
NO KIDDING.
HE SEEMS LIKE A CELEBRITY, BUT I'VE NEVER SEEN HIM BEFORE.
AZUMA.

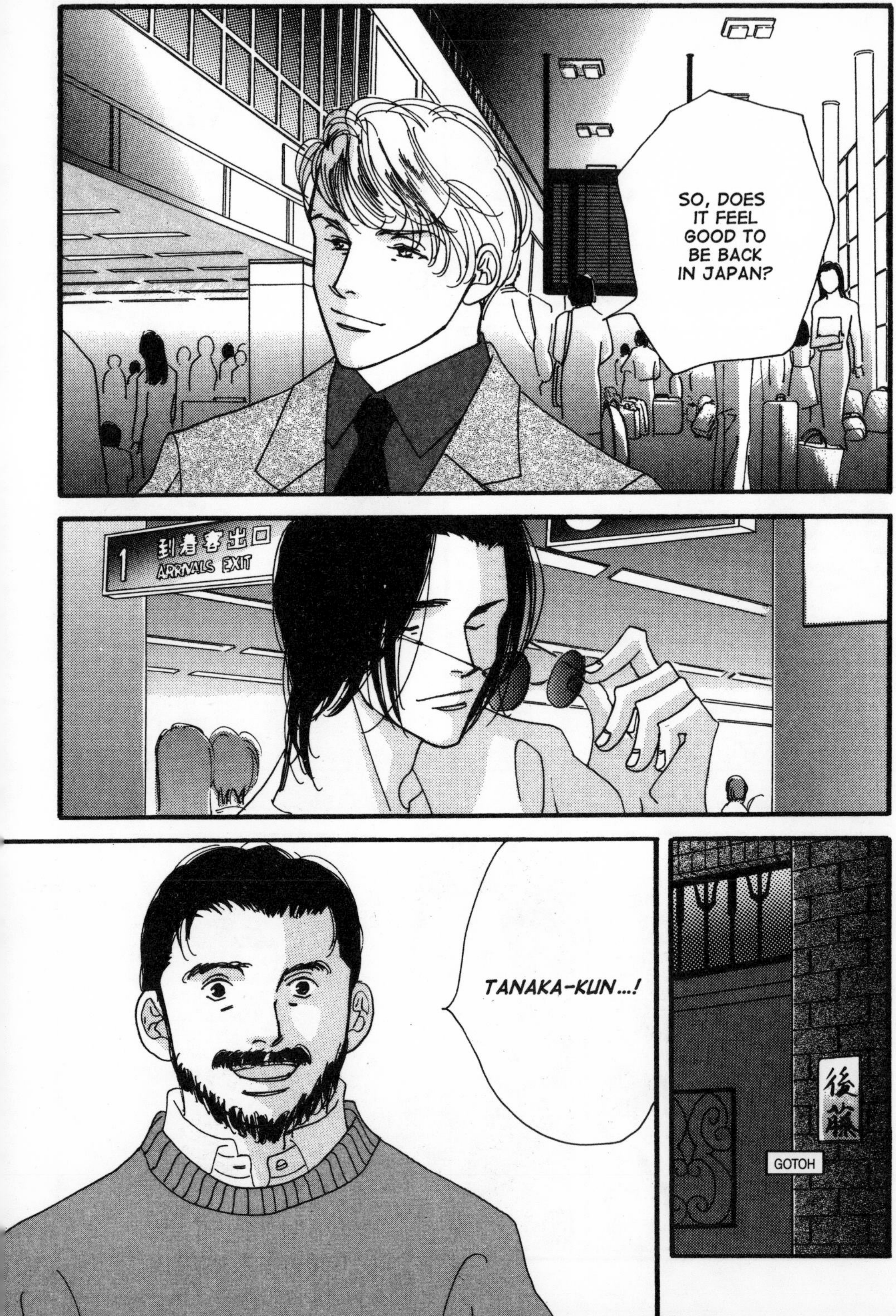
SO, DOES IT FEEL GOOD TO BE BACK IN JAPAN?
1 到着客出口 ARRIVALS EXIT
後藤
GOTOH
TANAKA-KUN...!

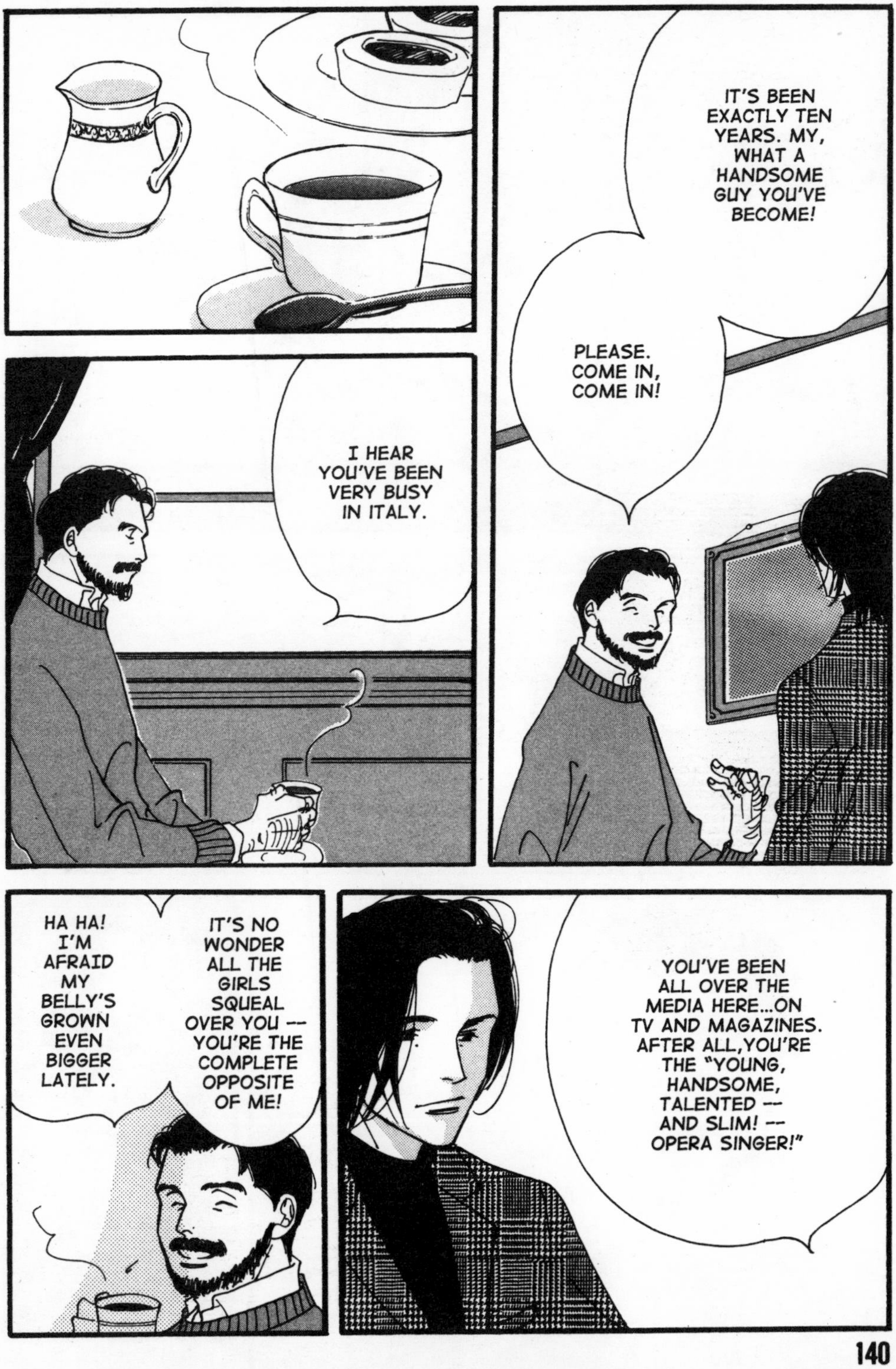
IT'S BEEN EXACTLY TEN YEARS. MY, WHAT A HANDSOME GUY YOU'VE BECOME!
PLEASE. COME IN, COME IN!
I HEAR YOU'VE BEEN VERY BUSY IN ITALY.
YOU'VE BEEN ALL OVER THE MEDIA HERE...ON TV AND MAGAZINES. AFTER ALL,YOU'RE THE "YOUNG, HANDSOME, TALENTED -- AND SLIM! -- OPERA SINGER!"
IT'S NO WONDER ALL THE GIRLS SQUEAL OVER YOU -- YOU'RE THE COMPLETE OPPOSITE OF ME!
HA HA! I'M AFRAID MY BELLY'S GROWN EVEN BIGGER LATELY.

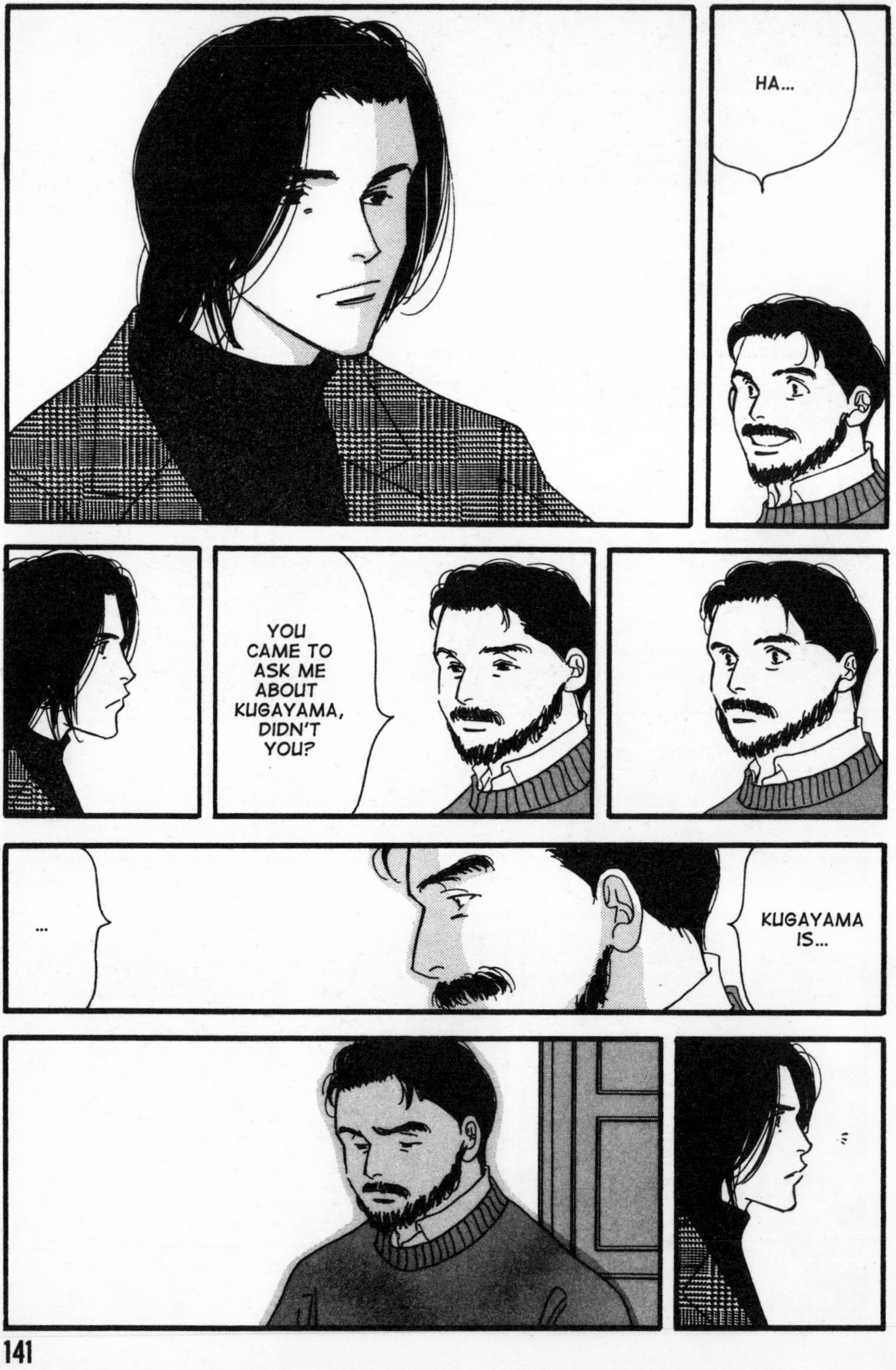
HA...
YOU CAME TO ASK ME ABOUT KUGAYAMA, DIDN'T YOU?
KUGAYAMA IS...
...

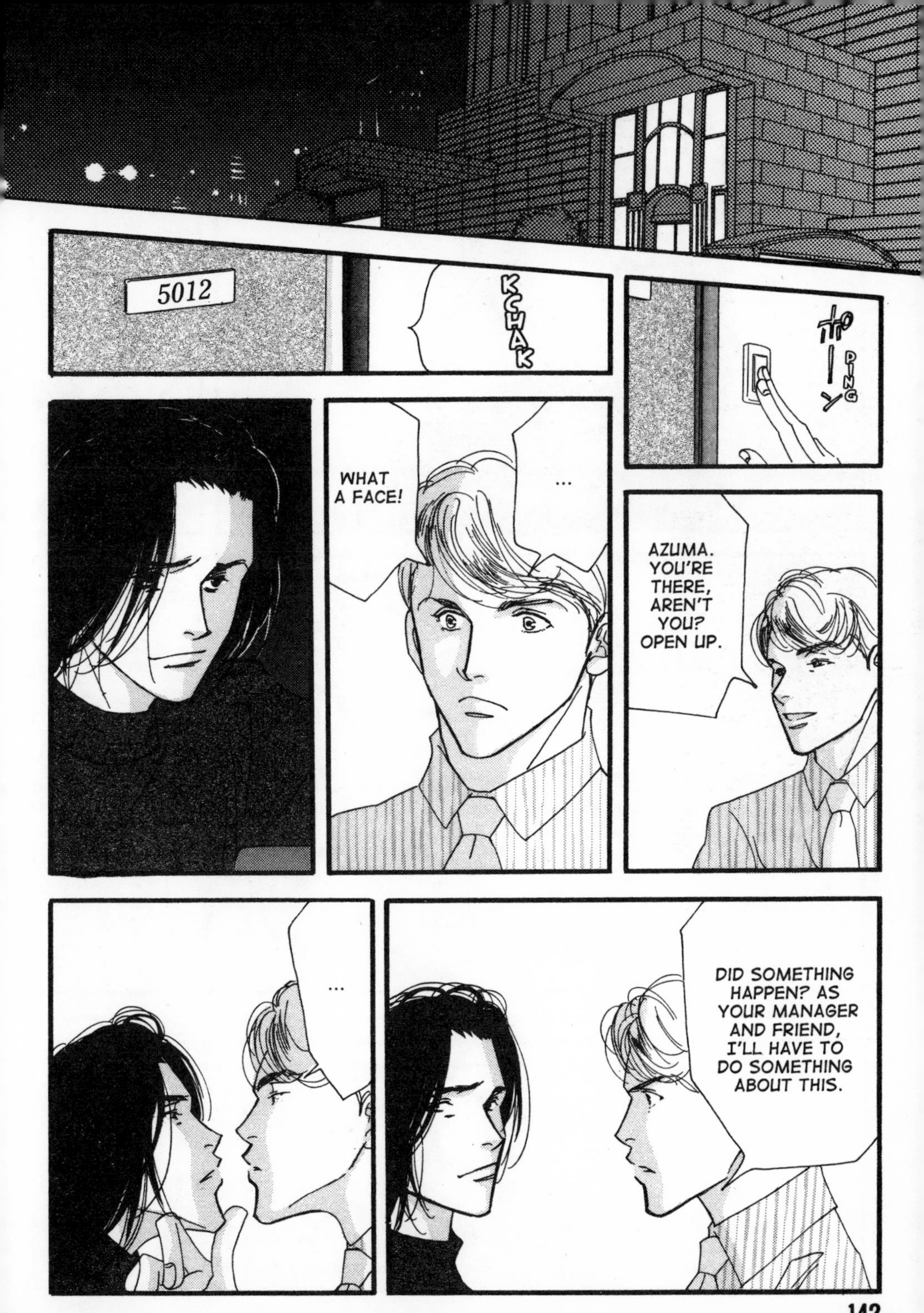
PING
KCHAK
5012
AZUMA. YOU'RE THERE, AREN'T YOU? OPEN UP.
...
WHAT A FACE!
DID SOMETHING HAPPEN? AS YOUR MANAGER AND FRIEND, I'LL HAVE TO DO SOMETHING ABOUT THIS.
...

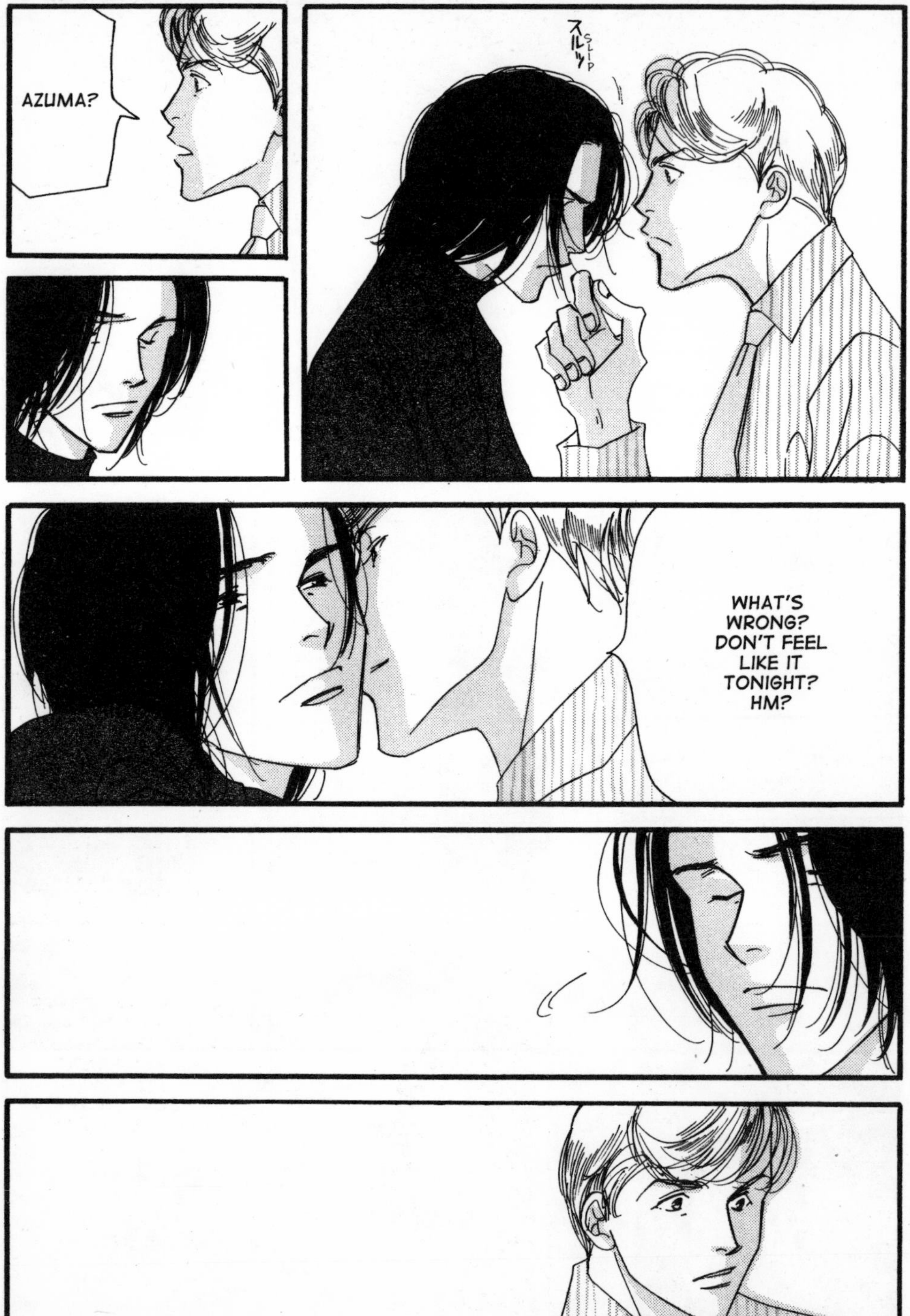
スルッ SLIP
AZUMA?
WHAT'S WRONG? DON'T FEEL LIKE IT TONIGHT? HM?

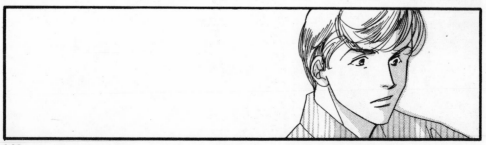

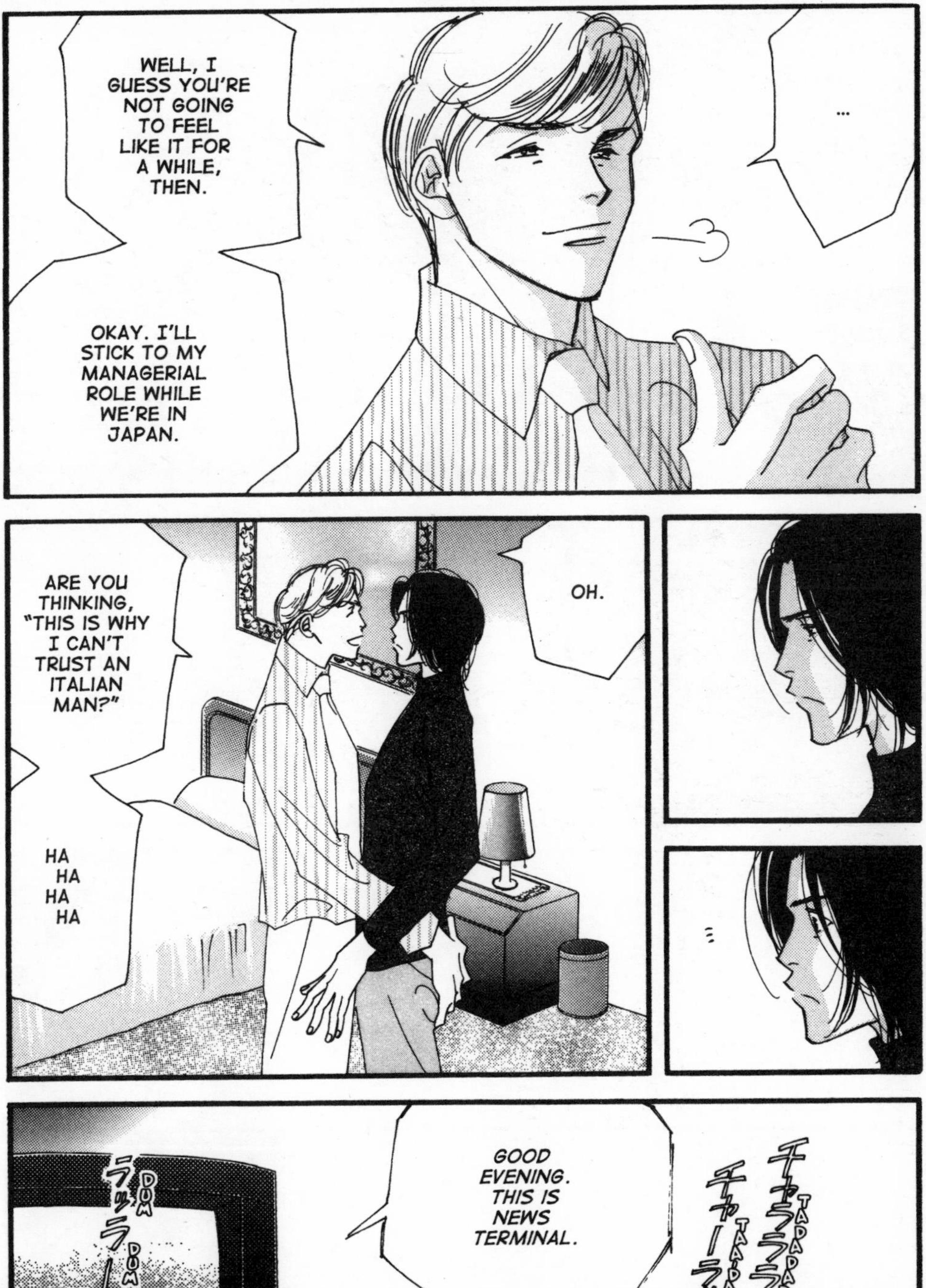
...
WELL, I GUESS YOU'RE NOT GOING TO FEEL LIKE IT FOR A WHILE, THEN.
OKAY. I'LL STICK TO MY MANAGERIAL ROLE WHILE WE'RE IN JAPAN.
OH.
ARE YOU THINKING, "THIS IS WHY I CAN'T TRUST AN ITALIAN MAN?"
HA HA HA HA
チャラララ
TADADADA
チャーラッラー
TAADA DUM
GOOD EVENING. THIS IS NEWS TERMINAL.
ラッラー
DUM DUM

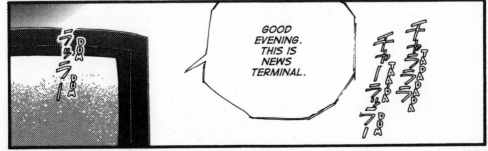

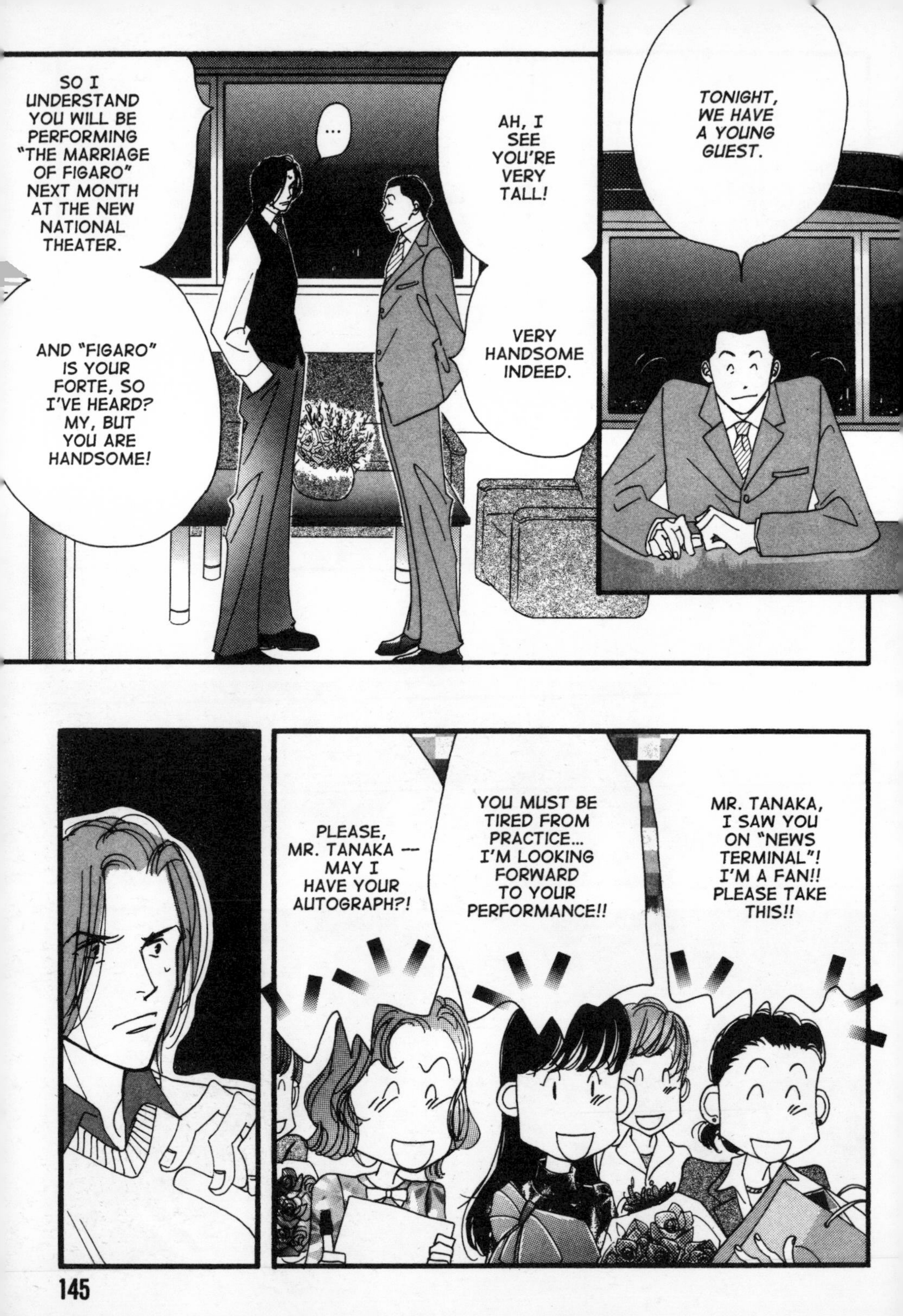
TONIGHT, WE HAVE A YOUNG GUEST.
AH, I SEE YOU'RE VERY TALL!
VERY HANDSOME INDEED.
...
SO I UNDERSTAND YOU WILL BE PERFORMING "THE MARRIAGE OF FIGARO" NEXT MONTH AT THE NEW NATIONAL THEATER.
AND "FIGARO" IS YOUR FORTE, SO I'VE HEARD? MY, BUT YOU ARE HANDSOME!
MR. TANAKA, I SAW YOU ON "NEWS TERMINAL"! I'M A FAN!! PLEASE TAKE THIS!!
YOU MUST BE TIRED FROM PRACTICE... I'M LOOKING FORWARD TO YOUR PERFORMANCE!!
PLEASE, MR. TANAKA -- MAY I HAVE YOUR AUTOGRAPH?!

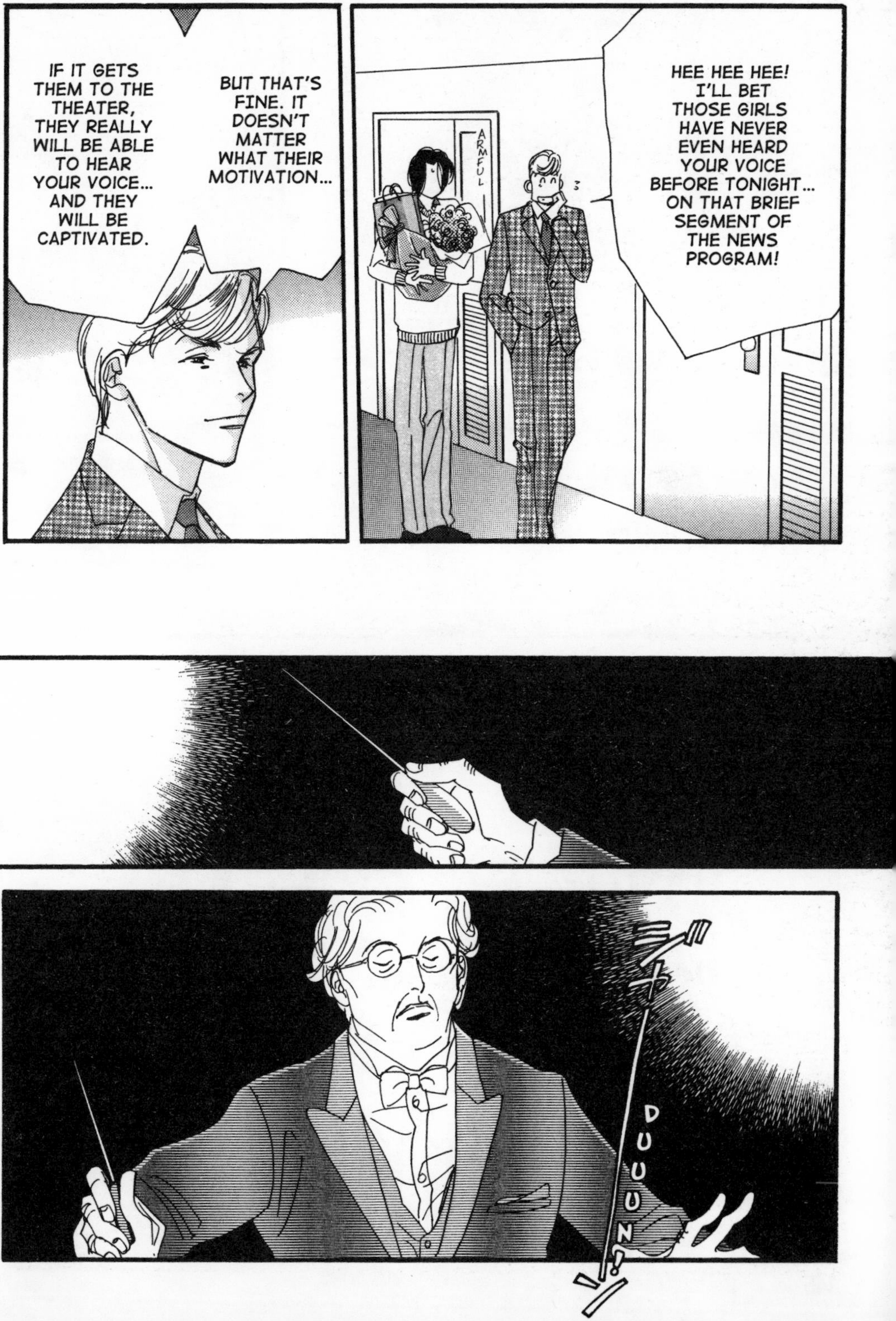
HEE HEE HEE! I'LL BET THOSE GIRLS HAVE NEVER EVEN HEARD YOUR VOICE BEFORE TONIGHT... ON THAT BRIEF SEGMENT OF THE NEWS PROGRAM!
ARMFUL
BUT THAT'S FINE. IT DOESN'T MATTER WHAT THEIR MOTIVATION...
IF IT GETS THEM TO THE THEATER, THEY REALLY WILL BE ABLE TO HEAR YOUR VOICE... AND THEY WILL BE CAPTIVATED.
DUUUN!

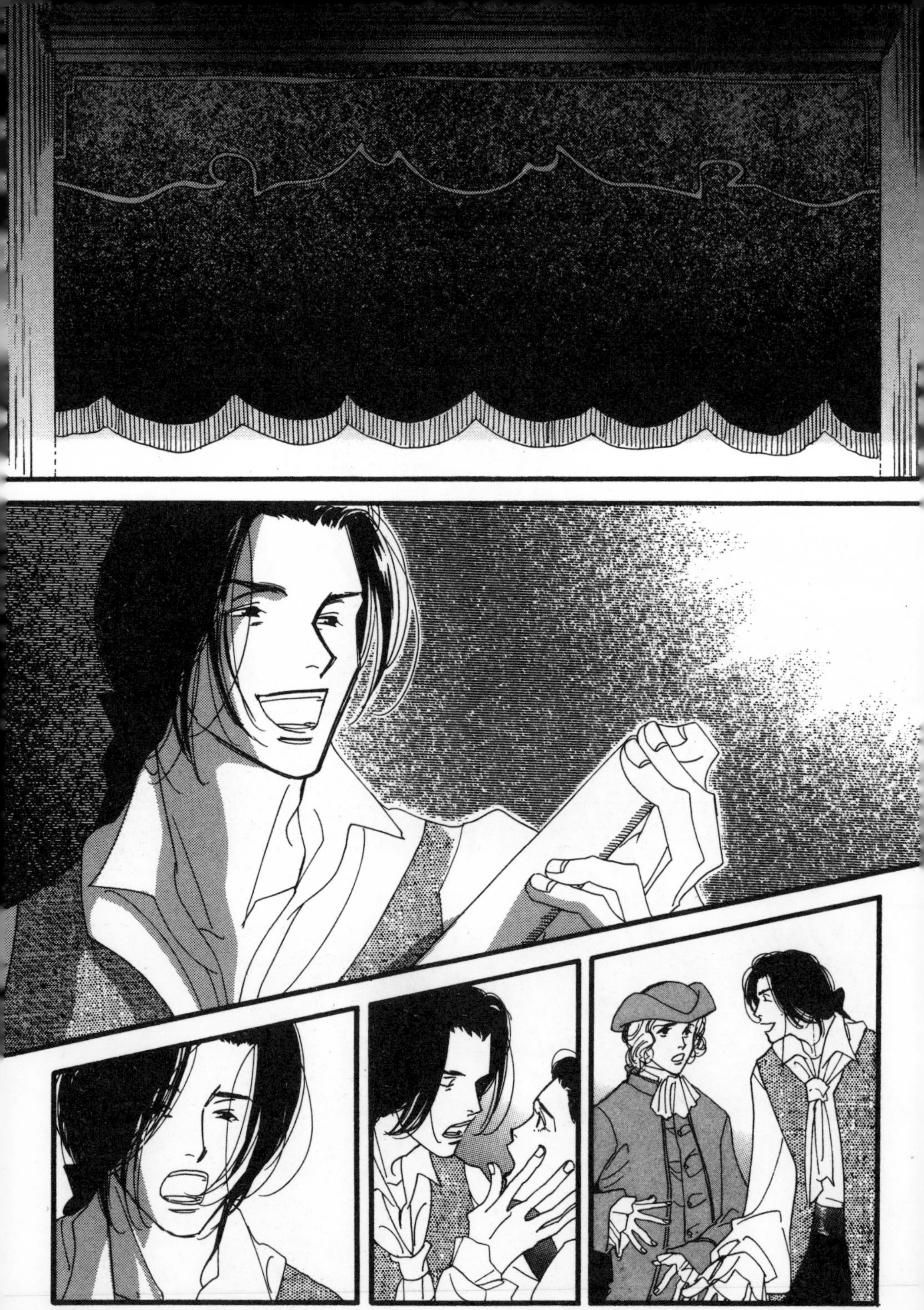

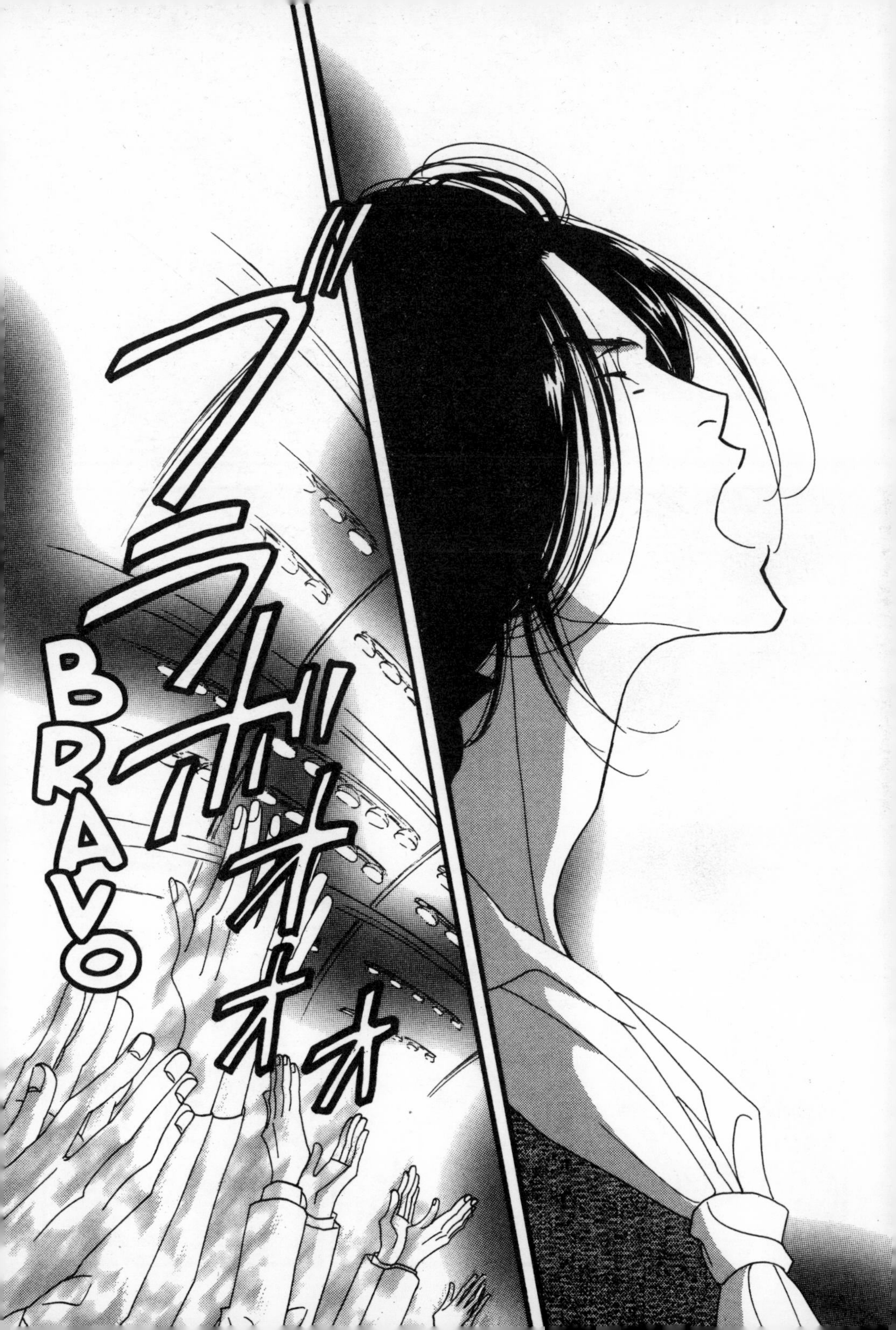
ブラボオオオ
BRAVO

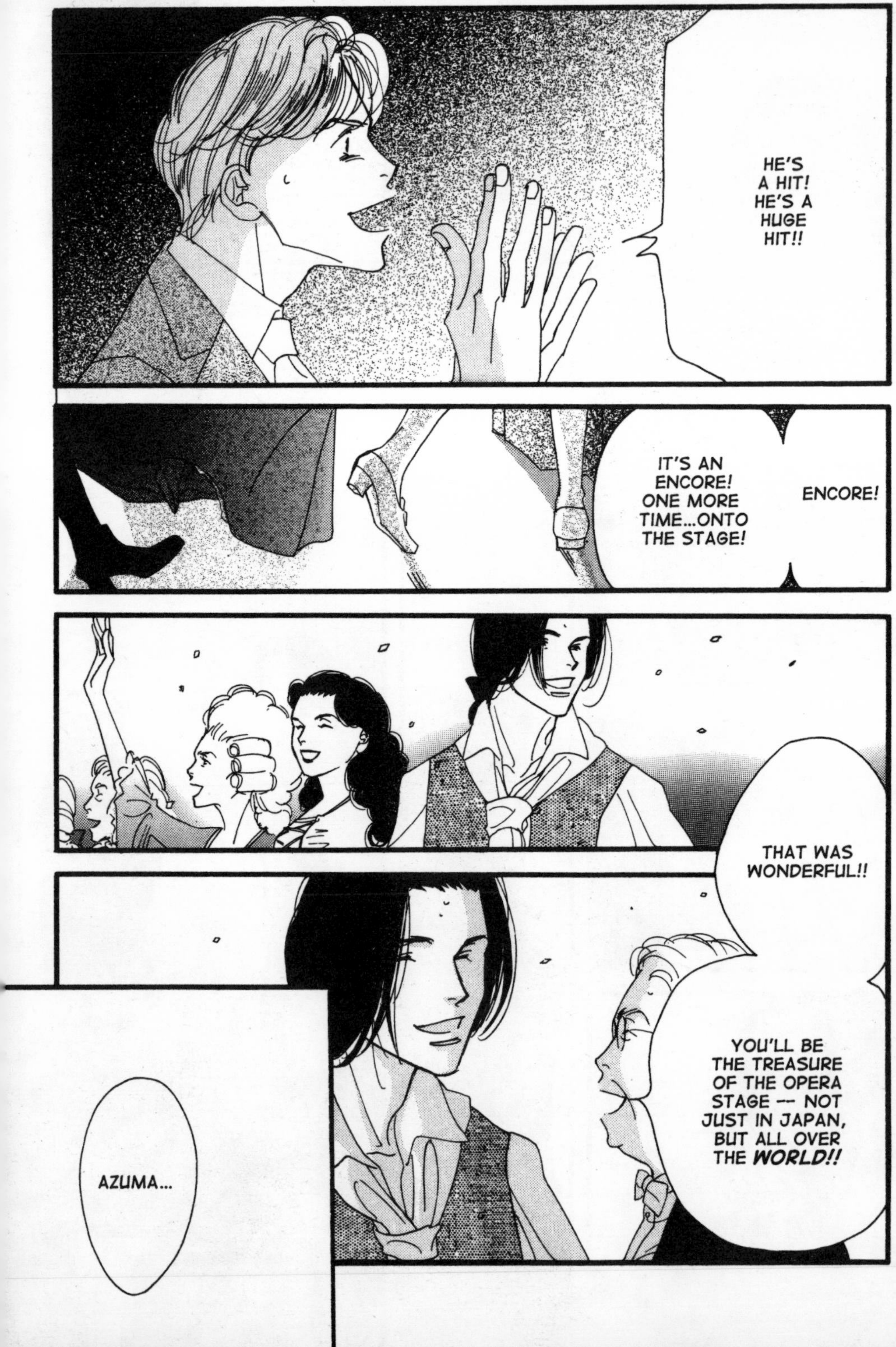
HE'S A HIT! HE'S A HUGE HIT!!
ENCORE!
IT'S AN ENCORE! ONE MORE TIME...ONTO THE STAGE!
THAT WAS WONDERFUL!!
YOU'LL BE THE TREASURE OF THE OPERA STAGE -- NOT JUST IN JAPAN, BUT ALL OVER THE ***WORLD!!***
AZUMA...

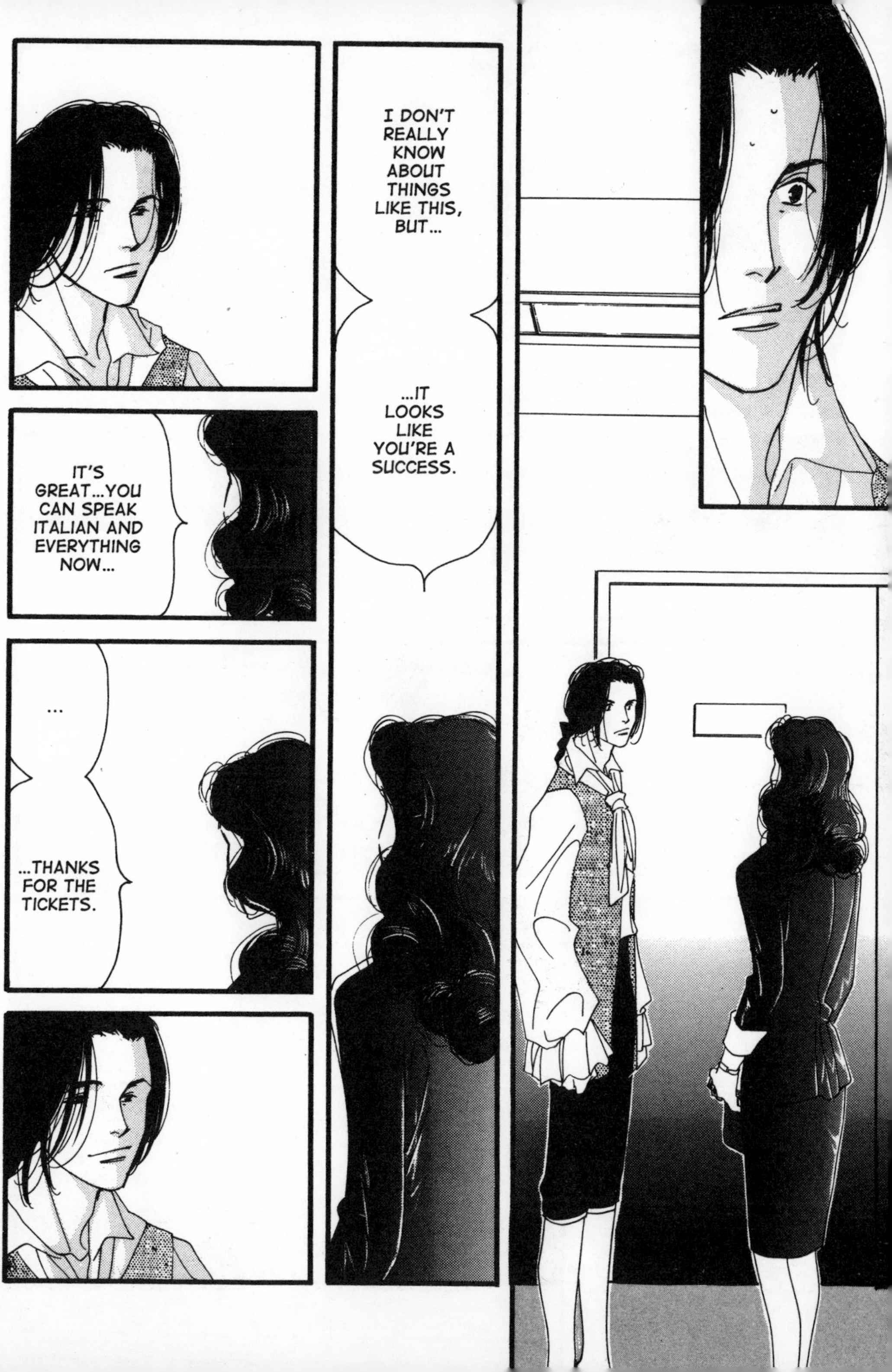
I DON'T REALLY KNOW ABOUT THINGS LIKE THIS, BUT...
...IT LOOKS LIKE YOU'RE A SUCCESS.
IT'S GREAT...YOU CAN SPEAK ITALIAN AND EVERYTHING NOW...
...
...THANKS FOR THE TICKETS.

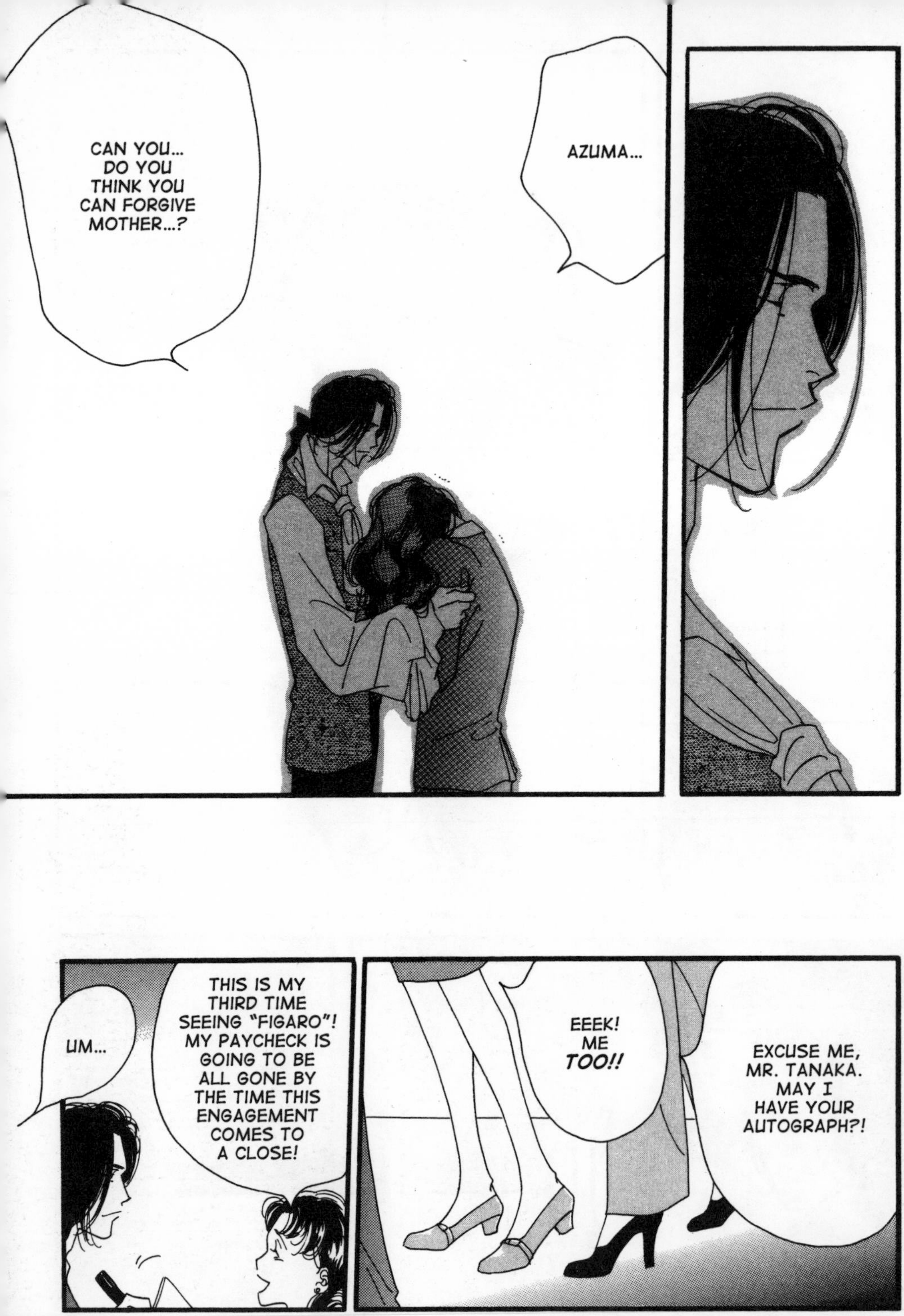
AZUMA...
CAN YOU... DO YOU THINK YOU CAN FORGIVE MOTHER...?
EXCUSE ME, MR. TANAKA. MAY I HAVE YOUR AUTOGRAPH?!
EEEK! ME *TOO!!*
THIS IS MY THIRD TIME SEEING "FIGARO"! MY PAYCHECK IS GOING TO BE ALL GONE BY THE TIME THIS ENGAGEMENT COMES TO A CLOSE!
UM...

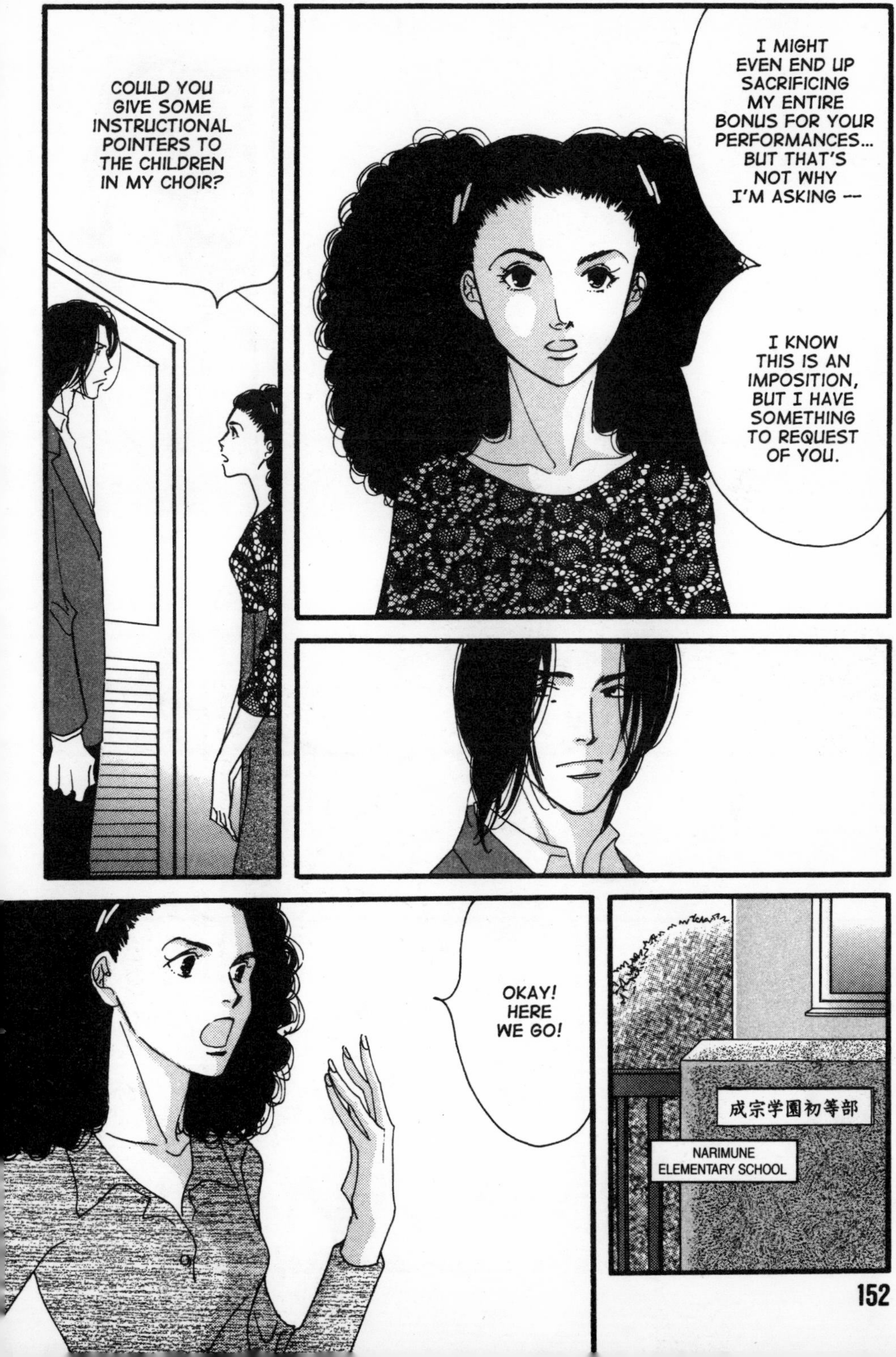
I MIGHT EVEN END UP SACRIFICING MY ENTIRE BONUS FOR YOUR PERFORMANCES... BUT THAT'S NOT WHY I'M ASKING --
I KNOW THIS IS AN IMPOSITION, BUT I HAVE SOMETHING TO REQUEST OF YOU.
COULD YOU GIVE SOME INSTRUCTIONAL POINTERS TO THE CHILDREN IN MY CHOIR?
成宗学園初等部
NARIMUNE ELEMENTARY SCHOOL
OKAY! HERE WE GO!

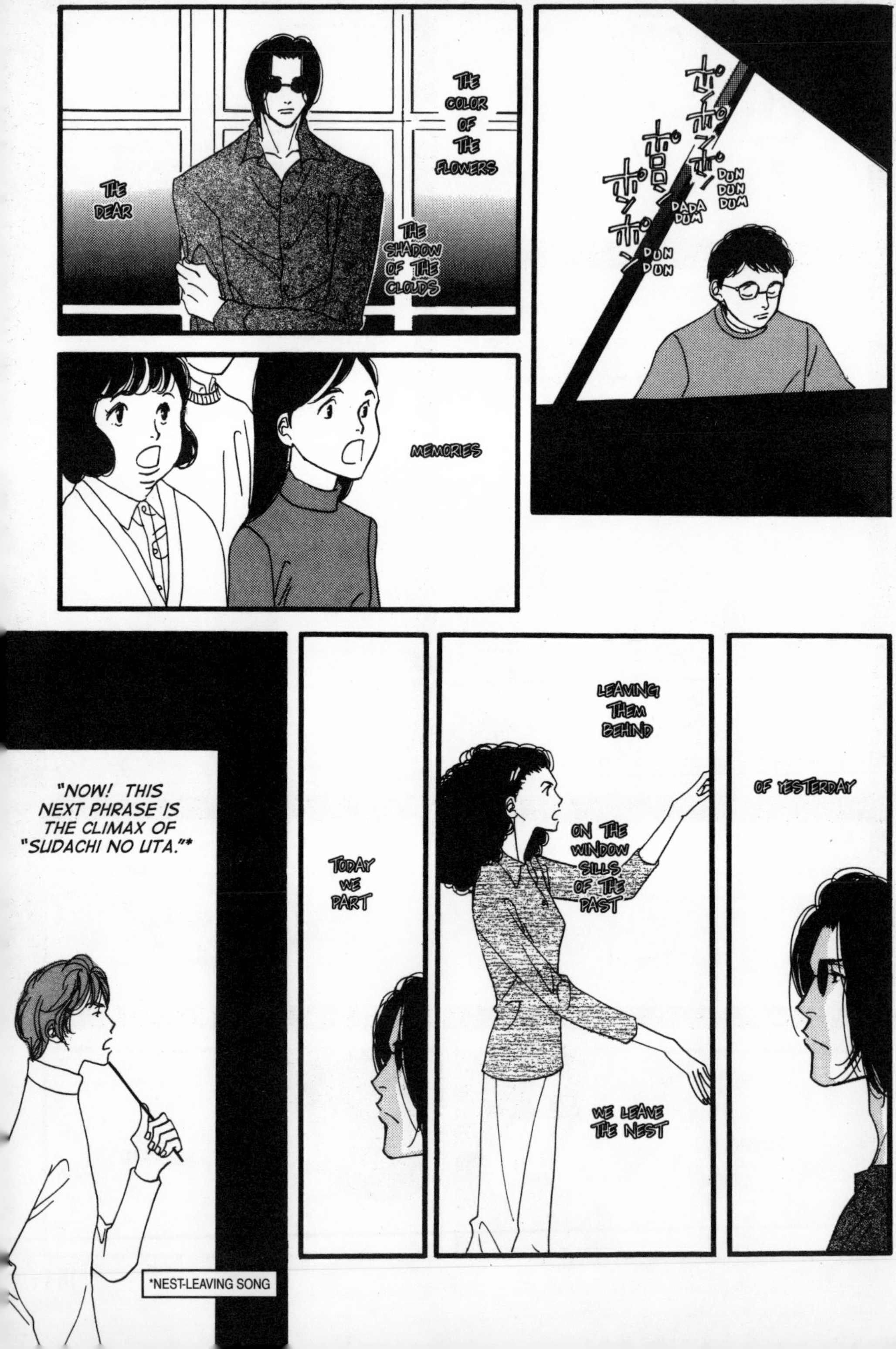
DUN DUN DUM
DADA DUM
DUN DUN
THE COLOR OF THE FLOWERS
THE SHADOW OF THE CLOUDS
THE DEAR
MEMORIES
OF YESTERDAY
LEAVING THEM BEHIND
ON THE WINDOW SILLS OF THE PAST
WE LEAVE THE NEST
TODAY WE PART
"NOW! THIS NEXT PHRASE IS THE CLIMAX OF "SUDACHI NO UTA."*
*NEST-LEAVING SONG

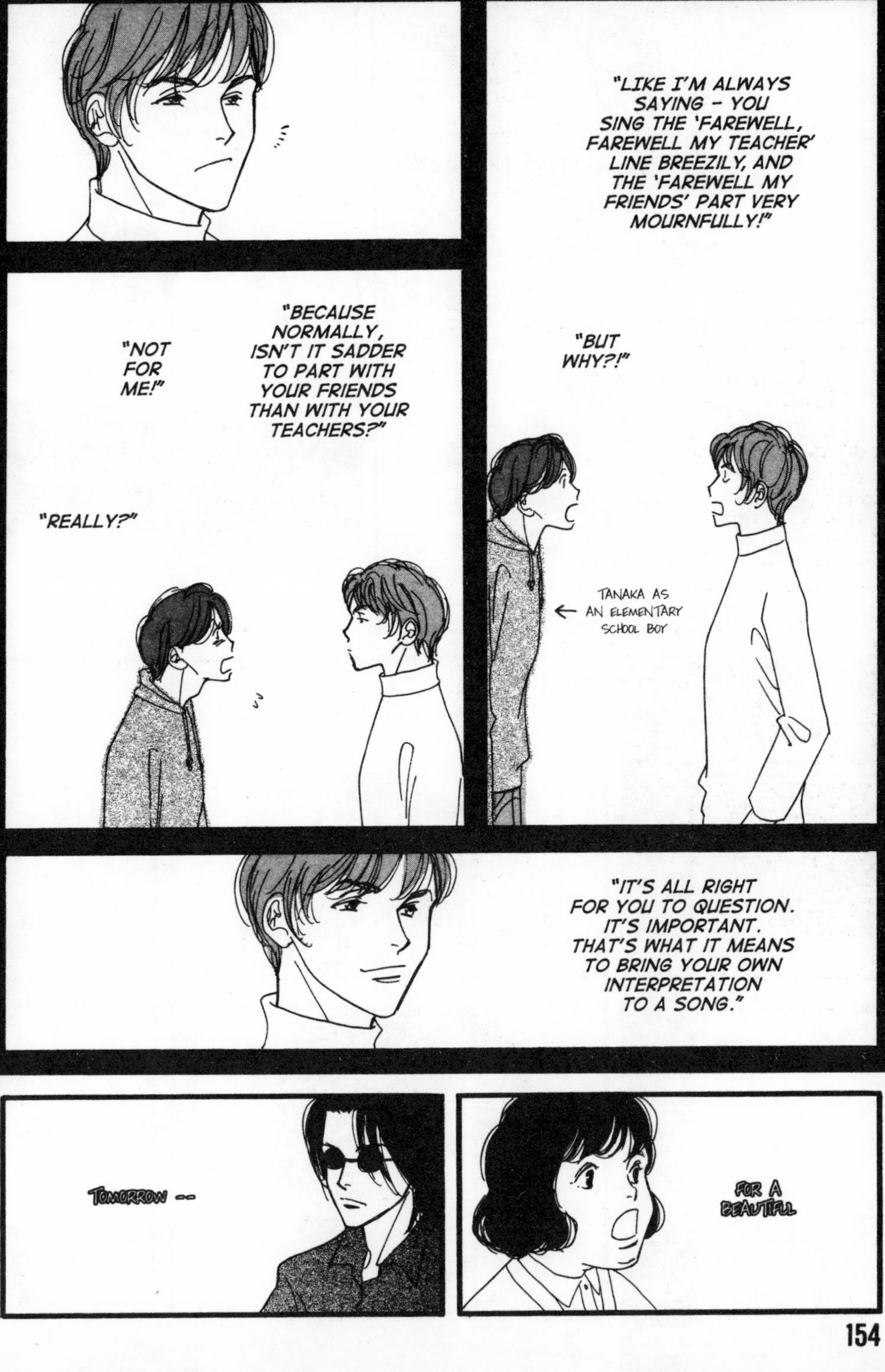
"LIKE I'M ALWAYS SAYING - YOU SING THE 'FAREWELL, FAREWELL MY TEACHER' LINE BREEZILY, AND THE 'FAREWELL MY FRIENDS' PART VERY MOURNFULLY!"
"BUT WHY?!"
TANAKA AS AN ELEMENTARY SCHOOL BOY
"BECAUSE NORMALLY, ISN'T IT SADDER TO PART WITH YOUR FRIENDS THAN WITH YOUR TEACHERS?"
"NOT FOR ME!"
"REALLY?"
"IT'S ALL RIGHT FOR YOU TO QUESTION. IT'S IMPORTANT. THAT'S WHAT IT MEANS TO BRING YOUR OWN INTERPRETATION TO A SONG."
FOR A BEAUTIFUL
TOMORROW --

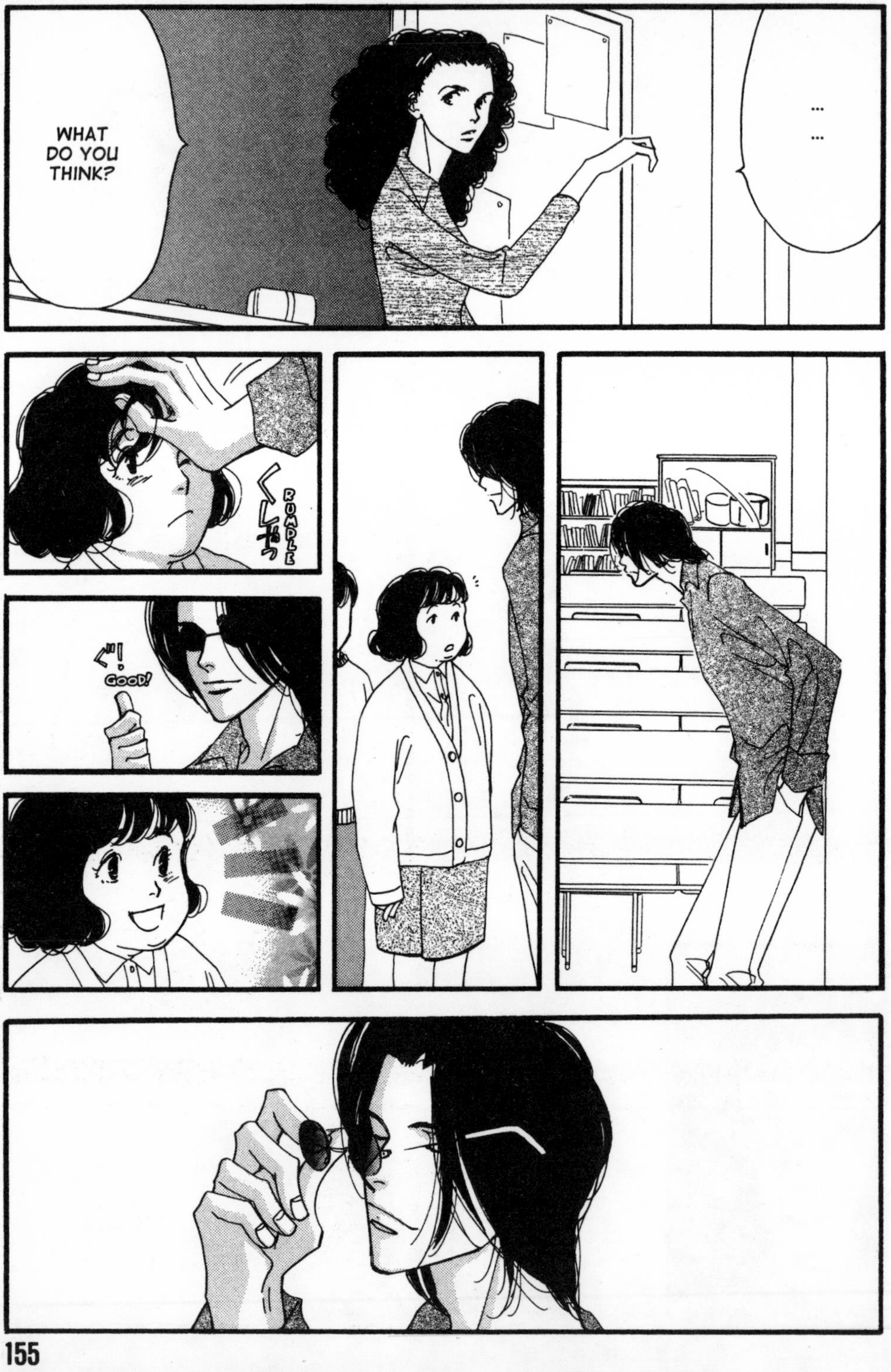
...
...
WHAT DO YOU THINK?
くしゃっ
RUMPLE
ぐ!
GOOD!

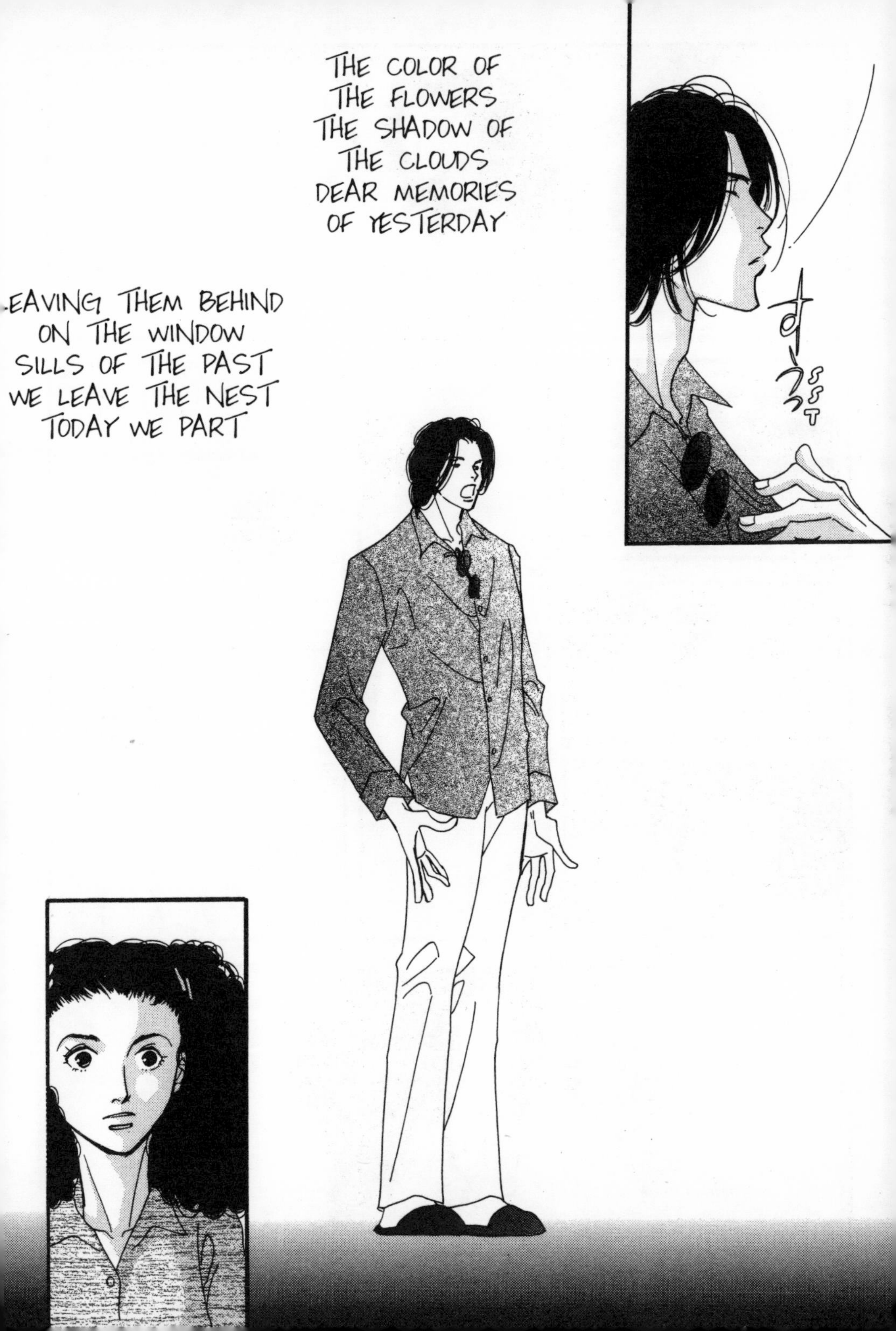
すーっ
SST
THE COLOR OF THE FLOWERS THE SHADOW OF THE CLOUDS DEAR MEMORIES OF YESTERDAY
EAVING THEM BEHIND ON THE WINDOW SILLS OF THE PAST WE LEAVE THE NEST TODAY WE PART

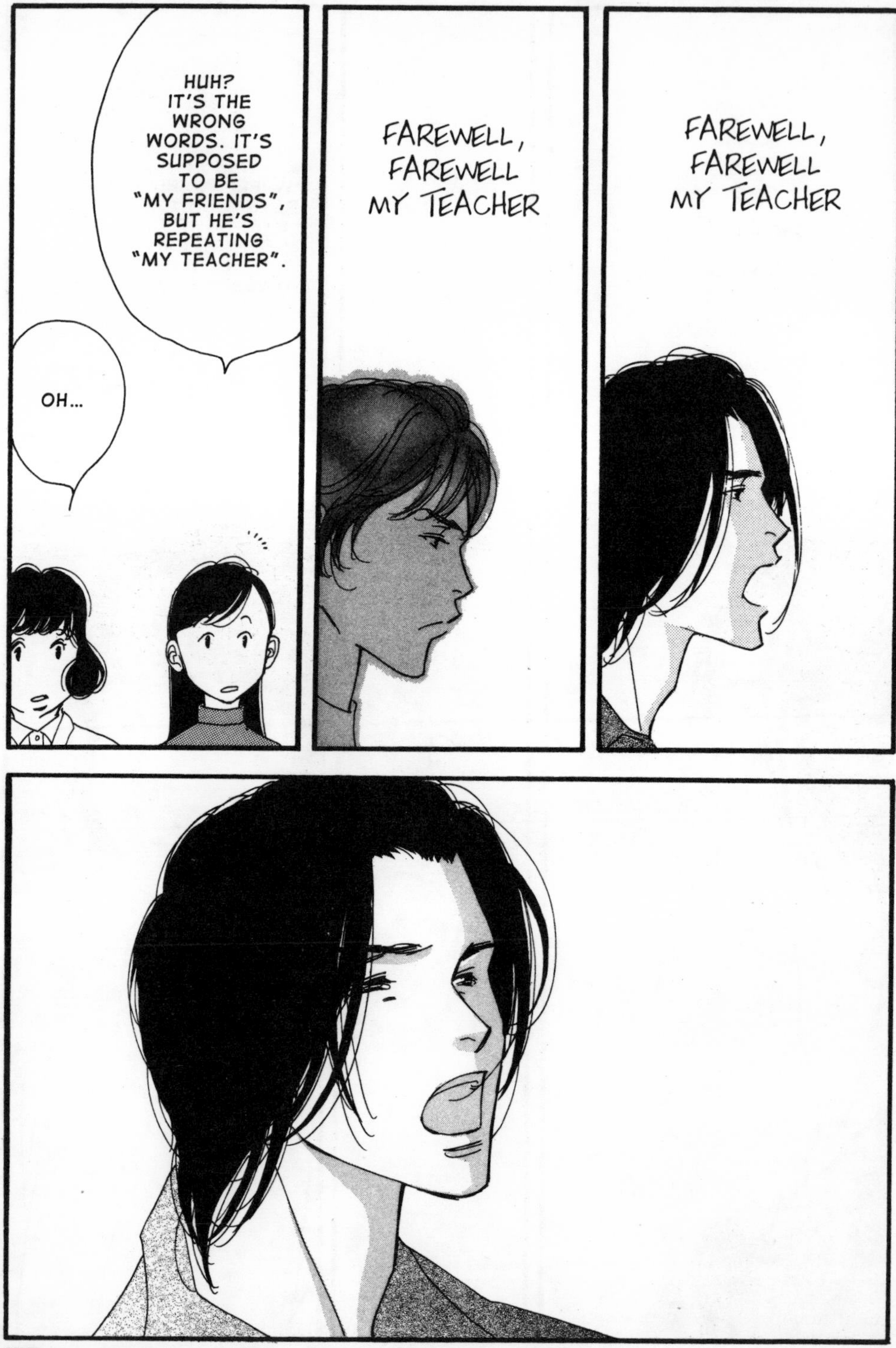
FAREWELL, FAREWELL MY TEACHER
FAREWELL, FAREWELL MY TEACHER
HUH? IT'S THE WRONG WORDS. IT'S SUPPOSED TO BE "MY FRIENDS", BUT HE'S REPEATING "MY TEACHER".
OH...

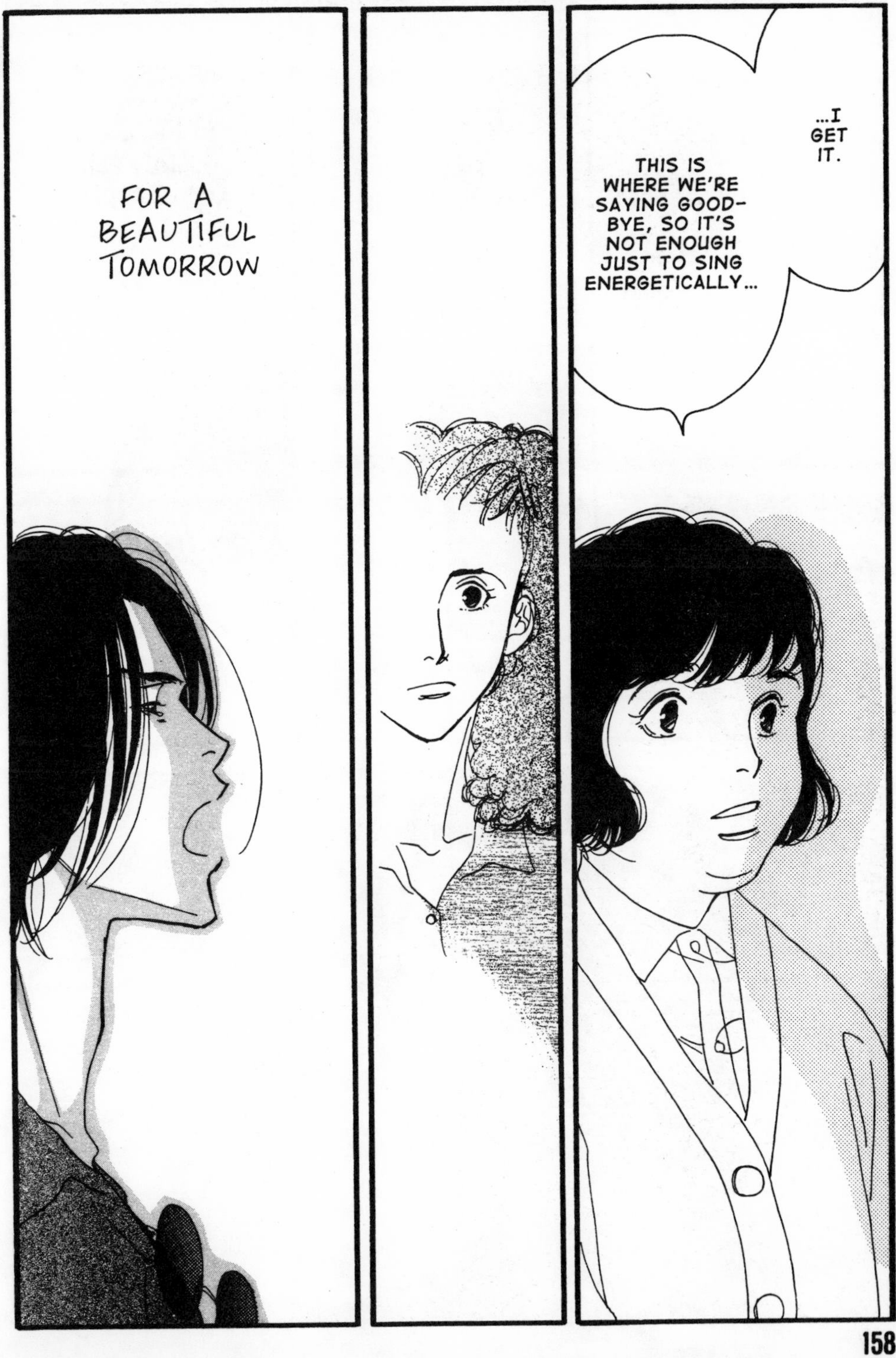
...I GET IT.
THIS IS WHERE WE'RE SAYING GOOD-BYE, SO IT'S NOT ENOUGH JUST TO SING ENERGETICALLY...
FOR A BEAUTIFUL TOMORROW

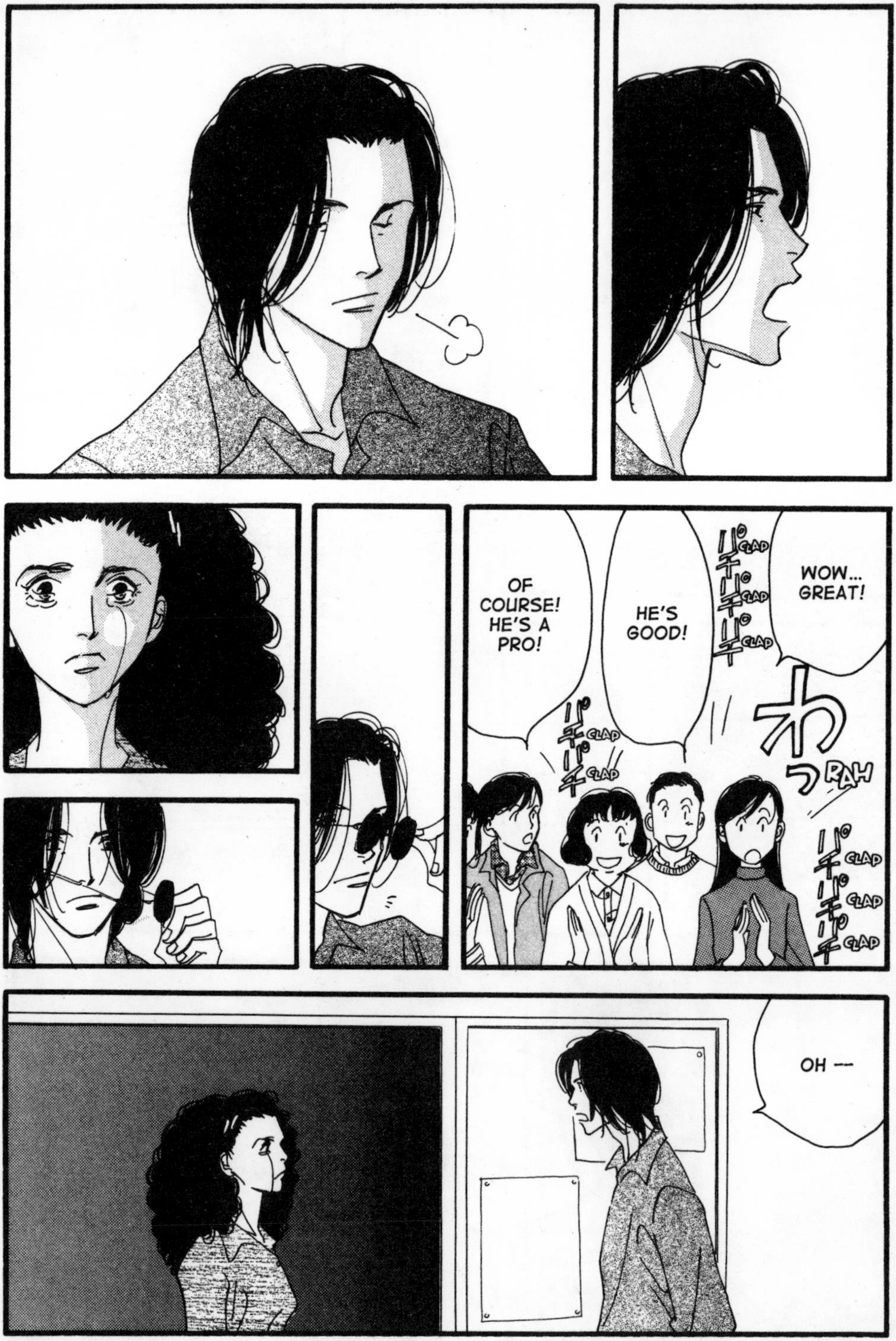
WOW... GREAT!
CLAP
CLAP
CLAP
HE'S GOOD!
OF COURSE! HE'S A PRO!
わっ
RAH
CLAP
CLAP
CLAP
CLAP
CLAP
OH --

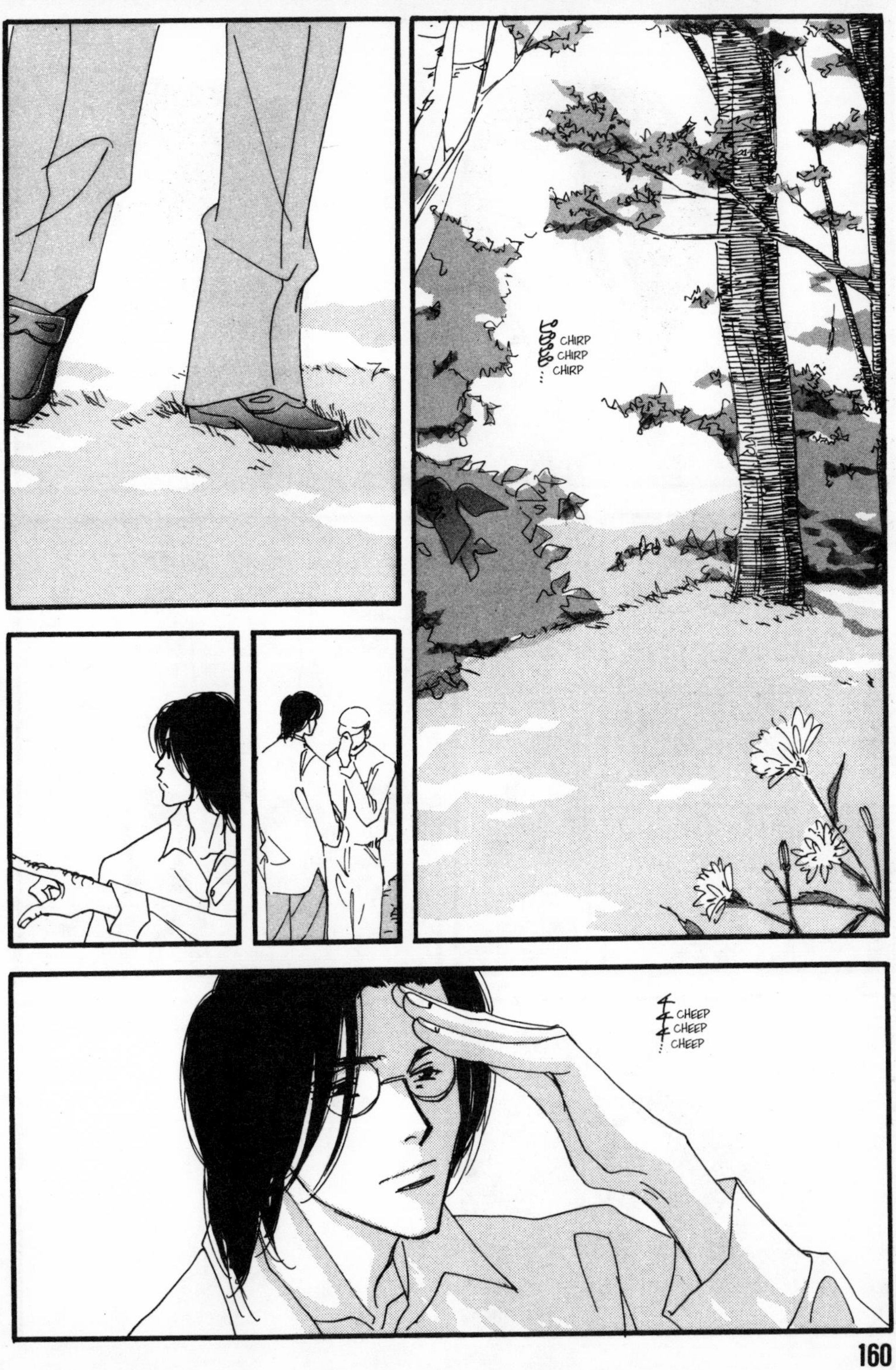
CHIRP CHIRP CHIRP
CHEEP CHEEP CHEEP

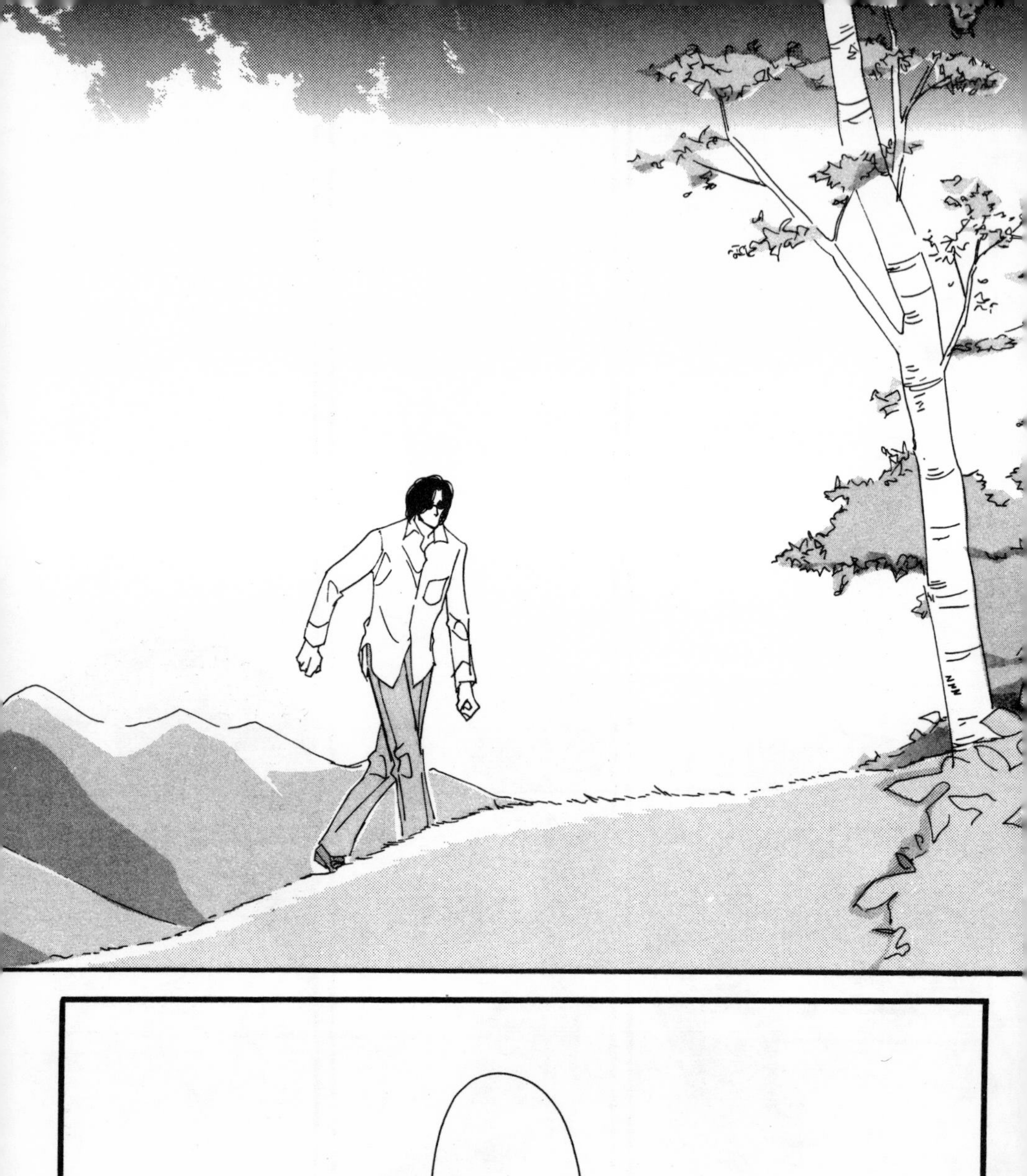

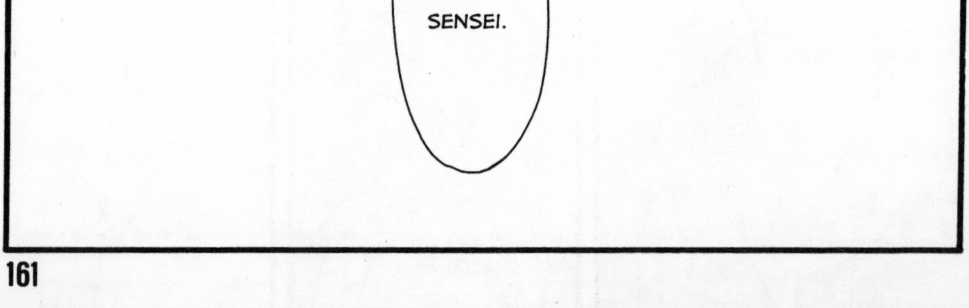
SENSEI.

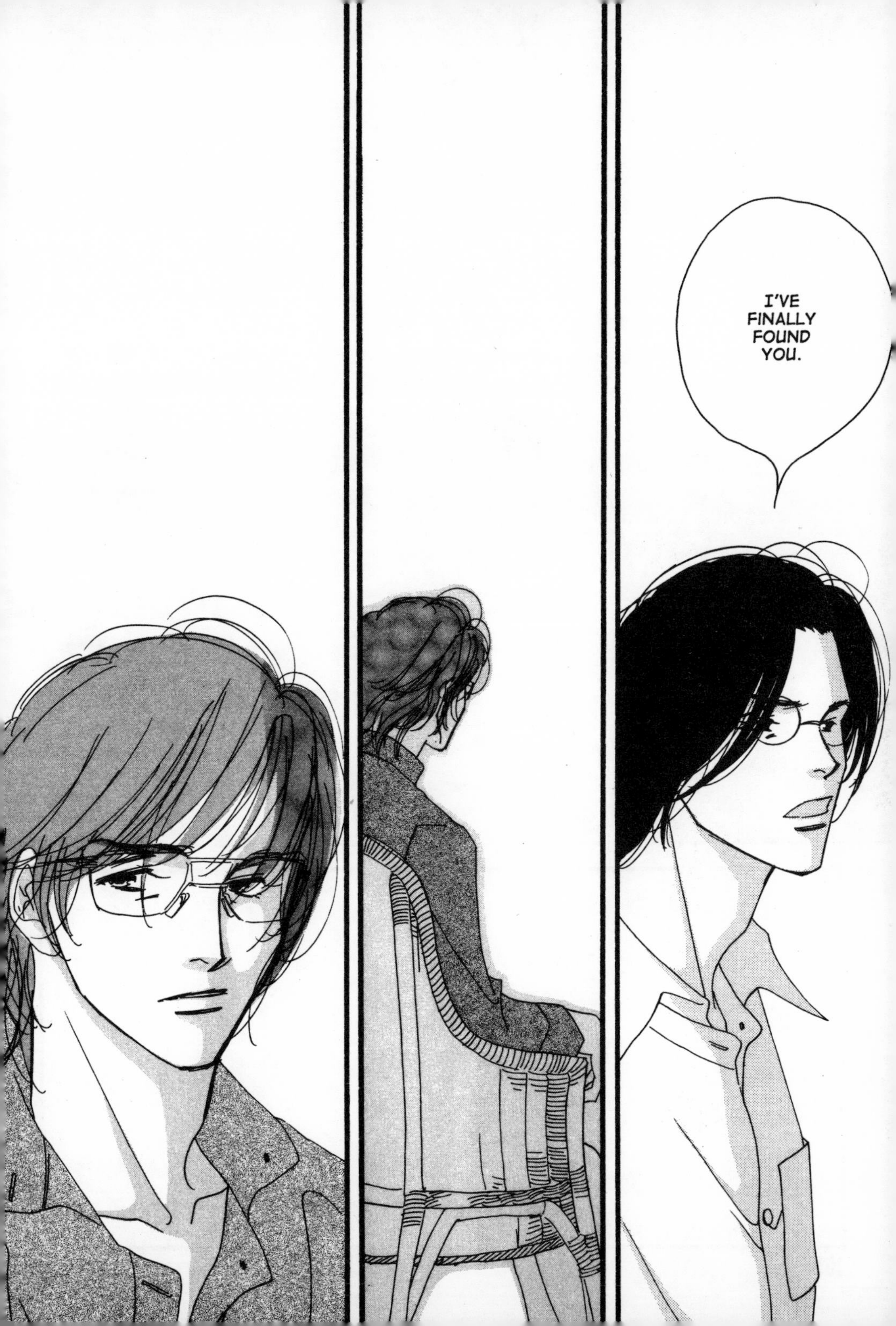
I'VE FINALLY FOUND YOU.

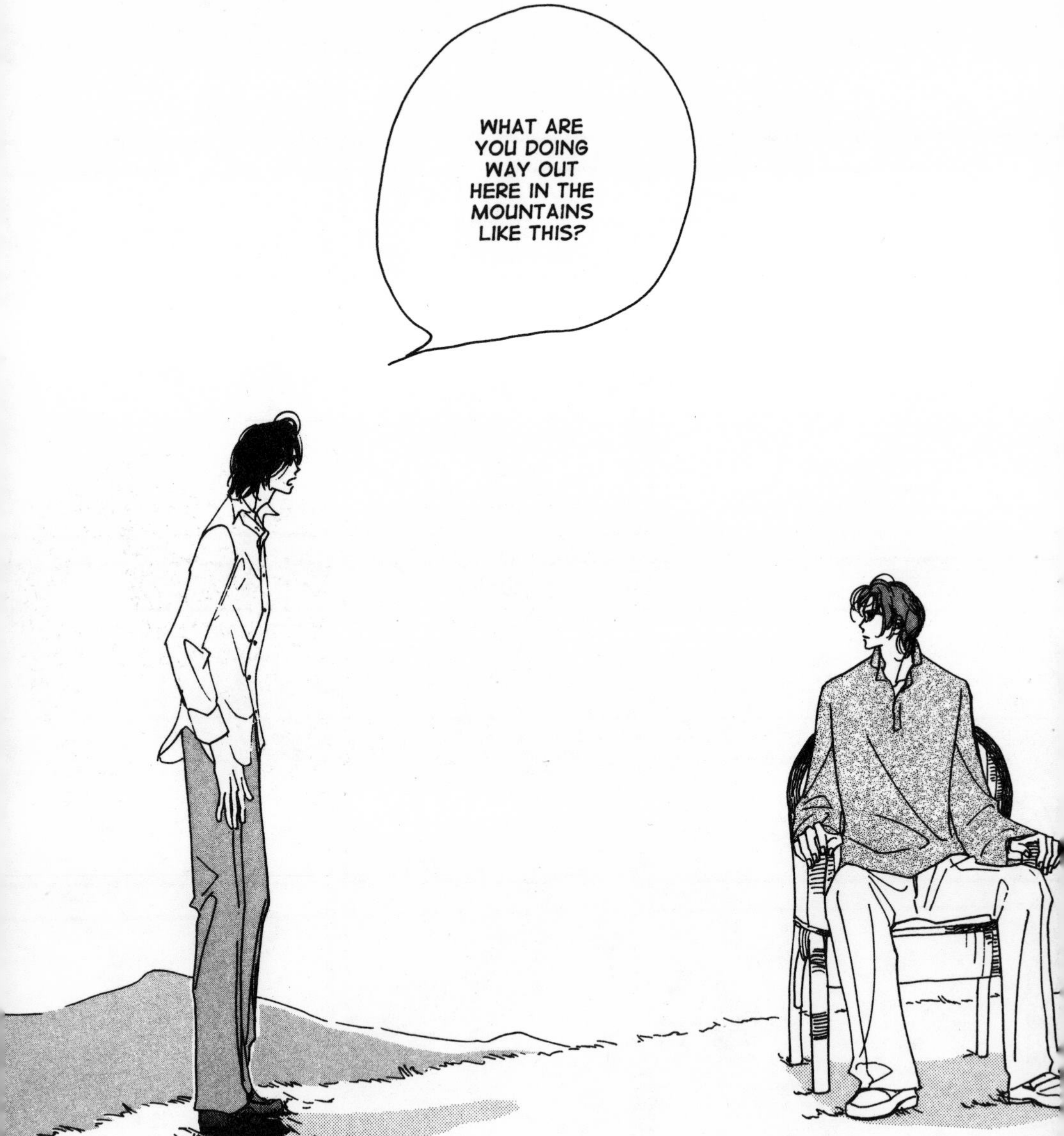
WHAT ARE YOU DOING WAY OUT HERE IN THE MOUNTAINS LIKE THIS?

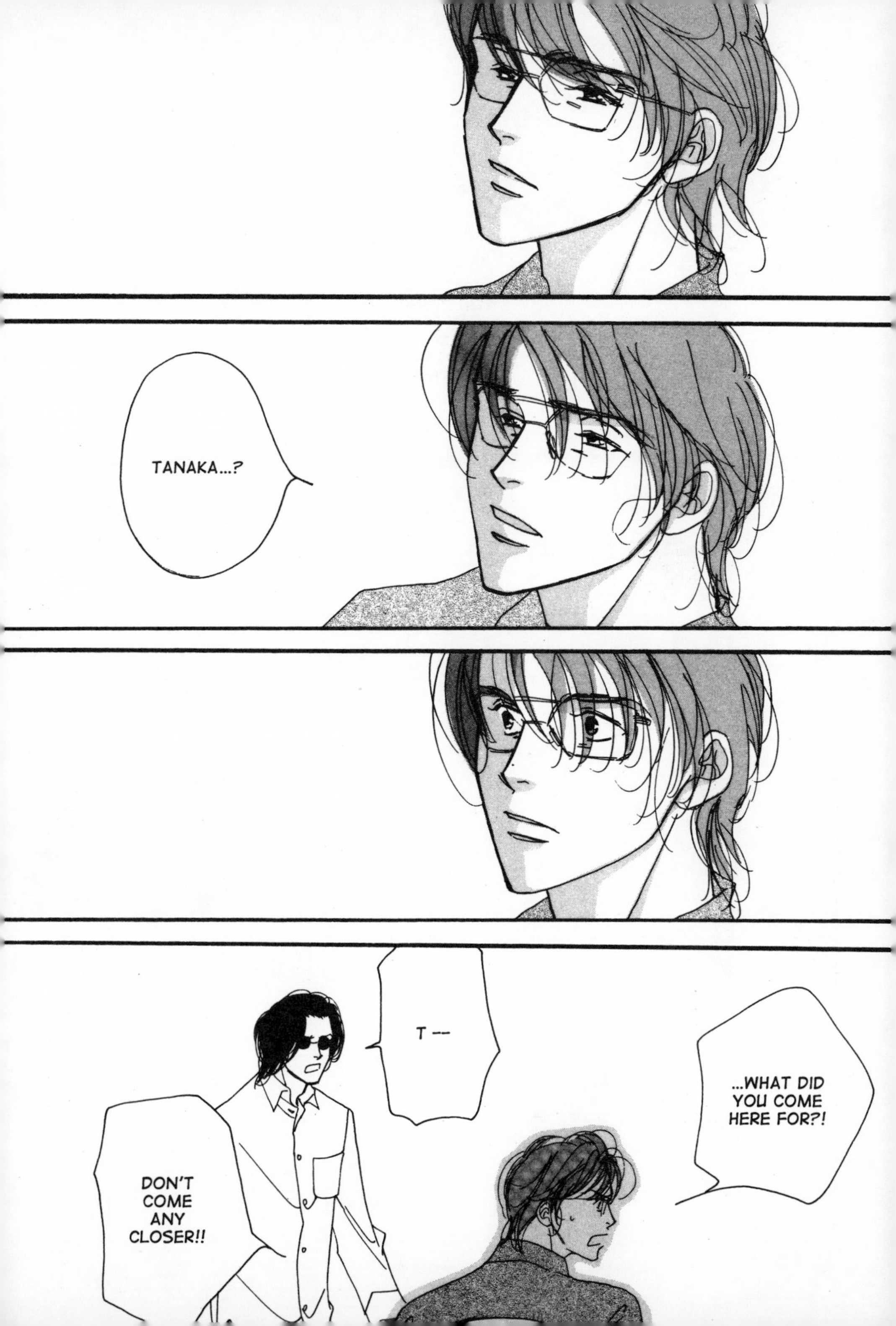
TANAKA...?
T --
...WHAT DID YOU COME HERE FOR?!
DON'T COME ANY CLOSER!!

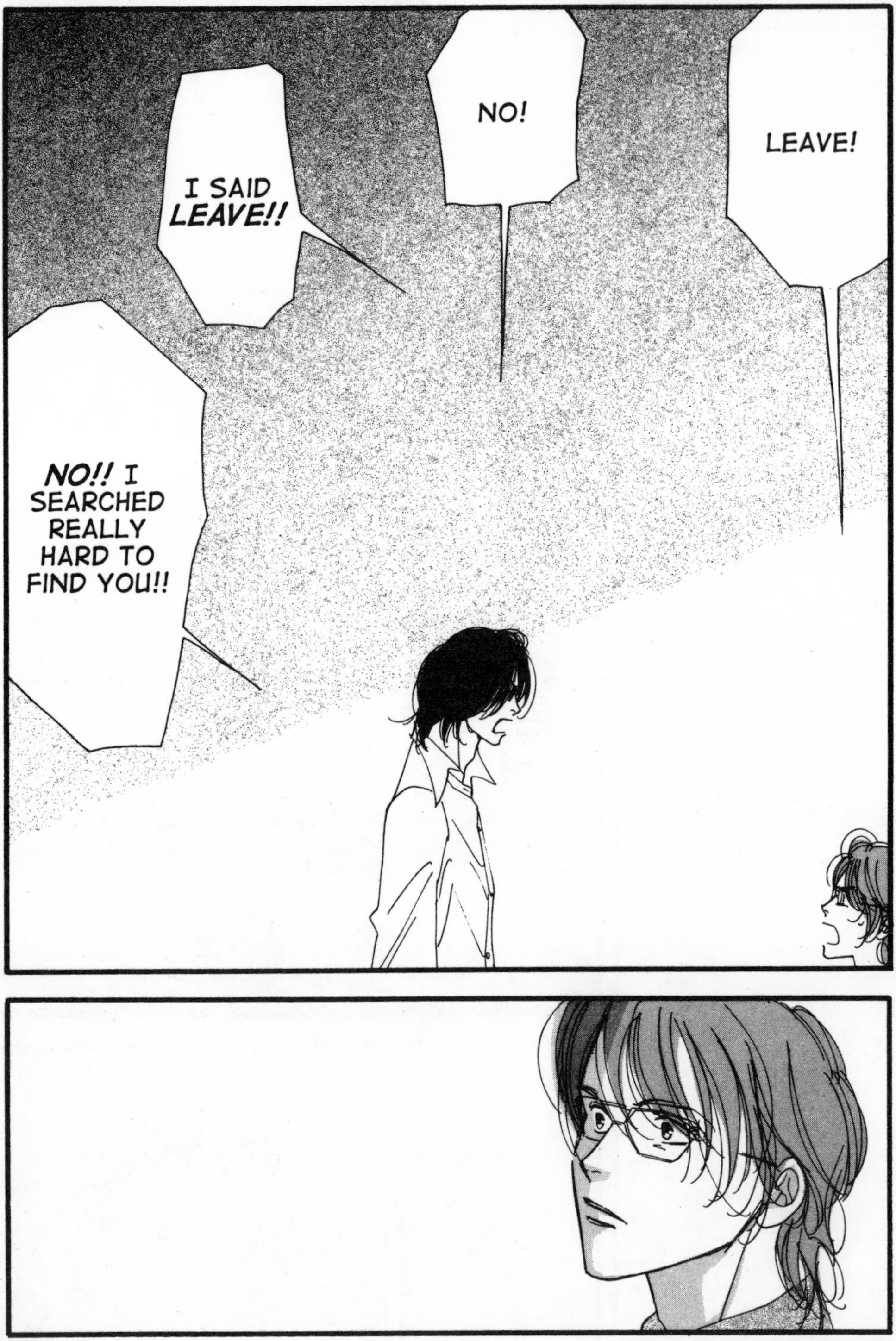
LEAVE!
NO!
I SAID LEAVE!!
NO!! I SEARCHED REALLY HARD TO FIND YOU!!

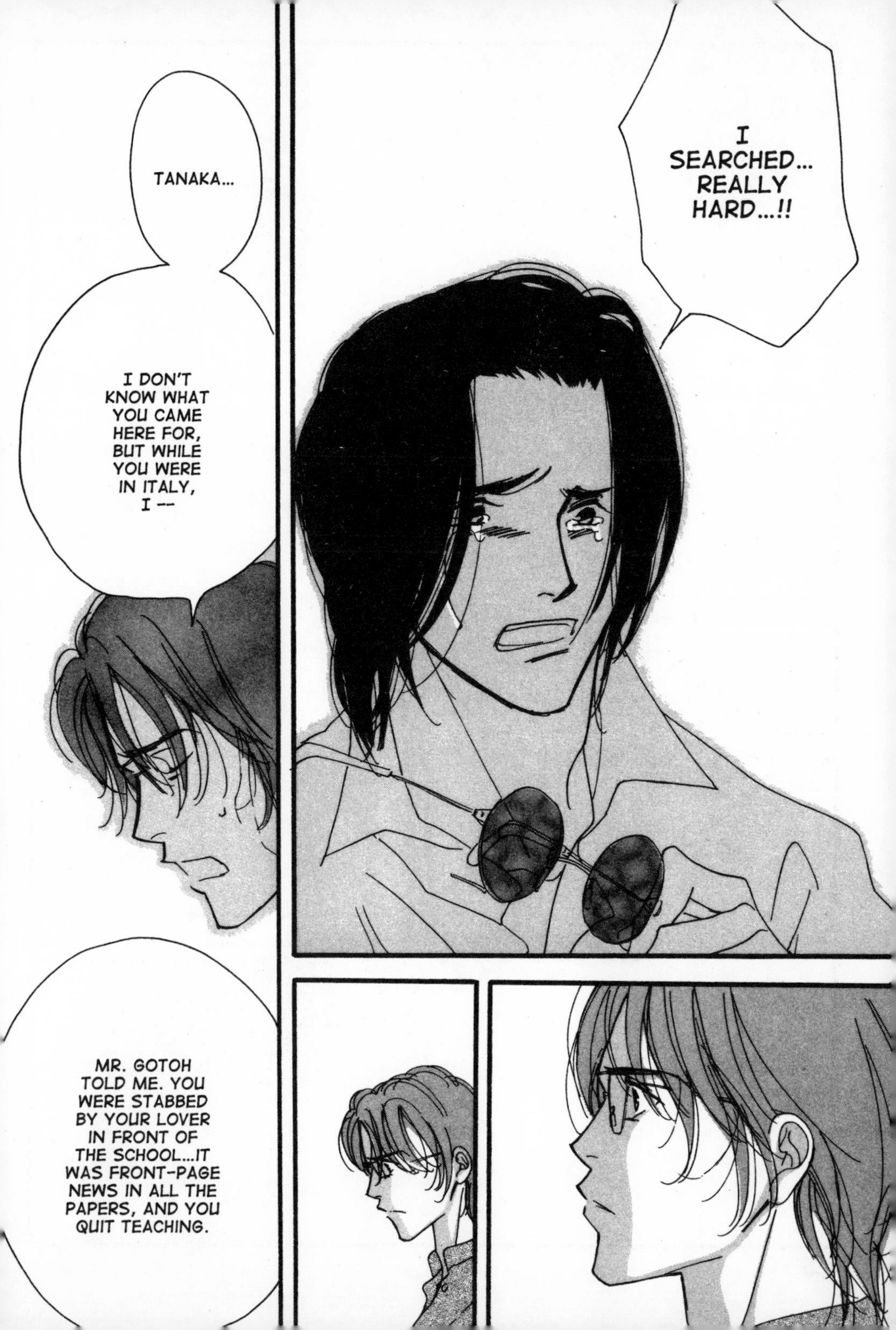
I SEARCHED... REALLY HARD...!!
TANAKA...
I DON'T KNOW WHAT YOU CAME HERE FOR, BUT WHILE YOU WERE IN ITALY, I --
MR. GOTOH TOLD ME. YOU WERE STABBED BY YOUR LOVER IN FRONT OF THE SCHOOL...IT WAS FRONT-PAGE NEWS IN ALL THE PAPERS, AND YOU QUIT TEACHING.

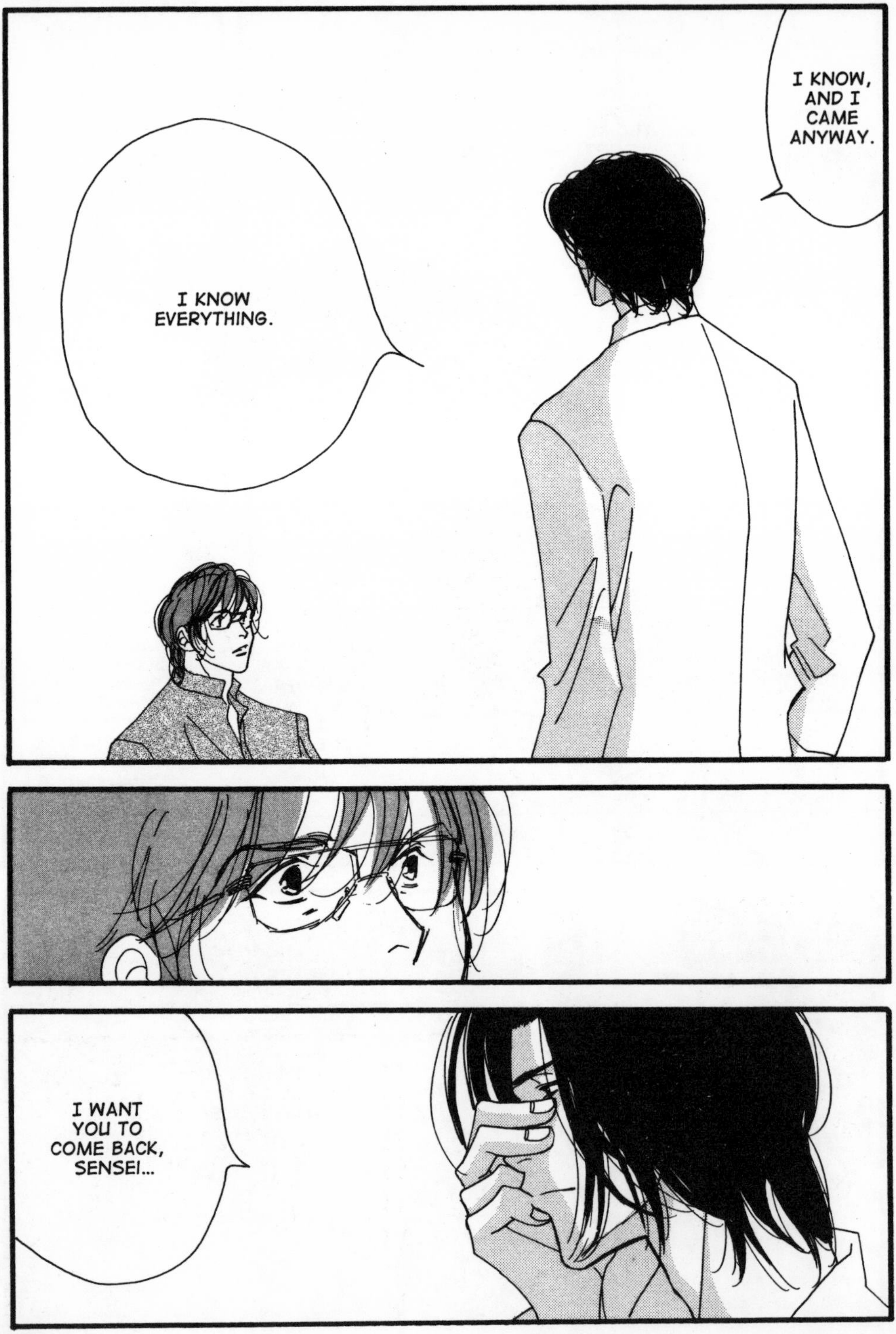
I KNOW, AND I CAME ANYWAY.
I KNOW EVERYTHING.
I WANT YOU TO COME BACK, SENSEI...

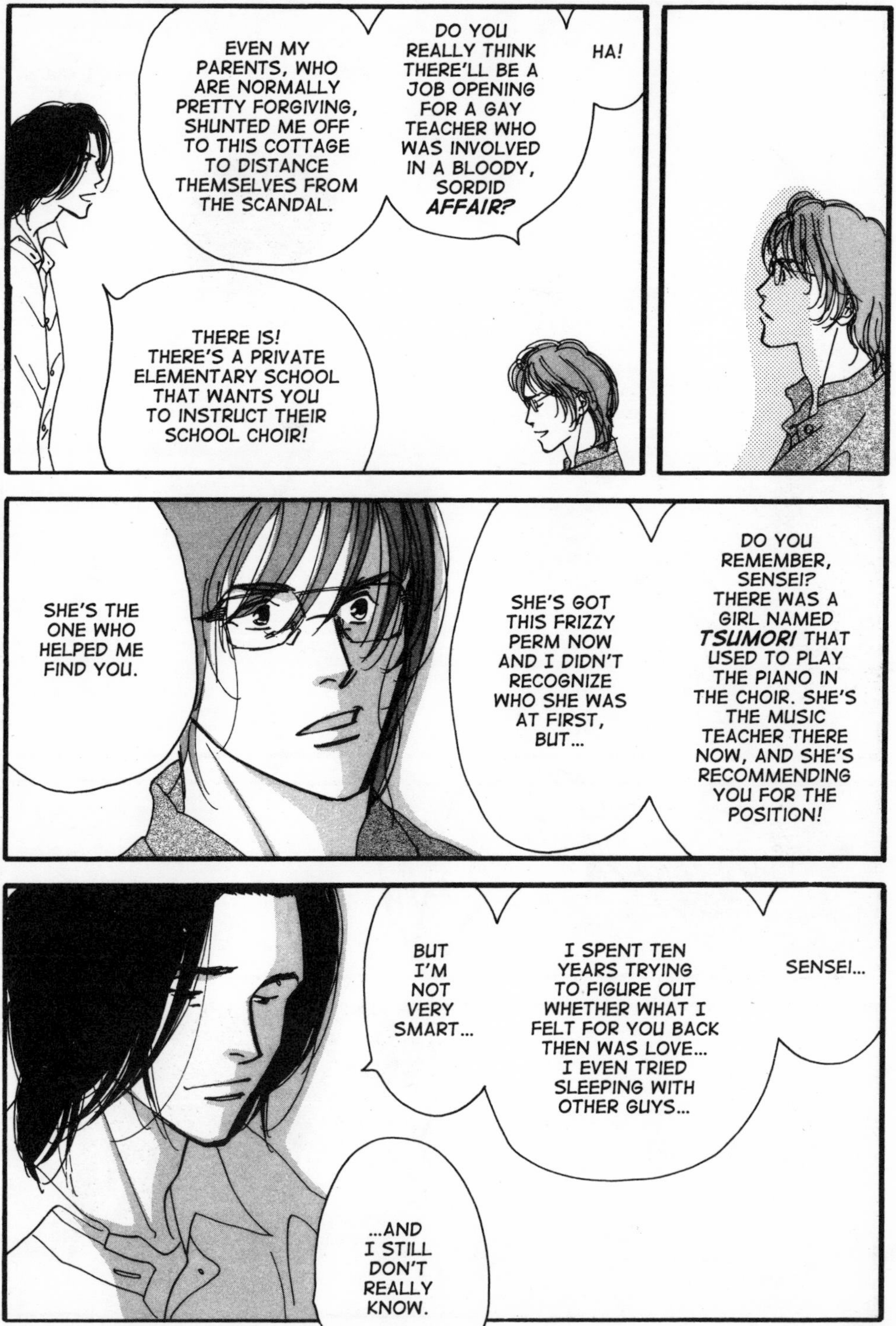
HA!
DO YOU REALLY THINK THERE'LL BE A JOB OPENING FOR A GAY TEACHER WHO WAS INVOLVED IN A BLOODY, SORDID *AFFAIR?*
EVEN MY PARENTS, WHO ARE NORMALLY PRETTY FORGIVING, SHUNTED ME OFF TO THIS COTTAGE TO DISTANCE THEMSELVES FROM THE SCANDAL.
THERE IS! THERE'S A PRIVATE ELEMENTARY SCHOOL THAT WANTS YOU TO INSTRUCT THEIR SCHOOL CHOIR!
DO YOU REMEMBER, SENSEI? THERE WAS A GIRL NAMED *TSUMORI* THAT USED TO PLAY THE PIANO IN THE CHOIR. SHE'S THE MUSIC TEACHER THERE NOW, AND SHE'S RECOMMENDING YOU FOR THE POSITION!
SHE'S GOT THIS FRIZZY PERM NOW AND I DIDN'T RECOGNIZE WHO SHE WAS AT FIRST, BUT...
SHE'S THE ONE WHO HELPED ME FIND YOU.
SENSEI...
I SPENT TEN YEARS TRYING TO FIGURE OUT WHETHER WHAT I FELT FOR YOU BACK THEN WAS LOVE... I EVEN TRIED SLEEPING WITH OTHER GUYS...
BUT I'M NOT VERY SMART...
...AND I STILL DON'T REALLY KNOW.

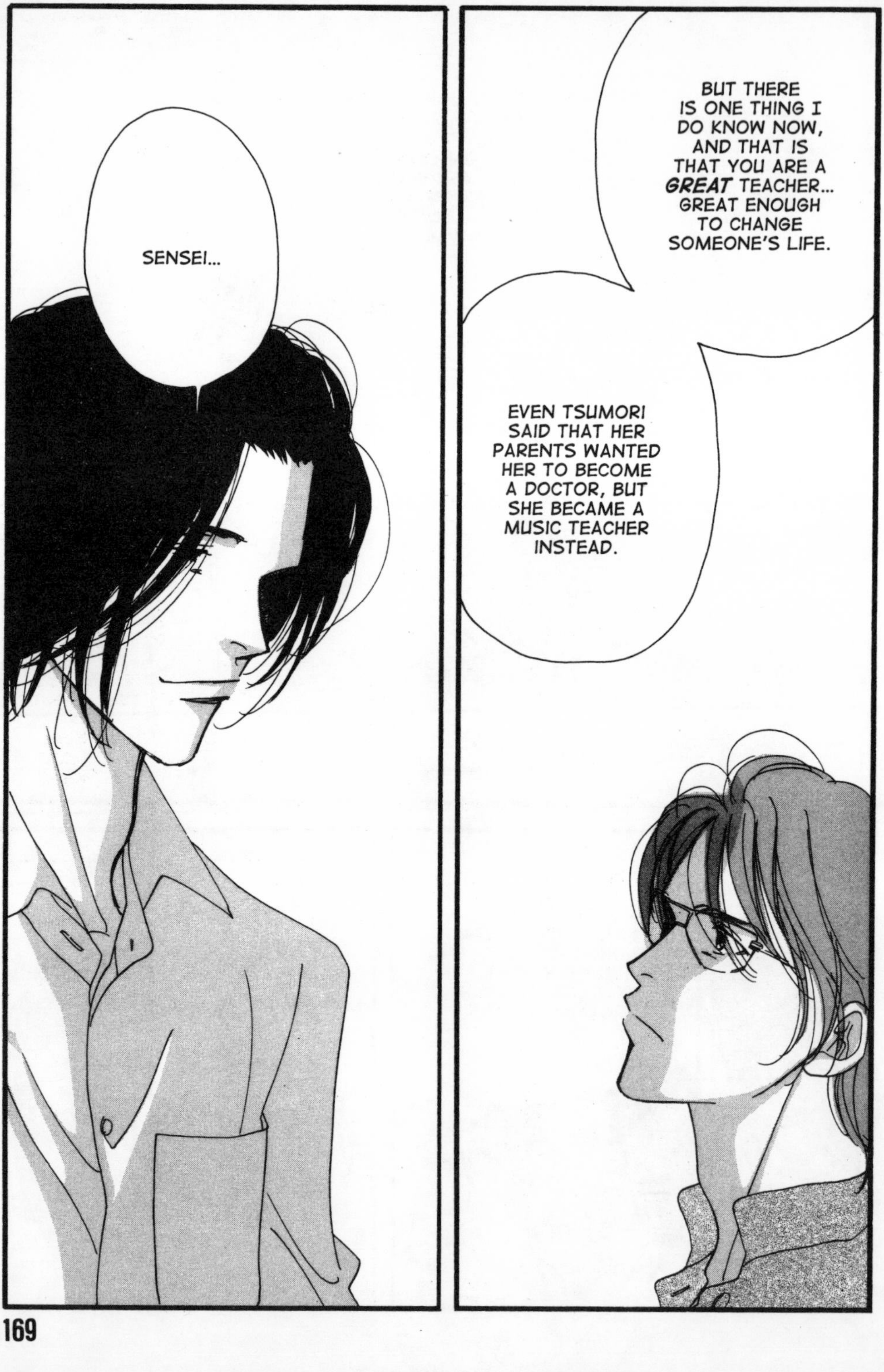
BUT THERE IS ONE THING I DO KNOW NOW, AND THAT IS THAT YOU ARE A **GREAT** TEACHER... GREAT ENOUGH TO CHANGE SOMEONE'S LIFE.
EVEN TSUMORI SAID THAT HER PARENTS WANTED HER TO BECOME A DOCTOR, BUT SHE BECAME A MUSIC TEACHER INSTEAD.
SENSEI...

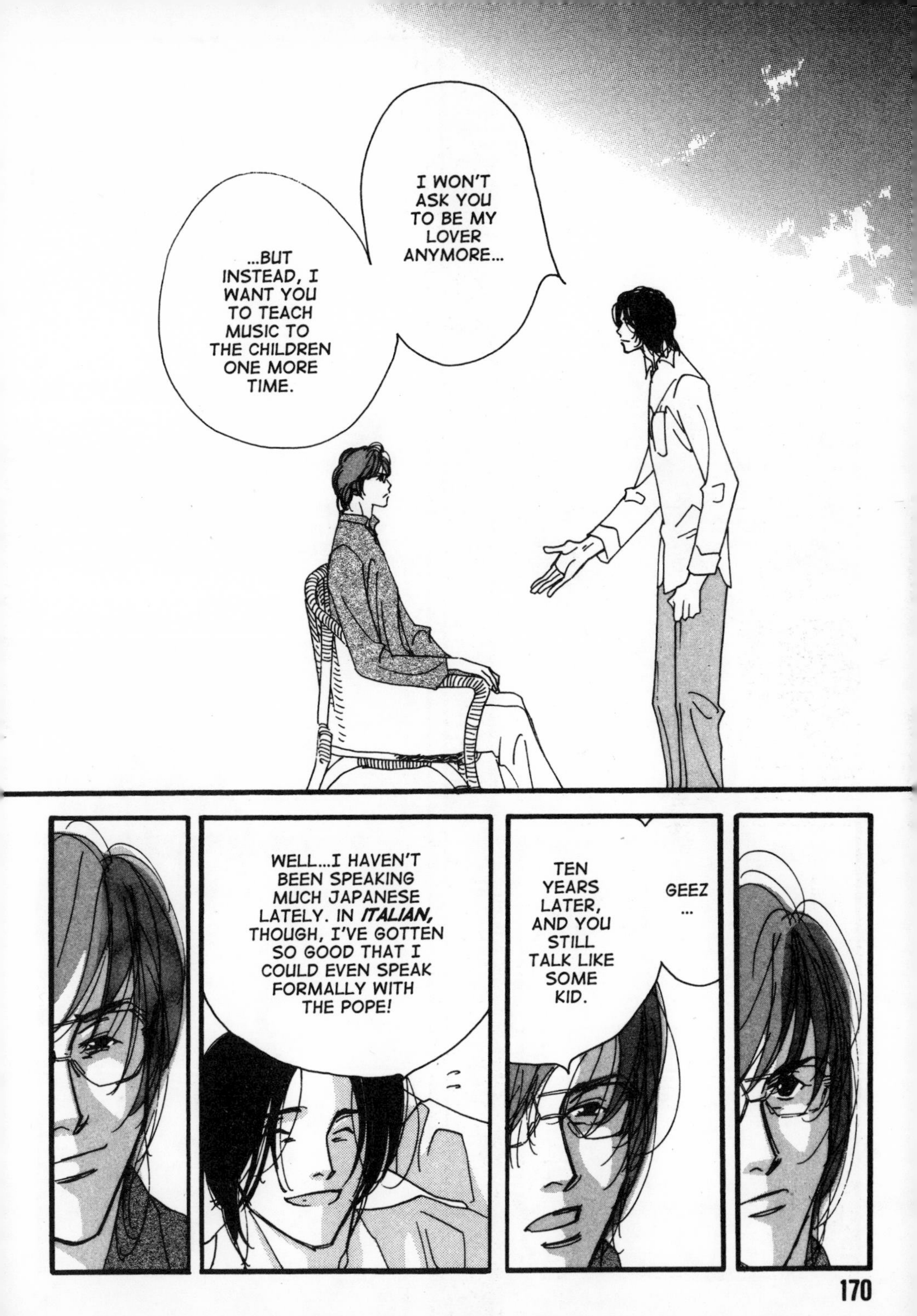
I WON'T ASK YOU TO BE MY LOVER ANYMORE...
...BUT INSTEAD, I WANT YOU TO TEACH MUSIC TO THE CHILDREN ONE MORE TIME.
GEEZ ...
TEN YEARS LATER, AND YOU STILL TALK LIKE SOME KID.
WELL...I HAVEN'T BEEN SPEAKING MUCH JAPANESE LATELY. IN *ITALIAN,* THOUGH, I'VE GOTTEN SO GOOD THAT I COULD EVEN SPEAK FORMALLY WITH THE POPE!

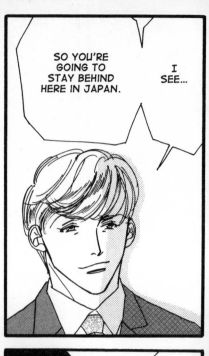

SO YOU'RE GOING TO STAY BEHIND HERE IN JAPAN.

I SEE...

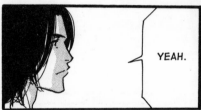

YEAH.

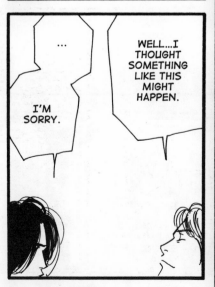

...

WELL...I THOUGHT SOMETHING LIKE THIS MIGHT HAPPEN.

I'M SORRY.

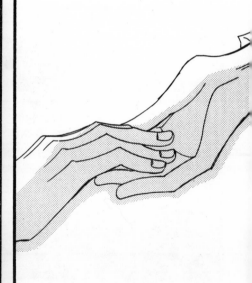

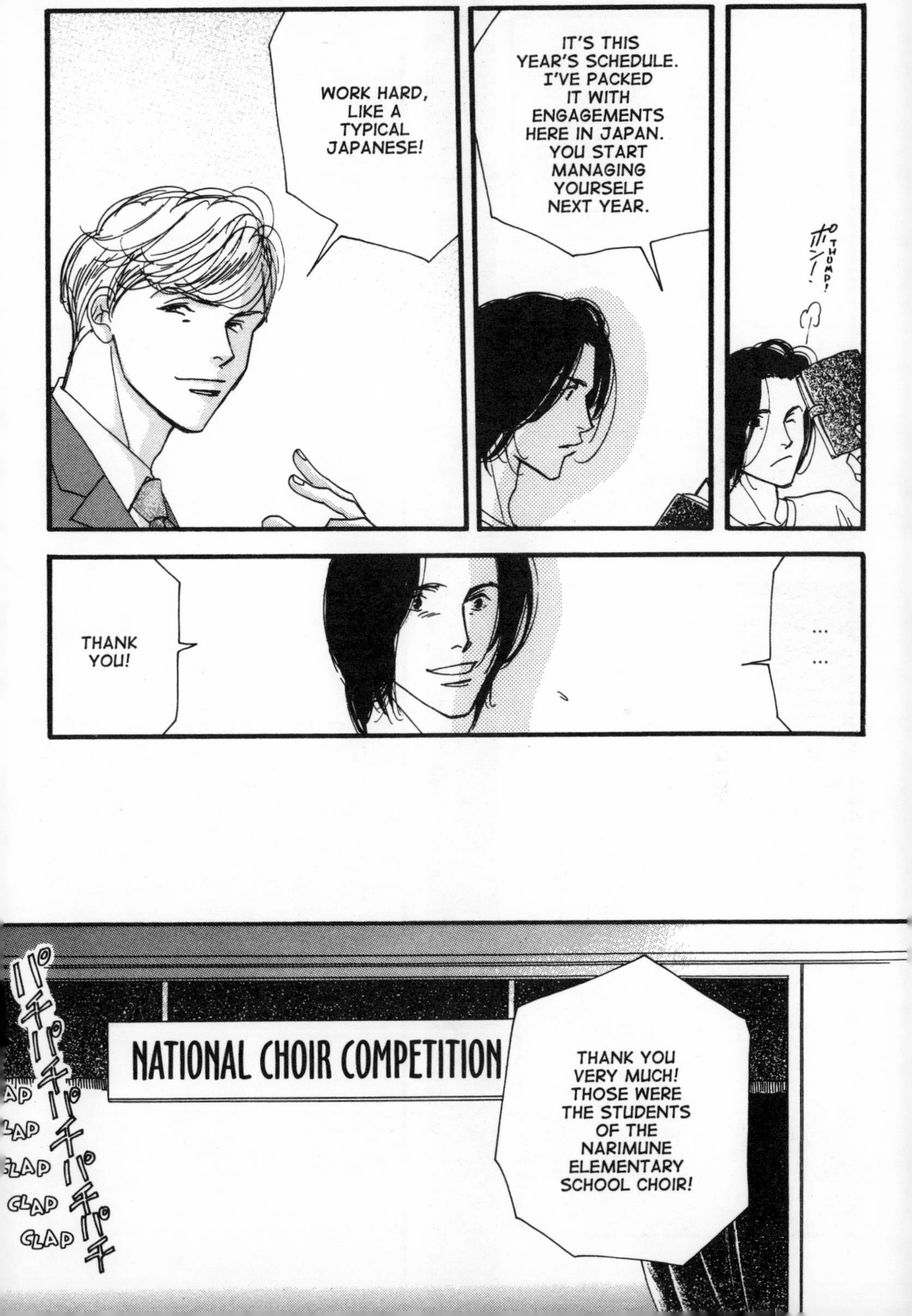
THUMP!
IT'S THIS YEAR'S SCHEDULE. I'VE PACKED IT WITH ENGAGEMENTS HERE IN JAPAN. YOU START MANAGING YOURSELF NEXT YEAR.
WORK HARD, LIKE A TYPICAL JAPANESE!
... ...
THANK YOU!
NATIONAL CHOIR COMPETITION
THANK YOU VERY MUCH! THOSE WERE THE STUDENTS OF THE NARIMUNE ELEMENTARY SCHOOL CHOIR!
CLAP
CLAP

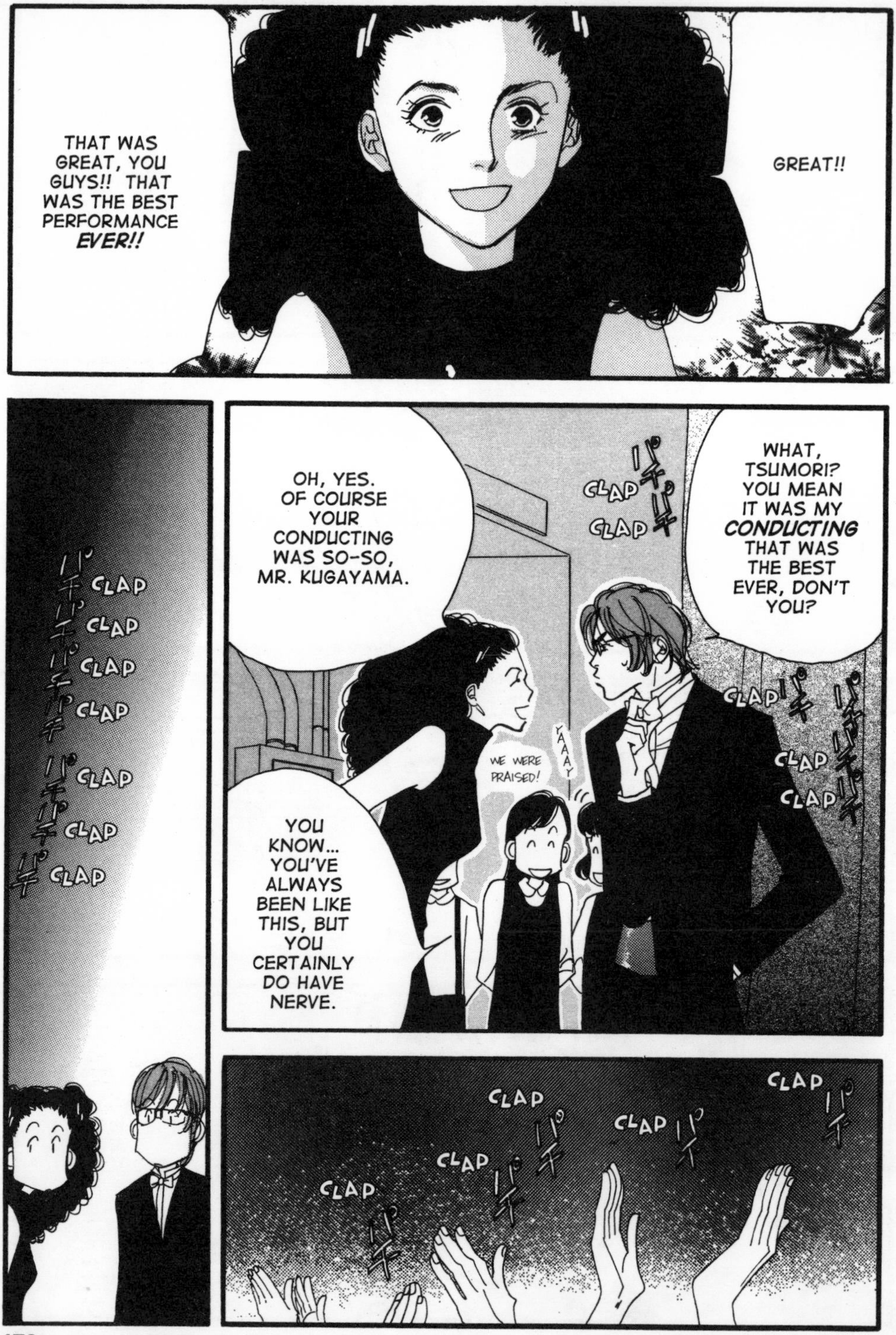
GREAT!!
THAT WAS GREAT, YOU GUYS!! THAT WAS THE BEST PERFORMANCE *EVER!!*
WHAT, TSUMORI? YOU MEAN IT WAS MY *CONDUCTING* THAT WAS THE BEST EVER, DON'T YOU?
CLAP
CLAP
OH, YES. OF COURSE YOUR CONDUCTING WAS SO-SO, MR. KUGAYAMA.
CLAP
CLAP
CLAP
YAAAY
WE WERE PRAISED!
YOU KNOW... YOU'VE ALWAYS BEEN LIKE THIS, BUT YOU CERTAINLY DO HAVE NERVE.
CLAP
CLAP
CLAP
CLAP
CLAP
CLAP
CLAP
CLAP
CLAP
CLAP
CLAP
CLAP
CLAP

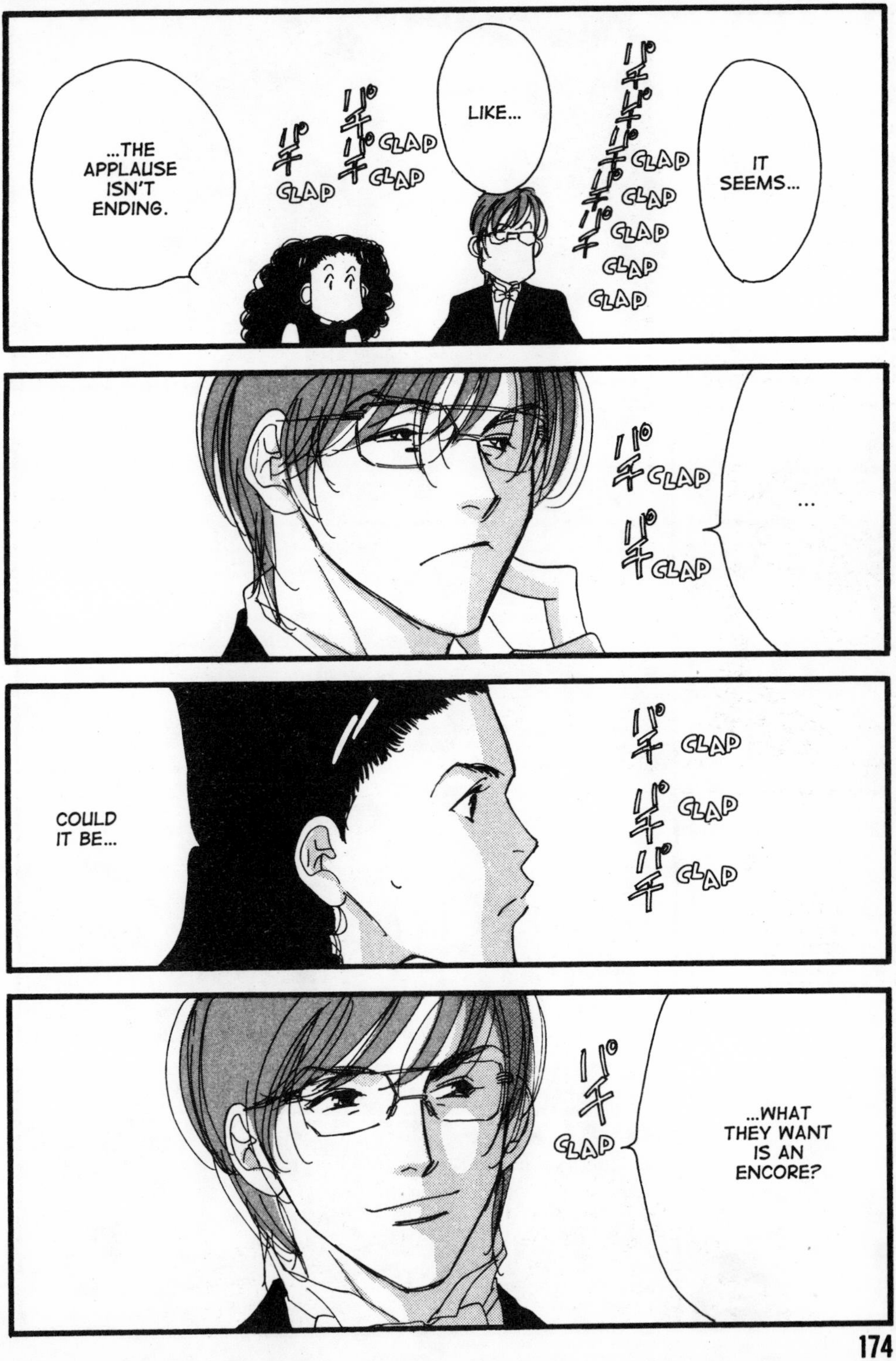
IT SEEMS...
CLAP CLAP CLAP CLAP CLAP
LIKE...
CLAP CLAP
CLAP
...THE APPLAUSE ISN'T ENDING.
...
CLAP
CLAP
CLAP
CLAP
CLAP
COULD IT BE...
CLAP
...WHAT THEY WANT IS AN ENCORE?

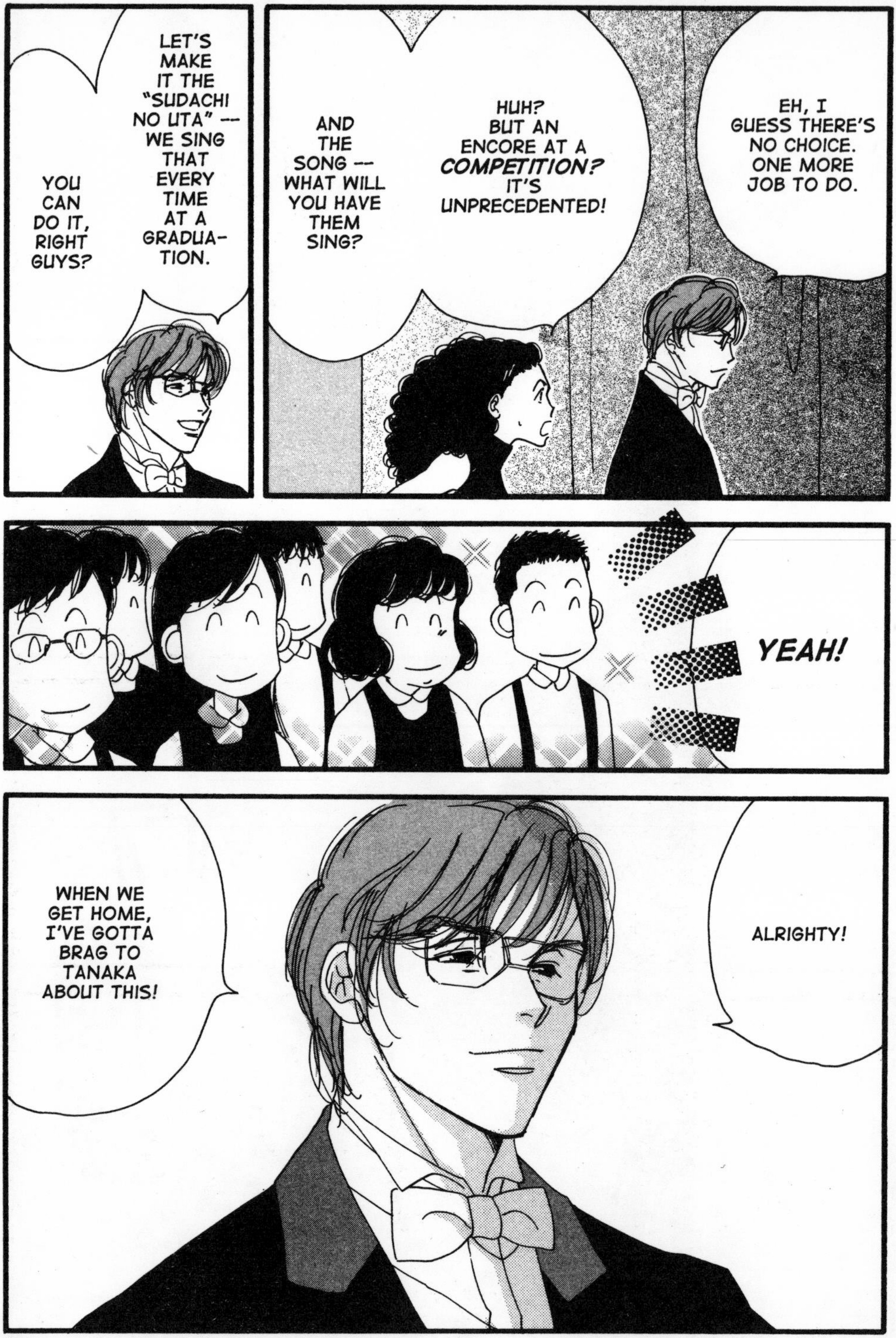
EH, I GUESS THERE'S NO CHOICE. ONE MORE JOB TO DO.
HUH? BUT AN ENCORE AT A *COMPETITION?* IT'S UNPRECEDENTED!
AND THE SONG -- WHAT WILL YOU HAVE THEM SING?
LET'S MAKE IT THE "SUDACHI NO UTA" -- WE SING THAT EVERY TIME AT A GRADUATION.
YOU CAN DO IT, RIGHT GUYS?
YEAH!
ALRIGHTY!
WHEN WE GET HOME, I'VE GOTTA BRAG TO TANAKA ABOUT THIS!

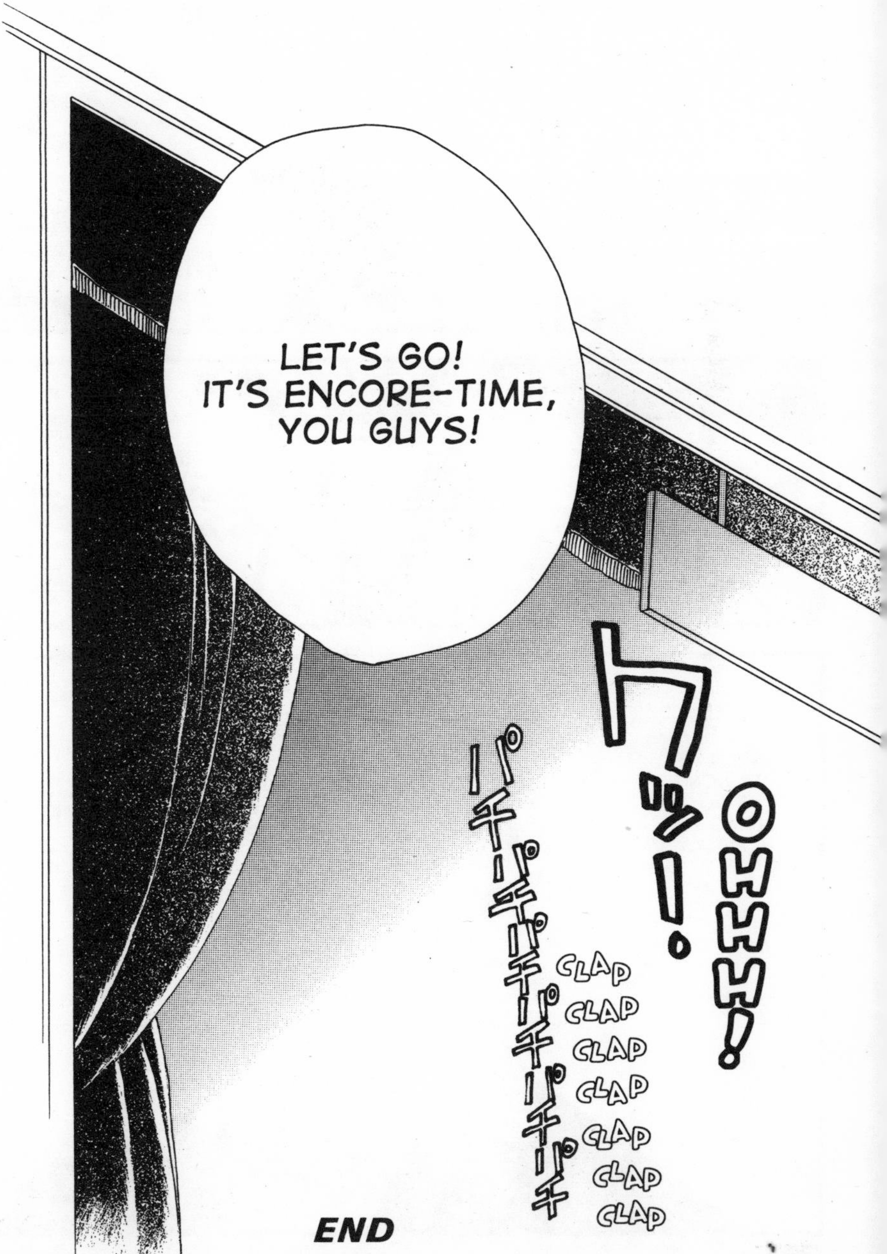
LET'S GO! IT'S ENCORE-TIME, YOU GUYS!
OHHHH!
CLAP CLAP CLAP CLAP CLAP CLAP CLAP

END

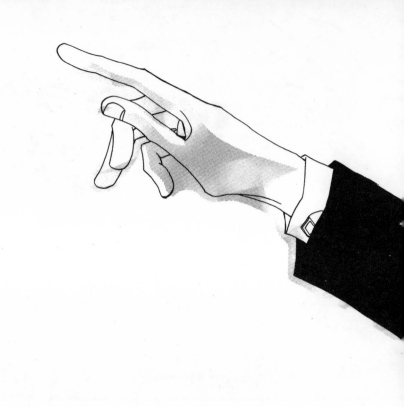

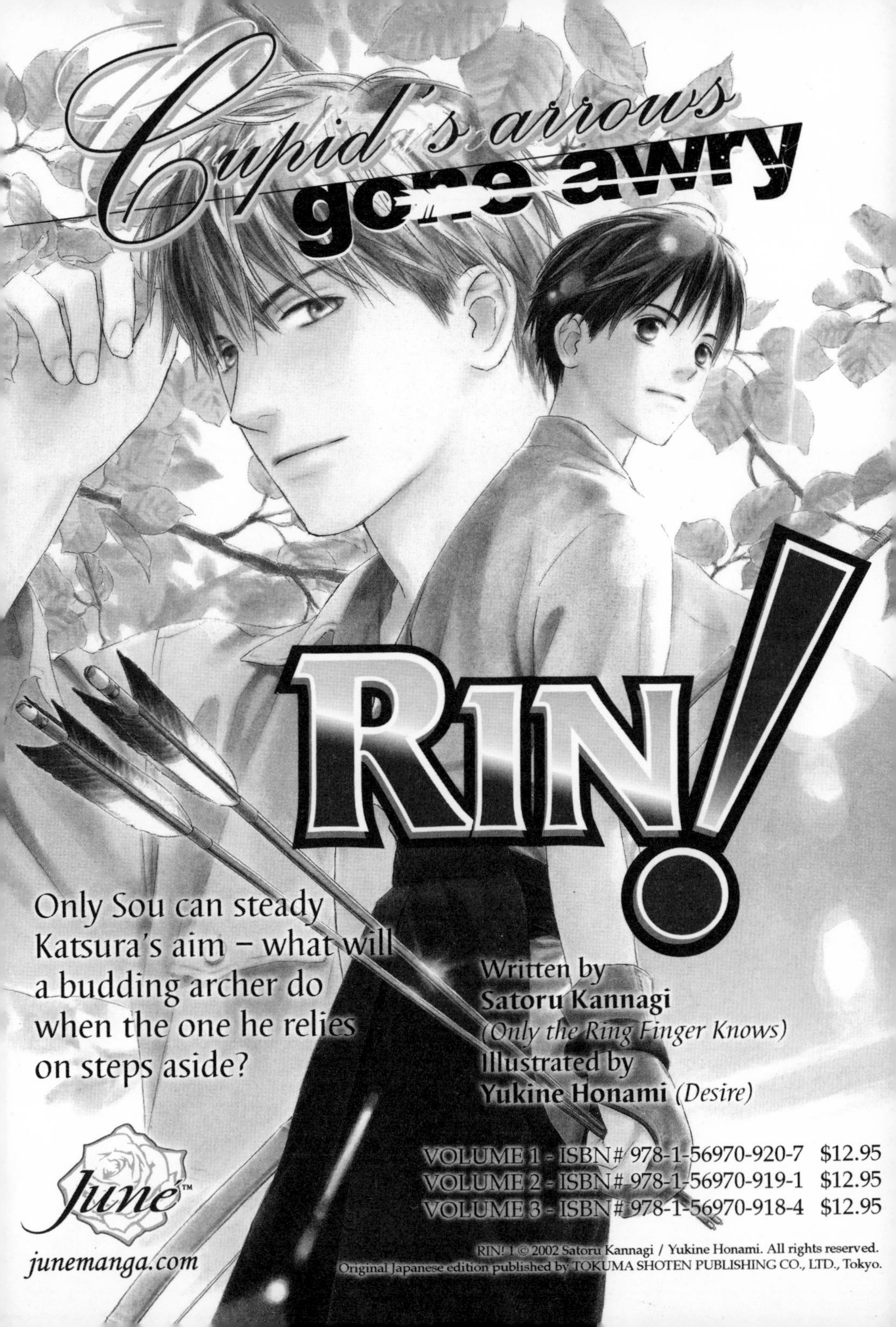
Cupid's arrows
gone awry
RIN!
Only Sou can steady Katsura's aim – what will a budding archer do when the one he relies on steps aside?
Written by
Satoru Kannagi
(Only the Ring Finger Knows)
Illustrated by
Yukine Honami (Desire)
VOLUME 1 - ISBN# 978-1-56970-920-7 $12.95
VOLUME 2 - ISBN# 978-1-56970-919-1 $12.95
VOLUME 3 - ISBN# 978-1-56970-918-4 $12.95
June™
junemanga.com
RIN! 1 © 2002 Satoru Kannagi / Yukine Honami. All rights reserved.
Original Japanese edition published by TOKUMA SHOTEN PUBLISHING CO., LTD., Tokyo.

THE Moon AND Sandals Vol. 1

月とサンダル

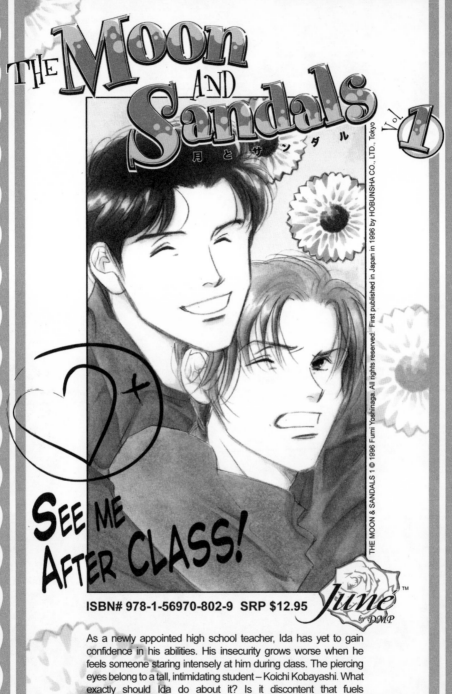

SEE ME AFTER CLASS!

ISBN# 978-1-56970-802-9 SRP $12.95

June
by DMP

As a newly appointed high school teacher, Ida has yet to gain confidence in his abilities. His insecurity grows worse when he feels someone staring intensely at him during class. The piercing eyes belong to a tall, intimidating student – Koichi Kobayashi. What exactly should Ida do about it? Is it discontent that fuels Kobayashi's sultry gaze… or could it be something else?

Written and Illustrated by:
Fumi Yoshinaga

junemanga.com

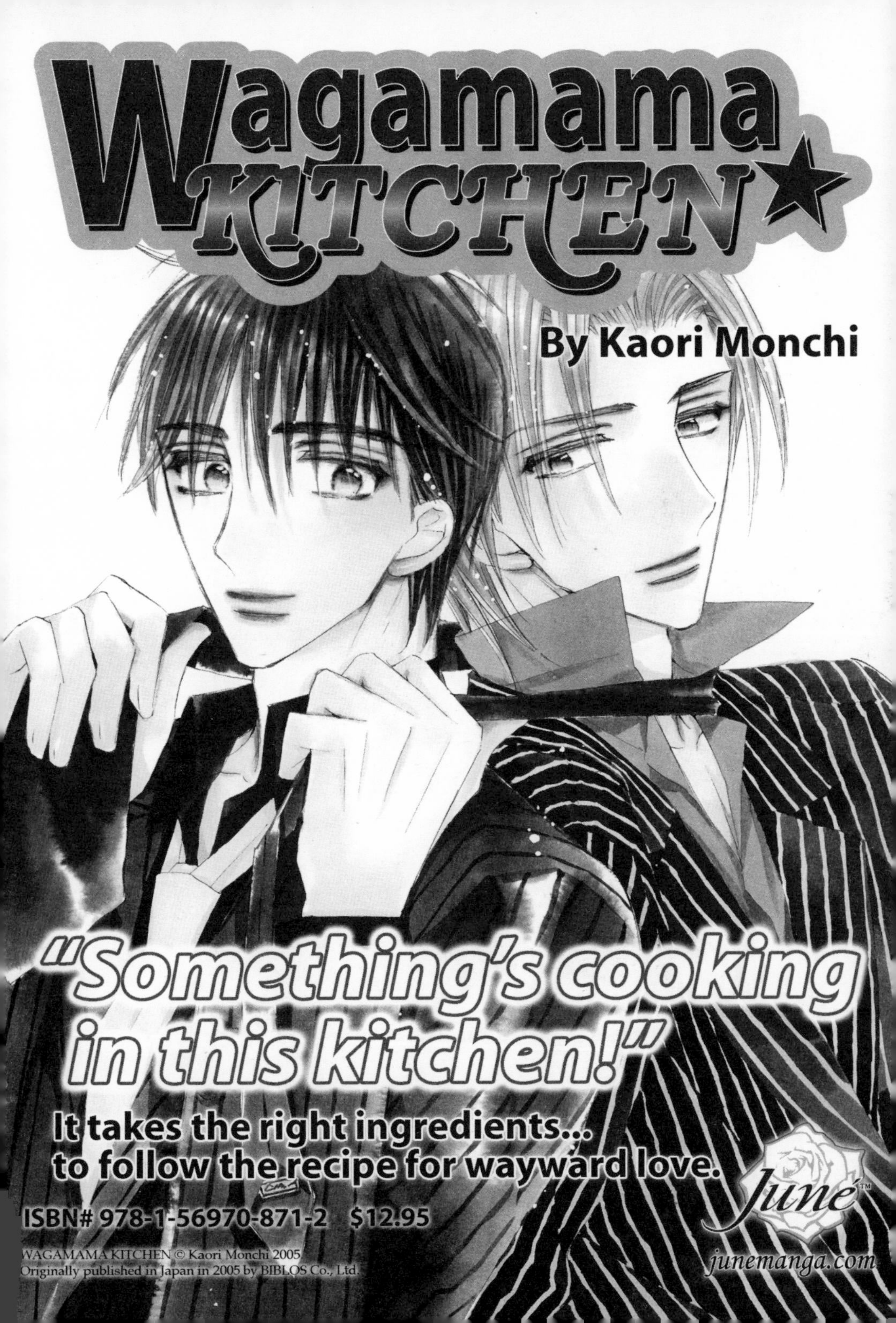
Wagamama KITCHEN★
By Kaori Monchi
"Something's cooking in this kitchen!"
It takes the right ingredients...
to follow the recipe for wayward love.
ISBN# 978-1-56970-871-2 $12.95
WAGAMAMA KITCHEN © Kaori Monchi 2005
Originally published in Japan in 2005 by BIBLOS Co., Ltd.
June™
junemanga.com

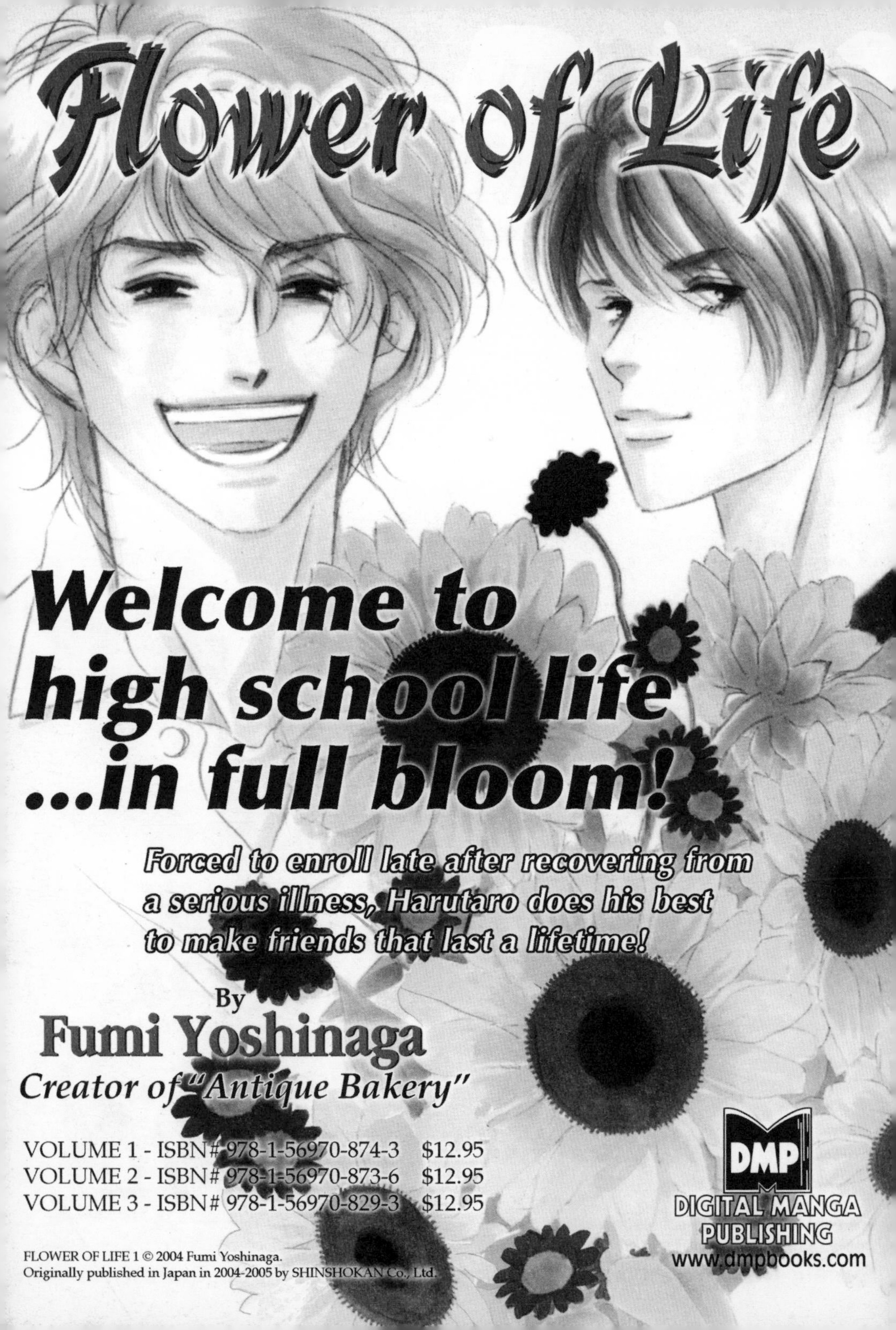
Flower of Life
Welcome to high school life ...in full bloom!
Forced to enroll late after recovering from a serious illness, Harutaro does his best to make friends that last a lifetime!
By
Fumi Yoshinaga
Creator of "Antique Bakery"
VOLUME 1 - ISBN# 978-1-56970-874-3 $12.95
VOLUME 2 - ISBN# 978-1-56970-873-6 $12.95
VOLUME 3 - ISBN# 978-1-56970-829-3 $12.95
DMP
DIGITAL MANGA PUBLISHING
www.dmpbooks.com
FLOWER OF LIFE 1 © 2004 Fumi Yoshinaga.
Originally published in Japan in 2004-2005 by SHINSHOKAN Co., Ltd.

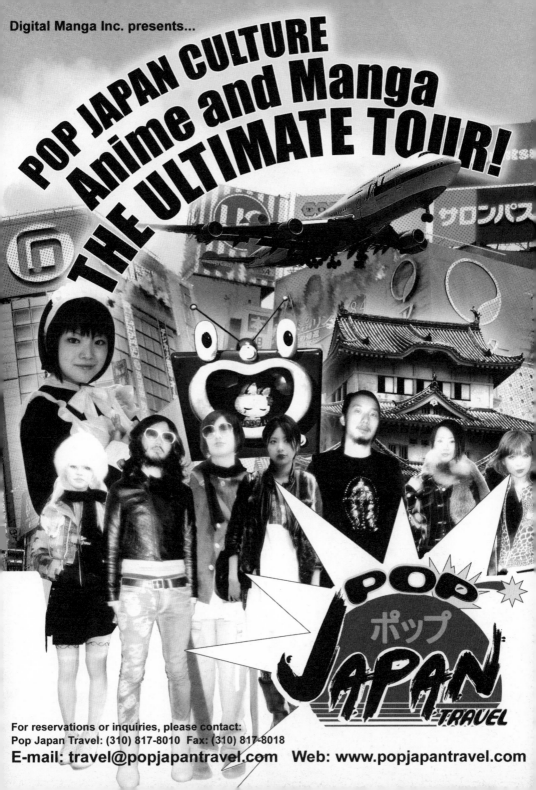

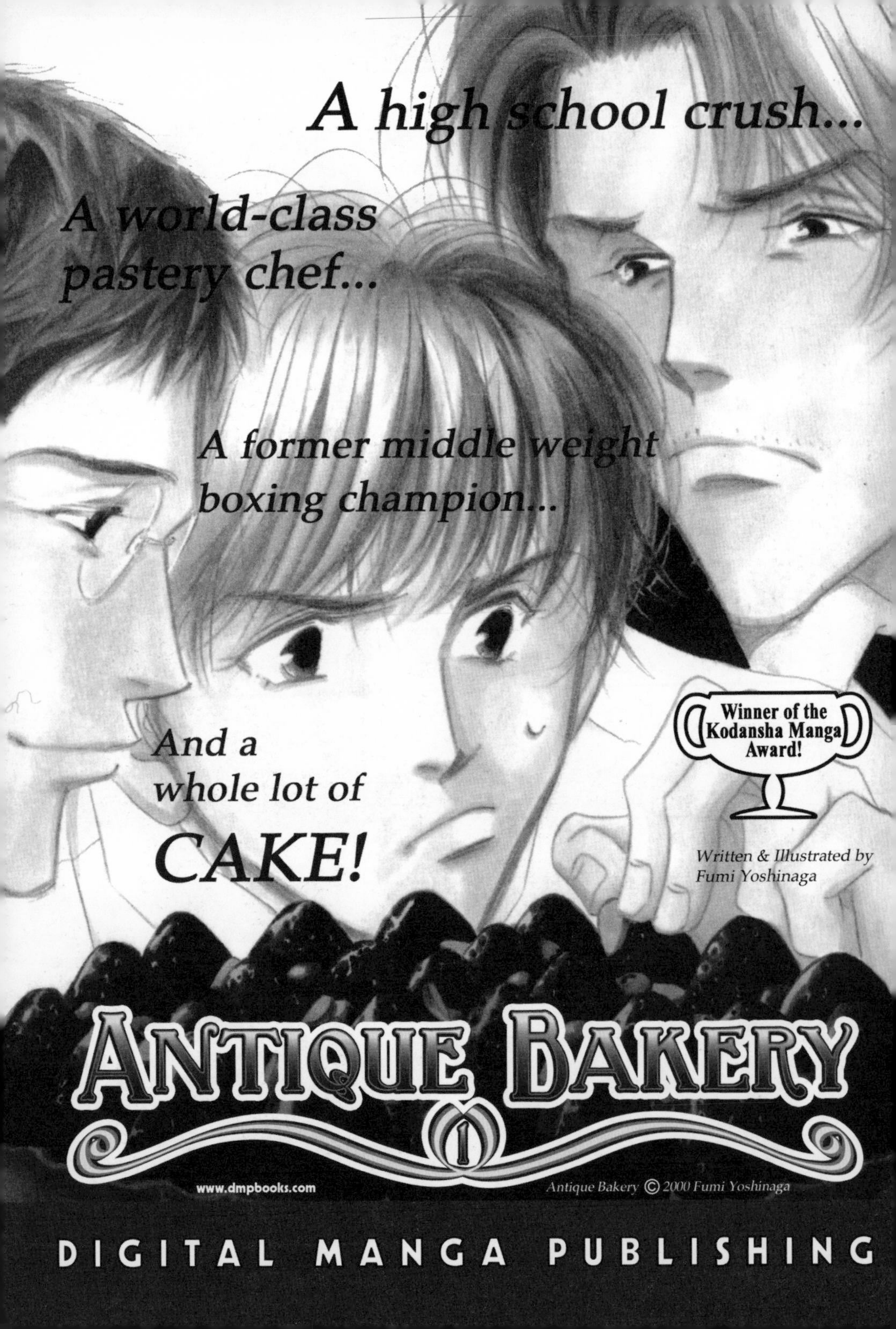
A high school crush...
A world-class pastery chef...
A former middle weight boxing champion...
And a whole lot of CAKE!
Winner of the Kodansha Manga Award!
Written & Illustrated by Fumi Yoshinaga
ANTIQUE BAKERY
1
www.dmpbooks.com
Antique Bakery © 2000 Fumi Yoshinaga
DIGITAL MANGA PUBLISHING

STOP

This is the back of the book!
Start from the other side.

NATIVE MANGA
readers read manga
from *right to left*.

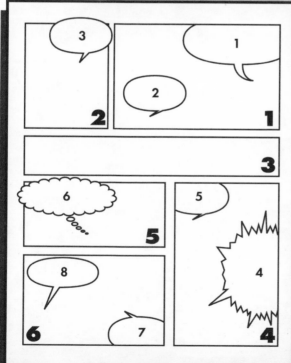

If you run into our **Native Manga** logo on any of our books... you'll know that this manga is published in it's true original native Japanese right to left reading format, as it was intended. Turn to the other side of the book and start reading from right to left, top to bottom.

Follow the diagram to see how its done.
Surf's Up!

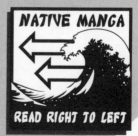

NATIVE MANGA

READ RIGHT TO LEFT